HELICON BOOK OF
days

HELICON BOOK OF
days

Helicon

Copyright © Helicon Publishing 1994

Helicon Publishing Ltd
42 Hythe Bridge Street
Oxford OX1 2EP

Printed and bound in Great Britain by
Biddles Ltd, Guildford and King's Lynn

ISBN 1 – 85986 – 064 – 8

British Cataloguing in Publication Data

A catalogue record for this book is available
from the British Library

Cover illustrations (clockwise): **1** Detail from a contemporary depiction of the
defeat of the Armada, *Society of Apothecaries, London*. **2** Roger Bannister
breaking the world record by running the mile in under four minutes *Topham
Picture Source*. **3** Detail from a portrait miniature of Queen Elizabeth I by
Nicholas Hilliard *Bridgeman Art Library*. **4** Channel Tunnel.

Contents

Editorial director
Michael Upshall

Contributors
Jane Anson
Sam Cridlan
Anna Farkas

Project editor
Sheila Dallas

Index
Jane Anson

Design and page make-up
TJ Graphics

Production
Tony Ballsdon

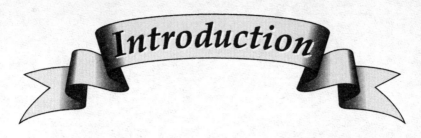

Introduction

'Every day should be passed as if it were to be our last.'
Pubilius Syrus, 1st century BC

Today is a significant anniversary! Don't let it pass without finding out why. Look through these pages and see the notable events – throughout time – for every day of the year.

The *Helicon Book of Days* is packed full of dates of important events, achievements of the famous and infamous, quotes of the day, news clippings, and sayings. It provides a wealth of ideas for those difficult speeches or presentations, or any other occasion when a quip, phrase, or coincidence can transform the good into excellent. Or just browse through and enjoy the serendipity.

Within the limitations of space we have aimed to achieve a balanced range of entries – historical, political, popular culture, and miscellany. Every day is allocated a page, showing the feasts that are traditionally celebrated on that date, followed by past events, then the names of people who were born or who died on that day.

In addition, every day has quotations that might be about any one of a wide range of topics from current affairs to ancient maxims, or be linked to an item on that day. An index enables the reader to start with the event and then find the right date.

There is further information, including a perpetual calendar and a list of the materials associated with wedding anniversaries, at the back of the book to enable the reader to make today's events extra special!

On This Day

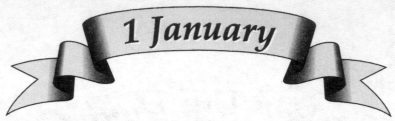

1 January

'Each age has deemed the new-born year. The fittest time for festal cheer.'
Walter Scott, *Marmion*

New Year's Day, and the national day of Cuba, Sudan, and Haiti. Feast day of St Felix of Bourges, St Almachius, St William of Dijon, St Eugendus or Oyend, St Peter of Atroa, St Odilo, and St Fulgentius of Ruspe.

≈ EVENTS ≈

1785 London's oldest daily paper *The Daily Universal Register* (renamed *The Times* in 1788) was first published. **1801** Italian astronomer Giuseppe Piazzi became the first person to discover an asteroid; he named it Ceres. **1887** Queen Victoria was proclaimed empress of India in Delhi. **1894** The Manchester Ship Canal was officially opened to traffic. **1901** The Commonwealth of Australia was formed. **1909** The first payments of old-age pensions were made in Britain, with persons over 70 receiving five shillings (25p) a week. **1958** The European Community came into existence. **1959** Fidel Castro overthrew the government of Fulgencio Batista, and seized power in Cuba. **1993** Czechoslovakia split into two separate states, the Czech Republic and Slovakia; the peaceful division had been engineered in 1992.

≈ BIRTHS ≈

Lorenzo de' Medici (The Magnificent), Florentine ruler, **1449**; Paul Revere, US patriot, **1735**; E M Forster, English novelist, **1879**; William Fox, US movie mogul, **1879**; J Edgar Hoover, director of the FBI, **1895**; J D Salinger, US author, **1919**; Joe Orton, English dramatist, **1933**.

≈ DEATHS ≈

William Wycherley, English dramatist, **1716**; James Stuart, the Old Pretender, **1766**; Heinrich Hertz, German physicist, **1894**; Edwin Landseer Lutyens, English architect, **1944**; Maurice Chevalier, French actor and singer, **1972**; L Ron Hubbard, US science-fiction writer and founder of Scientology, **1986**.

'Every New Year is the direct descendant,
isn't it, of a long line of proven criminals?'
Ogden Nash, 'Good-by, Old Year, You Oaf or Why Don't They Pay the Bonus?'

2 January

'An archaeologist is the best husband any woman can have:
the older she gets the more he is interested in her.'
Agatha Christie, reported on 2 Jan 1955

Feast day of St Seraphim of Sarov, St Basil, St Gregory Nazianzen, St Munchin, St Adalhard or Adelard, St Caspar of Bufalo, St Macarius of Alexandria, St Vincentian, and the Holy Name of Jesus.

❧ EVENTS ❧

1492 Granada, the last Moorish stronghold in Spain, surrendered to the Spaniards. **1635** Cardinal Richelieu established the Académie Française. **1839** French photographer Louis Daguerre took the first photograph of the Moon. **1946** King Zog of Albania, who had been residing in England since 1939, was deposed. **1959** The Russian uncrewed spacecraft *Luna I*, the first rocket to pass near the Moon, was launched. **1971** A barrier collapsed at the Ibrox Park football stadium in Glasgow, crushing 66 fans to death. **1979** The trial of Sid Vicious, the Sex Pistols' singer accused of murdering his girlfriend Nancy Spungen, began in New York.

❧ BIRTHS ❧

James Wolfe, British general, **1727**; George Murray, English classical scholar, **1866**; Michael Tippett, English composer, **1905**; Isaac Asimov, US biochemist and science-fiction writer, **1920**; Roger Miller, US singer and composer, **1936**; David Bailey, English photographer, **1938**.

❧ DEATHS ❧

Ovid, Roman poet, **17**; Livy, Roman historian, **17**; George Airy, English Astronomer Royal, **1892**; Emil Janning, US film actor, **1950**; Tex Ritter, US stage and screen singing cowboy, **1974**; Dick Emery, English comedian, **1983**.

'Time the devourer of everything.'
Ovid, *Metamorphoses*

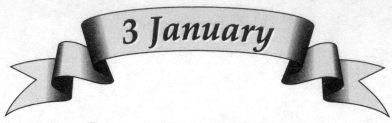

3 January

'Democracy means government by discussion,
but it is only effective if you can stop people talking.'
Clement Attlee

Feast day of St Peter Balsam, St Bertilia of Mareuil, St Antherus, pope, and St Genevieve or Genovefa.

EVENTS

1521 Pope Leo X excommunicated Martin Luther. **1777** The Battle of Princeton took place in the War of Independence, in which George Washington defeated the British forces, led by Cornwallis. **1924** English explorer Howard Carter discovered the sarcophagus of Tutankhamen in the Valley of the Kings, near Luxor, Egypt. **1959** Alaska became the 49th of the United States. **1962** Pope John XXIII excommunicated Cuban prime minister Fidel Castro. **1991** The British government announced that seven Iraqi diplomats, another embassy staff member and 67 other Iraqis were being expelled from Britain. **1993** US President George Bush and Russian President Boris Yeltsin signed the second Strategic Arms Reduction Treaty (START) in Moscow.

BIRTHS

Marcus Tullius Cicero, Roman orator and statesman, **106 BC**; Clement Attlee, British statesman, **1883**; J R R Tolkien, English writer, **1892**, Ray Milland, US film actor, **1907**; Victor Borge, Danish musician and comedian, **1909**; John Thaw, British actor, **1942**.

DEATHS

Josiah Wedgwood, English potter, **1795**; Pierre Larousse, French editor and encyclopedist, **1875**; Jaroslav Hasek, Czech novelist, **1923**; Conrad Hilton, US hotel magnate, **1979**; Joy Adamson, British naturalist and author, **1980**.

'Laws are silent in time of war.'
Marcus Tullius Cicero, Pro Milone

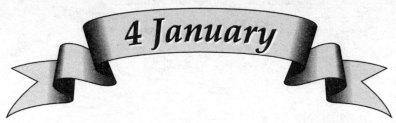

4 January

'Why should a married woman want a mortgage in her own name? We'll have husbands doing the housework next.'
Eric Nash, branch manager of the Magnet and Planet Building Society, reported on 4 Jan 1976

The national day of Myanmar. Feast day of St Gregory of Langres, St Roger of Ellant, St Elizabeth Bayley Seton, St Pharaïdis, and St Rigobert of Reims.

❧ EVENTS ❧

1884 The socialist Fabian Society was founded in London. **1885** The first successful surgical removal of an appendix was performed, in Iowa, USA. **1936** The first pop-music chart was compiled, based on record sales published in New York in Billboard. **1944** The attack on Monte Cassino was launched by the British Fifth Army in Italy. **1972** Rose Heilbron became the first woman judge in Britain at the Old Bailey, London. **1981** The Broadway show *Frankenstein* lost an estimated 2 million dollars, when it opened and closed on the same night. **1991** The UN Security Council voted unanimously to condemn Israel's treatment of the Palestinians in the occupied territories.

❧ BIRTHS ❧

Louis Braille, French deviser of an alphabet for the blind, **1809**; Augustus John, Welsh painter, **1878**; Floyd Patterson, US boxer, **1935**; Grace Bumbry, US opera singer, **1937**; Dyan Cannon, US actress, **1939**; John McLaughlin, British blues and jazz guitarist, **1943**.

❧ DEATHS ❧

Ralph Vaughan Williams, English composer, **1958**; Albert Camus, French novelist and dramatist, **1960**; T S Eliot, US poet and critic, **1965**; Brian Gwynne Horrocks, British general, **1985**; Christopher Isherwood, English novelist and dramatist, **1986**.

'The world is not a place where good is rewarded and evil punished.'
Canon Colin Semper, reported on 4 Jan 1981

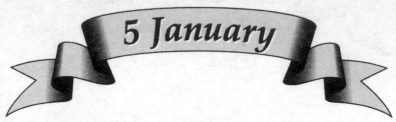

5 January

'The chief business of the American people is business.'
Calvin Coolidge

Feast day of St Simeon Stylites, St Gerlac, St Dorotheus the Younger, St Apollinaris, St Convoyon, St Syncletica, and St John Nepomucene Neumann.

✤ EVENTS ✤

1477 Charles the Bold, King of France, was killed at the Battle of Nancy. **1896** German physicist Röntgen gave the first demonstration of X-rays. **1938** Billie Holiday recorded 'When You're Smiling (the Whole World Smiles with You)' in New York. **1964** The London Underground's first automatic ticket barrier was installed, at Stamford Brook. **1964** On his tour of the Holy Land, Pope Paul VI met Patriarch Athenagoras I, the first meeting between the heads of the Roman Catholic and Orthodox Churches in over 500 years. **1976** French premier Giscard d'Estaing promulgated a law making French the only language permitted in advertising in France.

✤ BIRTHS ✤

Konrad Adenauer, German statesman, **1876**; Stella Gibbons, English poet and novelist, **1902**; Alfred Brendel, Austrian concert pianist, **1931**; Robert Duvall, US film actor, **1931**; Juan Carlos, King of Spain, **1938**; Diane Keaton, US film actress, **1946**.

✤ DEATHS ✤

English king Edward the Confessor, **1066**; Catherine de' Medici, Queen of France, **1589**; Count Radetzky, Austrian soldier, **1858**; Henry Shackleton, Irish Antarctic explorer, **1922**; Calvin Coolidge, 30th US president, **1933**; Amy Johnson, English aviator, **1941**.

'How could they tell?'
Dorothy Parker, on being told of the president's death

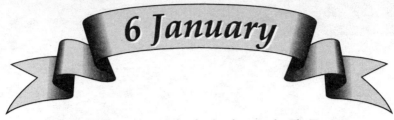

6 January

'I think I'd go to prison for the *Sun* but not for *The Times*.'
Rupert Murdoch, *Observer* 6 Jan 1985

Epiphany. Feast day of St John de Ribera, St Erminold, St Wiltrudis, St Guarinus.

✎ EVENTS ✎

871 English king Alfred defeated the Danes at the Battle of Ashdown. **1540** King Henry VIII was married to Anne of Cleves, his fourth wife. **1720** The Committee of Inquiry on the South Sea Bubble published its findings. **1838** The first public demonstration of the electric telegraph was given by its inventor, Samuel Morse. **1928** The River Thames flooded, drowning four people, and severely damaging paintings stored in the Tate Gallery's basement. **1945** The Battle of the Bulge, or Ardennes offensive, ended, with 130,000 German and 77,000 Allied casualties. **1988** La Coupole, the Parisian brasserie made famous by generations of notable artists and writers who frequented it, was sold for £6 million to be converted into an office block.

✎ BIRTHS ✎

King Richard II of England, **1367**; St Joan of Arc, **1412**; Gustave Doré, French artist and illustrator, **1833**; Carl Sandburg, US poet, **1878**; Loretta Young, US film actress, **1913**; Rowan Atkinson, English actor and comedian, **1957**; Kapil Dev, Indian cricketer, **1959**.

✎ DEATHS ✎

Fanny Burney, English novelist and diarist, **1840**; Gregor Mendel, Austrian monk and biologist, **1884**; Theodore Roosevelt, 26th US president, **1919**; Archibald Joseph Cronin, Scottish novelist, **1981**; Rudolf Nureyev, Russian dancer, **1993**; Dizzy Gillespie, US jazz trumpeter, **1993**.

'I am as strong as a bull moose and you can use me to the limit.'
Theodore Roosevelt

7 January

'My advice to all who want to attend a lecture on music is
"Don't: go to a concert instead." '
Ralph Vaughan Williams, reported on 7 Jan 1923

Christmas Day in the Orthodox Church. Feast day of St Valentine, St Raymund of Peñafort, St Aldric, St Lucian of Antioch, St Tillo, St Canute Lavard, and St Reinold.

EVENTS

1558 Calais, the last English possession on mainland France, was recaptured by the French. **1610** Italian astronomer Galileo discovered Jupiter's four satellites, naming them Io, Europa, Ganymede, and Callisto. **1785** The first aerial crossing of the English Channel was made by Jean Pierre Blanchard and Dr John Jeffries, in a hot-air balloon. **1927** The London–New York telephone service began operating, a three-minute call costing £15. **1975** OPEC agreed to raise crude oil prices by 10%, which began a tidal wave of world economic inflation. **1990** The Leaning Tower of Pisa was closed to the public, as its accelerated rate of 'leaning' raised fears for the safety of its many visitors.

BIRTHS

Joseph Bonaparte, King of Naples, **1768**; Carl Laemmle, US film producer, founder of Universal Pictures, **1867**; Adolph Zukor, US film magnate, **1873**; Charles Péguy, French poet and socialist, **1873**; Francis Poulenc, French composer, **1899**; Gerald Durrell, British author and naturalist, **1925**.

DEATHS

Catherine of Aragon, first wife of Henry VIII, **1536**; Nicholas Hilliard, English miniaturist painter, **1619**; André Maginot, French politician, **1932**; Trevor Howard, British actor, **1988**; Michinomiya Hirohito, Emperor of Japan, **1989**.

'As a cultural triumph, the evolution of societies without government
in which people detest violence in all forms should rank as high
as stealing an empire by mass murder or building ornate religious
edifices in which hardly anyone now worships.'
Robert Knox Denton, after living 30 years with a Malaysian forest people

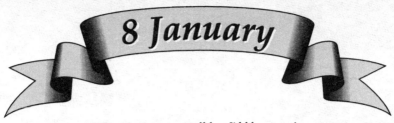

8 January

'I can't sing very well but I'd like to try.'
Elvis Presley, on first entering a studio

Feast day of St Severinus of Noricum, St Severinus of Septempeda, and St Wulsin.

EVENTS

1815 The Americans, under Andrew Jackson, defeated the British at the Battle of New Orleans. **1886** The Severn Railway Tunnel – Britain's longest – was opened. **1889** US inventor Herman Hollerith patented his tabulator, the first device for data processing; his firm would later become one of IBM's founding companies. **1916** The final withdrawal of Allied troops from Gallipoli took place. **1921** David Lloyd George became the first prime minister tenant at Chequers Court, Buckinghamshire. **1959** French general Charles de Gaulle became the first president of the Fifth Republic. **1993** Bosnian President Izetbegovic visited the USA to plead his government's case for Western military aid and intervention to halt Serbian aggression.

BIRTHS

Wilkie Collins, English novelist, **1824**; Elvis Presley, US rock singer, **1935**; Shirley Bassey, Welsh-born singer, **1937**; Stephen Hawking, English physicist and mathematician, **1942**; David Bowie, English rock singer and actor, **1947**; Calvin Smith, US athlete, **1961**.

DEATHS

Galileo Galilei, Italian astronomer, **1642**; Eli Whitney, US inventor of the cotton gin, **1825**; Paul Verlaine, French poet, **1895**; Zhou Enlai, Chinese leader, **1976**; Gregori Maximilianovich Malenkov, Soviet leader, **1988**; Terry- Thomas, English film comedy actor, **1990**.

'Each equation ... in the book would halve the sales.'
Stephen Hawking, A Brief History of Time

9 January

'One is not born a woman: one becomes one.'
Simone de Beauvoir, *Le deuxième sexe*

Feast day of Saints Julian and Basilissa, St Berhtwald of Canterbury, St Peter of Sebastea, St Waningus or Vaneng, and St Marciana of Rusuccur.

～ EVENTS ～

1799 British prime minister William Pitt the Younger introduced income tax, at two shillings (10p) in the pound, to raise funds for the Napoleonic Wars. **1902** New York State introduced a bill to outlaw flirting in public. **1969** The supersonic aeroplane *Concorde* made its first trial flight, at Bristol. **1972** The ocean liner *Queen Elizabeth* was destroyed by fire in Hong Kong harbour. **1972** British miners went on strike for the first time since 1926. **1991** US secretary of state Baker and Iraqi foreign minister Aziz met for 6½ hours in Geneva, but failed to reach any agreement that would forestall war in the Persian Gulf.

～ BIRTHS ～

Gracie Fields, English singer, **1898**; George Balanchine, US choreographer, **1904**; Simone de Beauvoir, French novelist and critic, **1908**; Richard Nixon, 37th US president, **1913**; Gypsy Rose Lee, US striptease artist and actress, **1914**; Joan Baez, US singer, **1941**.

～ DEATHS ～

Caroline Lucretia Herschel, English astronomer, **1848**; Napoleon III, French emperor, **1873**; Katherine Mansfield, New Zealand writer, **1923**; Tommy Handley, English radio comedian, **1949**; Frederick Gibberd, British architect, **1984**; Robert Mayer, British philanthropist, **1985**.

'God wants us to be rich and comfortable.'
Walter Hoving, chairman of Tiffany's, reported on 9 Jan 1983

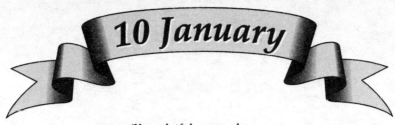

10 January

'You ask if they were happy.
This is not a European characteristic - that's for the cows.'
Coco Chanel

Feast day of St Marcian of Constantinople, St William of Bourges, St Agatho,
pope, St Dermot or Diarmaid, St Peter Orseolo, and St John the Good.

✎ EVENTS ✎

1840 The penny post, whereby mail was delivered at a standard charge rather than
paid for by the recipient, began in Britain. **1863** Prime Minister Gladstone opened
the first section of the London Underground Railway system, from Paddington to
Farringdon Street. **1920** The Treaty of Versailles was ratified, officially ending
World War I with Germany. **1920** The League of Nations held its first meeting in
Geneva. **1926** Fritz Lang's film *Metropolis* was first shown, in Berlin. **1946** The
first meeting of the United Nations General Assembly took place in London.
1949 Vinyl records were launched by RCA (45 r.p.m.) and Columbia (33.3
r.p.m.). **1992** An IRA bomb exploded in Whitehall, London, 300 m/975 ft from
Downing Street; the IRA threatened further attacks on the mainland.

✎ BIRTHS ✎

Michel Ney, French marshal, **1769**; Barbara Hepworth, English sculptor, **1903**;
Paul Henreid, Austrian actor, **1908**; Galina Ulanova, Russian ballerina, **1910**;
Johnny Ray, US singer, **1927**; Rod Stewart, English rock singer, **1945**.

✎ DEATHS ✎

Carolus Linnaeus, Swedish botanist, **1778**; Samuel Colt, US gunsmith, **1862**;
Sinclair Lewis, US novelist, **1951**; Dashiell Hammett, US detective-story writer,
1961; Coco (Gabrielle) Chanel, French fashion designer, **1971**; Anton Karas,
Austrian composer, **1985**.

'Nature does not make jumps.'
Carolus Linnaeus

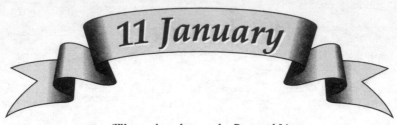

11 January

'We two kept house, the Past and I.'
Thomas Hardy, "The Ghost of the Past"

Feast day of St Salvius or Sauve of Amiens, and St Theodosius the Cenobiarch.

EVENTS

1569 England's first state lottery was held; tickets were obtainable from the West Door of St Paul's Cathedral, London. **1867** Benito Juarez returned to the Mexican presidency, following the withdrawal of French troops and the execution of Emperor Maximilian. **1922** Leonard Thompson became the first person to be successfully treated with insulin, at Toronto General Hospital. **1963** The first disco, called the 'Whisky-a-go-go', opened in Los Angeles, USA. **1973** The Open University awarded its first degrees. **1977** Rolling Stone Keith Richards was tried in London for possession of cocaine, found in his car after an accident, and fined £750. **1991** An auction of silver and paintings that had been acquired by the late Ferdinand Marcos and his wife, Imelda, brought in a total of $20.29 million at Christie's in New York.

BIRTHS

Ezra Cornell, US philanthropist, **1807**; Fred Archer, English jockey, **1857**; Henry Gordon Selfridge, US entrepreneur and founder of the London department store, 1864; Alan Paton, South African author, 1903; Rod Taylor, Australian film actor, **1929**; John Sessions, English actor and comedian, **1953**.

DEATHS

Hans Sloane, British physician and naturalist, **1753**; Thomas Hardy, English poet and novelist, **1928**; Alberto Giacometti, Swiss sculptor and painter, **1966**; Richmal Crompton, English author, **1969**; Padraic Colum, Irish poet, **1972**; Isidor Rabi, US physicist, **1988**.

'Tis the star-spangled banner; O long may it wave
O'er the land of the free, and the home of the brave.'
Francis Scott Key

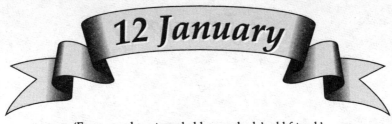

12 January

'Every murderer is probably somebody's old friend.'
Agatha Christie, *The Mysterious Affair at Styles*

Feast day of St Benedict or Benet Biscop, St Tatiana, St Margaret Bourgeoys, St Arcadius, St Caesaria, St Victorian, and St Eutropius.

EVENTS

1866 The Royal Aeronautical Society was founded in London. **1875** Kwang-su was made emperor of China. **1964** The Sultan of Zanzibar was overthrown, following an uprising, and a republic proclaimed. **1971** PLO terrorist Abu Davoud, leader of the Black September group responsible for the killing of 11 Israeli athletes at the Munich Olympics, was released from prison in France. **1970** The Boeing 747 aircraft touched down at Heathrow Airport at the end of its first transatlantic flight. **1991** US Congress passed a resolution authorising President Bush to use military power to force Iraq out of Kuwait. **1993** Sectarian violence continued for the eighth consecutive day in Bombay, India; 200 people died in nationwide clashes.

BIRTHS

Johann Pestalozzi, Swiss educational reformer, **1746**; John Singer Sargent, US painter, **1856**; Jack London, US author, **1876**; Hermann Goering, German Nazi leader, **1893**; P W Botha, South African politician, **1916**; Joe Frazier, US heavyweight boxer, **1944**.

DEATHS

Maximilian I, Holy Roman Emperor, **1519**; Jan Brueghel the Elder, Flemish painter, **1625**; Pierre de Fermat, French mathematician, **1665**; Isaac Pitman, English teacher and inventor of shorthand, **1897**; Nevil Shute, English novelist, **1960**; Agatha Christie, English detective-story writer, **1976**.

'Every time I paint a portrait I lose a friend.'
John Singer Sargent

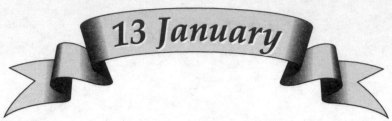

13 January

'Politics come from man. Mercy, compassion and justice come from God.'
Terry Waite, reported on 13 Jan 1985

Feast day of St Hilary of Poitiers, St Agrecius, and St Berno.

≈ EVENTS ≈

1893 The British Independent Labour Party was formed by Keir Hardie. **1898** French novelist Emile Zola published *J'accuse/I Accuse*, a pamphlet indicting the persecutors of Dreyfus. **1910** Opera was broadcast on the radio for the first time – Enrico Caruso singing from the stage of New York's Metropolitan Opera House. **1964** Capitol records released the Beatles' first single in the USA; 'I Wanna Hold Your Hand' sold one million copes in the first three weeks. **1978** NASA selected its first women astronauts, 15 years after the USSR had a female astronaut orbit the Earth. **1991** Soviet troops killed 15 protesters in Vilnius, capital of Lithuania, in a crackdown on pro-independence forces. **1993** Former East German leader Erich Honecker, who had been awaiting trial on charges of manslaughter, was released from a Berlin prison because of ill health.

≈ BIRTHS ≈

Sophie Tucker, US singer and vaudeville star, **1884**; Johannes Bjelke-Petersen, Australian politician, **1911**; Ted Willis, English dramatist, **1918**; Robert Stack, US film actor, **1919**; Michael Bond, English creator of the Paddington Bear stories for children, **1926**.

≈ DEATHS ≈

Edmund Spenser, English poet, **1599**; George Fox, English founder of the Society of Friends, **1691**; Stephen Foster, US songwriter, **1864**; James Joyce, Irish novelist, **1941**; Hubert Humphrey, US politician, **1978**.

'It bewilders Americans to be hated.'
Lance Morrow, reported on 13 Jan 1980

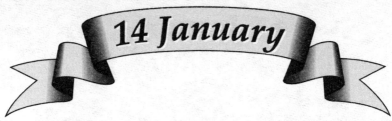

14 January

'The language down the pit is no worse than in a ladies' shoe shop.'
Tom Lindop, member of Newcastle-under-Lyme Industrial Tribunal,
reported on 14 Jan 1979

Feast day of The Martyrs of Mount Sinai, St Barbasymas or Barbascemin, St Antony Pucci, St Datius, St Macrina the Elder, St Sava, St Felix of Nola, and St Kentigern or Mungo.

✎ EVENTS ✎

1858 Attempt on the life of Napoleon III, in Paris. **1900** Puccini's opera *Tosca* was first performed, in Rome. **1907** An earthquake killed over 1,000 people in Kingston, Jamaica, virtually destroying the capital. **1943** US President Roosevelt and British Prime Minister Churchill met at Casablanca. **1954** Baseball hero Joe DiMaggio married film star Marilyn Monroe. **1993** Amid increasingly intrusive coverage about the private lives of the British royal family, the government pledged to introduce legislation to criminalise invasions of privacy by the press.

✎ BIRTHS ✎

Henri Fantin-Latour, French painter, **1836**; Albert Schweitzer, French missionary surgeon, **1875**; Cecil Beaton, British photographer and stage designer, **1904**; Joseph Losey, US film director, **1909**; Trevor Nunn, British stage director, **1940**; Faye Dunaway, US actress, **1941**.

✎ DEATHS ✎

Edmond Halley, English astronomer, **1742**; Jean Auguste Dominique Ingres, French painter, **1867**; Lewis Carroll, English mathematician and author, **1898**; Humphrey Bogart, US film actor, **1957**; Peter Finch, English actor, **1977**; Anaïs Nin, US novelist and diarist, **1977**.

' "What is the use of a book," thought Alice,
"without pictures or conversations?" '
Lewis Carroll, *Alice's Adventures in Wonderland*

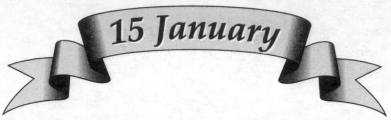

15 January

'If A is success in life, then A equals X plus Y plus Z. Work is X; Y is play; and Z is keeping your mouth shut.'
Albert Einstein, reported on 15 Jan 1950

Feast day of St Macarius the Elder, St Isidore of Alexandria, St Bonitus or Bonet, St Ita, and St John Calybites.

EVENTS

1559 The coronation of Queen Elizabeth I took place. **1759** The British Museum opened, at Montague House, Bloomsbury, London. **1797** London haberdasher James Hetherington was fined £50 for wearing his new creation, the top hat. **1880** The London Telephone Company published Britain's first telephone directory, listing 255 names. **1927** Captain Teddy Wakelam gave the first live rugby commentary on BBC radio of the match between Wales and England at Twickenham. **1971** The Aswan High Dam, on the Nile, financed by the USSR, was opened. **1973** President Nixon called a halt to the USA's Vietnam offensive. **1992** The EC granted diplomatic recognition to Slovenia and Croatia, essentially recognising the dismemberment of Yugoslavia.

BIRTHS

Molière, French dramatist, **1622**; Aristotle Onassis, Greek shipowner, **1906**; Lloyd Bridges, US film actor, **1913**; Gamal Nasser, Egyptian leader, **1918**; Martin Luther King, US civil-rights campaigner, **1929**; Margaret O'Brien, US film actress, **1937**.

DEATHS

Emma Hamilton, English courtesan, mistress to Lord Nelson, **1815**; Matthew B Brady, US Civil War photographer, **1896**; Rosa Luxemburg, German socialist, **1919**; Jack Teagarden, US jazz musician, **1964**; Sean MacBride, Irish politician, **1988**; Sammy Cahn, US lyricist, **1993**.

'I assure you that a learned fool is more foolish than an ignorant fool.'
Molière, *Les Femmes Savantes*

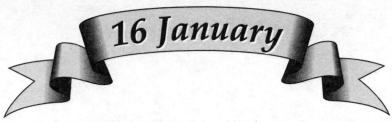

16 January

'We shall reach the helm within five years.'
Oswald Mosley, reported on 16 Jan 1938

Feast day of St Henry of Cocket, St Marcellus, pope, St Berard and Others, St Fursey, St Priscilla, and St Honoratus of Arles.

≈ EVENTS ≈

1547 Ivan the Terrible was crowned first tsar of Russia. **1809** The British defeated the French at the Battle of Corunna, in the Peninsular War. **1920** The 18th Amendment to the US Constitution was ratified, prohibiting the sale of alcoholic beverages. **1925** Leon Trotsky was dismissed as Chairman of the Revolutionary Council of the USSR. **1932** Duke Ellington and his Orchestra recorded 'It Don't Mean a Thing' in New York. **1970** Colonel Khaddafi became virtual president of Libya. **1991** A US-led international force launched Operation Desert Storm on Iraq and Iraqi-occupied Kuwait less than 17 hours after the expiration of the UN deadline for Iraqi withdrawal.

≈ BIRTHS ≈

Franz Brentano, German philosopher, **1838**; André Michelin, French tyremaker, **1853**; Diana Wynyard, British actress, **1906**, Alexander Knox, Canadian film actor, **1907**; Ethel Merman, US singer and actress, **1909**; Cliff Thorburn, snooker player, **1948**.

≈ DEATHS ≈

Léo Delibes, French composer, **1891**; Carole Lombard, US film actress, **1942**; Arturo Toscanini, Italian conductor, **1957**; Robert Van de Graff, US nuclear physicist, **1967**; Mohammed Reza Pahlavi, former Shah of Iran, **1979**; Florence Desmond, British actress, **1993**.

'God tells me how he wants this music played - and you get in his way.'
Arturo Toscanini

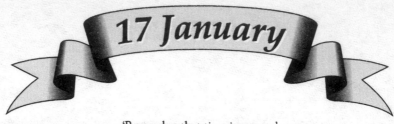

17 January

'Remember that time is money.'
Benjamin Franklin

Feast day of St Sabinus of Piacenza, St Julian Sabas, St Antony the Abbot, St Geulf or Genou, St Richimir, St Sulpicius II or Sulpice of Bourges, and Saints Speusippus, Eleusippus, and Meleusippus.

EVENTS

1377 The Papal See was transferred from Avignon back to Rome. **1773** Captain Cook's Resolution became the first ship to cross the Antarctic Circle. **1852** The independence of the Transvaal Boers was recognised by Britain. **1912** English explorer Robert Falcon Scott reached the South Pole; Norwegian Roald Amundsen had beaten him there by one month. **1959** Senegal and the French Sudan joined to form the Federal State of Mali. **1966** A B-52 carrying four H-bombs collided with a refuelling tanker, killing eight of the crew and releasing the bombs. **1977** US double murderer Gary Gilmore became the first to be executed in the USA in a decade; he chose to be executed by firing squad. **1992** An IRA bomb, placed next to a remote country road in County Tyrone, Northern Ireland, killed seven building workers and injured seven others.

BIRTHS

Benjamin Franklin, US statesman and scientist, **1706**; David Lloyd George, English statesman, **1863**; Nevil Shute, English novelist, **1899**; Al Capone, US gangster, **1899**; Muhammad Ali, US boxer, **1942**; Paul Young, English singer, **1956**.

DEATHS

Tomaso Giovanni Albinoni, Italian composer, **1751**; Quintin Hogg, English merchant and philanthropist, **1903**; Francis Galton, English anthropologist and explorer, **1911**; T W White, English writer, **1964**; Ruskin Spear, British artist, **1990**.

'Once in the racket you're always in it.'
Al Capone, Philadelphia Public Ledger 18 May 1929

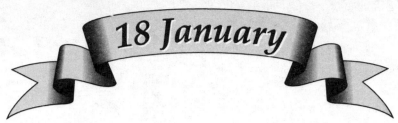

18 January

'Had the employers of past generations dealt fairly with men, there would have been no trade unions.'
Stanley Baldwin, reported on 18 Jan 1931

Feast day of St Prisca, St Peter's Chair, Rome, St Desle or Deicolus, and St Volusian.

EVENTS

1778 Captain Cook discovered the Sandwich Islands, now known as Hawaii. **1871** Wilhelm, King of Prussia from **1861**, was proclaimed the first German Emperor. **1911** The first landing of an aircraft on a ship's deck was made by US pilot Eugene Ely, in San Francisco Bay. **1919** The Versailles Peace Conference opened. **1944** The German siege of Leningrad, which began Sept 1941, was relieved. **1972** Former Rhodesian prime minister Garfield Todd and his daughter were placed under house arrest for campaigning against Rhodesian independence. **1977** In Australia, a Sydney-bound train derailed, killing 82 people.

BIRTHS

Peter Mark Roget, English lexicographer, **1779**; A A Milne, English author, **1882**; Oliver Hardy, US comedian, **1892**; Cary Grant, US film actor, **1904**; Danny Kaye, US film actor and comedian, **1913**; David Bellamy, English botanist, **1933**.

DEATHS

John Tyler, 10th US president, **1862**; Rudyard Kipling, English author, **1936**; Sydney Greenstreet, British film actor, **1954**; Hugh Gaitskell, British statesman, **1963**; Cecil Beaton, English photographer and designer, **1980**; George Markstein, British author, **1988**.

'Asia is not going to be civilized after the methods of the West. There is too much Asia and she is too old.'
Rudyard Kipling, *Life's Handicap* "The Man Who Was"

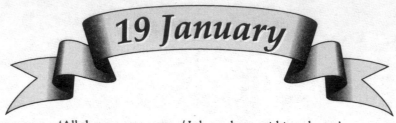

19 January

'All that we see or seem / Is but a dream within a dream.'
Edgar Allan Poe, "A Dream within a Dream"

Feast day of St Canute IV of Denmark, Saints Abachum and Audifax, St Fillan or Foelan, St Albert of Cashel, St Charles of Sezze, St Germanicus, Saints Marius and Martha, St Messalina, St Henry of Uppsala, St Nathalan, and St Wulfstan.

～ EVENTS ～

1764 John Wilkes was expelled from the British House of Commons for seditious libel. **1793** King Louis XVI was tried by the French Convention, found guilty of treason and sentenced to the guillotine. **1853** Verdi's opera *Il Trovatore* was first staged in Rome. **1915** More than 20 people were killed when German zeppelins bombed England for the first time; the bombs were dropped on Great Yarmouth and King's Lynn. **1942** The Japanese invaded Burma (now Myanmar). **1966** Indira Gandhi became prime minister of India. **1969** In protest against the Russian invasion of 1968, Czech student Jan Palach set himself alight in Prague's Wenceslas Square. **1993** IBM announced a loss of $4.97 billion for 1992, the largest single-year loss in US corporate history.

～ BIRTHS ～

James Watt, Scottish inventor, 1736; Edgar Allan Poe, US author and poet 1809; Paul Cézanne, French painter, **1839**; Janis Joplin, US rock singer, **1943**; Dolly Parton, US country singer, **1946**; Stefan Edberg, Swedish tennis player, **1966**.

～ DEATHS ～

Hans Sachs, German poet and composer, **1576**; William Congreve, English dramatist, **1729**; Louis Hérold, French composer, **1833**; Pierre-Joseph Proudhon, French journalist and anarchist, **1865**; Bhagwam Shree Rajneesh, Indian guru, **1990**.

'Property is theft.'
Pierre-Joseph Proudhon, *Qu'est-ce que la propriété*

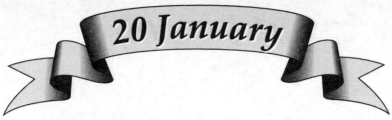
20 January

'Too bad all the people who know how to run the country
are busy driving cabs and cutting hair.'
George Burns

Feast day of St Sebastian, St Fabian, pope, St Euthymius the Great, and St Fechin.

✏ EVENTS ✏

1265 The first English parliament met in Westminster Hall, convened by the Earl of Leicester, Simon de Montfort. **1841** Hong Kong was ceded by China and occupied by the British. **1886** The Mersey Railway Tunnel was officially opened by the Prince of Wales. **1892** The game of basketball was first played at the YMCA in Springfield, Massachusetts. **1944** The RAF dropped 2,300 tons of bombs on Berlin. **1961** John F Kennedy was inaugurated as the 35th US president, and the first Roman Catholic to hold this office. **1981** Fifty-two Americans, held hostage in the US embassy in Teheran for 444 days by followers of Ayatollah Khomeini, were released. **1987** Terry Waite, the Archbishop of Canterbury's special envoy in the Middle East, disappeared on a peace mission in Beirut, Lebanon.

✏ BIRTHS ✏

Theobald Wolfe Tone, Irish nationalist, **1763**; George Burns, US comedian and actor, **1896**; Federico Fellini, Italian film director, **1920**; Patricia Neal, US film actress, **1926**; Edwin Aldrin, US astronaut, **1930**; Malcolm McLaren, British rock impresario, **1946**.

✏ DEATHS ✏

John Soane, English architect, **1837**; John Ruskin, English art critic and writer, **1900**; King George V, **1936**; Johnny Weissmuller, US film actor and swimmer, **1984**; Barbara Stanwyck, US film actress, **1990**; Audrey Hepburn, British film actress, **1993**.

'Life without industry is guilt, and industry without art is brutality.'
John Ruskin

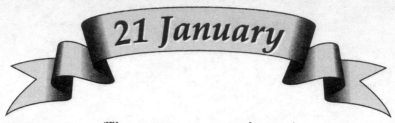
21 January

'We are winning international respect.'
Adolf Hitler, reported on 21 Jan 1934

Feast day of St Agnes, St Fructuosus of Tarragona, St Patroclus of Troyes, St Alban or Bartholomew Roe, St Epiphanius of Pavia, and St Meinrad.

∽ EVENTS ∽

1793 Louis XVI, King of France, was guillotined in Place de la Révolution. **1846** The first issue of the *Daily News*, edited by Charles Dickens, was published. **1911** The first Monte Carlo car rally was held; it was won seven days later by French racer Henri Rougier. **1941** The British communist newspaper, the *Daily Worker*, was banned due to wartime restrictions. **1954** The world's first nuclear submarine, the USS *Nautilus*, was launched. **1976** *Concorde* inaugurated its commercial service with simultaneous take-offs, from Paris to Rio de Janeiro and from London to Bahrain.

∽ BIRTHS ∽

John Charles Fremont, US explorer, **1813**; Thomas Jonathan ('Stonewall') Jackson, US Confederate general, **1824**; Christian Dior, French couturier, **1905**; Benny Hill, English comedian, **1924**; Jack Nicklaus, US golfer, **1940**; Placido Domingo, Spanish operatic tenor, **1941**.

∽ DEATHS ∽

Elisha Gray, US inventor, **1901**; V I Lenin, Russian leader, **1924**; Lytton Strachey, English critic and biographer, **1932**; George Orwell, British novelist, **1950**; Cecil B De Mille, US film director, **1959**.

'Comprehensive schools demonstrate that we are all members
of one family, of one society.'
Shirley Williams, reported on 21 Jan 1979

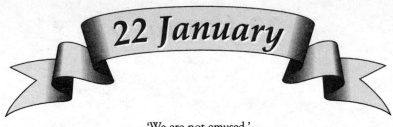

22 January

'We are not amused.'
Queen Victoria, Attr.

Feast day of St Dominic of Sora, St Berthwald of Ramsbury, St Anastasius the Persian, St Blesilla, St Vincent Pallotti, and St Vincent of Saragossa.

~ EVENTS ~

1771 The Falkland Islands were ceded to Britain by Spain. **1879** British troops were massacred by the Zulus at Isandhlwana. **1905** Insurgent workers were fired on in St Petersburg, resulting in 'Bloody Sunday'. **1924** Ramsay MacDonald took office as Britain's first Labour prime minister. **1959** British world racing champion Mike Hawthorn was killed while driving on the Guildford bypass. **1972** The United Kingdom, the Irish Republic, and Denmark joined the Common Market. **1973** US boxer George Foreman knocked out Joe Frazier in Kingston, Jamaica, becoming the world heavyweight boxing champion. **1992** Rebel soldiers seized the national radio station in Kinshasa, Zaire's capital, and broadcast a demand for the government's resignation.

~ BIRTHS ~

Ivan III (the Great), Grand Duke of Muscovy, **1440**; Francis Bacon, English politician and philosopher, **1561**; Lord Byron, English poet, **1788**; D W Griffith, US film producer and director, **1875**; John Hurt, English actor, **1940**; George Foreman, US boxer, **1948**.

~ DEATHS ~

William Paterson, Scottish financier, **1719**; David Edward Hughes, English inventor, **1900**; Queen Victoria, **1901**; Lyndon B Johnson, 36th US president, **1973**; Herbert Sutcliffe, English cricketer, **1978**; Arthur Bryant, British historian, **1985**.

'One of the minor pleasures in life is to be slightly ill.'
Harold Nicolson, reported on 22 Jan 1950

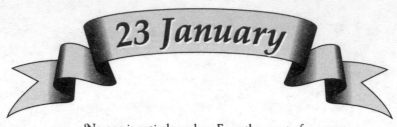

23 January

'No one is entirely useless. Even the worst of us
can serve as horrible examples.'
Editor, *State Prison Newspaper*, Salt Lake City, USA, 23 Jan 1949

Feast day of St Bernard of Vienne, Saints Clement and Agathangelus, St Asclas, St John the Almsgiver, St Emerentiana, St Maimbod, St Ildephonsus, and St Lufthidis.

EVENTS

1556 An earthquake in Shanxi Province, China, is thought to have killed some 830,000 people. **1571** The Royal Exchange in London, founded by financier Thomas Gresham, was opened by Queen Elizabeth I. **1849** English-born Elizabeth Blackwell graduated from a New York medical school to become the first woman doctor. **1924** The first Labour government was formed, under Ramsay MacDonald. **1943** The British captured Tripoli from the Germans. **1960** The US Navy bathyscaphe *Trieste*, designed by Dr Piccard, descended to a record depth of 10,750 m /35,820 ft in the Pacific Ocean. **1985** The proceedings of the House of Lords were televised for the first time.

BIRTHS

Stendhal, French novelist, **1783**; Edouard Manet, French painter, **1832**; Sergei Mikhailovich Eisenstein, Russian film director, **1898**; Alfred Denning, British judge and former Master of the Rolls, **1899**, Jeanne Moreau, French actress, **1928**; HSH Princess Caroline of Monaco, **1957**.

DEATHS

William Pitt the Younger, British prime minister, **1806**; Anna Pavlova, Russian ballerina, **1931**; Edvard Munch, Norwegian painter, **1944**; Pierre Bonnard, French painter, **1947**; Paul Robeson, US actor and singer, **1976**; Salvador Dali, Spanish painter and sculptor, **1989**.

Friend: 'Dali, you go too far.'
Dali: 'But that's where I've always wanted to go.'
Salvador Dali

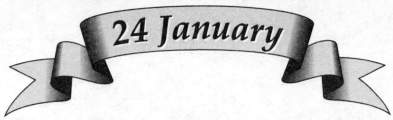

24 January

'Never in the field of human conflict was so much owed by so many to so few.'
Winston Churchill, *Hansard* 18 June 1940

Feast day of St Francis of Sales, St Babylas of Antioch, St Felician of Foligno, and St Macedonius the Barley-eater.

❧ EVENTS ❧

1848 James Marshall was the first to discover gold in California, at Sutter's Mill near Coloma. **1916** The US Supreme Court ruled that income tax is unconstitutional. **1916** Conscription was introduced in Britain. **1935** Beer in cans was first sold, in Virginia, USA, by the Kreuger Brewing Company. **1962** French film director François Truffaut's *Jules et Jim* premiered in Paris. **1978** A Russian satellite crashed near Yellow Knife in Canada's Northwest Territory. **1991** More than 15,000 Allied air sorties were flown in the Gulf War, with 23 aircraft lost.

❧ BIRTHS ❧

Hadrian, Roman emperor, **76**; Frederick the Great, King of Prussia, **1712**; Ernest Borgnine, US film actor, **1917**; Desmond Morris, English zoologist and writer, **1928**; Neil Diamond, US singer and songwriter, **1941**; Nastassja Kinski, German film actress, **1961**.

❧ DEATHS ❧

Caligula, Roman emperor, assassinated, AD **41**; Randolph Churchill, British politician, **1895**; Amadeo Modigliani, Italian artist, **1920**; Winston Churchill, British prime minister, **1965**; George Cukor, US film director, **1983**.

'Would that the Roman people had but one neck.'
Caligula

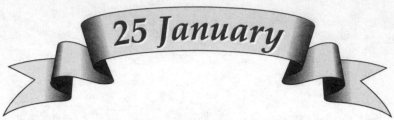

25 January

'It is quite an arguable proposition that mankind has owed as much to its bugbears as to its heroes.'
Winston Churchill, reported on 25 Jan 1925

Feast day of Saints Juventinus and Maximinimus, the Conversion of St Paul, St Apollo, St Artemas, St Publius, St Dwynwen, St Poppo, and Saint Praejectus or Prix.

≈ EVENTS ≈

1533 King Henry VIII and Anne Boleyn were secretly married. **1917** The USA purchased the Danish West Indies (now the Virgin Islands) for $25 million. **1924** The first Winter Olympic Games were inaugurated in Chamonix in the French Alps. **1938** Due to intense sunspot activity, the aurora borealis, or 'northern lights', were seen as far south as western Europe. **1971** Idi Amin led a coup that deposed Milton Obote and became president of Uganda. **1971** At a US court, Charles Manson and others were found guilty of murdering actress Sharon Tate and four others. **1981** Jiang Qing, Mao's widow, was tried for treason and received a death sentence, which was subsequently commuted to life imprisonment.

≈ BIRTHS ≈

Robert Boyle, Irish physicist and chemist, **1627**; Robert Burns, Scottish poet, **1759**; William Somerset Maugham, English author, **1874**; Virginia Woolf, English author, **1882**; Wilhelm Furtwängler, German conductor, **1886**; Edvard Shevardnadze, Russian politician, **1928**.

≈ DEATHS ≈

Marcus Cocceius Nerva, Roman emperor, **AD 98**; Lucas Cranach the Younger, German painter, **1586**; Dorothy Wordsworth, English writer, **1855**; Al Capone, US gangster, **1947**; Ava Gardner, US film actress, **1990**.

'I see the time when people will regard it as a duty to use contraception rather than a duty not to.'
Hugh Montefiore, reported on 25 Jan 1970

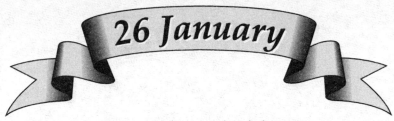

26 January

'India rarely changes and rarely forgets.'
F Yeats Brown, *Bengal Lancer*

The national day of Australia and of India. Feast day of St Timothy, St Margaret of Hungary, St Alberic, St Paula, St Conan of Man, St Titus, St Eystein, and St Thordgith or Theorigitha of Barking.

≫ EVENTS ≪

1500 Vincente Yanez Pinzon discovered Brazil and claimed it for Portugal. **1841** Hong Kong was proclaimed a British sovereign territory. **1871** England's Rugby Football Union was founded in London, by 20 clubs. **1905** The Cullinan diamond, weighing 1¼ lbs, was found by Captain Wells at the Premier Mine, near Pretoria, South Africa. **1939** In the Spanish Civil War, Franco's forces, with Italian aid, took Barcelona. **1950** India became a republic within the Commonwealth. **1965** Hindi was made the official language of India. **1992** Russian President Yeltsin announced that his country would stop targeting US cities with nuclear weapons.

≫ BIRTHS ≪

Douglas MacArthur, US general, **1880**; Stephane Grappelli, French jazz violinist, **1908**; Jimmy Van Heusen, US popular composer, **1913**; Paul Newman, US film actor, **1925**; Eartha Kitt, US singer, **1928**; Roger Vadim, French film director, **1928**.

≫ DEATHS ≪

Edward Jenner, English physician, **1823**; Charles George Gordon, British general, **1885**; Nikolaus August Otto, German engineer, **1891**; Edward G Robinson, US film actor, **1973**; Nelson Rockefeller, US statesman, **1979**; José Ferrer, US actor, **1992**.

'There is in our time no well-educated, literate population that is poor; there is no illiterate population that is other than poor.'
John Kenneth Galbraith

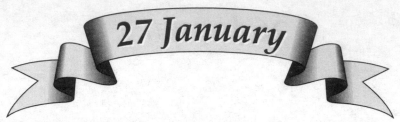
27 January

'It could never be a correct justification that, because the whites oppressed us yesterday when they had power, the blacks must oppress them today when they have power.'
Robert Mugabe

Feast day of St Julian of Le Mans, St Marius or May, St Angela Merici, and St Vitalian, pope.

EVENTS

1879 Thomas Edison patented the electric lamp. **1926** The first public demonstration of television was given by John Logie Baird, at his workshop in London. **1943** The US Air Force carried out its first bombing raid on Germany. **1967** Three US astronauts died in a fire which broke out aboard the spacecraft *Apollo* during tests at Cape Kennedy. **1973** The Vietnam cease-fire agreement was signed by North Vietnam and the USA. **1992** Former world boxing champion Mike Tyson went on trial for allegedly raping an 18-year-old contestant in the 1991 Miss Black America Contest.

BIRTHS

Wolfgang Amadeus Mozart, Austrian composer, **1756**; Wilhelm II, Emperor of Germany, **1859**; Jerome Kern, US composer, **1891**; John Eccles, Australian physiologist, **1903**; Mordecai Richler, Canadian novelist and dramatist, **1931**; John Ogden, English pianist, **1937**.

DEATHS

John Audubon, US artist and naturalist, **1851**; Giuseppe Verdi, Italian composer, **1901**; Giovanni Verga, Italian novelist and dramatist, **1922**; Carl Mannerheim, Finnish soldier and statesman, **1951**; Mahalia Jackson, US gospel singer, **1972**; Thomas Sopwith, British aircraft designer, **1989**.

'In 1969 I published a small book on Humility. It was a pioneering work which has not, to my knowledge, been superseded.'
Frank Longford

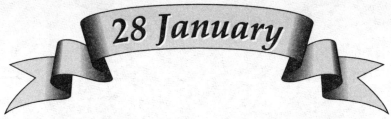
28 January

'Our members will do precisely what is in their contracts without a smile.'
Frank Huff, reported on 28 Jan 1979

Feast day of St Thomas Aquinas, St Amadeus of Lausanne, St Peter Nolasco, St Peter Thomas, and St Paulinus of Aquileia.

❧ EVENTS ❧

1521 The Diet of Worms began, at which Protestant reformer Luther was declared an outlaw by the Roman Catholic church. **1807** London became the world's first city to be illuminated by gas light, when the lamps on Pall Mall were lit. **1871** In the Franco-Prussian War, Paris fell to the Prussians after a five-month siege. **1935** Iceland became the first country to introduce legalised abortion. **1942** The British Eighth Army retreated to El Alamein. **1986** The US space shuttle *Challenger* exploded shortly after lift-off from Cape Canaveral, killing five men and two women on board. **1993** Solicitors for British prime minister John Major issued writs for libel against the *New Statesman* and *Scallywag* for publishing stories detailing rumours of an affair between Major and Clare Latimer, a caterer.

❧ BIRTHS ❧

Henry Morton Stanley, British journalist and explorer, **1841**; Auguste Piccard, Swiss balloonist and deep-sea explorer, **1884**; Ernst Lubitsch, US film director, **1892**; Jackson Pollock, US artist, **1921**; Alan Alda, US film actor and director, **1936**; Mikhail Baryshnikov, Russian ballet dancer, **1948**.

❧ DEATHS ❧

Charlemagne, Holy Roman emperor, **814**; Francis Drake, English buccaneer and explorer, **1596**; Thomas Bodley, English scholar and diplomat, **1613**; Vicente Blasco Ibáñez, Spanish writer and politician, **1928**; W B Yeats, Irish poet, **1939**; Klaus Fuchs, German spy, **1988**.

'I have spread my dreams under your feet;
Tread softly, because you tread on my dreams.'
W B Yeats, "He Wishes for the Cloths of Heaven"

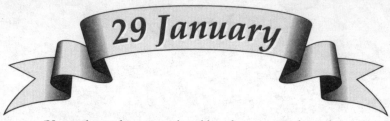

29 January

'Human beings have an inalienable right to invent themselves;
when that right is pre-empted it is called brain-washing.'
Germaine Greer, *The Times* 1 Feb 1986

Feast day of St Sainian of Troyes, St Sulpicius 'Severus', and St Gildas the Wise.

✎ EVENTS ✎

1728 John Gay's *The Beggar's Opera* was first performed at Lincoln's Inn Fields Theatre, London. **1848** Greenwich Mean Time was adopted by Scotland. **1856** Britain's highest military decoration, the Victoria Cross, was founded by Queen Victoria. **1886** The first successful petrol-driven motorcar, built by Karl Benz, was patented. **1916** Paris was bombed by German zeppelins for the first time. **1942** The BBC Radio 4 programme 'Desert Island Discs', devised and presented by Roy Plomley, was first broadcast. **1978** The use of environmentally damaging aerosol sprays was banned in Sweden. **1991** In the Gulf War, Iraq began its first major ground offensive into Saudi Arabia.

✎ BIRTHS ✎

Thomas Paine, English political writer and reformer, **1737**; W C Fields, US film actor and comedian, **1880**; Victor Mature, US film actor, **1915**; Paddy Chayefsky, US writer, **1923**; Germaine Greer, Australian feminist and author, **1939**; Katharine Ross, US film actress, **1943**.

✎ DEATHS ✎

King George III, **1820**; Alfred Sisley, English painter, **1899**; Douglas Haig, British field marshal, **1928**; Fritz Kreisler, US violinist, **1962**; Alan Ladd, US film actor, **1964**; Jimmy Durante, US comedian, **1980**.

'I am free of all prejudice. I hate everyone equally.'
W C Fields

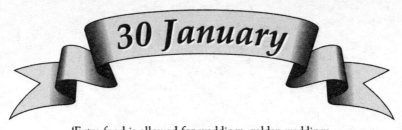
30 January

'Extra food is allowed for weddings, golden weddings,
funerals and other festivities.'
Edith Somerskill, on rationing after the war, reported on 30 Jan 1949

Feast day of St Martina, St Bathildis, St Adelelmus or Aleaume, St Aldegundis,
St Barsimaeus, and St Hyacintha Mariscotti.

❧ EVENTS ❧

1649 The Commonwealth of England was established upon the execution of
Charles I. **1790** The first purpose-built lifeboat was launched on the River Tyne.
1889 Rudolph, crown prince of Austria, and his 17-year-old mistress, Baroness
Marie Vetsera, were found shot in his hunting lodge at Mayerling, near Vienna.
1933 Adolf Hitler was appointed Chancellor of Germany. **1958** Yves Saint
Laurent, aged 22, held his first major fashion show in Paris. **1972** In
Londonderry, Northern Ireland, 13 civilians were shot by British troops during
riots following an illegal march – known as 'Bloody Sunday'.

❧ BIRTHS ❧

Anton Chekhov, Russian dramatist and writer, **1860**; Franklin D Roosevelt,
32nd US president, **1882**; Gene Hackman, US film actor, **1932**; Vanessa
Redgrave, English actress, **1937**; Boris Spassky, Russian chess champion, **1938**;
Phil Collins, English pop singer and drummer, **1951**.

❧ DEATHS ❧

King Charles I, **1649**; Frank Doubleday, US publisher and editor, **1934**; Orville
Wright, US aviation pioneer, **1948**; Mohandas Karamchand Gandhi, Indian
leader, assassinated, **1948**; Francis Poulenc, French composer, **1963**; Stanley
Holloway, English actor and singer, **1982**.

'Non-violence is the first article of my faith. It is also
the last article of my creed.'
Mohandas Karamchand Gandhi, speech 18 March 1922

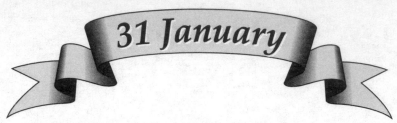
31 January

'No poet ever interpreted nature as freely as a lawyer interprets the truth.'
Jean Giraudoux

Feast day of Saints Cyrus and John of Alexandria, St Francis Xavier Bianchi, St Adamnan of Coldingham, St Aidan or Maedoc of Ferns, St Eusebius of St Gall, St Marcella of Rome, St John Bosco, and St Ulphia.

EVENTS

1606 The executions of Winter, Rockwood, Keys, and Guy Fawkes, the Gunpowder Conspirators, took place in London. **1747** The first clinic specialising in the treatment of venereal diseases was opened at London Dock Hospital. **1858** The *Great Eastern*, the five-funnelled steamship designed by Brunel, was launched at Millwall. **1876** All Native American Indians were ordered to move into reservations. **1929** The USSR exiled Leon Trotsky; he found asylum in Mexico. **1958** *Explorer I*, the first US Earth satellite, was launched from Cape Canaveral. **1983** The wearing of seat belts in cars became compulsory in Britain.

BIRTHS

Franz Schubert, Austrian composer, **1797**; Zane Grey, US novelist, **1872**; Anna Pavlova, Russian ballerina, **1882**; Freya Stark, English traveller and writer, **1893**; Norman Mailer, US novelist, **1923**; Jean Simmons, English film actress, **1929**.

DEATHS

Charles Edward Stuart, the Young Pretender, **1788**; John Galsworthy, English novelist, **1933**; Jean Giraudoux, French novelist and dramatist, **1944**; C B Cochran, British theatrical producer, **1951**; A A Milne, English author, **1956**; Samuel Goldwyn, US film producer, **1974**.

'Sentimentality is the emotional promiscuity of those who have no sentiment.'
Norman Mailer, *Cannibals and Christians*

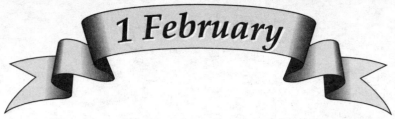

1 February

'You can run the office without a boss, but you can't run an office without the secretaries.'
Jane Fonda, reported on 1 Feb 1981

Feast day of St John of the Grating, St Henry Morse, St Pionius, St Bride or Brigid of Kildare, St Seiriol, and St Sigebert III of Austria.

EVENTS

1884 The first edition of the Oxford English Dictionary was published. **1893** Thomas Edison opened the first film studio – to produce films for peepshow machines – in New Jersey, USA. **1896** Puccini's opera *La Bohème* was first staged in Turin. **1930** *The Times* published its first crossword puzzle. **1958** The United Arab Republic was formed by a union of Egypt and Syria (it was broken 1961). **1965** Medical prescriptions on the NHS became free of charge (they remained so until June 1968). **1979** Ayatollah Khomeini returned to Iran after 16 years of exile.

BIRTHS

Victor Herbert, US composer, **1859**; John Ford, US film director, **1895**; Clark Gable, US film actor, **1901**; Stanley Matthews, English footballer, **1915**; Renata Tebaldi, Italian operatic soprano, **1922**; Don Everly, US rock singer, **1937**; Princess Stephanie of Monaco, **1966**.

DEATHS

René Descartes, French scientist and philosopher, **1650**; Mary Wollstonecraft Shelley, English novelist, **1851**; Carlos I, King of Portugal, assassinated, **1908**; Aritomo Yamagata, Japanese soldier and politician, **1922**; Piet Mondrian, Swiss painter, **1944**; Buster Keaton, US silent-film comedian, **1966**.

'I think, therefore I am.'
René Descartes

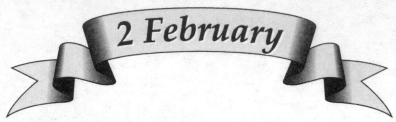

2 February

'You just pick a chord, go twang, and you've got music.'
Sid Vicious

Candlemas (Wives' Feast Day). Feast day of The Purification, St Joan de Lestonnac, St Adalbald of Ostrevant, and The Martyrs of Ebsdorf.

🐚 EVENTS 🐚

1801 The first parliament of the United Kingdom of Great Britain and Ireland assembled. **1852** Britain's first men's public flushing toilets opened on Fleet Street, London. **1878** Greece declared war on Turkey. **1943** The German army surrendered to the Soviet army at Stalingrad. **1972** The British Embassy in Dublin was burned down by protesters angered by the 'Bloody Sunday' shootings in Londonderry. **1986** Women in Liechtenstein went to the polls for the first time. **1989** The USSR's military occupation of Afghanistan ended after nine years. **1991** A protest against the Gulf War was held in London's Hyde Park, attended by more than 40,000 people.

🐚 BIRTHS 🐚

Nell Gwyn, English actress and mistress of Charles II, **1650**; Charles Maurice de Talleyrand-Périgord, French statesman and diplomat, **1754**; James Joyce, Irish author **1882**; Elaine Stritch, US actress, **1927**; Stan Getz, US jazz saxophonist, **1927**; Farrah Fawcett, US TV actress, **1946**.

🐚 DEATHS 🐚

Pope Clement XIII, **1769**; Dmitri Ivanovich Mendeleyev, Russian chemist, **1907**; Bertrand Russell, English philosopher, **1970**; Sid Vicious, British punk singer, **1979**; Alistair Maclean, Scottish novelist.

'Three passions, simple but overwhelmingly strong, have governed my life: the longing for love, the search for knowledge, and unbearable pity for the suffering of mankind.'
Bertrand Russell, *Autobiography*

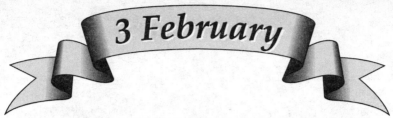

3 February

'The foreign newspapers ought to be ashamed of themselves for expressing disapproval of the recent shooting of a few score of anti-soviet terrorists.'
Vyatcheslav Mikhailovich Molotov, reported on 3 Feb 1925

Feast day of St Laurence of Spoleto, St Anskar, St Ia the Virgin, St Laurence of Canterbury, St Blaise, St Werburga, and St Margaret 'of England'.

EVENTS

1488 The Portuguese navigator Bartholomeu Diaz landed at Mossal Bay in the Cape – the first European known to have landed on the southern extremity of Africa. **1913** The 16th Amendment to the US Constitution, authorising the power to impose and collect income tax, was ratified. **1919** The League of Nations held its first meeting in Paris, with US President Wilson chairing. **1966** The first rocket-assisted controlled landing on the Moon was made by the Soviet space vehicle Luna IX. **1969** At the Palestinian National Congress in Cairo, Yassir Arafat was appointed leader of the PLO. **1989** South African politician P W Botha unwillingly resigned both party leadership and the presidency after suffering a stroke.

BIRTHS

Felix Mendelssohn, German composer, **1809**; Gertrude Stein, US author, **1874**; Alvar Aalto, Finnish architect, **1898**; James Michener, US novelist, **1907**; Simone Weil, French writer, **1909**; Frankie Vaughan, English singer, **1928**.

DEATHS

John of Gaunt, Duke of Lancaster, **1399**; Richard 'Beau' Nash, British dandy and gambler, **1762**; Woodrow Wilson, 28th US president, **1924**; Buddy Holly, US singer and guitarist, **1959**; Boris Karloff, US film actor, **1969**; John Cassavetes, US film actor and director, **1989**.

'In the United States, there is more space where nobody is, than where anybody is. That is what makes America what it is.'
Gertrude Stein

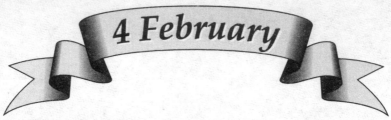

4 February

'If someone is confronting our essential liberties, if someone is inflicting injury and harm - by God I'll confront them.'
Margaret Thatcher, reported on 4 Feb 1979

The national day of Sri Lanka. Feast day of St Theophilus the Penitent, St Nicholas Studites, St Andrew Corsini, bishop, St Joan of Valois, St Isidore of Pelusium, St John de Britto, St Modan, St Phileas, St Joseph of Leonessa, and St Rembert.

EVENTS

1861 Seven secessionist southern states formed the Confederate States of America, in Montgomery, Alabama. **1904** The Russo-Japanese War began after Japan laid seige to Port Arthur. **1928** Black US entertainer Josephine Baker's provocative performance in Munich drew protests from members of the Nazi party. **1945** Allied leaders Roosevelt, Churchill, and Stalin met at Yalta, in the Crimea. **1968** The world's largest hovercraft was launched at Cowes, Isle of Wight. **1987** The US Stars and Stripes won the America's Cup back from Australia. **1993** Russian scientists unfurled a giant mirror in orbit and flashed a beam of sunlight across Europe during the night; observers saw it only as an instantaneous flash.

BIRTHS

Fernand Léger, French painter, **1881**; Jacques Prévert, French poet and novelist, **1900**; Charles Lindbergh, US aviator, **1902**; Ida Lupino, English actress, **1918**; Norman Wisdom, English comedian, **1920**; Alice Cooper, US pop singer, **1948**.

DEATHS

Lucius Septimius Severus, Roman emperor, **211**; Giambattista della Porta, Italian natural philosopher, **1615**; Robert Koldewey, German archaeologist, **1925**; Oliver Heaviside, English physicist, **1925**; Karen Carpenter, US singer, **1983**; Liberace, US entertainer, **1987**.

'My age is 39 plus tax.'
Liberace

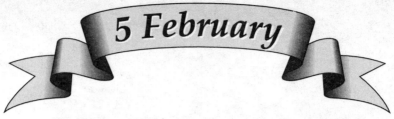

5 February

'Don't just move to the music, listen to what I'm saying.'
Bob Marley

Feast day of St Agatha, Saints Indractus and Dominica, St Adelaide of Bellich, St Bertulph or Bertoul of Renty, St Avitus of Vienne, and St Vodalus or Voel.

EVENTS

1782 The Spanish captured Minorca from the British. **1924** The BBC time signals, or 'pips', from Greenwich Observatory were heard for the first time; they are broadcast every hour. **1940** Glenn Miller recorded 'Tuxedo Junction' with his orchestra. **1961** The first issue of the *Sunday Telegraph* was published. **1967** Due to a Musicians' Union ban, the Rolling Stones were not allowed to play their hit 'Let's Spend the Night Together' when they appeared on an ITV show. **1974** Patricia Hearst, granddaughter of US newspaper tycoon William R Hearst, was kidnapped by the Symbionese Liberation Army. **1982** Laker Airways collapsed with debts of $270 million. **1983** Expelled from Bolivia, Nazi war criminal Klaus Barbie flew to France to be tried for crimes against humanity.

BIRTHS

Robert Peel, British politician, **1788**; Adlai Stevenson, US politician and ambassador, **1900**; John Carradine, US film actor, **1906**; William Burroughs, US novelist, **1914**; Bob Marley, Jamaican reggae singer, **1945**; Charlotte Rampling, British actress, **1946**.

DEATHS

Joost van den Vondel, Dutch poet and dramatist, **1679**; Thomas Carlyle, English author and historian, **1881**; A B 'Banjo' Paterson, Australian poet and journalist, **1941**; George Aliss, English actor, **1946**; Marianne Moore, US poet, **1972**; Joseph Mankiewicz, US director and author, **1993**.

'Time present and time past
Are both perhaps present in time future
And time future contained in time past.'
T S Eliot, *Four Quartets*

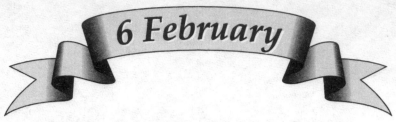

6 February

'Of the four wars in my lifetime none came about because the
United States was too strong.'
Ronald Reagan, speech

The national day of New Zealand. Feast day of St Paul Miki and his
Companions, St Vedast or Vaast, St Hidegund, St Amand, Saints Mel and
Melchu, and St Guarinus of Palestrina.

EVENTS

1508 Maximilian I assumed the title of Holy Roman Emperor. **1778** Britain
declared war on France. **1840** The Treaty of Waitangi was signed by Great
Britain and the Maori chiefs of New Zealand, granting British sovereignty. **1918**
Women over 30 were granted the right to vote in Britain. **1958** An aeroplane
carrying the Manchester United football team crashed on take-off at Munich,
killing seven players. **1964** Britain and France reached an agreement on the
construction of a Channel Tunnel. **1968** The 10th Winter Olympic games
opened in Grenoble, France. **1991** Debris from *Salyut 7*, a Soviet space station
abandoned in 1986, re-entered the Earth's atmosphere; it was believed that most
of it landed in the Atlantic Ocean.

BIRTHS

Christopher Marlowe, English dramatist, **1564**; Queen Anne, **1665**; Ronald
Reagan, 40th US president, **1911**; Zsa Zsa Gabor, Hungarian actress, **1920**;
François Truffaut, French film director, **1932**; Rick Astley, British pop singer, **1966**.

DEATHS

Lancelot 'Capability' Brown, English landscape gardener, **1783**; Carlo Goldoni,
Italian dramatist, **1793**; Joseph Priestley, English chemist, **1804**; Gustav Klimt,
Austrian painter, **1918**; Marghanita Laski, English author, **1988**; Arthur Ashe,
US tennis player, **1993**.

'Was this country settled by an Industrus people they would very soon be
suppl'd not only with the necessarys but many of the luxuries of life.'
Captain James Cook on New Zealand, *Journal*

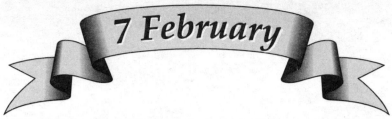
7 February

'There are strings ... in the human heart that had better not be wibrated.'
Charles Dickens, *Barnaby Rudge*

Feast day of St Luke the Younger, St Theodore of Heraclea, St Adaucus, St Moses, St Richard, 'King of the English', and St Silvin.

✑ EVENTS ✑

1301 Edward Caernarvon (later King Edward II) became the first Prince of Wales. **1792** Austria and Prussia formed an alliance against France. **1845** The Portland Vase, a Roman cameo glass vase dating to the 1st century BC, was smashed by a drunken visitor to the British Museum. **1863** HMS *Orpheus* was wrecked off the New Zealand coast, with the loss of 185 lives. **1947** The main group of the Dead Sea Scrolls, dating to about 150 BC–AD 68, was found in caves on the W side of the Jordan River. **1974** Grenada became a fully independent state within the Commonwealth. **1991** British prime minister Major and his senior cabinet ministers escaped an apparent assassination attempt when the IRA fired three mortar shells at 10 Downing Street from a parked van.

✑ BIRTHS ✑

Thomas More, English politician, **1478**; Philippe Buache, French cartographer, **1700**; Charles Dickens, English novelist, **1812**; Alfred Adler, Austrian psychoanalyst, **1870**; Sinclair Lewis, US novelist, **1885**; Peter Jay, British writer and broadcaster, **1937**.

✑ DEATHS ✑

William Boyce, English organist and composer, **1779**; Sheridan Le Fanu, Irish writer, **1873**; Adolphe Sax, Belgian inventor of the saxophone, **1894**; Daniel Malan, South African statesman, **1959**; Igor Vasilevich Kuchatov, Russian nuclear physicist, **1960**; Jimmy Van Heusen, US composer, **1990**.

'Neither side will win the sex war as there is far too much fraternization with the enemy.'
Anon.

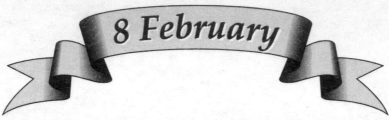

8 February

'As a rule, the motor cycle is driven by a hot-headed youth, without a hat, his hair flowing down behind; and everybody, except the young lady on the pillion behind him, hates him.'
Mr Justice Swift, reported on 8 Feb 1931

Feast day of St Jerome Emiliani, St John of Matha, St Cuthman, St Stephen of Muret, St Elfleda, St Nicetius or Nizier of Besançon, and St Meingold.

✎ EVENTS ✎

1725 Catherine I succeeded her husband, Peter the Great, to become Empress of Russia. **1740** The 'Great Frost' of London ended (began 25 Dec 1739). **1920** Odessa was taken by Bolshevik forces. **1924** The gas chamber was used in the USA for the first time, in the Nevada State Prison. **1969** The Boeing 747, the world's largest commercial plane, made its first flight. **1972** A concert by Frank Zappa and the Mothers of Invention was cancelled at the Albert Hall, London, because some of their lyrics were considered obscene. **1974** After 85 days in space, the US Skylab station returned to earth. **1993** All 132 persons aboard an Iran Air passenger jet were killed minutes after take-off when the plane collided with a military aircraft.

✎ BIRTHS ✎

John Ruskin, English writer, artist, and art critic, **1819**; William Sherman, US general, **1820**; Jules Verne, French novelist, **1828**; Lana Turner, US film actress, **1920**; Jack Lemmon, US film actor, **1925**; James Dean, US film actor, **1931**.

✎ DEATHS ✎

Mary, Queen of Scots, beheaded, **1587**; R B Ballantyne, Scottish writer, **1894**; Peter Alexeivich Kropotkin, Russian anarchist, **1921**; William Bateson, English biologist, **1926**; Max Liebermann, German painter and etcher, **1935**; Del Shannon, US pop singer, **1990**.

'When we build, let us think that we build for ever.'
John Ruskin, *The Seven Lamps of Architecture*

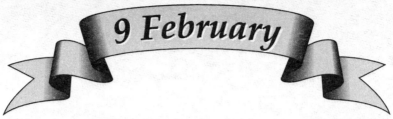

9 February

'Think of it, a second chamber selected by the whips - a seraglio of eunuchs.'
Michael Foot, on the House of Lords, reported on 9 Feb 1969

Feast day of St Apollonia, St Sabinus of Canossa, St Teilo, St Alto, St Ansbert, and St Nicephorus of Antioch.

❧ EVENTS ❧

1801 The Holy Roman Empire came to an end with the signing of the Peace of Luneville between Austria and France. **1830** Explorer Charles Sturt discovered the source of the Murray River in Australia. **1872** Lieutenant Dawson's expedition in search of Dr Livingstone began. **1942** Soap rationing began in Britain. **1949** US film actor Robert Mitchum was sentenced to two months in prison for smoking marijuana. **1972** The British government declared a state of emergency due to the miners' strike, which was in its third month. **1991** The republic of Lithuania held a plebiscite on independence which showed overwhelming support for secession from the USSR.

❧ BIRTHS ❧

Daniel Bernoulli, Swiss mathematician, **1700**; Mrs Patrick Campbell, English actress, **1865**; Alban Berg, Austrian composer, **1885**; Ronald Colman, English film actor, **1891**; Carole King, US singer and songwriter, **1941**; Mia Farrow, US film actress, **1945**.

❧ DEATHS ❧

Nevil Maskelyne, Astronomer Royal, **1811**; Fyodor Mikhailovich Dostoevsky, Russian novelist, **1881**; Sergei Vladimirovich Ilyushin, Russian aircraft designer, **1977**; Bill Haley, US rock musician, **1981**; Yuri Andropov, Russian leader, **1984**.

'Even the most hardened criminal a few years ago would help an old lady across the road and give her a few quid if she was skint.'
Charles Kray, 9 Feb 1986

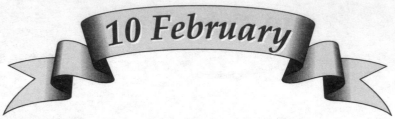

10 February

'The difference between perseverance and obstinacy is that perseverance means a strong will and obstinacy means a strong won't.'
Lord Dundee, reported on 10 Feb 1963

Feast day of St William of Maleval, St Scholastica, St Trumwin, St Austreberta, and St Soteris.

✎ EVENTS ✎

1354 A street battle between Oxford University students and townspeople resulted in several deaths and many injuries. **1763** Canada was ceded to Britain by the Peace of Paris. **1774** Andrew Becker demonstrated his practical diving suit in the River Thames. **1840** Queen Victoria and Prince Albert, both aged 20, were married in St James' Palace. **1931** New Delhi became the capital of India. **1942** The first gold disc – sprayed with gold by the record company RCA Victor – was presented to Glenn Miller for 'Chattanooga Choo Choo'. **1989** Jamaican-born Tony Robinson became Nottingham's first black sheriff.

✎ BIRTHS ✎

Harold Macmillan, British politician and publisher, **1894**; Bertolt Brecht, German dramatist and poet, **1898**; Robert Wagner, US actor, **1930**; Boris Pasternak, Russian novelist, **1890**; Mark Spitz, US swimmer, **1950**; Greg Norman, Australian golfer, **1955**.

✎ DEATHS ✎

Luca della Robbia, Italian sculptor, **1482**; Alexander Sergeyevich Pushkin, Russian author, **1837**; Wilhelm Konrad von Röntgen, German physicist, **1923**; Edgar Wallace, English thriller writer, **1932**; Billy Rose, US producer and lyricist, **1966**; Sophie Tucker, US singer, **1966**.

'Indeed, let's be frank about it; some of our people have never had it so good.'
Harold Macmillan, speech 20 July 1957

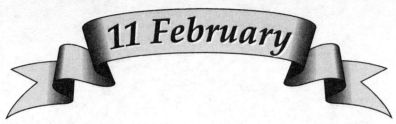

11 February

'I have cherished the idea of a democratic and free society in which all persons live together in harmony and with equal opportunity ... if needs be, it is an idea for which I am prepared to die.'
Nelson Mandela, on release after 26 years in jail

Feast day of Saints Saturninus and Dativus, St Benedict of Aniane, St Gregory II, pope, St Caedmon, St Pascal, pope, St Lazarus of Milan, St Lucius of Adrianople, and St Severinus of Agaunum.

≫ EVENTS ≪

1858 Bernadette Soubirous, a peasant girl, allegedly had a vision of the Virgin Mary in a grotto in Lourdes. **1878** The first weekly weather report was published by the Meteorological Office. **1945** The Yalta Conference ended, at which the Allied leaders planned the final defeat of Germany and agreed on the establishment of the United Nations. **1975** Margaret Thatcher became the first woman leader of a British political party. **1990** After more than 27 years in prison, ANC president Nelson Mandela walked to freedom from a prison near Cape Town, South Africa.

≫ BIRTHS ≪

Henry Fox Talbot, British photographic pioneer, **1800**; Thomas Edison, US inventor, **1847**; Vivian Fuchs, British Antarctic explorer, **1908**; Joseph Mankiewicz, US film writer and director, **1909**; Mary Quant, English fashion designer, **1934**; Burt Reynolds, US film actor, **1936**.

≫ DEATHS ≪

Lazaro Spallanzani, Italian physiologist and chemist, **1799**; Honoré Daumier, French caricaturist, **1879**; John Buchan, Canadian statesman and novelist, **1940**; Sergei Mikhailovich Eisenstein, Russian film director, **1948**; Silvia Plath, US poet, **1963**; Lee J Cobb, US actor, **1976**.

'I dreamt that I was making a speech in the House.
I woke up, and by Jove I was!'
Duke of Devonshire

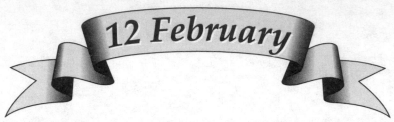

12 February

'In giving freedom to the slave we assure freedom to the free - honourable alike in what we give and what we preserve. We shall nobly save, or meanly lose, the last best hope of earth.'
Abraham Lincoln, annual message to Congress 1 Dec 1862

Feast day of St Julian the Hospitaller, St Ethelwald of Lindisfarne, St Antony Kauleas, St Marina or Pelagia, St Meletius, and St Ludan.

EVENTS

1554 Lady Jane Grey, queen of England for nine days, was executed on Tower Green for high treason. **1797** Over 1,000 French troops, led by Irish-American General William Tate, made an unsuccessful attempt to invade Britain, on the Welsh coast. **1818** Independence was proclaimed by Chile. **1831** Rubber galoshes first went on sale, in Boston, Massachusetts, USA. **1851** Prospector Edward Hargreaves made a discovery at Summerhill Creek, New South Wales, which set off a gold rush in Australia. **1912** China became a republic following the overthrow of the Manchu Dynasty. **1973** The first group of US prisoners of war were released from North Vietnam. **1993** The South African government and the ANC reached an agreement on a transitional 'government of national unity' in which both parties would be partners for five years.

BIRTHS

Thomas Campion, English composer and poet, **1567**; Abraham Lincoln, 16th US president, **1809**; Charles Darwin, English scientist, **1809**; George Meredith, English novelist, **1828**; Marie Lloyd, English music-hall star, **1870**; Franco Zeffirelli, Italian film director, **1923**.

DEATHS

Immanuel Kant, German philosopher, **1804**; Hans Guido von Bülow, German pianist and conductor, **1894**; Lillie Langtry, English actress, **1929**; Tom Keating, English painter and art forger, **1984**; Henry Hathaway, US filmmaker, **1985**.

'People with an over-abundance of dignity and an over-supply of power have always in the end been targets for laughter.'
Charlie (Charles) Chaplin, reported on 12 Feb 1939

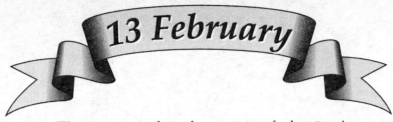
13 February

'Writing is not a profession but a vocation of unhappiness.'
Georges Simenon

Feast day of St Catherine dei Ricci, St Stephen of Rieti, St Ermenilda or Ermengild, St Martinian the Hermit, St Polyeuctes of Melitene, St Licinus or Lesin, and St Modomnoc.

EVENTS

1689 William of Orange and Mary ascended the throne of Great Britain as joint sovereigns. **1692** The massacre of the Macdonalds at Glencoe in Scotland was carried out by their traditional enemies, the Campbells. **1793** Britain, Prussia, Austria, Holland, Spain, and Sardinia formed an alliance against France. **1867** Strauss's waltz *The Blue Danube* was first played publicly, in Vienna. **1886** The James Younger gang made its first 'hit', robbing $60,000 from a bank in Missouri, USA. **1917** Dutch spy Mata Hari was arrested by the French. **1960** The French tested their first atomic bomb in the Sahara. **1974** Russian novelist Alexander Solzhenitsyn was expelled from the USSR.

BIRTHS

John Hunter, Scottish surgeon and anatomist, **1728**; Fyodor Chaliapin, Russian operatic bass singer, **1873**; Georges Simenon, Belgian novelist, **1901**; George Segal, US film actor, **1934**; Oliver Reed, British film actor, **1938**; Peter Gabriel, British pop musician, **1950**.

DEATHS

Catherine Howard, fifth wife of Henry VIII, executed, **1542**; Benvenuto Cellini, Italian sculptor and goldsmith, **1571**; Cotton Mather, US colonist and writer, **1728**; Richard Wagner, German composer, **1883**; Georges Rouault, French painter, **1958**; Jean Renoir, French film director, **1979**.

'The only way to get rid of a temptation is to yield to it.'
Oscar Wilde

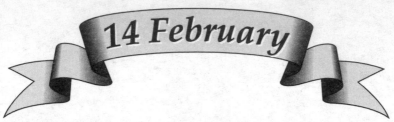
14 February

'Of all forms of caution, caution in love is perhaps the most fatal to true happiness.'
Bertrand Russell

St Valentine's Day. Feast day of St John the Baptist of the Conception, St Antoninus of Sorrento, St Maro, St Abraham of Carrhae, St Adolf of Osnabrück, St Auxentius, Saints Cyril and Methodius, and St Conran.

≈ EVENTS ≈

1779 Captain Cook was stabbed to death by natives in the Sandwich Islands (now Hawaii). **1797** The naval Battle of St Vincent took place off SW Portugal, in which Captain Nelson and Admiral Jervis defeated the Spanish fleet. **1852** Great Ormond Street children's hospital, in London, accepted its first patient. **1895** Oscar Wilde's *The Importance of Being Earnest* was first staged in London. **1929** The St Valentine's Day Massacre took place in Chicago, when seven members of Bugsy Moran's gang were gunned down in a warehouse. **1946** The Bank of England was nationalised. **1956** At the 20th Soviet Communist Party Conference, Nikita Khrushchev denounced the policies of Stalin. **1989** The Ayatollah Khomeini issued a fatwa edict calling on Muslims to kill Salman Rushdie for his blasphemous novel *The Satanic Verses*.

≈ BIRTHS ≈

Francesco Cavalli, Italian composer, **1602**; Thomas Malthus, English economist, **1766**; Christopher Sholes, US inventor of the typewriter, **1819**; Jack Benny, US comedian and actor, **1894**; Alan Parker, British film director, **1944**; Kevin Keegan, British footballer, **1951**.

≈ DEATHS ≈

King Richard II of England, **1400**; Fiorenzo di Lorenzo, Italian painter, **1525**; William Sherman, US general, **1891**; Julian Huxley, English biologist and philosopher, **1975**; P G Wodehouse, English novelist, **1975**; Frederick Loewe, US composer, **1988**.

'It is a good rule in life never to apologise. The right sort of people do not want apologies, and the wrong sort take a mean advantage of them.'
P G Wodehouse, *The Man Upstairs*

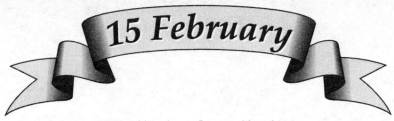

15 February

'Float like a butterfly, sting like a bee.'
Muhammad Ali (Cassius Clay)

Feast day of St Tanco or Tatto, St Agape of Terni, St Walfrid or Galfrid, and St Sigfrid of Växjö.

✒ EVENTS ✒

1882 The first shipment of frozen meat left New Zealand for England. **1898** The USS *Maine*, sent to Cuba on a goodwill tour, was struck by a mine and sank in Havana harbour, with the loss of 260 lives. **1922** The first session of the Permanent Court of International Justice in The Hague was held. **1942** Singapore surrendered to Japanese forces. **1971** Britain adopted the decimal currency system. **1974** The battle for the strategic Golan Heights between Israeli and Syrian forces began. **1978** Mohammad Ali lost his world heavyweight boxing title to Leon Spinks in Las Vegas. **1981** For the first time, English Football League matches were played on a Sunday.

✒ BIRTHS ✒

Pedro Menendez de Avilés, Spanish navigator, **1519**; Galileo Galilei, Italian astronomer, **1564**; Jeremy Bentham, English philosopher and writer, **1748**; Graham Hill, British racing driver, **1929**; Claire Bloom, English actress, **1931**; Jane Seymour, English actress, **1951**.

✒ DEATHS ✒

Gotthold Ephraim Lessing, German author, **1781**; Mikhail Ivanovich Glinka, Russian composer, **1857**; Herbert Henry Asquith, British statesman, **1928**; Nat King Cole, US singer and musician, **1965**; Ethel Merman, US singer and actress, **1984**.

'All punishment is mischief: all punishment in itself is evil.'
Jeremy Bentham

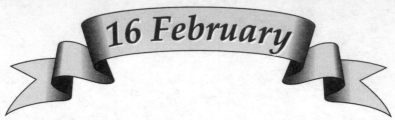

16 February

'I've a woman's ability to stick to a job and get on with it when everyone else walks off and leaves it.'
Margaret Thatcher, reported on 16 Feb 1975

Feast day of St Juliana of Cumae, St Onesimus the Slave, St Gilbert of Sempringham, and Saints Elias, Jeremy, and their Companions.

✑ EVENTS ✑

1659 The first British cheque was written. **1887** 25,000 prisoners in India were released to celebrate Queen Victoria's jubilee. **1932** Irish general election won by Fianna Fáil party, led by Éamon de Valera. **1937** US scientist W H Corothers obtained a patent for nylon. **1940** The British navy rescued about 300 British seamen who were held on board the German ship *Altmark*, in a Norwegian fjord. **1959** Fidel Castro became president of Cuba. **1960** The US nuclear submarine *Triton* set off to circumnavigate the world underwater.

✑ BIRTHS ✑

Giambattistsa Bodoni, Italian typographer, **1740**; Francis Galton, English scientist and founder of eugenics, **1822**; Ernst Haeckel, German naturalist and philosopher, **1834**; Geraint Evans, Welsh operatic baritone, **1922**; John Schlesinger, US film director, **1926**; John McEnroe, US tennis player, **1959**.

✑ DEATHS ✑

Alfonso III, king of Portugal, **1279**; Pierre-Paul Prudhon, French painter, **1823**; Lionel Lukin, English inventor of the lifeboat, **1834**; Henry Walter Bates, English naturalist and explorer, **1892**; Leslie Hore-Belisha, British politician who introduced driving tests and the Highway Code, **1957**.

'Madame, you must really be more careful. Suppose it had been someone else who found you like this.'
Duc de Richelieu, to his wife with her lover

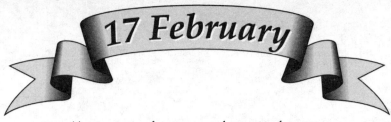
17 February

'A saint may embrace poverty but national poverty
won't breed a race of saints.'
Sir Miles Thomas, reported on 17 Feb 1957

Feast day of Saints Theodulus and Julian, St Evermod, St Loman, St Fintan of
Cloneenagh, and St Finan of Lindisfarne.

⁓ EVENTS ⁓

1461 Lancastrian forces defeated the Yorkists at the Battle of St Albans. **1859**
First production of Verdi's opera *Un Ballo in Maschera*, in Rome. **1864** The first
successful submarine torpedo attack took place when the USS *Housatonic* was
sunk by the Confederate submarine *Hunley* in Charleston harbour; however, the
force of the explosion was so great that the submarine itself was also blown up,
killing all on board. **1880** An attempt was made to assassinate the Russian tsar
Alexander II with a bomb at the Winter Palace, St Petersburg. **1904** First
production of Puccini's *Madame Butterfly*, in Milan. **1958** The Campaign for
Nuclear Disarmament (CND) was formed in London. **1968** French skier Jean-
Claude Killy won three gold medals at the Winter Olympics in Grenoble. **1972**
The House of Commons voted in favour of Britain joining the Common Market.

⁓ BIRTHS ⁓

Arcangelo Corelli, Italian composer, **1653**; Thomas Malthus, English
economist, **1766**; Marian Anderson, US operatic contralto, **1902**; Yassir Arafat,
Palestinian leader, **1929**; Barry Humphries, Australian actor and creator of
'Dame Edna Everidge', **1934**; Alan Bates, English actor, **1934**.

⁓ DEATHS ⁓

Tamerlane the Great, Mongol leader, **1405**; Molière, French dramatist, **1673**;
Heinrich Heine, German poet, **1856**; Geronimo, Apache leader, **1909**; Graham
Sutherland, English painter, **1980**; Lee Strasburg, US actor, **1982**; Thelonious
Monk, US jazz pianist, **1982**.

'Sleep is good, death is better; but of course, the best thing would be never to
have been born at all.'
Heinrich Heine, 'Morphine'

⁓ 49 ⁓

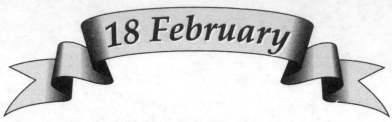
18 February

'I love men like some people like good food or wine.'
Germaine Greer, reported on 18 Feb 1979

National day of Gambia and Nepal. Feast day of St Colman of Lindisfarne, St Flavian of Jerusalem, St Simeon of Jerusalem, St Theotonius, and St Helladius of Toledo.

≈ EVENTS ≈

1678 Publication of John Bunyan's *Pilgrim's Progress*. **1861** Victor Emmanuel proclaimed king of a united Italy at the first meeting of the Italian parliament. **1876** A direct telegraph link was set up between Britain and New Zealand. **1930** US astronomer Clyde Tombaugh discovered the planet Pluto. **1948** After 16 years in power, the Fianna Fáil party was defeated in the Irish general elections. **1965** The Gambia became an independent state within the Commonwealth.

≈ BIRTHS ≈

Mary Tudor, daughter of Henry VIII and Catherine of Aragon, **1517**; Alessandro Volta, Italian scientist and inventor of the electric battery, **1745**; Niccolò Paganini, Italian violinist, **1784**; Andres Segovia, Spanish classical guitarist, **1894**; Helen Gurley Brown, US magazine editor, **1922**; Len Deighton, English novelist, **1929**.

≈ DEATHS ≈

Martin Luther, German founder of the Reformation, **1546**; Fra Angelico, Florentine painter, **1455**; George, Duke of Clarence, drowned in a butt of Malmsey on the orders of his brother, Richard, Duke of Gloucester, **1478**; Michelangelo Buonarroti, Italian painter and sculptor, **1564**; Richard Wagner, German composer, **1833**; Robert Oppenheimer, US physicist, inventor of the atomic bomb, **1967**.

'Whenever I'm caught between two evils, I take the one I've never tried.'
Mae West

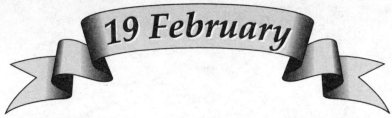
19 February

'Genius is one per cent inspiration, ninety-nine per cent perspiration.'
Thomas Edison

Feast day of St Boniface of Lausanne, St Barbatus, St Conrad of Piacenza, and St Mesrop.

⚘ EVENTS ⚘

1800 Napoleon Bonaparte proclaimed himself First Consul of France. **1878** US inventor Thomas Edison patented the phonograph. **1897** The Women's Institute was founded in Ontario, Canada, by Mrs Hoodless. **1906** William Kellogg established the Battle Creek Toasted Cornflake Company, selling breakfast cereals originally developed as a health food for psychiatric patients. **1959** Britain, Greece, and Turkey signed an agreement guaranteeing the independence of Cyprus. **1976** Iceland broke off diplomatic relations with Britain after negotiations failed to produce an agreement over fishing limits in the 'cod war'. **1985** The BBC broadcast the first episode of the soap opera *EastEnders*.

⚘ BIRTHS ⚘

Nicolaus Copernicus, Polish astronomer, **1473**; David Garrick, English actor and theatre manager, **1717**; Luigi Boccherini, Italian cellist and composer, **1743**; Adelina Patti, Italian soprano, **1843**; Merle Oberon, Tasmanian-born film actress, **1911**; Lee Marvin, US film actor, **1924**; Andrew, Duke of York, **1960**.

⚘ DEATHS ⚘

Georg Büchner, German poet and dramatist, **1837**; Charles Blondin, French tightrope walker, **1897**; Ernst Mach, Austrian physicist, **1916**; André Gide, French novelist, **1951**; Luigi Dallapiccola, Italian composer, **1975**; Michael Powell, English documentary filmmaker, **1990**.

'I intended to give some advice but now I remember how much is left over from last year unused.'
George Harris, to students at the start of a new academic year

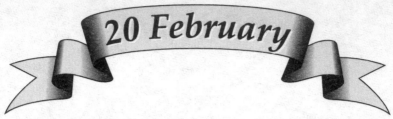
20 February

'I know of no method by which an aristocratic nation like England can become a democracy.'
Hilaire Belloc, reported on 20 Feb 1921

Feast day of St Eleutherius of Tournai, St Eucherius of Orléans, St Tyranno, St Zenobius, and St Wulfric.

EVENTS

1811 Austria declared itself bankrupt. **1938** Anthony Eden resigned as British foreign secretary after Prime Minister Neville Chamberlain decided to negotiate with Italian Fascist leader Benito Mussolini. **1947** Lord Louis Mountbatten was appointed viceroy of India, the last person to hold this office. **1962** US astronaut John Glenn orbited the Earth three times in the space capsule *Friendship 7.* **1985** The sale of contraceptives became legal in the Irish Republic. **1989** An army barracks at Tern Hill, Shropshire, was destroyed by an IRA bomb.

BIRTHS

Voltaire, French writer and philosopher, **1694**; Honoré Daumier, French painter, **1808**; Marie Rambert, British dancer and founder of the Ballet Rambert, **1888**; Enzo Ferrari, Italian car manufacturer, **1898**; Robert Altman, US film director, **1925**; Sidney Poitier, US film actor, **1927**.

DEATHS

King James I of Scotland, assassinated **1437**; Benedict Spinoza, Dutch philosopher, **1677**; Aurangzeb, last of the Mogul rulers of India, **1707**; Percy Grainger, Australian-born composer, **1961**; Walter Winchell, US journalist, **1972**; Mikhail Sholokhov, Russian author, **1984**.

'I have thousands of bad ideas all the time.'
Clive Sinclair, reported on 20 Feb 1985

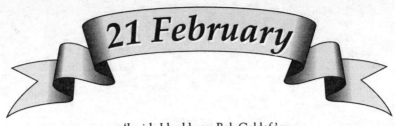

21 February

'I wish I had been Bob Geldof.'
Prince Charles, reported on 21 Feb 1988

Feast day of St Robert Southwell, St Peter Damian, St George of Amastris, and St Germanus of Granfel.

EVENTS

1804 British engineer Richard Trevithick demonstrated the first steam engine to run on rails. **1916** The Battle of Verdun began (it continued until 16th December). **1931** The *New Statesman* was first published. **1960** All private businesses in Cuba nationalised by Fidel Castro. **1972** US president Richard Nixon arrived in Beijing on a visit intended to improve US–Chinese relations. **1989** Czech writer Vaclav Havel jailed for anti-government demonstrations.

BIRTHS

Antonio Lopez de Santa Anna, Mexican revolutionary and dictator, **1794**; John Henry Newman, English cardinal and theologian, **1801**; W H Auden, English poet, **1907**; Robert Mugabe, first prime minister of Zimbabwe, **1924**; Nina Simone, US singer, **1934**; Jilly Cooper, English novelist and journalist, 1937.

DEATHS

Robert Southwell, English poet and Jesuit martyr, **1595**; Jethro Tull, English agriculturalist, **1741**; Nikolai Gogol, Russian novelist and dramatist, **1852**; George Ellery Hale, US astronomer, **1938**; Malcolm X, US Black Muslim leader, shot dead at a meeting, **1965**; Howard Walter Florey, Australian pathologist who developed penicillin, **1968**; Margot Fonteyn, English ballet dancer, **1991**.

'She has set herself an extremely low standard
which she has failed to maintain.'
Jilly Cooper, from school report *The Sunday Times* 16 July 1978

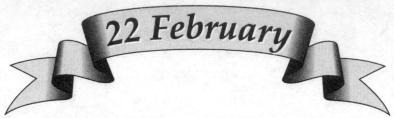

22 February

'Part of the problem is that many MPs never see the London that exists beyond the wine bars and brothels of Westminster.'
Ken Livingstone, reported on 22 Feb 1987

Feast day of St Baradates, St Margaret of Cortona, and Saints Thalassius and Limnaeus.

✑ EVENTS ✑

1797 Over 1,000 French troops landed at Fishguard, in South Wales, but were quickly taken prisoner. **1819** Spain ceded Florida to the USA. **1879** US storekeeper F W Woolworth opened his first 'five-and-ten-cent' store in Utica, New York. **1886** *The Times* newspaper published a classified personal column, the first newspaper to do so. **1940** Five-year-old Tenzin Gyatso was enthroned as the 14th Dalai Lama in Lhasa, Tibet. **1946** Dr Selman Abraham Waksman announced that he had discovered streptomycin, an antibiotic.

✑ BIRTHS ✑

George Washington, first president of the USA, **1732**; Arthur Schopenhauer, German philosopher, **1788**; Robert Baden-Powell, English soldier and founder of the Boy Scout movement, **1857**; Eric Gill, English sculptor and typographer, **1877**; Luis Buñuel, Spanish film director, **1900**; John Mills, English actor, **1908**; Kenneth Williams, English comedy actor, **1926**.

✑ DEATHS ✑

Amerigo Vespucci, Italian navigator after whom America is named, **1512**; Jean-Baptiste-Camille Corot, French painter, **1875**; Charles Lyell, English geologist, **1875**; Stefan Zweig, Austrian writer, **1942**; Elizabeth Bowen, Irish novelist, **1973**; Oskar Kokoschka, Austrian painter, **1980**.

'I am not conceited. It is just that I have a fondness for the good things in life and I happen to be one of them.'
Kenneth Williams

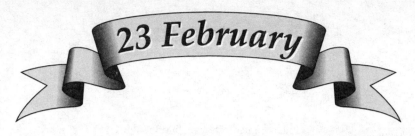

23 February

'I went out to Charing Cross, to see Major-general Harrison hanged, drawn, and quartered; which was done there, he looking as cheerful as any man could do in that condition.'
Samuel Pepys, *Diary* 13 Oct 1660

Feast day of St Polycarp of Smyrna, St Dositheus, St Milburga, St Alexander Akimites, St Boisil, and St Willigis.

EVENTS

1732 First performance of Handel's *Oratorio*, in London. **1820** Discovery of the Cato Street conspiracy; following a tip-off, police arrested revolutionaries who planned to blow up the British Cabinet. **1836** The siege of the Alamo began, under the Mexican general Santa Anna. **1863** Lake Victoria was proclaimed to be the source of the River Nile by British explorers John Speke and J A Grant. **1898** Emile Zola was imprisoned for writing his open letter *J'accuse*, accusing the French government of anti-Semitism and of wrongly imprisoning the army officer Captain Alfred Dreyfus. **1919** Benito Mussolini founded the Italian Fascist Party. **1970** Guyana became an independent republic within the Commonwealth. **1981** Spanish Fascist army officers led by Lt Colonel Antonio Tejero attempted a coup in the Cortes (parliament).

BIRTHS

Samuel Pepys, English civil servant and diarist, **1633**; George Frederick Handel, German-born British composer, **1685**; Victor Fleming, US film director who made *The Wizard of Oz*, **1883**; Erich Kästner, German children's author, **1899**; Peter Fonda, US film actor, **1940**.

DEATHS

Joshua Reynolds, English painter, **1792**; John Keats, English poet, **1821**; Karl Gauss, German mathematician and astronomer, **1855**; Nellie Melba, Australian opera singer, **1931**; Edward Elgar, English composer, **1994**; Stan Laurel, English-born US film comedian, **1965**; Adrian Boult, English conductor, **1983**; Andy Warhol, US Pop artist, **1987**.

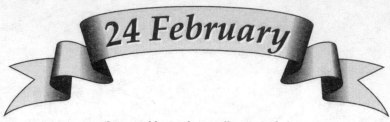

24 February

'I married beneath me, all women do.'
Lady Astor

Feast day of St Praetextatus and Saints Montanus, Lucius, and their Companions.

❧ EVENTS ❧

AD 303 Galerius Valerius Maximianus issued an edict demanding the persecution of Christians. **1582** The Gregorian Calendar was introduced by Pope Gregory XIII; it replaced the Julian Calendar, but was not adopted in Britain until **1752**. **1905** The Simplon Tunnel through the Alps was completed. **1920** Nancy Astor became the first woman to address the British Parliament. **1932** Malcolm Campbell beat his own land speed record in *Bluebird* at Daytona Beach, USA; he reached a speed of 408.88 kph/253.96 mph. **1938** Nylon toothbrush bristles were first produced in the USA – the first commercial use of nylon. **1946** Juan Perón was elected president of Argentina.

❧ BIRTHS ❧

Charles V, Holy Roman Emperor, **1500**; Wilhelm Grimm, German philologist and, with his brother Jakob, compiler of fairy tales, **1786**; Arnold Dolmetsch, Swiss maker and restorer of musical instruments, **1858**; Michel Legrand, French composer of film music, **1932**; Alain Prost, French racing driver, **1955**; Dennis Waterman, English actor, **1948**.

❧ DEATHS ❧

Henry Cavendish, English physicist, **1810**; Thomas Bowdler, English editor who produced 'bowdlerised' versions of great literary works such as Shakespeare and the Old Testament, **1825**; Nikolai Bulganin, Soviet prime minister, **1975**; Memphis Slim, US blues singer, **1987**; Bobby Moore, English footballer, **1993**.

'Wars come because not enough
people are sufficiently afraid.'
Hugh Schonfield

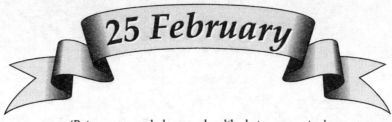

25 February

'Being a sex symbol was rather like being a convict.'
Raquel Welch, reported on 25 Feb 1979

National Day of Kuwait. Feast day of St Ethelbert of Kent, St Walburga, St Gerland, St Louis Versiglia, St Caesarius of Nazianzen, and St Calixto Caravario.

∾ EVENTS ∾

1308 Coronation of King Edward II of England. **1570** Pope Pius V excommunicated Queen Elizabeth I. **1913** English suffragette Emmeline Pankhurst went on trial for a bomb attack on the home of David Lloyd George, chancellor of the Exchequer. **1939** The first Anderson air-raid shelter was built in Islington, N London. **1955** HMS *Ark Royal* was completed, the largest aircraft carrier ever built in Britain. **1988** US televangelist Jimmy Swaggart was suspended after it became known that he had visited a prostitute for three years.

∾ BIRTHS ∾

Carlo Goldoni, Italian playwright, **1707**; Pierre-Auguste Renoir, French Impressionist painter, **1841**; Enrico Caruso, Italian operatic tenor, **1873**; Myra Hess, English pianist, **1890**; Anthony Burgess, English novelist, **1917**; David Puttnam, English film producer, **1941**; George Harrison, English pop musician and former member of the Beatles, **1943**.

∾ DEATHS ∾

Robert Devereux, Earl of Essex, executed for high treason, **1601**; Christopher Wren, English architect, **1723**; Paul Julius von Reuter, founder of Reuters international news agency, **1899**; John Tenniel, English artist and illustrator, **1914**; Mark Rothko, US painter, **1970**; Tennessee Williams, US dramatist, **1983**.

'Much of British management does not seem
to understand the human factor.'
Prince Charles, reported on 25 Feb 1979

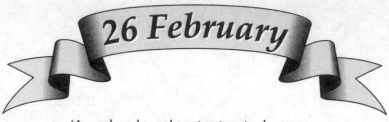

26 February

'A stand can be made against invasion by an army;
no stand can be made against invasion by an idea.'
Victor Hugo

Feast day of St Alexander of Alexandria, St Porphyry of Gaza, St Nestor of Magydus, and St Victor the Hermit.

❧ EVENTS ❧

1531 An earthquake in Lisbon, Portugal, killed 20,000 people. **1797** The first £ note was issued by the Bank of England. **1815** Napoleon escaped from exile on the island of Elba. **1839** The first Grand National Steeplechase was run at Aintree. **1935** Robert Watson-Watt gave the first demonstration of Radar at Daventry, England. **1936** Adolf Hitler launched the Volkswagen ('people's car'), intended to compete with Ford's Model T and boost the German economy.

❧ BIRTHS ❧

Victor Hugo, French novelist and playwright, **1802**; William Cody ('Buffalo Bill'), US showman, **1846**; Frank Bridge, English composer and conductor, **1879**; Fats Domino, US singer, **1928**; Johnny Cash, US country singer, **1932**.

❧ DEATHS ❧

Roger II, king of Sicily, **1154**; John Philip Kemble, English actor, **1823**, Richard Gatling, US inventor of the Gatling gun, **1903**; Harry Lauder, Scottish music-hall comedian, **1950**; Slim Gaillard, US jazz musician, **1991**.

'Convicts are the best audiences I ever played for.'
Johnny Cash, Attr.

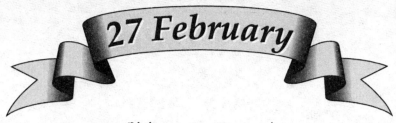

27 February

'I believe in private property.'
Svetlana Alliluyeva, reported on 27 Feb 1972

Feast day of St Alnoth, St Herefrith of Louth, and St Leander of Seville.

❧ EVENTS ❧

1557 The first Russian Embassy opened in London; exactly one year later, the first trade mission arrived. **1879** US chemists Ira Remsen and Constantine Fahlberg announced their discovery of saccharin. **1881** British troops were defeated by the Boers at Majuba Hill, Transvaal. **1933** The German Reichstag (parliament building) in Berlin was destroyed by fire; it is believed that the Nazis were responsible, though they blamed the Communists. **1948** The Communist Party seized power in Czechoslovakia. **1991** The Gulf War came to an end with the liberation of Kuwait and the retreat of Iraqi forces.

❧ BIRTHS ❧

Constantine, Roman emperor, AD 274; Henry Wadsworth Longfellow, US poet, 1807; Rudolf Steiner, Austrian philosopher, 1861; John Steinbeck US novelist, 1902; Lawrence Durrell, English poet and novelist, 1912; Elizabeth Taylor, English-born US film actress, 1932.

❧ DEATHS ❧

John Evelyn, English diarist, 1706; Alexander Borodin, Russian composer and chemist, 1887; Ivan Pavlov, Russian psychologist, 1936; Peter Behrens, German architect, 1940; Henry Cabot Lodge, US politician and diplomat, 1985; Lilian Gish, US film actress, 1993.

'Some of my best leading men have been dogs and horses.'
Elizabeth Taylor, *The Times* 18 Feb 1981

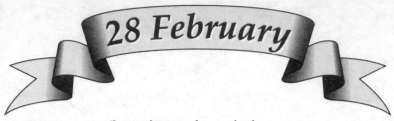
28 February

'It was about par for a rugby dinner -
from what I can remember.'
Colin Smart, reported on 28 Feb 1982

Feast day of St Oswald of Worcester, St Lupicinus, St Hilarius, pope, St Proterius, and St Romanus

EVENTS

1784 John Wesley, English founder of the Wesleyan faith, signed its deed of declaration. **1900** Relief forces under General Buller reached British troops besieged for four months at Ladysmith, Natal; Boer troops retreated. **1912** The first parachute jump was made, over Missouri, USA. **1948** The last British troops left India. **1975** A London underground train crashed at Moorgate station, killing 42 people. **1986** Swedish prime minister Olof Palme was shot dead as he walked home from a cinema in Stockholm.

BIRTHS

René Antoine de Réaumur, French scientist and inventor of a thermometer scale, **1683**; Linus Pauling, US physicist and chemist, **1909**; Stephen Spender, English poet and critic, **1909**; Vincente Minnelli, US film director, **1913**; Peter Medawar, English immunologist, **1915**; Barry McGuigan, Irish-born boxer, **1951**.

DEATHS

Alphonse de Lamartine, French poet, **1869**; Henry James, US-born British novelist, **1916**; Alfonso XIII, ex-king of Spain, **1941**; Rajendra Prasad, first president of India, **1963**; Henry Luce, US magazine publisher, **1967**.

'What is character but the determination of incident?
What is incident but the illustration of character?'
Henry James, *Partial Portraits*

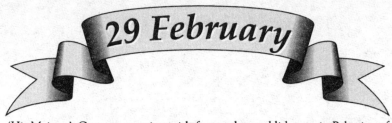

29 February

'His Majesty's Government view with favour the establishment in Palestine of a national home for the Jewish people, and will use their best endeavours to facilitate the achievement of this object, it being clearly understood that nothing shall be done which may prejudice the civil and religious rights of existing non-Jewish communities in Palestine.'
Arthur Balfour

Leap Year Day.

✎ EVENTS ✎

1880 The St Gotthard railway tunnel through the Alps was completed, linking Italy with Switzerland. **1948** The Stern Gang blew up a train carrying British soldiers from Cairo to Haifa; 27 soldiers were killed. **1956** Pakistan became an Islamic republic. **1960** An earthquake killed about 12,000 people in Agadir, Morocco. **1968** English astronomer Jocelyn Burnell announced the discovery of the first pulsar.

✎ BIRTHS ✎

Ann Lee, English founder of the American Society of Shakers, **1736**; Gioacchino Rossini, Italian composer, **1792**; John Holland, US submarine inventor, **1840**; Shri Morarji Desai, Indian politician, **1896**; Jimmy Dorsey, US bandleader, **1904**; Mario Andretti, Italian racing driver, **1940**.

✎ DEATHS ✎

St Hilarius, 46th pope, **468**; St Oswald, archbishop of York, **992**; Patrick Hamilton, Scottish Protestant martyr, **1528**; John Whitgift, archbishop of Canterbury, **1604**; John Landseer, English painter, **1852**; Roland Culver, English actor, **1984**.

'Wherever one wants to be kissed.'
Coco Chanel, when asked where one should wear perfume

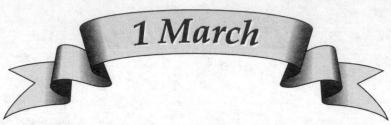

1 March

'The Welch are said to be so remarkably fond of cheese, that in cases of difficulty their midwives apply a piece of toasted cheese to the *janua vitae* to attract and entice the young Taffy, who on smelling it makes the most vigorous efforts to come forth.'
Francis Grose, *A Classical Dictionary of the Vulgar Tongue*

National Day of Wales. Feast day of St David, St Swithbert, and St Felix III, pope.

EVENTS

1780 Pennsylvania became the first US state to abolish slavery. **1845** The USA annexed Texas. **1940** English actress Vivien Leigh won an Oscar for her performance as Scarlett O'Hara in the film *Gone with the Wind*. **1949** US heavyweight boxing champion Joe Louis retired after successfully defending his title 25 times. **1954** The USA conducted its first hydrogen-bomb test at Bikini Atoll, in the Marshall Islands. **1966** The uncrewed Soviet spacecraft *Venus 3* landed on Venus.

BIRTHS

Frédéric Chopin, Polish composer, **1810**; Lytton Strachey, English biographer, **1880**; Glenn Miller, US bandleader, **1904**; David Niven, Scottish-born US film actor, **1910**, Harry Belafonte, US singer, **1927**; Roger Daltrey, English rock musician, singer with The Who, **1945**.

DEATHS

George Herbert, English poet, **1633**; Girolamo Frescobaldi, Italian composer, **1643**; George Grossmith, English singer and comedian, **1912**; Jackie Coogan, US film actor who in **1921** played the child in Charlie Chaplin's *The Kid*, **1984**.

'After playing Chopin, I feel as if I had been weeping over sins that I had never committed, and mourning over tragedies that were not my own.'
Oscar Wilde, *The Critic as Artist*

2 March

'No party has a monopoly over what is right.'
Mikhail Gorbachev, reported on 2 March 1986

Feast day of St Chad and St Joavan.

∽ EVENTS ∾

1717 The first ballet, *The Loves of Mars and Venus* was performed at the Theatre Royal, Drury Lane, London. **1882** An attempt was made to assassinate Queen Victoria at Windsor. **1949** US Airforce Captain James Gallagher returned to Fort Worth, Texas, after flying non-stop around the world in 94 hours with a crew of 13 men; tanker aircraft refuelled their plane four times during the flight. **1955** Severe flooding in N and W Australia killed 200 people. **1969** The French-built supersonic aircraft *Concorde* made its first test flight from Toulouse. **1970** Rhodesia proclaimed itself a republic.

∽ BIRTHS ∾

Thomas Bodley, founder of the Bodleian Library, Oxford, **1545**; Bedrich Smetana, Czech composer, **1824**; Kurt Weill, German composer who worked with Bertolt Brecht, **1900**; Basil Hume, archbishop of Westminster, **1923**; Mikhail Gorbachev, Soviet leader, **1931**; J P R Williams, Welsh rugby player, **1949**; Ian Woosnam, Welsh golfer, **1958**.

∽ DEATHS ∾

John Wesley, English founder of Methodism, **1791**; Horace Walpole, novelist and historian, **1797**; D H Lawrence, English novelist, **1930**; Howard Carter, English Egyptologist who discovered Tutankhamen's tomb, **1939**; Joan Greenwood, English film actress, **1987**; Randolph Scott, US film actor, **1987**.

'Jesus said love one another.
He didn't say love the whole world.'
Mother Teresa, reported on 2 March 1980

3 March

'Morocco is like a tree nourished by roots deep in the soil of Africa which breathes through foliage rustling to the winds of Europe.'
King Hassan II of Morocco, *The Challenge*

National Day of Morocco. Feast day of St Ailred of Rievaulx, St Cunegund, empress, St Marinus of Caesarea, St Non, St Winwaloe, St Anselm of Nonantola, St Artelais, St Chef, and St Emeterius.

EVENTS

1802 Beethoven's 'Moonlight Sonata' published. **1875** The first performance of Bizet's opera Carmen was staged at the Opéra Comique, Paris. **1931** 'The Star-Spangled Banner' was adopted as the US national anthem. **1969** US spacecraft *Apollo 9* was launched. **1985** British miners voted to go back to work after a year of striking over pit closures. **1991** Latvia and Estonia voted to secede from the Soviet Union.

BIRTHS

George Pullman, US designer of luxury railway carriages, **1831**; Alexander Graham Bell, Scottish-born inventor of the telephone, **1847**; Jean Harlow, US film actress, **1911**; Ronald Searle, English artist and cartoonist, **1920**; Miranda Richardson, English actress, **1958**; Fatima Whitbread, English javelin champion, **1961**.

DEATHS

Robert Hooke, English physicist, **1703**; Robert Adam, Scottish architect, **1792**; Giandomenico Tiepolo, Italian artist, **1804**; Lou Costello, US comedian, **1959**; Arthur Koestler, Hungarian-born writer and supporter of euthanasia, committed suicide, **1983**; Danny Kaye, US comedian, **1987**.

'I do not expect to be impeached.'
Richard Nixon, reported on 3 March 1974

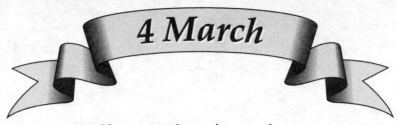

4 March

> 'No pain, no palm; no thorns, no throne;
> no gall, no glory; no cross, no crown.'
> **William Penn,** *No Cross, No Crown*

Feast day of St Peter of Cava, St Casimir of Poland, and St Adrian and his Companions.

⚘ EVENTS ⚘

1681 King Charles II granted a Royal Charter to William Penn, entitling Penn to establish a colony in North America. **1861** Abraham Lincoln was sworn in as the 16th president of the USA. **1877** The Russian Imperial Ballet staged the first performance of the ballet *Swan Lake* in Moscow. **1882** Britain's first electric trams came into operation in Leytonstone, East London. **1890** The Forth railway bridge, Scotland was officially opened. **1968** Tennis authorities voted to admit professional players to Wimbledon, previously open only to amateur players.

⚘ BIRTHS ⚘

Prince Henry the Navigator, Portuguese patron of explorers, **1394**; Antonio Vivaldi, Italian composer, **1678**; Patrick Moore, English astronomer, **1928**; Bernard Haitink, Dutch conductor, **1929**; Miriam Makeba, South African singer, **1931**; Kenny Dalgleish, Scottish footballer, **1951**.

⚘ DEATHS ⚘

Saladin, Kurdish-born Muslim leader who defeated the Crusaders, **1193**; Thomas Malory, English writer of the *Morte d'Arthur*, **1470**; Jean-François Champollion, French Egyptologist, **1832**; Nikolai Gogol, Russian novelist and playwright, **1852**; William Carlos Williams, US poet, **1963**.

> 'If acute and rapid tones are evil, Vivaldi has much of the
> sin to answer for.'
> **Charles Burney,** *A General History of Music*

5 March

'We have become a grandmother.'
Margaret Thatcher, reported on 5 March 1989

Feast day of St Piran, St Gerasimus, Saints Adrian and Eubulus, St Eusebius, St John Joseph of the Cross, St Kieran of Saighir, St Phocas of Antioch, and St Virgil of Arles.

EVENTS

1461 King Henry VI of England was deposed; he was succeeded by Edward IV. **1770** British troops killed five civilians when they fired into a crowd of demonstrators in Boston; the incident became known as the 'Boston Massacre'. **1850** English engineer Robert Stephenson's tubular bridge was opened, linking Anglesey with mainland Wales. **1933** The Nazi Party won almost half the seats in the elections. **1936** The British fighter plane *Spitfire* made its first test flight from Eastleigh, Southampton. **1946** The term 'iron curtain' was first used, by Winston Churchill in a speech in Missouri, USA.

BIRTHS

King Henry II of England, **1133**; Gerardus Mercator, Flemish cartographer, **1512**; Augusta Gregory, Irish playwright, **1852**; Heitor Villa-Lobos, Brazilian composer **1887**; Rex Harrison, English actor, **1908**; Elaine Page, English musical actress, **1952**.

DEATHS

Antonio Correggio, Italian painter, **1534**; Friedrich Mesmer, Austrian physician and founder of mesmerism, or 'animal magnetism', **1815**; Alessandro Volta, Italian physicist, **1827**; Joseph Stalin, Soviet dictator, **1953**; Sergei Prokofiev, Russian composer, **1953**; Tito Gobbi, Italian operatic baritone, **1984**.

'This diamond has so many carats, it's almost a turnip.'
Richard Burton, on his present to Elizabeth Taylor,
reported on 5 March 1972

6 March

'Luck and destiny are the excuses of the world's failures.'
Henry Ford, reported on 6 March 1927

National Day of Ghana. Feast day of Saints Baldred and Billfrith, St Chrodegang, St Colette, St Conon, St Cyneburga, St Fridolin, and St Tibba.

EVENTS

1836 The 12-day siege of the Alamo ended, with only six survivors out of the original force of 155. **1899** Aspirin was patented by chemist Felix Hoffman. **1930** Clarence Birdseye's first frozen foods went on sale in Springfield, Massachusetts, USA. **1957** Ghana became independent, the first British colony to do so. **1987** A cross-channel ferry left Zeebrugge, Belgium, with its bow doors open; it capsized suddenly outside the harbour, killing over 180 passengers. **1988** British SAS men shot dead three IRA members in a street in Gibraltar, claiming that they had been about to attack a military parade.

BIRTHS

Cyrano de Bergerac, French novelist and playwright, **1619**; Elizabeth Barrett Browning, English poet, **1806**; Frankie Howerd, English comedian, **1922**; Andrzej Wajda, Polish film director, **1926**; Valentina Tereshkova, Soviet astronaut, **1937**; Kiri Te Kanawa, New Zealand soprano, **1944**.

DEATHS

Louisa May Alcott, US novelist, **1888**; Gottlieb Daimler, German motor engineer who invented the motorcycle, **1900**; Ivor Novello, Welsh composer and actor, **1951**; George Formby, English entertainer, **1961**; Pearl Buck, US novelist, **1971**; Donald Maclean, English-born Soviet spy, **1984**.

'Perish the Universe, provided I have my revenge.'
Cyrano de Bergerac, La Mort d'Agrippine

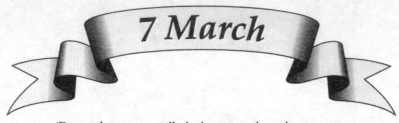

7 March

'Destroy him as you will, the bourgeois always bounces up -
execute him, expropriate him, starve him out en masse,
and he reappears as your children.'
Cyril Connolly, reported on 7 March 1937

Feast day of St Eosterwine, St Perpetua, and St Felicitas.

EVENTS

1838 Swedish singer Jenny Lind gave her debut performance in *Der Freischutz*.
1876 Alexander Graham Bell patented the telephone. **1912** French aviator
Henri Seimet made the first non-stop flight from Paris to London. **1926** A radio-
telephone link was established between London and New York. **1969** The
Victoria line was opened as part of London's underground railway. **1971** Women
in Switzerland achieved the right to vote and hold federal office.

BIRTHS

Tomas Masaryk, Czech leader, **1850**; Piet Mondrian, Dutch painter, **1872**;
Maurice Ravel, French composer, **1875**; Viv Richards, Antiguan cricketer, **1952**;
Ivan Lendl, Czech tennis player, **1960**; Rik Mayall, English comedian, **1958**.

DEATHS

Antoninus Pius, Roman emperor, AD **161**; St Thomas Aquinas, Christian
philosopher, **1274**; Herman Mankiewicz, US screenwriter, **1953**; Percy
Wyndham Lewis, English writer and artist, **1957**; Stevie Smith, English poet
and novelist, **1971**.

'Nationalisation will be the Magna Carta
of the twentieth century.'
H G Wells, reported on 7 March 1920

8 March

'There is nothing - absolutely nothing - half so much worth
doing as simply messing about in boats.'
Kenneth Grahame, *The Wind in the Willows*

Feast day of St Felix of Dunwich, St Duthac, St Julian of Toledo, St Pontius of
Carthage, St Veremund, St Senan, and St John of God.

EVENTS

1702 Anne became queen of Britain after William III died in a riding accident.
1910 The first pilot's licences were issued, to an Englishman, J T C Moore
Brabazon, and a Frenchwoman, Elise Deroche. **1917** The February Revolution
began in Petrograd (St (Petersburg), Russia. **1930** In India, a campaign of civil
disobedience began, led by Mahatma Gandhi. **1965** 3,500 US marines landed in
South Vietnam. **1971** US boxer Muhammad Ali was defeated by Joe Frazier.

BIRTHS

Kenneth Grahame, Scottish author of *The Wind in the Willows*, **1859**; Otto
Hahn, German physicist and chemist, **1879**; Douglas Hurd, British politician,
1930; James Dean, US film actor, **1931**; Lynn Seymour, Canadian ballet dancer,
1939; Norman Stone, English historian, **1941**.

DEATHS

Abraham Darby, English ironmaster, the first to use coke for smelting iron,
1717; Hector Berlioz, French composer, **1869**; John Ericsson, Swedish-born US
inventor of the screw propeller, **1889**; William Howard Taft, 27th president of
the USA, **1930**; Thomas Beecham, English conductor, **1961**; Harold Lloyd, US
comedian and silent-film actor, **1971**.

'Jazz will endure just as long as people hear it through
their feet instead of their brains.'
John Philip Sousa

9 March

'Resolve to free yourselves from the slavery of the tea and
coffee and other slop-kettle.'
William Cobbett, *Advice to Young Men*

Feast day of the Forty Martyrs of Sebaste, St Frances of Rome, St Bosa, St
Constantine, St Gregory of Nyssa, St Pacianus, and St Dominic Savio.

EVENTS

1074 Pope Gregory VII excommunicated all married priests. **1796** French army
commander Napoleon Bonaparte married Josephine de Beauharnais. **1831** The
French Foreign Legion was founded in Algeria; its headquarters moved to France
in **1962**. **1918** The Russian capital was transferred from Petrograd (St Petersburg)
to Moscow. **1923** Lenin retired as Soviet leader after suffering a severe stroke; he
died the following year. **1956** Archbishop Makarios of Cyprus was deported to the
Seychelles to prevent his involvement in terrorist activities. **1961** Russian dog
Laika was launched into space aboard the spacecraft *Sputnik 9*.

BIRTHS

William Cobbett, author and politician, **1763**; Vita Sackville-West, English
novelist, **1892**; Yuri Gagarin, Soviet astronaut, the first man in space, **1934**;
Bobby Fischer, US chess champion, **1943**; Vyacheslav Molotov, Soviet
politician, **1890**; Bill Beaumont, English rugby player, **1952**.

DEATHS

David Rizzio, secretary to Mary Queen of Scots, murdered **1566**; Jules Mazarin,
French cardinal and politician, **1661**; Frank Wedekind, German playwright,
1918; Wilhelm I of Prussia, **1888**; Bob Crosby, US bandleader, **1993**.

'Now they're calling drugs an epidemic - that's
'cos white folks are doing it.'
Richard Pryor

10 March

'If you pick up a starving dog and make him prosperous he
will not bite you. This is the principal difference
between a dog and a man.'
Mark Twain, *What is Man?*

Feast day of St Kessog, St John Ogilvie, St Attalas, St Hymelin, St Macarius of
Jerusalem, St Simplicius, pope, and St Anastasia Patricia.

∽ EVENTS ∽

1801 The first census was begun in Britain. **1886** Cruft's Dog Show was held in
London for the first time – since 1859 it had been held in Newcastle. **1906** The
Bakerloo line was opened on the London underground railway. **1914** English
suffragette Mary Richardson slashed Velasquez' *Rokeby Venus* with a meat
cleaver. **1969** James Earl Ray was sentenced to 99 years' imprisonment after
pleading guilty to the murder of civil-rights leader Martin Luther King. **1974** A
Japanese soldier was discovered hiding on Lubang Island in the Philippines. He
was unaware that World War II had ended, and was waiting to be picked up by
his own forces.

∽ BIRTHS ∽

Marcello Malpighi, Italian physiologist, **1628**; Tamara Karsavina, Russian ballet
dancer, **1885**; Arthur Honegger, French composer, **1892**; Bix Beiderbecke, US
jazz musician and composer, **1903**; Prince Edward, youngest son of Queen
Elizabeth II, **1964**.

∽ DEATHS ∽

Giuseppe Mazzini, Italian nationalist, **1832**; Mikhail Bulgakov, Russian novelist
and playwright, **1940**; Jan Masaryk, Czech politician, allegedly committed
suicide after Communist takeover, **1948**; Konstantin Chernenko, Soviet leader,
1985; Ray Milland, US film actor, **1986**.

'You know, by the time you reach my age, you've made plenty
of mistakes if you've lived your life properly.'
Ronald Reagan

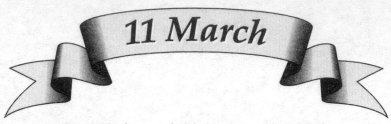

11 March

'Being a thief is a terrific life, but the trouble is they do
put you in the nick for it.'
John McVicar, reported on 11 March 1979

Feast day of St Oengus, St Vindician, St Sophronius of Jerusalem, St Constantine of Cornwall, St Eulogius of Cordova, St Aurea, St Benedict of Milan, and St Teresa Margaret Redi.

∞ EVENTS ∞

1682 The Royal Chelsea Hospital for soldiers was founded by Charles II. **1702** The first successful English daily newspaper, the *Daily Courant* was published in London. **1941** US Congress passed the Lend-Lease Bill, authorising huge loans to Britain to finance World War II. **1985** Mikhail Gorbachev became leader of the USSR. **1988** The Bank of England replaced pound notes with pound coins. **1990** US tennis player Jennifer Capriati, aged 13, became the youngest-ever finalist in a professional contest.

∞ BIRTHS ∞

Urbain Leverrier, French astronomer, **1811**; Malcolm Campbell, English speed record holder, **1885**; Harold Wilson, British politician, **1916**; Rupert Murdoch, Australian newspaper proprietor, **1931**; Douglas Adams, English author of *The Hitch-Hiker's Guide to the Galaxy*, **1952**; Nigel Lawson, British politician, **1932**.

∞ DEATHS ∞

Rolf Boldrewood, Australian author, **1915**; David Beatty, British admiral, **1936**; Alexander Fleming, Scottish bacteriologist who discovered penicillin, **1955**; Richard Evelyn Bird, US aviator and explorer, **1957**; Erle Stanley Gardner, US lawyer and crime writer, **1970**.

' "Life," said Marvin,
"Don't talk to me about life." '
Douglas Adams, *The Hitch Hiker's Guide to the Galaxy*

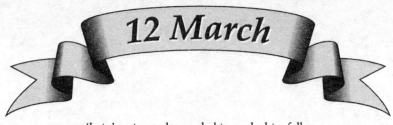
12 March

'I ain't going to let no darkies and white folks
segregate together in this town.'
Eugene Connor, police commissioner of Birmingham,
Alabama, USA, reported on 12 March 1950

Feast day of St Alphege, St Bernard of Winchester, St Gregory, St Maximilian of Theveste, St Mura, St Paul Aurelian, St Theophanes, and St Pionius.

EVENTS

1609 Bermuda became a British colony. **1881** France made Tunisia a protectorate. **1904** Britain's first mainline electric train ran from Liverpool to Southport. **1912** The Girl Guides movement (later called Scouts) was founded in the USA. **1930** Indian leader Mahatma Gandhi began his walk to the sea, known as the Salt March, in defiance of the British government's tax on salt and monopoly of the salt trade in India. **1938** Germany annexed Austria. **1940** The Russo-Finnish war ended with Finland signing over territory to the USSR.

BIRTHS

John Aubrey, English antiquary and author of *Brief Lives*, **1626**; Thomas Arne, English composer who wrote 'Rule Britannia', **1710**; Kemal Ataturk, Turkish leader, **1881**; Vaslav Nijinsky, Russian ballet dancer, **1890**; Max Wall, English actor and comedian, **1908**; Liza Minnelli, US film actress and singer, **1946**.

DEATHS

St Gregory, pope, **604**; Cesare Borgia, Italian cardinal and politician, **1507**; Sun Yat-sen, Chinese revolutionary leader, **1925**; Anne Frank, Dutch Jewish diarist, died in a Nazi concentration camp, **1945**; Charlie Parker, US jazz saxophonist, **1955**; Eugene Ormandy, US conductor, **1985**.

'I don't know what effect these men will have on the enemy,
but, by God, they frighten me.'
Duke of Wellington, as his forces occupied Bordeaux

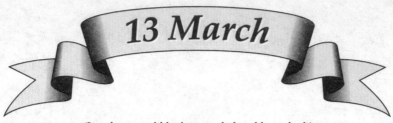

13 March

'Laughter would be bereaved if snobbery died.'
Peter Ustinov, reported on 13 March 1955

Feast day of St Gerald of Mayo, St Mochoemoc, St Nicephorus of Constantinople, Saints Roderic and Salomon, St Ansovinus, and St Euphrasia.

EVENTS

1781 German-born British astronomer William Herschel discovered the planet Uranus. **1881** Tsar Alexander II of Russia died after a bomb was thrown at him in St Petersburg. **1894** The first public striptease act was performed in Paris. **1928** 450 people drowned when a dam burst near Los Angeles, USA. **1930** US astronomer Clyde Tombaugh discovered the planet Pluto; its existence had been predicted 14 years earlier by US astronomer Percy Lowell. **1979** A Marxist coup led by Maurice Bishop took place in Grenada while Prime Minister Edward Gairy was in New York at a meeting of the United Nations.

BIRTHS

Joseph Priestley, English scientist, **1733**; Percy Lowell, US astronomer, **1855**; Hugh Walpole, English novelist, **1884**; Henry Hathaway, US film director, **1898**; Neil Sedaka, US singer and songwriter, **1939**; Joe Bugner, Hungarian-born British boxer, **1950**.

DEATHS

Richard Burbage, English actor who built the Globe Theatre, **1619**; Susan Anthony, US feminist, **1906**; Stephen Benet, US poet who wrote 'John Brown's Body', **1943**; Angela Brazil, English writer of stories about girls' schools, **1947**; John Middleton Murry, English writer and critic, **1957**.

'I never hated a man enough to give him his diamonds back.'
Zsa Zsa Gabor

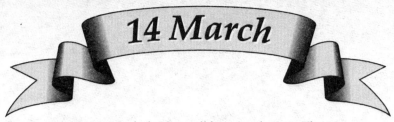

14 March

'I seriously doubt if we will have another war. This
[Vietnam] is probably the last.'
Richard Nixon, reported on 14 March 1971

Feast day of St Matilda, St Eutychius, and St Leobinus.

EVENTS

1492 Queen Isabella of Castile ordered the expulsion of 150,000 Jews from
Spain, unless they accepted Christian baptism. **1757** British admiral John Byng
was executed by firing squad at Plymouth, for having failed to relieve Minorca
from the French fleet. **1864** English explorer Samuel Baker was the first
European to see the lake he named Lake Albert. **1885** Gilbert and Sullivan's
Mikado was first performed at the Savoy Theatre, London. **1891** The submarine
Monarch laid the first underwater telephone cable.

BIRTHS

Georg Telemann, German composer, **1681**; Mrs Isabella Beeton, English
cookery writer, **1836**; Maxim Gorky, Russian playwright and novelist, **1868**;
Albert Einstein, German-born Swiss physicist, **1879**; Michael Caine, English
film actor, **1933**; Jasper Carrott, English comedian, **1946**.

DEATHS

John Jervis, English admiral, **1823**; Karl Marx, German philosopher, **1883**;
George Eastman, inventor of the Kodak camera, **1932**; Nikolai Bukharin,
Russian politician, **1938**; Busby Berkeley, US film choreographer, **1976**.

'Equations are more important to me because politics is for
the present, but an equation is something for eternity.'
Albert Einstein

15 March

'There is no more sense in students participating in the management of universities than there would be in a union of housewives participating in the management of Marks and Spencer's stores.'
Enoch Powell, reported on 15 March 1970

Feast day of St Longinus, St Louise de Marillac, St Zacharias, pope, St Lucretia, St Matrona, and St Clement Mary Hofbauer.

⁓ EVENTS ⁓

1892 US inventor Jesse Reno patented the first escalator. **1909** US entrepreneur G S Selfridge opened Britain's first department store in Oxford Street, London. **1917** Tsar Nicholas II of Russia abdicated. **1933** Nazi leader Adolf Hitler proclaimed the Third Reich in Germany; he also banned left-wing newspapers and kosher food. **1949** Clothes rationing in Britain ended. **1964** Actors Elizabeth Taylor and Richard Burton were married in Montreal.

⁓ BIRTHS ⁓

Andrew Jackson, seventh president of the USA, **1767**; William Lamb, Viscount Melbourne, British prime minister, **1779**; John Snow, English physician who pioneered the use of ether as an anaesthetic, **1813**; Emil von Behring, German bacteriologist, **1854**; Mike Love, US pop singer, member of the Beach Boys, **1941**; Ry Cooder, US guitarist, **1947**.

⁓ DEATHS ⁓

Julius Caesar, Roman emperor, assassinated, **44 BC**; Henry Bessemer, English metallurgist who invented the Bessemer converter, **1898**; Aristotle Onassis, Greek shipping tycoon, **1975**; Rebecca West, English novelist, **1983**; Tommy Cooper, English comedian, **1984**; Farzad Barzoft, Iranian-born journalist working for the *Observer*, hanged as a spy in Iraq, **1990**.

'Funny really. When you look at the things that go on these days my life story reads like Noddy.'
Diana Dors, reported on 15 March 1970

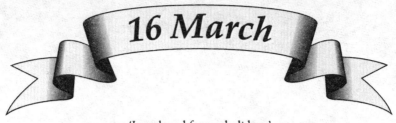
16 March

Feast day of St Finan Lobur, St Abraham Kidunaia, St Julian of Antioch, St Eusebia of Hamage, St Heribert of Cologne, and St Gregory Makar.

EVENTS

1660 The Long Parliament of England was dissolved, after sitting for 20 years. **1802** The US Military Academy was established at West Point, New York State. **1872** The Wanderers beat the Royal Engineers 1–0 in the first FA Cup Final, at Kennington Oval. **1926** The first rocket fuelled by petrol and liquid oxygen was successfully launched by US physicist Robert Goddard. **1973** The new London Bridge was opened.

BIRTHS

Matthew Flinders, English navigator who explored the coast of Australia, **1774**; Georg Ohm, German physicist, **1787**; Leo McKern, Australian actor, **1920**; Jerry Lewis, US comedy actor, **1926**; Bernardo Bertolucci, Italian film director, **1941**.

DEATHS

Tiberius Claudius Nero, Roman emperor, AD **37**; Aubrey Beardsley, English illustrator, **1898**; Miguel Primo de Rivera, Spanish politician and dictator, **1930**; Austen Chamberlain, British politician who negotiated the Locarno Pact, **1937**; William Henry Beveridge, English economist who wrote the report on which the British welfare state was founded, **1963**.

'The gift of rhetoric has been responsible for more bloodshed
on this earth than all the guns and explosives
that were ever invented.'
Stanley Baldwin, reported on 16 March 1924

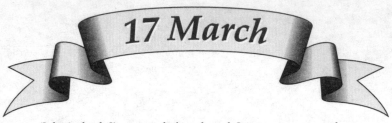

17 March

'I don't think I'm particularly awkward. It just seems to me that everybody else is awkward.'
Elvis Costello

National Day of Ireland. Feast day of St Patrick, St Withburga, St Gertrude of Nivelles, St Joseph of Arimathea, St Paul of Cyprus, and the Martyrs of the Serapaeum.

EVENTS

1897 English-born New Zealand boxer Bob Fitzsimmons won the heavyweight title from US champion Jim Corbett. **1899** The first-ever radio distress call was sent, summoning assistance to a merchant ship aground on the Goodwin Sands, off the Kent coast. **1921** English doctor Marie Stopes opened The Mothers' Clinic in London, to advise women on birth-control. **1969** Golda Meir, aged 70, took office as prime minister of Israel, the first woman to do so. **1978** The oil tanker *Amoco Cadiz* ran aground on the coast of Brittany, spilling over 220,000 tons of crude oil and causing extensive pollution. **1990** The Bastille opera house, Paris, was opened.

BIRTHS

Edmund Kean, English actor, **1787**; Kate Greenaway, English children's book illustrator, **1846**; Nat 'King' Cole, US singer, **1919**; Penelope Lively, English children's novelist, **1933**; Rudolf Nureyev, Russian ballet dancer, **1938**; Robin Knox-Johnston, the first person to sail single-handed, non-stop around the world, **1939**.

DEATHS

Marcus Aurelius, Roman emperor, AD **180**; Daniel Bernoulli, Swiss mathematician and physicist **1782**; Christian Doppler, Austrian physicist, **1853**; Lawrence Oates, English Antarctic explorer, a member of Scott's expedition, who walked into a blizzard, saying 'I am just going outside, and may be some time', **1912**; George Wilkins, Australian polar explorer, **1958**; John Glubb (Glubb Pasha), English soldier, founder of the Arab Legion, **1986**.

'Brigands demand your money or your life; women require both.'
Samuel Butler

18 March

'We have recognised that it is for the good of the country
that we should abdicate the Crown of the Russian state, and lay
down the supreme power.'
Tsar Alexander II of Russia, reported on 18 March 1917

Feast day of St Cyril of Jerusalem, St Alexander of Jerusalem, St Christian, St Edward the Martyr, St Finan of Aberdeen, St Anselm of Lucca, St Frigidian, and St Salvator of Horta.

✑ EVENTS ✑

1662 The first public bus service began operating, in Paris. **1834** Six farm labourers from Tolpuddle, Dorset, were sentenced to transportation to Australia for forming a trade union. **1891** The London–Paris telephone link came into operation. **1922** Indian leader Mahatma Gandhi was jailed for six years for sedition. **1931** The first electric razors were manufactured in the USA. **1965** Soviet astronaut Alexei Leonov made the first 'walk' in space.

✑ BIRTHS ✑

Nikolai Rimsky-Korsakov, Russian composer, **1844**; Rudolf Diesel, German engineer who invented the engine named after him, **1858**; Neville Chamberlain, British prime minister who tried unsuccessfully to make peace with Hitler, **1869**; Lavrenti Beria, Soviet chief of secret police, **1889**; Wilfred Owen, English World War I poet, **1893**; Robert Donat, English film actor, **1905**.

✑ DEATHS ✑

Edward the Martyr, king of England, murdered at Corfe Castle, **978**; Fra Angelico, Italian monk and painter, **1455**; Ivan IV, 'the Terrible' **1584**; Robert Walpole, first prime minister of Britain, **1745**; Laurence Sterne, Irish novelist, **1768**; Percy Thrower, English gardener and broadcaster, **1988**.

'I believe it is peace in our time ... peace with honour.'
Neville Chamberlain

19 March

'Hatred is always in the depths, self hatred.'
James Baldwin

Feast day of St Alcmund, St Joseph, St John of Panaca, and St Landoald.

 EVENTS

721 BC The first-ever recorded solar eclipse was seen from Babylon. **1628** The New England Company was formed in Massachusetts Bay. **1913** Russian composer Modest Mussorgsky's opera *Boris Godunov* was first performed in full at the Metropolitan Opera, New York. **1932** The Sydney Harbour Bridge, New South Wales, Australia, was opened; it was the world's longest single-span arch bridge, at 503 m/1,650 ft. **1969** British troops landed on the Caribbean island of Anguilla, after the island declared itself a republic; they were well received, and the island remained a UK dependency.

BIRTHS

Georges de la Tour, French painter, **1593**; Tobias Smollett, Scottish physician and author, **1721**; David Livingstone, Scottish missionary and explorer, **1813**; Richard Burton, English explorer and scholar, **1821**; Wyatt Earp, US law officer, **1848**; Sergei Diaghilev, Russian ballet impresario, **1872**.

DEATHS

Thomas Killigrew, English playwright, **1683**; Mary Anning, English paleontologist who discovered the first ichthyosaurus, **1847**; Arthur James Balfour, British prime minister, **1930**; Edgar Rice Burroughs, US novelist who wrote the Tarzan stories, **1950**; Alan Badel, English actor, **1965**.

'At 50 everyone has the face he deserves.'
George Orwell

20 March

'Half the country is middle class:
the other half is trying to be.'
Alan Ayckbourn, reported on 20 March 1977

Feast day of St Cuthbert, St Wolfram, St Herbert of Derwentwater, St Martin of Braga, St Photina and her Companions, and the Martyrs of Mar Saba.

✎ EVENTS ✎

1602 The Dutch government founded the Dutch East India Company. **1806** The foundation stone of Dartmoor Prison was laid. **1815** Napoleon returned to Paris from banishment on the island of Elba to begin his last 100 days of power that ended with defeat and exile. **1852** US author Harriet Beecher Stowe's novel *Uncle Tom's Cabin* was published. **1956** Tunisia achieved independence from France. **1980** Pirate radio ship Radio Caroline sank.

✎ BIRTHS ✎

Ovid, Roman poet, **43** BC; Henrik Ibsen, Norwegian playwright, **1828**; Beniamino Gigli, Italian operatic tenor, **1890**; Michael Redgrave, English actor, **1908**; Vera Lynn, English singer, **1917**; Madan Lal, Indian cricketer, **1951**.

✎ DEATHS ✎

King Henry IV of England, **1413**; Thomas Seymour, Lord High Admiral of England, executed, **1549**; Isaac Newton, English scientist, **1727**; Lajos Kossuth, Hungarian revolutionary leader, **1894**; Ferdinand Foch, French Army marshal, **1929**; Brendan Behan, Irish playwright, **1964**.

'What ought a man to be? Well, my short answer is "himself".'
Henrik Ibsen, *Peer Gynt*

21 March

'I was obliged to work hard.
Whoever is equally industrious will succeed just as well.'
J S Bach

Feast day of St Benedict, St Enda, St Nicholas of Flue, St Fanchea, and St Serapion of Thmuis.

EVENTS

1933 Germany's first Nazi parliament was officially opened in a ceremony at the garrison church in Potsdam. **1946** British minister Aneurin Bevan announced the Labour government's plans for the National Health Service. **1952** Kwame Nkrumah was elected prime minister of the Gold Coast (later Ghana). **1960** The Sharpeville Massacre – in South Africa a peaceful demonstration against the pass laws ended with about 70 deaths when police fired on demonstrators. **1963** Alcatraz, the maximum-security prison in San Francisco Bay, USA, was closed. **1990** A demonstration in London against the poll tax became a riot, in which over 400 people were arrested.

BIRTHS

Johann Sebastian Bach, German composer, **1685**; Paul Tortelier, French cellist, **1914**; Peter Brook, English stage and film director, **1925**; Michael Heseltine, British politician, **1933**; Brian Clough, English footballer and manager, **1935**; Ayrton Senna, Brazilian racing driver, **1960**.

DEATHS

Thomas Cranmer, archbishop of Canterbury, burned at the stake, **1556**; James Ussher, Irish theologian and archbishop of Armagh, who fixed the date of the Creation at 4004 BC, **1656**; Robert Southey, English poet, **1843**; Alexander Glazunov, Russian composer, **1936**; Philip Wilson Steer, English painter, **1942**; Harry H Corbett, English actor, **1982**.

'I can recommend you go to jail for a while, to see, because you open your eyes and see the system exactly. You have to go to the bottom of society to understand it.'
Nawal al-Saadawi

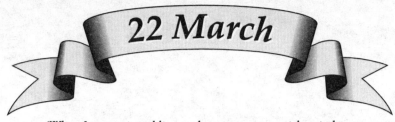

22 March

'When I appear in public people expect me to neigh, grind my teeth, paw the ground and swish my tail.'
Princess Anne, reported on 22 March 1977

The earliest possible date for Easter. Feast day of St Deogratius, St Basil of Ancyra, St Paul of Narbonne, St Nicholas Owen, and St Benvenuto of Osimo.

∾ EVENTS ∾

1824 The British parliament voted to buy 38 pictures at a cost of £57,000, to establish the national collection which is now housed in the National Gallery, Trafalgar Square, London. **1888** The English Football League was formed. **1895** French cinema pioneers Auguste and Louis Lumière gave the first demonstration of celluloid film, in Paris. **1942** The BBC began broadcasting in morse code to the French Resistance. **1945** The Arab League was founded in Cairo. **1946** Jordan achieved independence from British rule.

∾ BIRTHS ∾

Maximilian I, Holy Roman Emperor, **1459**; Anthony van Dyck, Flemish painter, **1599**; Karl Malden, US film actor, **1913**; Marcel Marceau, French mime, **1923**; Stephen Sondheim, US composer and lyricist, **1930**; Andrew Lloyd Webber, English composer of musicals, **1948**.

∾ DEATHS ∾

Jean Lully, French composer, **1687**; John Canton, English physicist, **1772**; Johann Wolfgang von Goethe, German poet, novelist, and playwright, **1832**; Thomas Hughes, English author of *Tom Brown's Schooldays*, **1896**; Mike Todd, US film producer, **1958**.

'History has been made in this church today. By me.'
Reverend Sylvia Mutch, the first woman to conduct a marriage ceremony in the Church of England, reported on 22 March 1987

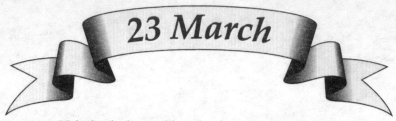

23 March

'Nobody who has wealth to distribute ever omits himself.'
Leon Trotsky, reported on 23 March 1937

National Day of Pakistan. Feast day of St Gwinear, St Turibius, St Benedict the Hermit, St Victorian, St Ethelwald the Hermit, and St Joseph Oriol.

✑ EVENTS ✑

1765 The British parliament passed the Stamp Act, imposing a tax on all publications and official documents in America. **1861** London's first trams began operating, in Bayswater. **1891** Goal nets, invented by Liverpudlian J A Brodie, were used for the first time in an FA Cup Final. **1919** The Italian Fascist Party was formed by Benito Mussolini. **1925** Authorities in the state of Tennessee, USA, forbade the teaching of Darwinian theory in schools. **1956** Pakistan was declared an Islamic republic within the Commonwealth.

✑ BIRTHS ✑

Juan Gris, Spanish painter, **1887**; Joan Crawford, US film actress, **1904**; Akira Kurosawa, Japanese film director, **1910**; Wernher von Braun, German-born US rocket engineer, **1912**; Jimmy Edwards, English comedian, **1920**; Roger Bannister, English neurologist who, as a student, was the first person to run a mile in under four minutes (3 min 59.4 sec), **1929**.

✑ DEATHS ✑

Stendhal, French novelist, **1842**; Steve Donoghue, English jockey, **1945**; Raoul Dufy, French painter, **1953**; Peter Lorre, Hungarian-born US film actor, **1964**; Claude Auchinleck, British Field Marshal, **1981**; Mike Hailwood, English champion motor cyclist, **1981**.

'To be an artist means never to look away.'
Akira Kurosawa

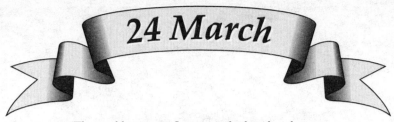
24 March

'The world is so overflowing with absurdity that it is
difficult for the humorist to compete.'
Malcolm Muggeridge, on becoming editor of *Punch*

Feast day of St Dunchad, St Hildelith, St Macartan, St Aldemar, St Simon of
Trent, St William of Norwich, St Catherine of Vadstena, and St Irenaeus of
Sirmeum.

〰 EVENTS 〰

1401 Tamerlane the Great captured Damascus. **1603** The crowns of England
and Scotland were united when King James VI of Scotland succeeded to the
English throne. **1877** The Oxford–Cambridge boat race ended in a dead heat,
the only time this has happened. **1922** Only three of the 32 horses in the Grand
National Steeplechase finished the race. **1942** The national loaf was introduced
in Britain. **1976** Isabel Perón, president of Argentina, was deposed.

〰 BIRTHS 〰

William Morris, English socialist and craftsman, **1834**; Roscoe 'Fatty' Arbuckle,
US silent film actor, **1887**; Ub Iwerks, US animator who worked with Walt
Disney on the creation of Mickey Mouse, **1901**; Steve McQueen, US film actor,
1930; Malcolm Muggeridge, English writer and broadcaster, **1903**; Archie
Gemmill, Scottish footballer, **1947**.

〰 DEATHS 〰

Elizabeth I, queen of England, **1603**; Henry Wadsworth Longfellow, US poet,
1882; Jules Verne, French novelist, **1905**; J M Synge, Irish playwright, **1909**;
Orde Charles Wingate, British general, **1944**; Bernard, Viscount Montgomery of
Alamein, British Field Marshal, **1976**.

'I will make you shorter by the head.'
Queen Elizabeth I

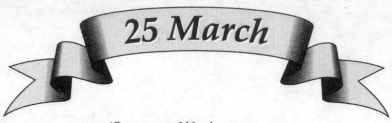

25 March

'Communism I like, but communist
intellectuals are savages.'
Jean-Paul Sartre, reported on 25 March 1956

National Day of Greece. Feast day of St Barontius, St Alfwold, St Dismus, St
Lucy Filippini, St Hermenland, and St Margaret Clitherow.

EVENTS

1306 Robert I 'the Bruce' was crowned king of Scots. **1609** English explorer
Henry Hudson set off from Amsterdam, on behalf of the Dutch East India
Company, in search of the North West Passage. **1807** The British parliament
abolished the slave trade. **1843** A pedestrian tunnel was opened beneath the
Thames in London, linking Wapping with Rotherhithe. **1876** In the first
football international between Wales and Scotland, played in Glasgow, Scotland
won 4–0. **1957** Six European countries (France, Belgium, Luxembourg, West
Germany, Italy, and the Netherlands) signed the Treaty of Rome, establishing
the European Community.

BIRTHS

Henry II, **1133**; Arturo Toscanini, Italian conductor, **1867**; Béla Bartók,
Hungarian composer, **1881**; A J P Taylor, English historian, **1906**; David Lean,
English film director, **1900**, Aretha Franklin, US singer, **1942**; Elton John,
English pop singer and songwriter, **1947**.

DEATHS

Anna Seward, English novelist who wrote *Black Beauty*, **1809**; Nicholas
Hawksmoor, English architect, **1836**; Frédéric Mistral, French poet, **1914**;
Claude Debussy, French composer, **1918**; King Faisal of Saudi Arabia,
assassinated by his nephew, **1975**.

'The most dangerous thing in the world is to make a friend of
an Englishman, because he'll come sleep in your closet rather
than spend ten shillings on a hotel.'
Truman Capote, reported on 25 March 1966

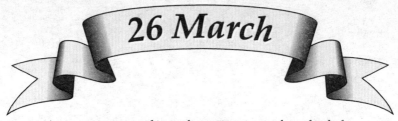

26 March

'Any contemporary of ours who wants peace and comfort before anything has chosen a bad time to be born.'
Leon Trotsky, reported on 26 March 1933

Feast day of St William of Norwich, St Liudger, St Felix of Trier, St Castulus of Rome, St Braulio, and St Basil of Rome.

❧ EVENTS ❧

1839 The annual rowing regatta at Henley-on-Thames was established. **1886** The funeral of the first person to be officially cremated in Britain took place in Woking, Surrey. **1920** The British special constables known as the Black and Tans arrived in Ireland. **1934** Driving tests were introduced in Britain. **1973** The first women were allowed on the floor of the London Stock Exchange. **1979** Israeli prime minister Menachem Begin and Egyptian president Anwar Sadat signed a peace treaty after two years of negotiations.

❧ BIRTHS ❧

A E Housman, English poet, **1859**; Robert Frost, US poet, **1874**; Pierre Boulez, French conductor and composer, **1925**; Leonard Nimoy, US actor who played Mr Spock in the TV series *Star Trek*; James Caan, US film actor, **1939**; Diana Ross, US singer, **1944**.

❧ DEATHS ❧

John Vanbrugh, English playwright and architect, **1726**; Ludwig von Beethoven, German composer, **1827**; Walt Whitman, US poet, **1892**; Cecil Rhodes, English-born South African politician, **1902**; Sarah Bernhardt, French actress, **1923**; Raymond Chandler, US novelist who created private eye Philip Marlowe, **1959**; Noël Coward, English playwright and entertainer, **1973**.

'It was a blonde to make a bishop kick a hole in a stained glass window.'
Raymond Chandler, *Farewell My Lovely*

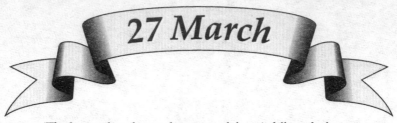

27 March

'The hungry hare has no frontiers and doesn't follow ideologies.
The hungry hare goes where it finds the food.
And the other hares don't block its path with the tanks.'
Lech Walesa

Feast day of St Rupert, St Athilda, and St John of Egypt.

EVENTS

1794 The United States Navy was formed. **1871** England and Scotland played their first rugby international, in Edinburgh; Scotland won. **1914** The first successful blood transfusion was performed, in a Brussels hospital. **1958** Nikita Khrushchev became leader of the Soviet Union. **1964** The ten Great Train Robbers who were caught were sentenced to a total of 307 years in prison. **1977** Pan Am and KLM jumbo jets collided on the runway at Tenerife airport, in the Canary Islands, killing 574 people.

BIRTHS

Henry Royce, English car designer and manufacturer, **1863**; Ludwig Mies van der Rohe, German architect, **1886**; Gloria Swanson, US film actress, **1899**; Cyrus Vance, US secretary of state, **1917**; Sarah Vaughan, US jazz singer, **1924**; Mstislav Rostropovich, Russian cellist and conductor, **1927**; Duncan Goodhew, English Olympic swimmer, **1957**.

DEATHS

King James I of Great Britain, **1625**; Giovanni Battista Tiepolo, Italian painter, **1770**; George Gilbert Scott, English architect, **1878**; James Dewar, Scottish physicist and chemist who invented the thermos flask, **1923**; Arnold Bennett, English novelist, **1931**; Anthony Blunt, English art historian and Soviet spy, **1983**.

'When a woman behaves like a man,
why doesn't she behave like a nice man?'
Edith Evans

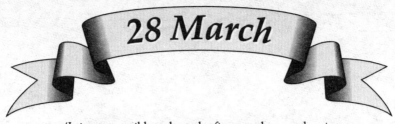

28 March

'It is now possible to hear the finest cockney spoken in first-class railway carriages.'
William Pett Ridge, reported on 28 March 1920

Feast day of St Alkelda of Middleham, St Gontran, and St Tutilo.

～ EVENTS ～

1910 The first seaplane took off near Marseille, S France. **1912** Both the Oxford and the Cambridge boats sank in the University boat race. **1930** The cities of Angora and Constantinople, in Turkey, changed their names to Ankara and Istanbul respectively. **1939** The Spanish Civil War came to an end as Madrid surrendered to General Franco. **1945** Germany dropped its last V2 bomb on Britain. **1979** The nuclear power station at Three Mile Island, Pennsylvania, suffered a meltdown in the core of one of its reactors.

～ BIRTHS ～

Raphael, Italian painter, **1483**; St Teresa of Avila, Carmelite nun, **1515**; King George I, **1660**; Flora Robson, English actress, **1902**; Dirk Bogarde, English actor and author, **1921**; Neil Kinnock, British politician, **1942**,

～ DEATHS ～

James Thomas Brudenell, 7th earl of Cardigan, leader of the disastrous Charge of the Light Brigade at Balaclava, **1868**; Virginia Woolf, English novelist, **1941**; Sergei Rachmaninov, Russian composer, **1943**; Marc Chagall, Russian-born French painter, **1985**; W C Handy, US blues composer, **1958**; Dwight Eisenhower, 34th president of the USA, **1969**.

'Perhaps this country needs an Iron Lady.'
Margaret Thatcher, reported on 28 March 1976

29 March

'Great God! This is an awful place.'
Robert Falcon Scott, diary entry on the South Pole

Feast day of Saints Gwynllyw and Gwladys, St Cyril of Heliopolis, St Berthold, St Mark of Arethusa, St Rupert of Salzburg, Saints Jonas, Barachisius and Others, Saints Armogastes, Masculas, Achinimus, and Saturus.

❧ EVENTS ❧

1461 Over 28,000 people are said to have been killed in the Battle of Towton, N Yorkshire; the Lancastrians under Henry VI were defeated. **1871** The Albert Hall, London, was opened by Queen Victoria. **1886** Coca Cola went on sale in the USA; it was marketed as a 'Brain Tonic' and claimed to relieve exhaustion. **1971** In the USA, Lt. William Calley was sentenced to life imprisonment after being found guilty of the murder of civilians in the South Vietnamese village of My Lai in 1969. **1973** The last US troops left Vietnam. **1974** US spacecraft *Mariner 10* took close-up photographs of the planet Mercury.

❧ BIRTHS ❧

Elihu Thomson, US inventor, **1853**; Edwin Lutyens, English architect, **1869**; William Walton, English composer, **1902**; Pearl Bailey, US singer, **1918**; Norman Tebbit, British politician, **1931**; John Major, British prime minister, **1943**.

❧ DEATHS ❧

Charles Wesley, English evangelist and hymn-writer, **1788**; Maria Fitzherbert, mistress of King George IV, **1837**; Georges-Pierre Seurat, French painter, **1891**; Robert Falcon Scott, Antarctic explorer, **1912**; Joyce Cary, Irish novelist, **1957**; Vera Brittain, English socialist writer, **1970**.

'I grew up in the thirties with our unemployed father.
He did not riot, he got on his bike and looked for work.'
Norman Tebbit, speech 15 Oct 1981

30 March

'The English are probably the most tolerant,
least religious people on earth.'
Rabbi David Goldberg, reported on 30 March 1980

Feast day of St Osburga, St John Climacus, St Zosimus of Syracuse, St Ludolf, St Leonard Murialdo, and St Rieul.

EVENTS

1775 The British parliament passed an Act forbidding its North American colonies to trade with anyone other than Britain. **1842** Ether was first used as an anaesthetic during surgery, by US doctor Crawford Long. **1856** The Crimean War was brought to an end by the signing of the Treaty of Paris. **1867** The USA bought Alaska from Russia for $7.2 million (oil had not yet been discovered). **1893** Thomas Bayard, the USA's first ambassador to Great Britain, arrived in London. **1981** In Washington DC, USA, would-be assassin John Hinckley shot President Reagan in the chest.

BIRTHS

Francisco de Goya, Spanish painter, **1746**; Paul Verlaine, French poet, **1844**; Vincent Van Gogh, Dutch painter, **1853**; Sean O'Casey, Irish playwright, **1880**; Melanie Klein, Austrian-born British psychologist, **1882**; Eric Clapton, English guitarist, **1945**.

DEATHS

William Hunter, Scottish anatomist and obstetrician, **1783**; 'Beau' Brummel, English dandy, **1840**; Rudolf Steiner, Austrian philosopher, **1925**; Friedrich Bergius, German scientist, **1949**; Léon Blum, French politician, **1950**; James Cagney, US film actor, **1986**.

'Oh, the beautiful sun of midsummer! It beats upon my head,
and I do not doubt it makes one a little queer.'
Vincent Van Gogh, letter to his brother Theo

31 March

'I have never been anywhere really.
I came from school, went to work and then got married.'
Princess of Wales, reported on 31 March 1985

Feast day of St Benjamin, St Balbina, St Acacius, and St Guy of Pomposa.

EVENTS

1282 The Sicilian Vespers, a massacre of the French in Sicily, begun the previous evening, ended. **1889** In Paris, the Eiffel Tower, built for the Universal Exhibition, was inaugurated. **1896** The first zip fastener was patented in the USA by its inventor, Whitcomb Judson. **1959** Tibetan Buddhist leader the Dalai Lama fled from Chinese-occupied Tibet. **1973** Racehorse Red Rum set a record of 9 min 1.9 sec for the Grand National Steeplechase. **1986** Hampton Court Palace, near Richmond, SW London, was severely damaged by a fire which broke out in the south wing.

BIRTHS

René Descartes, French philosopher and mathematician, **1596**; Andrew Marvell, English poet, **1621**; Franz Joseph Haydn, Austrian composer, **1732**; Nikolai Gogol, Russian novelist, **1809**; Robert Bunsen, German chemist, **1811**; John Fowles, English novelist, **1927**.

DEATHS

King Francis I of France, **1547**; King Philip III of Spain, **1621**; John Donne, English poet, **1631**; John Constable, English painter, **1837**; Charlotte Brontë, English novelist, **1855**; Jesse Owens, US athlete, **1980**; Enid Bagnold, English novelist, **1981**.

'Common sense is the best-distributed commodity in the world,
for every man is convinced that he is well supplied with it.'
René Descartes

1 April

'Let us be thankful for the fools.
But for them the rest of us could not succeed.'
Mark Twain, *Following the Equator*

All Fools' Day. Feast day of St Agilbert, St Gilbert of Caithness, St Tewdric, St Walaric, St Catharine of Palma, St Melito, St Valery, St Hugh of Bonnevaux, and St Hugh of Grenoble.

EVENTS

1908 The British Territorial Army was founded. **1918** The Royal Air Force was formed when the Royal Naval Air Service and the Royal Flying Corps were merged. **1947** Britain's school-leaving age was raised to 15. **1948** The USSR began its blockade of Berlin. **1960** The USA launched the world's first weather satellite, *Tiros I*. **1973** In Britain, Value Added Tax (VAT) replaced Purchase Tax and Selective Employment Tax.

BIRTHS

William Harvey, English physician who explained the circulation of the blood, **1578**; Otto von Bismarck, first chancellor of the German Empire, **1815**; Edmond Rostand, French playwright, author of Cyrano de Bergerac, **1868**; Lon Chaney, US silent-film actor, **1883**; Ali McGraw, US film actress, 1938; David Gower, English cricketer, **1957**.

DEATHS

Eleanor of Aquitaine, queen of England and France, **1204**; King Robert III of Scotland, **1406**; Scott Joplin, US composer, **1917**; Karl Franz Josef, emperor of Austria, **1922**; Max Ernst, German Surrealist painter, **1976**; Marvin Gaye, US singer, **1984**.

'Games are the last recourse to those who do not know how to idle.'
Robert Lynd, reported on 1 April 1923

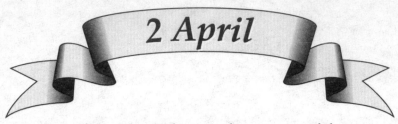

2 April

'Every advance in science leaves morality in its ancient balance;
and it depends still on the inscrutable soul of man
whether any discovery is mainly a benefit or mainly a calamity.'
G K Chesterton, reported on 2 April 1922

Feast day of St Francis of Paola, St Mary of Egypt, St John Payne, St Zosimus, St Nicetius of Lyons, and Saints Apphian and Theodosia.

❧ EVENTS ❧

1792 The first mint was established in the USA. **1801** The British and Danish fleets met in the Battle of Copenhagen, during which Nelson put his telescope to his blind eye and ignored Admiral Parker's signal to stop fighting; the British fleet won. **1849** Britain annexed the Punjab. **1860** The first parliament of the united Italy met at Turin. **1946** The Royal Military Academy at Sandhurst, Berkshire, was founded. **1979** Israeli Prime Minister Menachem Begin became the first Israeli leader to visit Cairo when he met Egyptian President Sadat. **1982** Argentina invaded the Falkland Islands.

❧ BIRTHS ❧

Charlemagne, king of the Franks, **742**; Hans Christian Andersen, Danish author, **1805**; Emile Zola, French novelist, **1840**; Alec Guinness, English actor, **1914**; Jack Brabham, Australian racing driver, **1926**; Penelope Keith, English actress, **1939**.

❧ DEATHS ❧

Honoré Mirabeau, French politician and writer, **1791**; Richard Cobden, British politician, **1865**; Samuel Morse, US inventor, **1872**; C S Forester, English novelist, **1966**; Georges Pompidou, president of France, **1974**.

'A statesman is a politician who places himself at the
service of the nation. A politician is a statesman who places
the nation at his service.'
Georges Pompidou

3 April

'In one or two generations the nobility in England will be
forced to go to work.'
Gordon Selfridge, reported on 3 April 1921

Feast day of Saints Agape, Chionia, and Irene, St Pancras of Taormina, St
Richard of Chichester, St Nicetas, St Burgundofara, and St Sixtus I, pope.

≋ EVENTS ≋

1721 Robert Walpole became the first prime minister of Britain. **1860** In the
USA, the Pony Express came into operation, with despatch riders regularly
making the 3,000-km /2,000-mi trip from St Joseph, Missouri to San Francisco,
California. **1922** In the USSR, Stalin was appointed as general secretary of the
Communist Party. **1930** Haile Selassie became emperor of Ethiopia. **1987** At an
auction in Geneva, jewellery belonging to the late Duchess of Windsor raised
over £31 million.

≋ BIRTHS ≋

King Henry IV, first Lancastrian king of England, **1367**; Washington Irving, US
historian and short-story writer, **1783**; Doris Day, US film actress and singer,
1924; Marlon Brando, US actor, **1924**; Helmut Kohl, German politician, **1930**;
Eddie Murphy, US film actor, **1961**.

≋ DEATHS ≋

Bartolomé Murillo, Spanish painter, **1682**; James Clark Ross, English explorer,
1862; Johannes Brahms, German composer, **1897**; Jesse James, US outlaw,
1882; Graham Greene, English novelist, **1991**; Martha Graham, US dancer and
choreographer, **1991**; Dieter Plage, German wildlife photographer, **1993**.

'Any cook should be able to run the country.'
V I Lenin

4 April

'Peace cannot be kept by force. It can only be achieved by understanding.'
Albert Einstein, *Notes on Pacifism*

National Day of Hungary. Feast day of St Ambrose, St Isidore, St Plato, St Tigernach, St Benedict the Black, and Saints Agathopus and Theodulus.

〜 EVENTS 〜

1541 Spanish Jesuit Ignatius de Loyola became the order's first superior-general. **1581** English navigator Francis Drake returned home after sailing around the world, and was knighted by Queen Elizabeth I. **1933** In the USA, 73 people died when the helium-filled airship *Akron* crashed into the sea off the New Jersey coast. **1934** 'Cat's-eye' reflective studs were first used on roads near Bradford, Yorkshire. **1949** The North Atlantic Treaty Organization (NATO) was formed in Washington DC, USA; 11 countries signed the treaty. **1958** Members of the Campaign for Nuclear Disarmament (CND) held the first Aldermaston March, walking from Hyde Park Corner, London, to the Atomic Weapons Research Establishment at Aldermaston, Berkshire.

〜 BIRTHS 〜

Grinling Gibbons, Dutch-born woodcarver and sculptor, **1648**; William Siemens, German-born British metallurgist and inventor, **1823**; Marguerite Duras, French author, **1914**; Muddy Waters, US blues singer, **1915**; Maya Angelou, US author, **1928**; Anthony Perkins, US actor, **1932**.

〜 DEATHS 〜

John Napier, Scottish mathematician who invented logarithms, **1617**; Oliver Goldsmith, Irish playwright, **1774**; Karl Benz, German motor-car engineer, **1929**; André Michelin, French tyre manufacturer, **1931**; Martin Luther King, US civil-rights leader, assassinated, **1968**; Zulfikar Ali Bhutto, Pakistani prime minister, executed, **1979**.

'We must learn to live together as brothers or perish together as fools.'
Martin Luther King

5 April

'True and False are attributes of speech not of things. And where speech is not, there is neither Truth nor Falsehood.'
Thomas Hobbes, *Leviathan*

Feast day of St Derfel, St Vincent Ferrer, St Ethelburga of Lyminge, St Albert of Montecorvino, and St Gerald of Sauve-Majeure.

✎ EVENTS ✎

1614 In England, the Addled Parliament began sitting, so called because it passed no Bills. **1874** Johann Strauss's opera *Die Fledermaus* was first performed, in Vienna. **1955** British prime minister Winston Churchill resigned. **1964** Automatic, driverless trains began operating on the London Underground. **1976** Harold Wilson resigned as prime minister of Britain, and was succeeded by James Callaghan.

✎ BIRTHS ✎

Thomas Hobbes, English philosopher, **1588**; Elihu Yale, American merchant and founder of the college named after him, **1649**; Spencer Tracey, US film actor, **1900**; Bette Davis, US film actress, **1908**; Herbert von Karajan, Austrian conductor, **1908**; Gregory Peck, US film actor, **1916**.

✎ DEATHS ✎

Georges Danton, French revolutionary leader, guillotined, **1794**; John Wisden, English cricketer who compiled the almanacs named after him, **1884**; Douglas MacArthur, US general, **1964**; Chiang Kai-shek, Chinese soldier and politician, **1975**; Howard Hughes, US industrialist and multi-millionaire, **1976**; George Herbert, earl of Carnarvon, British Egyptologist, **1923**.

'We shall not talk lightly about sacrifice until we are driven to the last extremity which makes sacrifice inevitable.'
Chiang Kai-shek

6 April

'The modern Olympic Games symbolise the struggle between
man's ideals and the reality within which he must live.'
Richard Espy, *The Politics of the Olympic Games*

Feast day of St Elstan, St Irenaeus of Sirmium, St Celestine I, pope, St
Marcellinus of Carthage, St Prudentius of Troyes, St Eutychius of
Constantinople, and St William of Eskilsoè.

EVENTS

1580 An earth tremor damaged several London churches, including the old St
Paul's Cathedral. **1830** Joseph Smith founded the Mormon Church in New York
State. **1896** The first modern Olympic Games began in Athens. **1909** US
explorer Robert Peary became the first person to reach the North Pole. **1917**
The USA declared war on Germany. **1965** Early Bird, the first commercial
communications satellite, was launched by the USA.

BIRTHS

Gustave Moreau, French painter, **1826**; Harry Houdini, US escapologist, **1874**;
John Betjeman, English poet, **1906**; James Watson, US biologist, **1928**; André
Previn, US conductor, **1929**; Paul Daniels, English magician and entertainer,
1938

DEATHS

King Richard I, 'the Lion-Heart', **1199**; Albrecht Dürer, German painter, **1528**;
Francis Walsingham, English politician, **1590**; Jules Bordet, Belgian
bacteriologist, **1961**; Igor Stravinsky, Russian composer, **1971**; Isaac Asimov,
US scientist, **1992**.

'There's only one thing I miss. It's the smell of summer in
the countryside in Cornwall.'
Ronald Biggs, reported on 6 April 1986

7 April

'Mom and pop were just a couple of kids when they got married. He was 18, she was 16 and I was 3.'
Billie Holiday, *Lady Sings the Blues*

Feast day of St Celsus, St Goran, St Finan Cam, St George the Younger, St Hegesippus, St Aphraates, St Henry Walpole, St Herman Joseph, and St John Baptist de la Salle.

≋ EVENTS ≋

1827 The first matches were sold in Stockton, England, by their inventor, chemist John Walker. **1853** Chloroform was used as an anaesthetic on Queen Victoria, during the birth of her eighth child, Prince Leopold. **1906** A major eruption of the Italian volcano, Vesuvius, took place. **1939** Italy invaded Albania. **1948** The World Health Organization (WHO) was established.

≋ BIRTHS ≋

St Francis Xavier, Spanish Jesuit missionary, **1506**; William Wordsworth, English poet, **1770**; Billie Holiday, US jazz singer, **1915**; Ravi Shankar, Indian sitar player, **1920**; David Frost, English TV presenter and interviewer, **1939**; Francis Ford Coppola, US film director, **1939**.

≋ DEATHS ≋

El Greco, Greek-born Spanish painter, **1614**; Dick Turpin, English highwayman, **1739**; Phineas T Barnum, US showman, **1891**; Henry Ford, US car manufacturer, **1947**; Theda Bara, US silent-film actress, **1955**; Jim Clark, English racing driver, killed in a crash, **1968**.

'Poetry is the spontaneous overflow of powerful feelings: it takes its origin from emotion recollected in tranquillity.'
William Wordsworth, *Lyrical Ballads*

8 April

'The truth is that men are tired of liberty.'
Benito Mussolini, reported on 8 April 1923

Feast day of St Walter of Pontoise, St Julia Billart, St Perpetuus of Tours, and St Dionysus of Corinth.

EVENTS

1513 Spanish explorer Juan Ponce de Leon arrived in Florida and claimed it for Spain. **1838** Isambard Brunel's steamship *Great Western* set off on its first voyage, from Bristol to New York; the journey took 15 days. **1898** Lord Kitchener defeated Sudanese leader the Mahdi, at the Battle of Atbara. **1908** Herbert Asquith became prime minister of Britain. **1939** In Albania, King Zog abdicated after Italy occupied the country. **1946** The League of Nations met for the last time. **1953** British colonial authorities in Kenya sentenced Jomo Kenyatta to seven years' imprisonment for allegedly organising the Mau Mau guerrillas.

BIRTHS

Adrian Boult, English conductor, **1889**; Mary Pickford, US film actress, **1893**; Ian Smith, Rhodesian prime minister, **1919**; Eric Porter, English actor, **1928**; Dorothy Tutin, English actress, **1931**; Hywel Bennett, Welsh actor, **1944**.

DEATHS

Caracalla, Roman emperor, assassinated, AD **217**; Domenico Donizetti, Italian composer, **1848**; Elisha Graves Otis, US inventor of the safety lift, **1861**; Pablo Picasso, Spanish painter, **1973**; Marian Anderson, US contralto, **1993**.

'I paint objects as I think them, not as I see them.'
Pablo Picasso

9 April

'Life in the South is much better now, for both blacks and whites. Martin always said it would be a fine place to live when the prejudice was gone.'
Mrs King (wife of Martin Luther) reported on 9 April 1978

Feast day of St Madrun, St Uramar, St Hugh of Rouen, St Gaucherius, St Mary Cleophas, and St Waldetrudis.

EVENTS

1747 The Scottish Jacobite Lord Lovat was beheaded on Tower Hill, London, for high treason; he was the last man to be executed in this way in Britain. **1770** English navigator James Cook arrived in Botany Bay, Australia, the first European to do so. **1865** The American Civil War came to an end when Confederate General Robert E Lee surrendered to Union General Ulysses S Grant, at Appomatox, Virginia. **1869** The Hudson Bay Company agreed to transfer its territory to Canada. **1917** In France, during World War I, Canadian forces began the assault on Vimy Ridge, and the Battle of Arras began. **1969** The British supersonic aircraft *Concorde* made its first test flight, from Bristol to Fairford, Gloucestershire.

BIRTHS

Isambard Kingdom Brunel, English engineer, **1806**; Charles Baudelaire, French poet, **1821**; Paul Robeson, US actor and singer, **1898**; Hugh Gaitskell, British politician, **1906**; Jean-Paul Belmondo, French film actor, **1933**; Severiano Ballesteros, Spanish golfer, **1957**.

DEATHS

Edward IV of England, **1483**; Lorenzo de'Medici, Florentine ruler, **1492**; Francis Bacon, English philosopher and politician, **1626**; Dante Gabriel Rossetti, English painter and poet, **1882**; Dietrich Bonhoeffer, German theologian, **1945**; Frank Lloyd Wright, US architect, **1959**.

'If a man will begin with certainties, he shall end in doubts, but if he will be content to begin with doubts, he will end in certainties.'
Sir Francis Bacon

10 April

'The poll tax is thatcherism taken to its ultimate absurdity.'
John Smith, reported on 10 April 1988

Feast day of St Hedda of Peterborough, Saints Beocca and Hethor, St Bademus, St Macarius of Ghent, St Paternus of Abdinghhof, St Michael de Sanctis, St Fulbert of Chartres, and the Martyrs under the Danes.

EVENTS

1633 Bananas, never seen before in England, were on sale in a London shop. **1820** The first British settlers landed at Algoa Bay, South Africa. **1841** The US newspaper *New York Tribune* was first published. **1849** The safety pin was patented in the USA; unaware of this, a British inventor patented his own safety pin later the same year. **1864** Austrian Archduke Maximilian was made Emperor of Mexico. **1972** Earthquakes in Iran killed over 3,000 people.

BIRTHS

King James V of Scotland, **1512**; William Hazlitt, English essayist and critic, **1778**; William Booth, English founder of the Salvation Army, **1829**; Joseph Pulitzer, US newspaper proprietor who founded the Pulitzer Prize for literature and journalism, **1847**; Max von Sydow, Swedish actor, **1929**; Omar Sharif, Egyptian film actor, **1932**.

DEATHS

Joseph-Louis Lagrange, French mathematician, **1813**; Algernon Charles Swinburne, English poet, **1909**; Emiliano Zapata, Mexican revolutionary leader, shot by government troops, **1919**; Auguste Lumière, French cinema pioneer, **1954**; Evelyn Waugh, English novelist, **1966**; Chris Hani, South African ANC leader, asssassinated, **1993**.

'Anyone who has been to an English public school will always
feel comparatively at home in prison.'
Evelyn Waugh, *Decline and Fall*

11 April

'Never despise what it says in the women's magazines: It may
not be subtle but neither are men.'
Zsa Zsa Gabor, reported on 11 April 1976

Feast day of St Guthlac, St Stanislas, St Godeberta, St Barsanuphius, St Gemma
Galgani, St Isaac of Spoleto, and St Stanislaus of Cracow.

❧ EVENTS ❧

1689 The coronation of William III and Mary II took place in London. **1713**
The War of the Spanish Succession was ended by the signing of the Treaty of
Utrecht; France ceded Newfoundland and Gibraltar to Britain. **1814** Napoleon
abdicated and was exiled to the island of Elba; Louis XVIII became king of
France. **1855** Britain's first pillar boxes were put up in London; there were just
six of them, and they were painted green. **1945** Allied troops liberated the Nazi
concentration camp at Buchenwald. **1951** US General Douglas MacArthur was
relieved of his command in Korea, after a disagreement with President Truman.
1961 Nazi war criminal Adolf Eichmann went on trial in Jerusalem after being
kidnapped from Argentina, where he had fled after World War II.

❧ BIRTHS ❧

James Parkinson, English physician who discovered Parkinson's disease, **1755**;
George Canning, British prime minister, **1770**; Charles Hallé, German-born
British pianist and conductor, **1819**; Dean Acheson, US politician, **1893**; Dan
Maskell, British tennis player, coach, and commentator, **1908**; Joel Grey, US
actor and singer, **1933**.

❧ DEATHS ❧

Donato Bramante, Italian architect who began St Peter's, Rome, **1514**; Thomas
Wyatt, English soldier and conspirator, **1554**; Luther Burbank, US botanist,
1926; Archibald McIndoe, New Zealand-born plastic surgeon, **1960**; John
O'Hara, US novelist, **1970**; Erskine Caldwell, US novelist, **1987**.

'The most delightful advantage of being bald - one can hear snowflakes.'
R G Daniels

12 April

'There is something wrong with a man if he does not want to break the Ten Commandments.'
G K Chesterton, reported on 12 April 1925

Feast day of St Zeno of Verona, St Julius I, pope, St Sabas the Goth and Others, and St Alferius.

≈ EVENTS ≈

1204 Soldiers taking part in the Fourth Crusade under the direction of the Doge of Venice, captured the Byzantine city of Constantinople. **1606** The Union Jack was adopted as the official flag of England. **1782** The British fleet under Admiral Rodney defeated the French fleet in the Battle of the Saints in the West Indies. **1861** The American Civil War began when Confederate troops fired on the Federal garrison at Fort Sumter. **1961** Soviet cosmonaut Yuri Gagarin became the first person to orbit the Earth. **1981** The US space shuttle Columbia was launched from Cape Canaveral.

≈ BIRTHS ≈

Henry Clay, American politician, **1777**; Lionel Hampton, US bandleader, **1913**; Raymond Barre, French politician, **1924**; Alan Ayckbourn, English playwright, **1939**; Bobby Moore, English footballer, **1941**.

≈ DEATHS ≈

William Kent, English architect and landscape gardener, **1748**; Fyodor Chaliapin, Russian operatic bass, **1938**; Franklin Delano Roosevelt, 32nd president of the USA, **1945**; Josephine Baker, US-born French singer and dancer, **1975**; Alan Paton, South African novelist and politician, **1988**.

'Few women care to be laughed at and men not at all, except for large sums of money.'
Alan Ayckbourn

13 April

'In view of the success of my economic revolution in Uganda,
I offer myself to be appointed Head of the Commonwealth.'
Idi Amin, reported on 13 April 1975

Feast day of St Guinoch, St Martin I, pope, Saints Carpus, Papylus, and Agathonice, St Hermenegild, and St Martius.

✺ EVENTS ✺

1598 Henry IV of France issued the Edict of Nantes, giving religious freedom to the Huguenots. **1668** English poet John Dryden became the first Poet Laureate. **1829** The British Parliament passed the Catholic Emancipation Act, lifting restrictions imposed on Catholics at the time of Henry VIII. **1919** The Amritsar Massacre took place in the Punjab, India; British troops fired into a crowd of 10,000 which had gathered to protest at the arrest of two Indian Congress Party leaders, 379 people were killed and 1,200 wounded. **1936** Luton Town footballer Joe Payne set a goal-scoring record when he scored ten goals in one match against Bristol Rovers. **1980** Spanish golfer Severiano Ballesteros became the youngest-ever winner of the US Masters Tournament.

✺ BIRTHS ✺

Thomas Jefferson, 3rd president of the USA, **1743**; Richard Trevithick, English engineer, **1771**; F W Woolworth, US founder of chain stores, **1852**; John Braine, English novelist, **1922**; Seamus Heaney, Irish poet, **1939**; Gary Kasparov, Russian chess player, **1963**.

✺ DEATHS ✺

Boris Godunov, Russian tsar, **1605**; Jean de La Fontaine, French writer of fables, **1695**; William Orchardson, Scottish painter, **1910**; Abdul Salam Arif, president of Iraq, **1966**; Christmas Humphreys, English judge, **1983**.

'It's a recession when your neighbour loses his job: it's a
depression when you lose yours.'
Harry S Truman, reported on 13 April 1958

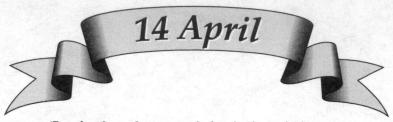

14 April

'Die when I may, I want it said of me by those who know me
best, that I have always plucked a thistle and planted a
flower where I thought a flower would grow.'
Abraham Lincoln

Feast day of St Tiburtius and Companions, St Caradoc, St Lambert of Lyons, St
Ardalion, Saints Anthony, John, and Eustace, St Benezet, St John of Vilna, St
Bernard of Tiron or Abbeville, and the Martyrs of Lithuania.

EVENTS

1471 The Battle of Barnet took place in the Wars of the Roses, in which Yorkist
forces defeated the Lancastrians, leading to the restoration of Edward IV. **1828**
US lexicographer Noah Webster published his *American Dictionary of the English
Language*. **1929** The first Monaco Grand Prix was held in Monte Carlo. **1931**
Spanish King Alfonso XIII fled the country after Republican successes in
elections. **1931** The British Ministry of Transport published the first Highway
Code. **1983** The first cordless telephone went on sale in Britain.

BIRTHS

Christiaan Huygens, Dutch astronomer and physicist, **1629**; Peter Behrens,
German architect and designer, **1868**; John Gielgud, English actor, **1904**;
François Duvalier, Haitian dictator, **1907**; Rod Steiger, US film actor **1925**;
John Roberts, English historian, **1928**.

DEATHS

Richard Neville, 'the Kingmaker', killed at the Battle of Barnet, **1471**; Thomas
Otway, English playwright, **1685**; George Frederick Handel, English composer,
1759; Lazarus Zamenhof, Polish linguist who devised Esperanto, **1917**; Ernest
Bevin, British politician and trade-union leader, **1951**; Simone de Beauvoir,
French feminist writer, **1986**.

'If you save five shillings you put a man out of work for a day.'
J M Keynes, reported on 18 Jan 1931

15 April

'Even I, I the Pope, to cross the streets of Rome to visit a parish, have to be guarded and defended by so many policemen.
My God! All this is inconceivable.'
Pope John Paul II, reported on 15 April 1979

Feast day of St Ruadhan, St Paternus of Wales, St Hunna, and Saints Anastasia and Basilissa.

EVENTS

1755 English lexicographer Dr Samuel Johnson published his *Dictionary*; he had taken eight years to compile it. **1797** Sailors at Spithead, near Portsmouth, mutinied, demanding better conditions; the British government met their demands. **1891** US inventor Thomas Edison gave a public demonstration of his kinetoscope, a moving-picture machine. **1912** Over 1,500 people died when the passenger liner *Titanic* sank after colliding with an iceberg on its first voyage. **1922** Insulin was discovered by Canadian physiologist Frederick Banting and J J R Macleod. **1942** The George Cross was awarded to the island of Malta, for bravery under heavy attack by German and Italian forces during World War II.

BIRTHS

Guru Nanak, founder of Sikhism, **1469**; Henry James, US-born British novelist, **1843**; Joe Davis, English snooker player, **1901**; Neville Marriner, British conductor, **1924**; Jeffrey Archer, English politician and novelist, **1940**; Emma Thompson, English actress, **1959**.

DEATHS

Mme de Pompadour, mistress of French King Louis XV, **1764**; Abraham Lincoln, 16th president of the USA, assassinated **1865**; Matthew Arnold, English poet and educationalist, **1888**; Father Damien, Belgian missionary, **1889**; Jean-Paul Sartre, French philosopher and writer, **1980**; Arthur Lowe, English actor, **1982**.

'Manners are especially the need of the plain. The pretty can get away with anything.'
Evelyn Waugh, reported on 15 April 1962

16 April

'All I need to make a comedy is a park, a policeman and a pretty girl.'
Charlie (Charles) Chaplin, My *Autobiography*

Feast day of St Bernadette, St Magnus, St Paternus of Avranches, St Encratis, St Fructuosus Braga, St Turibius of Astorga, St Drogo, St Joseph Benedict Labre, and St Optatus and the Martyrs of Saragossa.

≈ EVENTS ≈

1746 Charles Edward Stuart (Bonnie Prince Charlie) was defeated at the Battle of Culloden. **1883** Paul Kruger became president of South Africa. **1912** US pilot Harriet Quimby became the first woman to fly across the English Channel. **1951** Seventy-five people died when the British submarine *Affray* sank in the English Channel. **1954** The first stock-car race meeting was held in Britain, at the Old Kent Road stadium, London. **1972** The US spacecraft *Apollo 16* was launched.

≈ BIRTHS ≈

John Franklin, English Arctic explorer who discovered the Northwest Passage, **1786**; Wilbur Wright, US aviator, **1867**; Charlie Chaplin, English-born film actor and director, **1889**; Spike Milligan, English comedian and writer, **1918**; Peter Ustinov, English actor and novelist, **1921**; Kingsley Amis, English novelist, **1922**.

≈ DEATHS ≈

Aphra Behn, English playwright, **1689**; Francisco de Goya, Spanish painter, **1828**; Marie Tussaud, French wax-modeller, **1850**; St Bernadette of Lourdes, French saint, **1879**; Samuel Smiles, Scottish social reformer and author of *Self-Help*, **1904**; David Lean, English film director, **1991**.

'As children we learn to laugh / As we grow up, we learn to laugh AT / As adults we learn to laugh WITH.'
Sam Hall

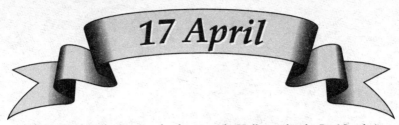

17 April

'If New York is the Big Apple, then tonight Hollywood is the Big Nipple.'
Bernardo Bertolucci, on collecting his Oscar, reported on 17 April 1988

National Day of Syria. Feast day of St Donnan, St Aybert, St Stephen Harding, St Innocent of Tortona, St Mappalicus and Others, and St Robert of Chaise-Dieu.

∾ EVENTS ∾

1521 The Diet of Worms excommunicated German church reformer Martin Luther. **1961** US troops and Cuban exiles failed in their attempt to invade Cuba at the Bay of Pigs. **1956** The first Premium Bonds were issued in Britain. **1957** Archbishop Makarios returned to Greece after over a year in exile in the Seychelles. **1969** The age at which a person is eligible to vote in Britain was lowered from 21 to 18. **1975** The Cambodian communist Khmer Rouge captured the capital, Pnomh Penh. **1980** Southern Rhodesia became Zimbabwe.

∾ BIRTHS ∾

John Ford, English playwright, **1586**; Leonard Woolley, English archaeologist, **1880**; Nikita Khrushchev, Soviet leader, **1894**; Thornton Wilder, US novelist, **1897**; Sirimavo Bandaranaike, first woman prime minister of Sri Lanka, **1916**; Lindsay Anderson, British film and stage director, **1923**.

∾ DEATHS ∾

Mme de Sévigné, French writer, **1696**; Joseph I, Holy Roman Emperor, **1711**; Benjamin Franklin, American scientist and politician, **1790**; Kawabata Yasunari, Japanese novelist, **1972**; Scott Brady, US actor, **1985**; Turgut Ozal, Turkish politician, **1993**.

'All these scripts, certainly in Hollywood, are essentially exactly the same, only now you're a doctor or a surgeon or a psychiatrist, but you turn out to be
a) stupid; b) in love with whoever the actual hero is; and
c) for some reason or other you have to get into a tight dress.'
Emma Thompson

18 April

'I, Woodrow Wilson, President of the United States of America, do hereby proclaim to all whom it may concern that a state of war exists between the United States and the Imperial German Government.'
Woodrow Wilson, reported on 18 April 1917

Feast day of St Laserian, St Galdinus, St Idesbald, St Apollonius, and Saints Eleutherius and Anthia.

EVENTS

1775 At the outbreak of the War of American Independence, US patriot Paul Revere rode from Charleston to Lexington, warning people as he went that British troops were on their way. **1881** The Natural History Museum in South Kensington, London, was opened. **1906** An earthquake and the fire that followed it destroyed most of the city of San Francisco, and killed over 450 people. **1934** The first launderette, called a 'washeteria', was opened in Fort Worth, Texas. **1949** Eire proclaimed itself the Republic of Ireland. **1968** The old London Bridge was sold to a US company, who shipped it, stone by stone, to Arizona, where it was re-erected.

BIRTHS

Lucrezia Borgia, duchess of Ferrara, **1480**; Leopold Stokowski, US conductor and composer, **1882**; Clarence Darrow, US lawyer, **1857**; Barbara Hayle, US film actress, **1922**; Hayley Mills, English actress, **1946**; Malcolm Marshall, West Indian cricketer, **1958**.

DEATHS

Albert Einstein, German-born US physicist, **1955**; George Jeffreys, the 'hanging judge', **1689**; Erasmus Darwin, English physician and writer, **1802**; Ottorino Respighi, Italian composer, **1936**; Will Hay, English comedian, **1949**; Benny Hill, English comedian, **1992**; Elisabeth Frink, English sculptor, **1993**.

'To see ourselves as others see us is a most salutary gift. Hardly less important is the capacity to see others as they see themselves. '
Aldous Huxley

19 April

'Rent is that portion of the earth which is paid to the landlord for the use of the original and indestructible powers of the soil.'
David Ricardo

Feast day of St Leo IX, pope, St Alphege, St Geroldus, and St Expeditus.

❧ EVENTS ❧

1587 In the incident known as 'singeing the King of Spain's beard', English navigator Francis Drake sank the Spanish fleet in Cadiz harbour. **1775** The first battle in the War of American Independence took place at Lexington, Massachusetts. **1951** The first 'Miss World' contest was held in London; it was won by a Swedish contestant. **1958** Footballer Bobby Charlton played his first international match for England. **1956** US film actress Grace Kelly married Prince Rainier III of Monaco. **1972** Bangladesh joined the Commonwealth.

❧ BIRTHS ❧

David Ricardo, English economist, **1772**; Richard Hughes, English novelist, **1900**; Jayne Mansfield, US film actress, **1933**; Dudley Moore, English-born comedy film actor, **1935**; Murray Perahia, US pianist and conductor, **1947**; Trevor Francis, English footballer, **1954**.

❧ DEATHS ❧

Paolo Veronese, Italian painter, **1588**; George Gordon Byron, English poet, died of malaria on his way to fight for Greek independence, **1824**; Benjamin Disraeli, British politician and novelist, **1881**; Charles Darwin, English biologist who developed the theory of evolution, **1882**; Pierre Curie, French chemist and physicist, **1906**; Konrad Adenauer, German politician, **1967**.

'There are three kinds of lies: lies, damned lies, and statistics.'
Benjamin Disraeli, Attr.

20 April

'If they [artists] do see the fields blue they are deranged,
and should go to an asylum. If they only pretend to see them
blue, they are criminals and should go to prison.'
Adolf Hitler

Feast day of St Caedwalla, St Agnes of Montepulciano, St Marcellinus of
Embrun, St Marcian of Auxerre, St Hildegund, and St Peter of Verona.

❧ EVENTS ❧

1526 A Mogul army led by Babur defeated an Afghan army at the Battle of
Panipat, taking the cities of Delhi and Agra. **1534** French explorer Jacques
Cartier arrived on the coast of Labrador, North America. **1657** English Admiral
Robert Blake defeated the Spanish fleet in Santa Cruz Bay, off the Canary Islands.
1770 English navigator James Cook reached New South Wales, Australia. **1949**
The Badminton Horse Trials were held for the first time, at Badminton,
Gloucestershire. **1969** Pierre Trudeau became prime minister of Canada.

❧ BIRTHS ❧

Adolf Hitler, German fascist dictator, **1889**; Joan Miró, Spanish painter, **1893**;
Harold Lloyd, US silent-film comedian, **1893**; Donald Wolfit, English actor,
1902; Ray Brooks, English actor, **1939**; Ryan O'Neal, US film actor, **1941**.

❧ DEATHS ❧

Jean Louis Petit, French surgeon, **1750**; Canaletto, Italian landscape painter,
1768; Pontiac, American Indian leader, **1769**; Bram Stoker, Irish author of
Dracula, **1912**; Christian X, king of Denmark, 1947.

'If we've put panes of glass in the windows and China wants
to smash them after 1997, that will need explaining in Hong
Kong and internationally.'
Chris Patten

21 April

'The men of violence are not going to bomb their way to the conference table. Nor must they be allowed to bomb Northern Ireland into the abyss.'
Harold Wilson, reported on 21 April 1974

Feast day of St Anselm, St Beuno, St Maelrubba, St Ethilwald, St Anastasius of Antioch, St Conrad of Prazham, and St Simeon Barsabas and Others.

∽ EVENTS ∽

753 BC Traditionally, the date on which the city of Rome was founded. **1509** Henry VIII became king of England. **1960** The new city of Brasilia was declared the capital of Brazil, replacing Rio de Janeiro. **1964** BBC 2 began broadcasting. **1967** King Constantine II of Greece was removed in an army coup, and martial law was imposed. **1983** One-pound coins replaced notes in England and Wales. **1989** Over 100,000 Chinese students gathered in Tiananmen Square, ignoring government warnings of severe punishment.

∽ BIRTHS ∽

Friedrich Froebel, German educationalist, **1782**; Henri de Montherlant, French novelist and playwright, **1896**; Richard Beeching, British Rail chairman, **1913**; Anthony Quinn, US film actor, **1915**; John Mortimer, English author and playwright, **1923**; Queen Elizabeth II, **1926**.

∽ DEATHS ∽

Henry VII, king of England, **1509**; Jean-Baptiste Racine, French playwright, **1699**; Mark Twain, US novelist, **1910**; Manfred von Richtofen, 'the Red Baron', German fighter pilot, **1918**; John Maynard Keynes, English economist, **1946**; Richard Stafford Cripps, English lawyer and politician, **1952**.

'All you need in this life is ignorance and confidence; then success is sure.'
Mark Twain

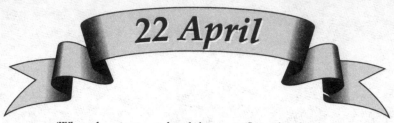

22 April

'When the tape is good and the music flows the elation is
like making love.'
Art Garfunkel, reported on 22 April 1979

Feast day of St Theodore of Sykeon, St Opportuna, St Agipatus I, pope, St
Leonides of Alexandria, and Saints Epipodius and Alexander.

≈ EVENTS ≈

1500 Portuguese explorer Pedro Cabral claimed Brazil for Portugal. **1662** King
Charles II granted a charter to the Royal Society of London, which became an
important centre of scientific activity in England. **1834** The South Atlantic
island of St Helena was declared a British Crown Colony. **1838** The first
steamship to cross the Atlantic, the British ship *Sirius*, arrived at New York; it
made the crossing in 18 days. **1969** Sailor Robin Knox Johnston returned to
Falmouth after a 312-day solo voyage around the world. **1972** The first people
to row across the Pacific Ocean, Sylvia Cook and John Fairfax, arrived in
Australia; they had been at sea for 362 days.

≈ BIRTHS ≈

Henry Fielding, English novelist, **1707**; Immanuel Kant, German philosopher,
1724; Mme de Staël, French writer, **1766**; Robert Oppenheimer, US physicist
who invented the atom bomb, **1904**; Kathleen Ferrier, English contralto, **1912**;
Yehudi Menuhin, US-born British violinist, **1916**; George Cole, English actor,
1925; Jack Nicholson, US film actor, **1937**.

≈ DEATHS ≈

John Tradescant, English naturalist, **1662**; James Hargreaves, English inventor
of the spinning jenny, **1778**; John Crome, English landscape painter, **1821**;
Thomas Rowlandson, English caricaturist, **1827**; Henry Campbell-Bannerman,
British politician, **1908**.

'You only lie to two people: your girlfriend and the police.
Everyone else you tell the truth to.'
Jack Nicholson

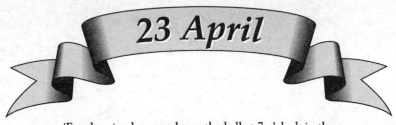

23 April

'Freedom is when one hears the bell at 7 o'clock in the morning and knows it is the milkman and not the Gestapo.'
Georges Bidault, reported on 23 April 1950

National Day of England. Feast day of St George, St Gerard of Toul, St Ibar, St Adalbert of Prague, and Saints Felix, Fortunatus, and Achilleus.

EVENTS

1349 English King Edward III founded the Order of the Garter. **1661** Charles II was crowned king of Great Britain and Ireland. **1662** Connecticut was declared a British colony. **1879** The Shakespeare Memorial Theatre was opened at Stratford-upon-Avon. **1924** The British Empire Exhibition opened at Wembley. **1932** The New Shakespeare Memorial Theatre opened at Stratford-upon-Avon. **1968** Britain's first decimal coins, the 5p and 10p, were issued in preparation for decimalisation

BIRTHS

William Shakespeare, English playwright and poet, **1564**; J M W Turner, English painter, **1775**; Max Planck, German physicist, **1858**; Ngaio Marsh, New Zealand novelist, **1899**; James Donleavy, Irish novelist, **1926**; Roy Orbison, US singer, **1936**.

DEATHS

William Shakespeare, **1616**; Miguel de Cervantes Saavedra, Spanish author of *Don Quixote*, **1616**; William Wordsworth, English poet, **1850**; Rupert Brooke, English poet, **1915**; Otto Preminger, US film director, **1986**; Satyajit Ray, Indian film director, **1992**.

'To be, or not to be: that is the question:
Whether 'tis nobler in the mind to suffer
The slings and arrows of outrageous fortune,
Or to take arms against a sea of troubles,
And by opposing end them?'
William Shakespeare, *Hamlet*

24 April

'The history of every country begins in the heart of a man or woman.'
Willa Cather, O *Pioneers!*

Feast day of St Mellitus, St Egbert, St Wilfrid, St Ives, St Fidelis, St Mary Euphrasia Pelletier, and St William Firmatus.

≈ EVENTS ≈

1558 Mary, Queen of Scots married the French Dauphin. **1800** The US Library of Congress was founded in Washington DC. **1895** US sailor Joshua Slocum set off from Boston, USA, to sail single-handed around the world; the voyage took just over three years. **1916** The Easter Rising – a Republican protest against British rule – took place in Dublin. **1949** Sweet-rationing in Britain came to an end. **1970** The Gambia was declared a republic within the Commonwealth.

≈ BIRTHS ≈

Anthony Trollope, English novelist, **1815**; Henri-Philippe Pétain, French politician and soldier, **1856**; William Joyce, 'Lord Haw-Haw', British traitor, **1906**; Bridget Riley, English painter, **1931**; Shirley MacLaine, US actress, **1934**; John Williams, Australian guitarist, **1941**; Barbra Streisand, US film actress and singer, **1942**.

≈ DEATHS ≈

Daniel Defoe, English author, **1731**; Willa Cather, US novelist, **1947**; Bud Abbott, US comedian, **1974**; the Duchess of Windsor, **1986**; Bill Edrich, English cricketer, **1986**.

'I think English culture is basically homosexual in the sense that the men only really care about other men.'
Germaine Greer, reported on 24 April 1988

25 April

'They [the homeless] are not on the streets because they have
to be on the streets. It is a strange way of life that some of
them choose to live.'
John Major

Anzac Day in Australia. Feast day of St Mark the Evangelist, St Heribald, and
St Anianus of Alexandria.

EVENTS

1792 The guillotine was first used in Paris. **1859** Work began on the Suez
Canal, supervised by the French engineer Ferdinand de Lesseps, who designed it.
1915 In World War I, Australian and New Zealand troops landed at Gallipoli.
1925 Paul von Hindenburg was elected President of Germany. **1959** The St
Lawrence Seaway was officially opened by Queen Elizabeth II and President
Eisenhower, linking the Atlantic with ports on the Great Lakes. **1975** The first
free elections for 50 years were held in Portugal, resulting in a precarious
Socialist government.

BIRTHS

Oliver Cromwell, Puritan leader in the English Civil War, **1599**; Mark Isambard
Brunel, French-born British engineer, **1769**; Walter de la Mare, English poet
and novelist, **1873**; Guglielmo Marconi, Italian inventor and pioneer in the
development of radio, **1874**; Ella Fitzgerald, US jazz singer, **1918**; Al Pacino, US
film actor, **1940**; Johann Cruyff, Dutch footballer, **1947**.

DEATHS

Torquato Tasso, Italian poet, **1595**; Anders Celsius, Swedish astronomer who
invented the centigrade thermometer, **1744**; William Cowper, English poet, **1800**;
Carol Reed, English film director, **1976**; Celia Johnson, English actress, **1982**.

'Strange to say what delight we married people have to see
these poor fools decoyed into our condition.'
Samuel Pepys

26 April

'There is no English value which we should defend more
vigorously than this tradition of tolerance.'
William Whitelaw, reported on 26 April 1981

Feast day of St Cletus, St Riquier, St Stephen of Perm, St Peter of Braga, St
Franca of Piacenza, and St Paschasius Radbertus.

EVENTS

1923 The Duke of York and Elizabeth Bowes-Lyon, later King George VI and
Queen Elizabeth, were married in Westminster Abbey. **1937** The Spanish town
of Guernica was almost destroyed by German bombers acting in support of the
Nationalists in the Spanish Civil War. **1957** English astronomer Patrick Moore
presented the first broadcast of *The Sky at Night*. **1964** Tanganyika and Zanzibar
merged to become the Republic of Tanzania. **1968** The largest underground
nuclear device ever to be tested in the USA exploded in Nevada. **1986**
Radioactive material was leaked from a damaged nuclear reactor at Chernobyl,
Ukraine; the effects could be measured thousands of miles away.

BIRTHS

Marcus Aurelius, Roman emperor, AD **121**; John James Audubon, US naturalist
and painter, **1785**; Eugène Delacroix, French painter, **1798**; Michel Fokine,
Russian ballet dancer and choreographer, **1880**; Ludwig Wittgenstein, Austrian
philosopher, **1889**; Rudolf Hess, German Nazi leader, **1894**.

DEATHS

Karl Bosch, German metallurgist and chemist, **1940**; Gypsy Rose Lee, US
dancer and striptease artist, **1970**; Cicely Courtneidge, British actress, **1980**;
Count Basie, US bandleader, **1984**; Broderick Crawford, US film actor, **1986**.

'There's no such thing as a bad Picasso,
but some are less good than others.'
Pablo Picasso

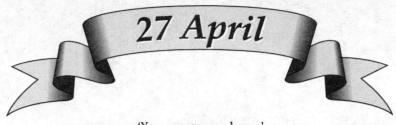

27 April

'Your country needs you.'
British conscription poster

Feast day of St Zita, St Machalus, St Floribert of Liège, St Asicus, St Anthimus of Nicomedia, and Saints Castor and Stephen.

∾ EVENTS ∾

1296 An English army, led by Edward I, defeated the Scots at the Battle of Dunbar. **1749** The first official performance of Handel's *Music for the Royal Fireworks* finished early due to the outbreak of fire. **1937** King George VI performed the official opening of the National Maritime Museum at Greenwich. **1939** Conscription for men aged 20–21 was announced in Britain. **1947** Norwegian anthropologist Thor Heyerdahl set off from Callao, Peru, heading for Polynesia to prove his theory that the original Polynesian islanders could have come from Peru. **1960** French Togoland became independent as the Republic of Togo. **1961** Sierra Leone became an independent republic within the Commonwealth.

∾ BIRTHS ∾

Edward Gibbon, English historian who wrote *The Decline and Fall of the Roman Empire*, **1737**; Mary Wollstonecraft Godwin, English feminist author, **1759**; Samuel Morse, US inventor of Morse Code, **1791**; Ulysses Simpson Grant, US general and 18th president, **1822**; Cecil Day Lewis, English poet, **1904**; Anouk Aimée, French film actress, **1932**; Sandy Dennis, US film actress, **1937**.

∾ DEATHS ∾

Ferdinand Magellan, Portuguese navigator, murdered by islanders in the Philippines, **1521**; Ralph Waldo Emerson, US poet and essayist, **1882**; Alexander Skryabin, Russian composer, **1915**; Harold Hart Crane, US poet, **1932**; Kwame Nkrumah, president of Ghana, **1972**.

'The Lord prefers common-looking people.
That is why he makes so many of them.'
Abraham Lincoln

28 April

'The moment you have protected an individual you have protected society.'
Kenneth Kaunda, reported on 6 May 1962

Feast day of St Louis de Montfort, St Vitalis, St Peter Mary Chanel, St Cyril of Turov, St Valeria, St Pollio, Saints Theodora and Didymus, St Pamphilus of Sulmona, and St Cronan Roscrea.

⁓ EVENTS ⁓

1603 Queen Elizabeth I's funeral took place at Westminster Abbey. **1770** English navigator Captain James Cook and his crew, including the botanist Joseph Banks, landed in Australia, at the place which was later named Botany Bay. **1789** The crew of the ship *Bounty*, led by Fletcher Christian, mutinied against their captain, William Bligh. **1919** The League of Nations was founded. **1923** The first FA Cup Final was held at Wembley Stadium. **1965** US marines intervened in an attempted communist coup in the Dominican Republic. **1969** French president General de Gaulle resigned.

⁓ BIRTHS ⁓

King Edward IV of England, **1442**; James Monroe, 5th president of the USA, **1758**; Charles Sturt, British explorer of Australia, **1795**; Lionel Barrymore, US actor, **1878**; Kenneth Kaunda, president of Zambia, **1924**; Ann-Margret, Swedish actress, **1941**; Mike Brearley, English cricketer, **1942**.

⁓ DEATHS ⁓

Gavrilo Princip, Bosnian revolutionary assassin who caused World War I by killing Archduke Franz Ferdinand and his wife, **1918**; King Fuad I of Egypt, **1936**; Benito Mussolini, **1945**; Francis Bacon, Irish-born painter, **1992**; Olivier Messiaen, French composer, **1992**.

'The triumph of hope over experience.'
Samuel Johnson, on second marriages

29 April

'We should strive not to be a powerful country, but to be a caring country.'
Tomiichi Murayama, Japan's first socialist prime
minister and longtime pacifist, 1 Aug 1994

National Day of Japan. Feast day of St Catherine of Siena, St Wilfrid the Younger, St Hugh of Cluny, St Endellion, St Joseph Cottolengo, St Robert of Molesme, and St Peter the Martyr.

EVENTS

1429 The Siege of Orléans was lifted by a French army under the leadership of Joan of Arc. **1884** Oxford University agreed to admit female students to examinations. **1913** Swedish-born US inventor Gideon Sundback patented the zip fastener in its modern form – earlier versions had not been successful. **1916** Republican rebels destroyed the Post Office in Dublin. **1945** The German army in Italy surrendered to the Allies under the British General Alexander.

BIRTHS

Thomas Beecham, English conductor, **1879**; 'Duke' Ellington, US composer and bandleader, **1899**; Emperor Hirohito of Japan, **1901**; Fred Zinneman, US film director, **1907**; Peter de la Bilière, British commander in the Gulf War, **1934**; Zubin Mehta, Indian conductor, **1936**; Saddam Hussein, president of Iraq, **1937**.

DEATHS

George Farquhar, Irish playwright, **1707**; Constantinos Cavafy, Greek poet, **1933**; Wallace Carothers, US chemist who patented nylon, **1937**; Alfred Hitchcock, English film director, **1980**; Andrew Cruikshank, English actor, **1988**.

'Here you have a different kind of poverty. A poverty of
spirit, of loneliness and being unwanted. And that is the
worst disease in the world: not tuberculosis or leprosy.'
Mother Teresa, reported on 29 April 1973

30 April

'You'd think, with all these tourists about, they would build an elevator.'
American lady climbing up to the Parthenon
reported on 30 April 1972

National Day of the Netherlands. Feast day of St Erkenwald, St Pius V, pope, St Forannan, St Wolfhard, St Maximus of Ephesus, St Eutropius of Saintes, and Saints Marianus, James, and Others.

EVENTS

1789 George Washington became the first president of the USA. **1803** France sold Louisiana to the USA. **1902** Debussy's opera *Pelléas et Mélisande* had its first performance, in Paris. **1975** The Vietnam War ended, with the South surrendering unconditionally to the North. **1979** The Jubilee Line on the London Underground was officially opened. **1980** Queen Juliana of the Netherlands abdicated and was succeeded by her daughter, Beatrix.

BIRTHS

David Thompson, English explorer, **1770**; Karl Gauss, German mathematician and astronomer, **1777**; Franz Lehár, Hungarian composer, **1870**; Jaroslav Hasek, Czech novelist, **1883**; Queen Juliana of the Netherlands, **1909**; Cloris Leachman, US film actress, **1926**; King Carl XVI Gustav of Sweden, **1946**.

DEATHS

Robert Fitzroy, English admiral and meteorologist, **1865**; Edouard Manet, French painter, **1883**; Otto Jespersen, Danish philologist, **1943**; Adolf Hitler, German fascist dictator, **1945**; Eva Braun, German mistress and later wife of Adolf Hitler, **1945**; Muddy Waters, US blues singer, **1983**; George Balanchine, Russian choreographer, **1983**.

'All my life, I was having trouble with women ... I've done a
lot of writing about women. Then, after I quit having trouble
with them, I could feel in my heart that somebody would always
have trouble with them, so I kept writing those blues.'
Muddy Waters

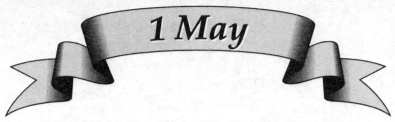

1 May

'The ideal voice for radio should have no substance, no sex,
no owner, and a message of importance for every housewife.'
Ed Murrow, reported on 1 May 1949

May Day. Feast day of St Asaph, St Corentin, St Joseph, St Brioc, St Amator, St Marcoul, Saints Philip and James, St Peregrine Laziosi, St Sigismund of Burgundy, and St Theodard of Narbonne.

EVENTS

1517 In 'Evil May Day' riots in London, apprentices attacked foreign residents. Wolsey suppressed the rioters, of whom 60 were hanged. **1707** The Union of England and Scotland was proclaimed. **1786** The first performance of Mozart's opera *The Marriage of Figaro* was given in Vienna. **1851** Queen Victoria opened the Great Exhibition in Hyde Park, London. **1925** Cyprus became a Crown Colony. **1926** British miners began a strike that continued until 19 November. **1931** The Empire State Building, New York, was completed; it had cost $41 million to build. **1933** A telephone link between Britain and India was established. **1960** A US U-2 aircraft piloted by Gary Powers, was shot down as it flew over the USSR. **1961** Betting shops became legal in Britain.

BIRTHS

Arthur Wellesley, Duke of Wellington, **1769**; Glenn Ford, US film actor, **1916**; Joseph Heller, US novelist, **1923**; Sonny Ramadhin, West Indies cricketer, **1929**; Una Stubbs, English actress, **1937**; Joanna Lumley, English actress, **1946**.

DEATHS

John Dryden, English poet, **1700**; David Livingstone, Scottish missionary, **1873**; Antonín Dvořák, Czech composer, **1904**; Joseph Goebbels, German Nazi propaganda minister, **1945**; William Fox, US film producer, **1952**; Harold Nicolson, English diplomat and author, **1968**.

'In a democracy everybody has the right to be represented,
including the jerks.'
Chris Patten

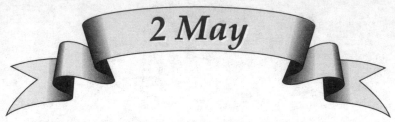

2 May

'Whatever exists in the universe, whether in essence, in act, or in the imagination, the painter has first in his mind and then in his hands.'
Leonardo da Vinci, *Notebooks*

Feast day of St Gennys, St Athanasius, St Mefalda, St Wiborada, St Waldebert, Saints Exuperius and Zoe, and St Ultan of Fosses.

❧ EVENTS ❧

1251 Simon de Montfort suppressed the Gascon rebellion. **1482** Venice, in alliance with the Papacy, declared war on Ferrara, which was supported by Florence, Milan and Naples. **1536** Queen Anne Boleyn was sent to the Tower of London. **1611** The Authorised Version of the Bible (King James Version) was first published. **1670** The Hudson Bay Company was incorporated. **1926** US troops landed to preserve order in Nicaraguan revolt. **1936** Ethiopian Emperor Haile Selassie and his family fled from Addis Ababa, three days before it fell to Italian forces. **1945** Germany surrendered to Allied forces. **1969** The passenger liner *Queen Elizabeth II* set off from Southampton on its first voyage. **1989** Martial law was imposed in China as the government took a firmer stand against pro-democracy demonstrators in Tiananmen Square.

❧ BIRTHS ❧

Catherine II 'the Great' of Russia, **1729**; Jerome K Jerome, English novelist and playwright, **1859**; Theodor Herzl, Hungarian founder of Zionism, **1860**; Benjamin Spock, US childcare specialist, **1903**; Bing Crosby, US singer, **1904**; Peggy Mount, English actress, **1916**; Clive Jenkins, British trade-union leader, **1926**; David Suchet, British actor, **1946**.

❧ DEATHS ❧

Leonardo da Vinci, Florentine artist and scientist, **1519**; Joseph McCarthy, US politician who investigated suspected communists, **1957**; Nancy Astor, first British woman MP, **1964**; J Edgar Hoover, US director of the FBI, **1972**.

'It is impossible to enjoy idling thoroughly unless
one has plenty of work to do.'
Jerome K Jerome

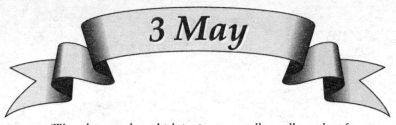

3 May

'We only want that which is given naturally to all peoples of
the world to be masters of our own fate, only of our fate, not
of others, and in co-operation and friendship with others.'
Golda Meir

Feast day of St Glywys, St Juvenal of Narni, Saints Alexander, Eventius, and
Theodulus, and Saints Timothy and Maura.

≋ EVENTS ≋

1381 The weavers of Ghent, led by Philip van Artevelde, took Bruges; other
Flemish towns revolted. **1493** Pope Alexander VI published the first bull *Inter
cetera* dividing the New World between Spain and Portugal. **1497** A rising broke
out in Cornwall, provoked by taxation; James Tutchet, Lord Audley, led an army
of 15,000 from Taunton through the southern counties to attack London. **1747**
The Battle of Cape Finisterre took place, at which the British defeated the
French. **1808** A duel was fought from two hot-air balloons over Paris, the first of
its kind. **1841** New Zealand was declared a British colony. **1898** Bread riots in
Milan were put down with heavy loss of life. **1906** The Sinai Peninsula became
Egyptian territory after Turkey renounced its claims. **1951** British King George
VI opened the Festival of Britain. **1958** US President Eisenhower proposed
demilitarisation of Antarctica, subsequently accepted by the countries concerned.

≋ BIRTHS ≋

Niccoló Machiavelli, Italian politician, **1469**; John Scott Haldane, Scottish
physiologist, **1860**; Golda Meir, Russian-born Israeli prime minister, **1898**;
Sugar Ray Robinson, US boxer, **1920**; Norman Thelwell, English cartoonist,
1923; James Brown, US singer, **1933**; Henry Cooper, English boxer, **1934**.

≋ DEATHS ≋

Eglon van der Neer, Dutch painter, **1703**; Thomas Hood, English poet, **1845**;
Henry Cornelius, South African-born film director, **1958**; Karl Freund, Czech-
born US film cameraman and photographer, **1969**.

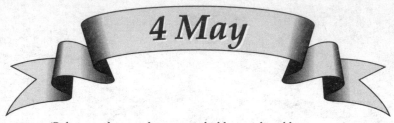
4 May

'Politics is the art of acquiring, holding and wielding power.'
Indira Gandhi, reported on 4 May 1975

Feast day of St Pelagia of Tarsus, St Florian of Lorch, St Robert Lawrence, St Augustine Webster, St Gothard, St John Houghton, St Venerius of Milan, and St Cyriacus.

EVENTS

1471 The Battle of Tewkesbury, the last battle in the Wars of the Roses, took place; the Yorkists defeated the Lancastrians. **1780** The first Derby was run at Epsom; the winner was Diomed. **1896** The first issue of the *Daily Mail* was published in London. **1904** Work began on the Panama Canal. **1926** The General Strike began in Britain, with almost half of the country's 6,000,000 trade-union members participating; it continued until 12 May. **1973** The world's tallest building, Sears Tower, Chicago, was completed. **1979** Margaret Thatcher became prime minister of Britain.

BIRTHS

Thomas Huxley, English naturalist, **1825**; John Speke, English explorer who discovered the source of the Nile, **1827**; Alice Liddell, the girl for whom Lewis Carroll wrote *Alice in Wonderland*, **1852**; Sylvia Pankhurst, English suffragette, **1882**; Eric Sykes, English comedian, **1923**; Audrey Hepburn, Dutch-born US film actress, **1929**.

DEATHS

William Froude, English engineer and mathematician, **1879**; Georges Enesco, Romanian composer, **1955**; Osbert Sacheverell Sitwell, English author, **1969**; Josip Broz Tito, Yugoslavian soldier and president, **1980**; Diana Dors, English film actress, **1984**.

'We will never have nuclear weapons, I promise you.
Who can we use them against?'
Kim Il Sung, president of North Korea, denying
reports that his country has the bomb, 2 May 1994

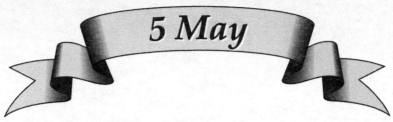

5 May

'Religion ... is the opium of the people.'
Karl Marx

———

Feast day of St Hydroc, St Hilary of Arles, St Hilary of Galeata, St Angelo, St Jutta, St Avertinus, and St Mauruntius.

≈ EVENTS ≈

1525 The Peasants' Revolt in south Germany was suppressed and the Anabaptist preacher Thomas Münzer was hanged a few days later. **1751** Portuguese foreign secretary Sebastião Pombal curbed the power of the Inquisition in Portugal by decreeing that no auto da fé should take place without government approval. **1762** The Treaty of St Petersburg was signed between Russia and Prussia; Russia restored all territory taken and formed an alliance with Prussia. **1816** Carl August of Saxe-Weimar granted the first German constitution. **1863** In the American Civil War, Confederate troops defeated Federal forces at the Battle of Chancellorsville, but 'Stonewall' Jackson died of his wounds five days later. **1864** The indecisive Battle of the Wilderness was fought in Virginia, between Federal troops under Ulysses S Grant and Confederate troops under Robert E Lee. **1865** A revolt in San Domingo forced Spain to renounce sovereignty.

≈ BIRTHS ≈

Godfrey of Bouillon, Norman crusader, first king of Jerusalem, **1061**; Gerardus Mercator (Gerhard Kremer), German cartographer, **1512**; Leopold III, Holy Roman Emperor, **1747**; George Borrow, English author, **1803**; Sören Kierkegaard, Danish philosopher, **1813**; Karl Marx, German philosopher and author, **1818**; Archibald, Lord Wavell, British soldier, **1883**.

≈ DEATHS ≈

Charles, Duke of Bourbon, **1527**; Edward Young, English poet, **1765**; Napoleon Bonaparte, French emperor, **1821**; Francis Bret Harte, US author, **1902**.

———

'The philosophers have only interpreted the world in various ways; the point is to change it.'
Karl Marx

6 May

'Analogies prove nothing, that is quite true, but they can make
one feel more at home.'
Sigmund Freud

Feast day of St Edbert, Saints Marian and James, St Evodius of Antioch, St
Petronax, and St John Before the Latin Gate.

≈ EVENTS ≈

1527 The Sack of Rome, when imperialist troops under Charles, Duke of
Bourbon (who was killed), mutinied, pillaging the city and killing some 4,000 of
the inhabitants. Valuable art treasures were looted. Law was not restored until
Feb 1528. **1576** The Fifth War of Religion in France ended; the Huguenots were
granted freedom of worship in all places except Paris. **1626** Dutch settler Peter
Minuit bought the island of Manhattan from native Americans for goods worth
about $25. **1840** The Penny Black, the first postage stamp, was issued in Britain.
1882 Fenians murdered Irish chief secretary, Lord Frederick Cavendish, and T
H Burke, Irish under-secretary, in Phoenix Park, Dublin. **1910** George V became
king of the United Kingdom on the death of Edward VII. **1937** The German
zeppelin *Hindenburg* caught fire in New Jersey, USA, killing 36 passengers.

≈ BIRTHS ≈

Pope Marcellus II, **1501**; Pope Innocent X, **1574**, Thomas William Coke, Earl of
Leicester, **1754**; André Massena, French soldier, **1756**; Maximilien François
Robespierre, French revolutionary leader, **1758**; François Guillaume Andrieux
1759; Sigmund Freud, Austrian psychoanalyst, **1856**; Robert Edwin Peary, US
Arctic explorer, **1856**; Rabindranath Tagore, Indian poet and philosopher, **1861**.

≈ DEATHS ≈

Juan Luis Vives, Spanish philosopher, **1540**; Francesco Guicciardini, Italian
historian, **1540**; Robert Cotton, English antiquary, **1631**; Cornelius Jansen,
Dutch theologian, **1638**; Alexander von Humboldt, German explorer, **1859**;
Henry David Thoreau, US poet, **1862**; Maurice Maeterlinck, Belgian
playwright, **1949**; Marlene Dietrich, German-born singer and actress, **1992**.

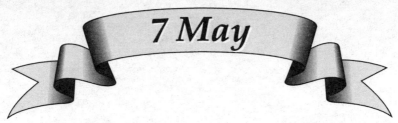
7 May

'I was the seventh of nine children. When you come from that far down you have to struggle to survive.'
Robert Kennedy

Feast day of St John of Beverley, St Letard, St Domitian of Maestricht, and Saints Serenicus and Serenus.

✑ EVENTS ✑

1793 The second partition of Poland was effected, with Russia taking Lithuania and W Ukraine, and Prussia taking Danzig, Thorn, Posen, Gnesen, and Kalisch. **1821** The Africa Company was dissolved because of heavy expenses incurred, and Sierra Leone, Gambia, and Gold Coast were taken over by the British government to form British West Africa. **1832** Greece became an independent kingdom. **1848** Polish rebels surrendered after Prussian troops put down an insurrection in Warsaw. **1915** German forces sank the liner *Lusitania* off the Irish coast, with the loss of 1,198 lives; the USA was brought to the verge of war with Germany. **1928** Women's suffrage in Britain was reduced from the age of 30 to 21. **1954** Dien Bien Phu fell to Communist Vietnamese. **1960** Leonid Brezhnev replaced Marshal Voroshilov as President of the USSR.

✑ BIRTHS ✑

David Hume, Scottish philosopher and historian, **1711**; Robert Browning, English poet, **1812**; Johannes Brahms, German composer, **1833**; Peter Iljitch Tchaikovsky, Russian composer, **1840**; Archibald Philip Primrose, Lord Rosebery, British politician, **1847**; Gary Cooper, US film actor, **1901**.

✑ DEATHS ✑

Jacques de Thou, French historian and politician, **1617**; Mary of Modena, consort of James II, **1718**; Henry, Lord Brougham, British politician, **1868**; Paul Doumer, French president, assassinated, **1932**; George Lansbury, British politician, **1940**; James George Frazer, Scottish anthropologist, **1941**.

'I let down my friends, I let down my country,
I let down our system of government.'
Richard Nixon

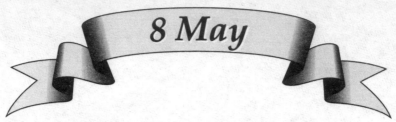

8 May

'Girls and boys grow up more normally together than apart.'
Daphne Rae, wife of the headmaster of Westminster,
reported on 8 May 1988

Feast day of St Indract, St Odger, St Victor, St Wiro, St Peter of Tarentaise, St Benedict II, pope, St Boniface IV, pope, St Gibrian, St Plechelm, St Desideratus of Bourges, and St Acacius.

EVENTS

1559 Queen Elizabeth I of England signed the Act of Uniformity. **1886** The Presidential Succession law was passed in the USA, providing for succession to presidency in the event of the deaths of both the President and the Vice-President. **1892** A ban was imposed on natives of the Congo, prohibiting them from collecting rubber and ivory other than for the state. **1902** On the Caribbean island of Martinique, the volcano Mount Pelée erupted, killing 30,000 people. **1950** Douglas MacArthur appointed commander of UN forces in Korea. **1958** J F Dulles stated in Berlin House of Representatives that an attack on Berlin would be regarded as an attack on the Allies.

BIRTHS

Peter Martyr (Pieto Martire Vermigli), Italian religious reformer, **1500**; Phineas Fletcher, English poet, **1582**; Francis Quarles, English poet, **1592**; Claude de Villars, French soldier, **1653**; Alain René Lesage, French novelist and playwright, **1668**; Henry Baker, English naturalist, **1698**; François Mignet, French historian, **1796**; Ruggiero Leoncavallo, Italian composer, **1858**; Harry S Truman, 33rd president of the USA, **1884**; David Attenborough, English naturalist and broadcaster, **1926**.

DEATHS

Palla Strozzi, founder of the first public library in Florence, **1462**; Antoine Laurent Lavoisier, French chemist, guillotined, **1794**; Vittorio Alfieri, Italian poet, **1803**; John Stuart Mill, English philosopher, **1873**; Gustave Flaubert, French novelist, **1880**; Oswald Spengler, German philosopher, **1936**; Henry Gordon Selfridge, US-born British store-owner, **1947**; Emmanuel Shinwell, British politician, **1986**.

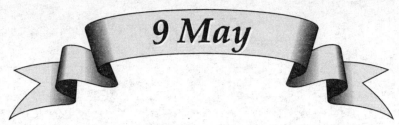

9 May

'I am a lone monk walking the world with a leaky umbrella.'
Mao Zedong, reported on 9 May 1971

Feast day of St Beatus of Lungern, St Gerontius of Cervia, St Beatus of Vendôme, and St Pachomius.

EVENTS

1386 The Treaty of Windsor, between kings Richard and John, made a perpetual alliance between England and Portugal. **1695** The Scottish Parliament met and enquired into the massacre of Glencoe. **1828** The British Test and Corporation Acts were repealed so that Catholic and Protestant Nonconformists could hold public office in Britain. **1939** British prime minister Winston Churchill urged military alliance with USSR. **1940** RAF began night bombing of Germany. **1940** Romania placed itself under German protection. **1945** Russian troops took Prague. **1946** Victor Emmanuel III of Italy abdicated and Umberto II proclaimed himself king.

BIRTHS

Giovanni Paisiello, Italian composer, **1741**; Jean Sismondi, Swiss historian and economist, **1773**; John Brown, US abolitionist, **1800**; J M Barrie **1860**; Howard Carter, British Egyptologist, **1873**; Joan Sims, English actress, **1930**; Alan Bennett, English actor and playwright, **1934**; Glenda Jackson, English actress, **1936**.

DEATHS

James Lancaster, English navigator, **1618**; William Bradford, English-born American colonist, **1657**; Dietrich Buxtehude, Danish organist and composer, **1707**; Louis-Joseph Gay-Lussac, French physicist and chemist, **1850**; Helena Blavatsky, Russian founder of the Theosophical Society, **1891**; Ethel Smyth, English composer and suffragette, **1944**.

'The Irish people do not gladly suffer common sense.'
Oliver St John Gogarty, reported on 9 May 1935

10 May

'I just put my feet in the air and move them around.'
Fred Astaire

Feast day of St Catald, St Conleth, Saints Gordian and Epimachus, St Antoninus, St Alphius, St Calepodius, St Solange, and St John of Avila.

EVENTS

994 The Danes devastated Anglesey. **1804** Pitt returned to office. **1857** A revolt of Sepoys at Meerut began the Indian Mutiny against British rule. **1893** Natal was granted self-government. **1910** The British House of Commons resolved that the maximum lifetime of Parliament be reduced from seven to five years. **1916** Ernest Shackleton and companions reached South Georgia after sailing 1,300 km/800 mi in 16 days in an open boat to seek help for the remaining members of their party, marooned on Elephant Island, Antarctica. **1941** The House of Commons was destroyed in London's heaviest air raid.

BIRTHS

Sir John Sinclair, Scottish politician and agriculturalist, **1754**; Augustin Thierry, French historian, **1795**; James Bryce, British politician and diplomat, **1838**; Benito Pérez Galdós, Spanish novelist and playwright, **1845**; Karl Barth, Swiss theologian and author, **1886**; Fred Astaire, US dancer, **1899**; David O Selznick, US film producer, **1902**.

DEATHS

Leonhard Fuchs, German physician and botanist, **1566**; Jean de la Bruyère, French writer, **1696**; Paul Revere, American hero, **1818**; Katsushuka Hokusai, Japanese artist, **1849**; Henry Morton Stanley, US journalist and explorer, **1904**; Joan Crawford, US film actress, **1977**.

'Never, never, and never again shall it be that this beautiful land will again experience the oppression of one by another and suffer the indignity of being the skunk of the world.'
Nelson Mandela, inaugural speech 10 May 1994

11 May

'You cannot govern nations without a mailed fist and an iron will.'
Benito Mussolini, reported on 11 May 1924

Feast day of St Comgall, St Credan, St Maieul, St Tudy, St Ansfrid, St Walter of l'Esterp, St Richard Reynolds, St Francis di Girolamo, St Ignatius of Laconi, St Asaph, St Gengulf, and Mamertus.

EVENTS

973 Edgar crowned at Bath as King of all England; he then went to Chester, where eight Scottish and Welsh kings rowed him on the Dee. **1534** English King Henry VIII made peace with his nephew, James V of Scotland. **1709** The first mass emigration of Germans from the Palatinate to North America began. **1812** British prime minister Spencer Perceval was assassinated in House of Commons. **1824** British forces took Rangoon, Burma. **1949** Siam changed its name to Thailand. **1949** Israel was admitted to United Nations.

BIRTHS

Hector Berlioz, French composer, **1803**; Chang and Eng, Chinese Siamese twins, **1811**; Irving Berlin, US composer, **1888**; Paul Nash, English painter, **1889**; Margaret Rutherford, English actress, **1892**; Mikhail Sholokhov, Russian novelist, **1905**.

DEATHS

'Abd-al-Mu'min, Almohad ruler of Muslim Spain and NW Africa, **1163**; Matteo Ricci, Jesuit missionary, **1610**; William Pitt, Earl of Chatham, British politician, **1778**; John Herschel, English astronomer, **1871**; William Dean Howells, US novelist and critic, **1920**; Kim Philby, English-born Soviet spy, **1988**.

'I do not see the EEC as a great love affair. It is more like
nine middle-aged couples with failing marriages meeting at a
Brussels hotel for a group grope.'
Kenneth Tynan reported on 11 May 1975

12 May

'I must go down to the seas again, to the lonely sea and the sky,
And all I ask is a tall ship and a star to steer her by.'
John Masefield, 'Sea Fever'

Feast day of St Dominic of the Causeway, St John Stone, St Ethelhard, St Fremund, Saints Nereus and Achilleus, St Pancras of Rome, St Epiphanius of Salamis, St Germanus of Constantinople, St Modoaldus, and St Rictrudis.

≋ EVENTS ≋

1394 Malik Sarvar founded the Muslim kingdom of Jaunpur, on the middle Ganges. **1536** Sir Francis Weston, Mark Smeaton and other alleged lovers of Anne Boleyn were tried for treason; they were executed on the 17th. **1809** Arthur Wellesley defeats French under Soult at Oporto and forces them to retreat from Portugal. **1881** Tunisia became a French protectorate. **1949** Berlin blockade was officially lifted. **1961** United States of the Congo founded, with Léopoldville the federal capital. **1962** South African General Law Amendment bill imposed the death penalty for sabotage. **1965** West Germany established diplomatic relations with Israel; Arab states broke off relations with Bonn.

≋ BIRTHS ≋

Claudio Monteverdi, Italian composer, **1567**; Augustus II of Poland and Elector of Saxony, **1670**; Joseph Nicolas Delisle, French astronomer, **1688**; John Bannister, English comedian, **1760**; Justus von Liebig, German chemist, **1803**; Florence Nightingale, English nursing pioneer, **1820**; Dante Gabriel Rossetti, English painter and poet, **1828**; Jules Massenet, French composer, **1842**.

≋ DEATHS ≋

George Chapman, English playwright, **1634**; Thomas Wentworth, Earl of Strafford, English politician, executed, **1641**; Bedřich Smetana, Czech composer, **1884**; Joris Karl Huysmans, French novelist, **1907**; Alfred, Lord Milner, British politician, **1925**; Arthur Quiller-Couch ('Q'), English writer, **1944**; Erich von Stroheim, Austrian-born US silent-film actor and director, **1957**; John Masefield, English poet, **1967**.

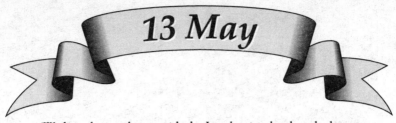

13 May

'We have been tolerant with the Jews but just let them look out.
I warn them for the last time.'
Josef Goebbels, reported on 13 May 1934

Feast day of St Andrew Hubert Fournet, St John the Silent, St Servatius, St Mucius, St Peter Regalatus, St Erconwald, St Euthymius the Enlightener, St Glyceria of Heraclia, and St Robert Bellarmine.

❦ EVENTS ❦

1203 Byzantine emperor Alexius Comnenus seized Trebizond and established a new Greek empire there. **1607** Riots took place in Northamptonshire and other Midland counties of England in protest at widespread enclosure of common land. **1643** Oliver Cromwell defeated Royalists at Grantham. **1846** Formal declaration of war by USA against Mexico. **1888** Serfdom was abolished in Brazil. **1915** The names of Emperors of Germany and Austria were struck off the roll of Knights of the Garter. **1927** 'Black Friday' with the collapse of Germany's economic system.

❦ BIRTHS ❦

Dante Alighieri, Italian poet, **1265**; Lazare Nicolas Marguerite Carnot, French revolutionary leader, **1753**; Pope Pius IX, **1792**; Alphonse Daudet, French novelist, **1840**; Arthur Sullivan, English composer, **1842**; Ronald Ross, British bacteriologist, **1857**; Daphne du Maurier, English novelist, **1907**; Joe Louis, US boxer, **1914**; Stevie Wonder, US singer, **1950**.

❦ DEATHS ❦

Johan van Oldenbarneveldt, Dutch lawyer and politician, **1619**; Georges Cuvier, French zoologist, **1832**; John Nash, English architect, **1835**; Friedrich Henle, German anatomist, **1885**; Fridtjof Nansen, Norwegian Arctic explorer, **1930**; Gary Cooper, US film actor, **1961**.

'I used to say that politics was the second oldest profession,
and I have come to know that it bears a gross similarity to the first.'
Ronald Reagan, reported on 13 May 1979

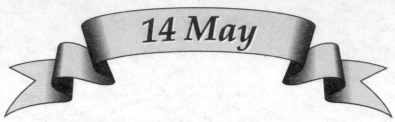

14 May

'A room is a place where you hide from the wolves outside
and that's all any room is.'
Jean Rhys

Feast day of St Mary Mazzarello, St Pontius of Cimiez, St Carthage the Younger,
St Erembert, St Matthias, St Gemma Galgani, and St Michael Garicoïts.

EVENTS

1080 Walcher, Bishop of Durham and Earl of Northumberland was murdered;
William (the Conqueror) consequently ravaged the area; he also invaded
Scotland and built the castle at Newcastle-upon-Tyne. **1264** The English barons
under Simon de Montfort defeated Henry III at the Battle of Lewes. **1147**
Conrad and the German crusaders departed from Regensburg. **1897** By treaty
with Ethiopia Britain abandoned certain claims in Somaliland but Emperor
Menelek refused to surrender his claims to lands near the Nile. **1921** 29 Fascists
returned in Italian elections. **1946** Anti-Jewish pogrom in Kielce, Poland. **1948**
As the British mandate in Palestine came to an end, a Jewish provisional
government was formed in Israel with Chaim Weizmann as president and David
Ben-Gurion as premier.

BIRTHS

Marguérite de Valois, queen of Navarre, **1553**, Gabriel Daniel Fahrenheit,
German physicist, the first to use mercury in thermometers, **1686**; Robert
Owen, Welsh social reformer, **1771**; Squire Bancroft, English actor, **1841**; Hall
Caine, English novelist, **1853**; Otto Klemperer, German conductor, **1885**;
Hastings Banda, president of Malawi, **1905**.

DEATHS

Jean Grolier, French diplomat and bibliophile, **1565**; Henry IV of France,
assassinated, **1610**; Daniel Auber, French composer, **1871**; August Strindberg,
Swedish playwright, **1912**; Henry Rider Haggard, English novelist, **1925**; Jean
Rhys, British novelist, **1979**.

'Every director bites the hand that lays the golden egg.'
Sam Goldwyn

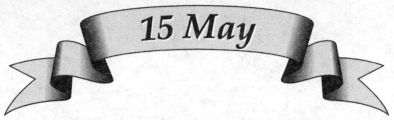

15 May

'If I'd been a ranch, they'd have named me the Bar Nothing.'
Rita Hayworth

Feast day of St Berchtun, St Dympna, St Pachomius, Saints Bertha and Rupert, St Isidore of Chios, St Gerebernus, St Hallvard, St Isias of Rostov, St Hilary of Galeata, St Peter of Lampsacus, St Isidore the Farmer, and St Torquatus and his Companions.

EVENTS

1567 Mary Queen of Scots married Bothwell in Edinburgh. **1649** The Levellers were defeated at Burford. **1848** A communist rising began in Paris, after news of suppression of Polish revolt; workers overturned the government and set up a provisional administration which immediately collapsed. **1902** Portugal declared itself bankrupt. **1922** Germany ceded Upper Silesia to Poland. **1937** Muslim rising in Albania. **1946** US President Truman signed a bill of credit for $3.75 billion for Britain. **1948** Egyptian troops intervened in Palestine on the side of the Arabs. **1957** Britain exploded the first British thermonuclear bomb in megaton range at Christmas Island, in the Central Pacific.

BIRTHS

Clemens Prince Metternich, Austrian politician, **1773**; Pierre Curie, French physicist, **1859**; Arthur Schnitzler, Austrian novelist and playwright, **1862**; James Mason, US film actor, **1909**; Ted Dexter, English cricketer, **1935**; Ralph Steadman, British cartoonist, **1936**.

DEATHS

Ephraim Chambers, English encyclopedist, **1740**; Richard Wilson, Welsh landscape painter, **1782**; Daniel O'Connell, Irish leader, **1847**; Emily Dickinson, US poet, **1886**; Leslie Ward ('Spy'), English caricaturist, **1922**; Rita Hayworth, US film actress, **1987**.

'I can't believe people bring their telephones to a match.
If they are so indispensable, they should stay in the office.'
Martina Navratilova

16 May

'Men are not in any sense irreplaceable, except in one's private life.'
Edith Cresson

Feast day of St Brendan the Navigator, St Carantoc, St Peregrine of Auxerre, St Simon Stock, St Domnolus of Le Mans, St Honoratus of Amiens, St Germerius, St John Nepomucen, St Possidius, and St Ubaldus of Gubbio.

❧ EVENTS ❧

1152 Henry II married Eleanor of Aquitaine. **1203** Baldwin, Count of Flanders, was crowned Latin Emperor of Constantinople. **1220** Henry II laid the foundation stone of a new Lady Chapel at Westminster Abbey, thus beginning the new abbey-church (1245). **1770** The Dauphin of France (later Louis XVI) married Marie Antoinette, daughter of the Empress Maria Theresa of Austria. **1804** Napoleon was declared Emperor. **1907** The Pact of Cartagena was declared between Britain, France, and Spain to counter German designs on the Balearic and Canary Islands. **1949** Chinese Nationalists organised a Supreme Council under Chiang Kai-shek, which began to remove forces to Formosa.

❧ BIRTHS ❧

Charles IV, Holy Roman Emperor, **1316**; John Sell Cotman, English watercolourist, **1782**; Maria Gaetana Agnesi, Italian scholar, **1718**; Claude Joseph Rouget de Lisle, French soldier who wrote the Marseillaise, **1760**; Henry Fonda, US film actor, **1905**; Roy Hudd, English comedian, **1936**.

❧ DEATHS ❧

Héloise, French nun, **1164**; Peter the Lombard, Bishop of Paris, **1164**; Charles Perrault, French writer of fairy tales, **1703**; Edward Gibbon Wakefield, British colonial politician, **1862**; Edward Augustus Freeman, English historian, **1892**; Bronislaw Malinowski, Polish anthropologist, **1942**.

'The concept of two people living together for 25 years without a cross word suggests a lack of spirit only to be admired in sheep.'
A P Herbert

17 May

'Writing free verse is like playing tennis with the net down.'
Robert Frost

Feast day of St Madron, St Paschal Baylon, and St Bruno of Würzburg.

〜 EVENTS 〜

1215 The English barons in revolt against King John took possession of London. **1527** Archbishop Warham began a secret inquiry at Greenwich into Henry VIII's marriage with Catherine of Aragon, the first step in divorce proceedings. **1536** Archbishop Cranmer declared Henry VIII's marriage to Anne Boleyn invalid; she was executed on the 19th. **1742** Frederick II defeated the Austrians at Chotusitz. **1885** Germany annexed Northern New Guinea and the Bismarck Archipelago. **1900** The Relief of Mafeking by British troops against the besieging Boer forces. **1939** Sweden, Norway and Finland rejected Germany's offer of non-aggression pacts, but Denmark, Estonia and Latvia accepted. **1960** The Kariba Dam, Rhodesia, was opened.

〜 BIRTHS 〜

Maria Theresa, empress, **1717**; Edward Jenner, English pioneer of vaccination, **1749**; Timothy Healy, Irish nationalist leader, **1855**; Erik Satie, French composer, **1866**; Dennis Hopper, US film actor, Bhagwat Chandrasekhar, Indian cricketer, **1945**; Sugar Ray Leonard, US boxer, **1956**.

〜 DEATHS 〜

Sandro Botticelli, Italian painter, **1510**; Matthew Parker, archbishop of Canterbury, **1575**; Samuel Clarke, English philosopher, **1729**; Charles de Talleyrand-Périgord, French politician, **1838**; Cass Gilbert, US architect, **1934**.

'I always say beauty is only sin deep.'
Saki

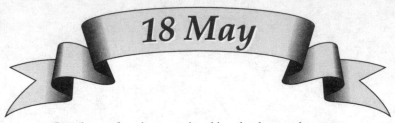
18 May

'Boredom is therefore a vital problem for the moralist, since half the sins of mankind are caused by the fear of it.'
Bertrand Russell

Feast day of St Elgiva, St John I, pope, St Eric, king of Sweden, St Felix of Cantalicio, St Potamon, and Saints Theodotus and Thecusa.

EVENTS

1302 A French garrison was massacred in the 'Matins of Bruges', when the Flemings revolted against the French occupation. **1764** The British Parliament amended the Sugar Act from a commercial to a fiscal measure, to tax American colonists. **1878** Colombia granted a French company a nine-year concession to build the Panama Canal. **1900** Tonga became a British protectorate. **1936** An army revolt under Emilio Mola and Francisco Franco began the Spanish Civil War. **1940** At Japan's request Britain prohibited the passage of war materials for China passing through Burma. **1944** Monte Cassino, Italy, was taken by Allied forces. **1980** Mount St Helens, USA, erupted for the first time since 1857, devastating an area of 600 sq km/230 sq mi.

BIRTHS

Pieter Brueghel, Flemish painter, **1525**; George Gascoigne, English poet and playwright, **1525**; Charles, Cardinal of Lorraine, **1525**; John Stow, English historian, **1525**; Joseph Butler, English philosopher, **1692**; Bertrand Russell, English philosopher, **1872**; Walter Gropius, US architect, **1883**; Pierre Balmain, French fashion designer, **1914**.

DEATHS

Elias Ashmole, English antiquarian, **1692**; Pierre Augustin Caron de Beaumarchais, French playwright, **1799**; Johann Gottfried von Herder, German critic and poet, **1803**; George Meredith, English novelist, **1909**; Gustav Mahler, Austrian composer, **1911**; Paul Dukas, French composer, **1935**; Werner Sombart, German economist, **1941**.

'Work is the curse of the drinking classes.'
Oscar Wilde

19 May

'We may be in some degree whatever character we choose.'
James Boswell

Feast day of St Dunstan, St Pudentiana, St Peter Celestine, Saints Calocerus and Parthenius, St Ivo of Kermartin, St Crispin of Viterbo, and St Peter Morrone.

EVENTS

1585 English shipping in Spanish ports was confiscated as a reprisal for depredations across the Line; this served as a declaration of war on England. **1643** The Confederation of New England was formed by Connecticut, New Haven, Plymouth and Massachusetts Bay. **1649** England was declared a Commonwealth. **1662** The Act of Uniformity gave consent to the revised English Prayer Book and denied the right to take up arms against the king; Presbyterianism in the Church was destroyed and many ministers who did not confirm were ejected. A Licensing Act forbade imports of literature contrary to Christian faith. **1930** White women were enfranchised in South Africa. **1964** The USA complained to Moscow about microphones concealed in its Moscow embassy.

BIRTHS

Johann Gottlieb Fichte, German philosopher, **1762**; Nellie Melba, Australian singer, **1861**; Ho Chi Minh, Vietnamese leader, **1890**; Max Perutz, Austrian-born British molecular biologist, **1914**; Sandy Wilson, British composer and playwright, **1924**; Michael Balcon, English film producer, **1896**.

DEATHS

Alcuin of York, English poet, **804**; James Boswell, Scottish biographer and diarist, **1795**; Nathaniel Hawthorne, US novelist, **1864**; William Ewart Gladstone, British politician, **1898**; T E Lawrence, English soldier and writer, **1935**; Charles Ives, US composer, **1954**; Ogden Nash, US poet, **1971**; John Betjeman, English poet, **1984**.

'The ballot is stronger than the bullet.'
Abraham Lincoln, speech

20 May

'Man is neither good nor bad; he is born with instincts and abilities.'
Honoré de Balzac

Feast day of St Bernardino of Siena, St Ethelbert of East Anglia, St Basilla, St Austregisilus, St Baudelius, and Saints Thalelaeus, Asterius, Alexander, and Others.

❧ EVENTS ❧

1191 Richard I 'the Lion Heart' conquered Cyprus from its independent Greek ruler, then joined the Crusaders before Acre. **1449** Afonso V of Portugal defeated a rebellion by his brother, Peter, who was killed, at Alfarrobeira. **1631** Flemish commander Count Tilly's imperialist army sacked Magdeburg; terrible carnage ensued and the city caught fire, leaving only the cathedral standing. **1927** By the treaty of Jeddah Britain recognised the independence of Saudi Arabia. **1941** German forces invaded Crete. **1941** British ministerial changes, with Brendan Bracken as Minister of Information and R A Butler as President of Board of Education. **1944** Nazi officers attempted to assassinate Hitler at a staff meeting. **1946** A bill for nationalisation of British coal mines passed the Commons stage. **1950** The US Senate committee denied Senator Joseph McCarthy's charges of Communist infiltration of the State Department.

❧ BIRTHS ❧

Donato d'Agnolo Bramante de Urbino, Italian architect, **1444**; Sandro Botticelli, Italian painter, **1444**; Honoré de Balzac, French novelist, **1799**; Thomas Lovell Beddoes, English poet and physiologist, **1803**; John Stuart Mill, English philosopher, **1806**; James Stewart, US film actor, **1908**; Moshe Dayan, Israeli military leader, **1915**.

❧ DEATHS ❧

St Bernardino of Siena, **1444**; Christopher Columbus, Genoese navigator, **1506**; Caterina Sforza, Countess of Forli, **1509**; Nicholas Brady, Anglican clergyman, **1726**; John Clare, English poet, **1864**; Clara Schumann, German pianist, **1896**; Max Beerbohm, English writer and caricaturist, **1956**; Barbara Hepworth, English sculptor, **1975**.

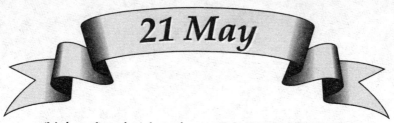

21 May

'Madam, if you don't know by now, DON'T MESS WITH IT!'
Fats Waller, reply to question, 'What is Jazz?'

Feast day of St Godric, St Collen, St Andrew Bobola, and St Theophilus of Corte.

✺ EVENTS ✺

1662 Charles II married Catherine de Braganza, daughter of John IV of Portugal. **1674** John Sobieski was elected King of Poland as John III. **1767** Townshend introduced taxes on imports of tea, glass, paper, and dyestuffs in American colonies to provide revenue for colonial administration. **1840** Britain claimed complete sovereignty over New Zealand. **1851** Gold was first discovered in Australia. **1894** The official opening of the Manchester Ship Canal took place. **1946** A world wheat shortage led to bread rationing in Britain.

✺ BIRTHS ✺

King Philip II of Spain, **1527**; Alexander Pope, English poet and satirist, **1688**; Francis Egerton, Duke of Bridgwater, builder of Britain's first canal, **1736**; Elizabeth Fry, English prison reformer, **1780**; Fats Waller, US jazz pianist and composer, **1904**; Harold Robbins, US novelist, **1916**.

✺ DEATHS ✺

King Henry VI of England, **1471**; Tomaso Campanella, Italian philosopher, **1639**; James, Marquess of Montrose, Scottish general, **1650**; Edward Montagu, Earl of Manchester, Parliamentarian leader in the English Civil War, **1671**; Robert Harley, Earl of Oxford, British politician, **1724**; Karl Wilhelm Scheele, Swedish chemist, **1786**; Geoffrey de Havilland, British aircraft designer, **1965**.

'I've always found it much more dangerous to fool with a
man's mistress than his wife.'
Harold Robbins, *The Inheritors*

22 May

'I'm a European because I believe it is in people's self-interest to exploit for Britain the potential of the European movement.'
Michael Heseltine

Feast day of St Helen of Carnavon, St Rita of Cascia, St Julia of Corsica, St Aigulf of Bourges, St Romanus, Saints Castus and Aemilius, St Humility, St Joachima de Mas, and St Quiteria.

✑ EVENTS ✑

853 A Greek expedition captured Damietta, in Egypt. **853** Olaf the White, son of the King of Norway, received the submission of Vikings and Danes in Ireland and made Dublin his capital. **1455** In the Wars of the Roses, Richard of York and the Nevilles attacked the court at St Albans, capturing Henry VI and killing Edmund Beaufort, Duke of Somerset. **1498** A death sentence was pronounced on Savonarola, former Prior of St Mark's and effective ruler of Florence, who had been excommunicated in June 1497 for attempting to seek the deposition of Pope Alexander VI. **1912** The Reichstag (German parliament) was adjourned following Socialist attacks on German emperor. **1914** Britain acquired control of oil properties in Persian Gulf from Anglo-Persian Oil Company. **1923** Stanley Baldwin formed a Conservative ministry, with Neville Chamberlain as Chancellor of Exchequer. **1972** US President Richard Nixon visited Moscow to discuss arms limitations with Soviet President Leonid Brezhnev.

✑ BIRTHS ✑

Richard Wagner, German composer, **1813**; Aston Webb, English architect, **1849**; Arthur Conan Doyle, English novelist, **1859**; Laurence Olivier, English actor, **1907**; Charles Aznavour, French singer, **1924**; George Best, Irish footballer, **1946**.

✑ DEATHS ✑

Thomas Southerne, Irish playwright, **1746**; Augustin Thierry, French historian, **1856**; John French, Earl of Ypres, British soldier, **1925**; Ernst Toller, German poet and playwright, **1939**; Cecil Day Lewis, English poet, **1972**; Rajiv Gandhi, Indian leader, assassinated, **1991**.

23 May

'Actually, I believe in marriage, having done it three times myself.'
Joan Collins

Feast day of Saints Montanus and Lucius, St William of Rochester, St Aldhelm, St Euphrosyne of Polotsk, St Ivo of Chartres, St Leontius of Rostov, St Desiderius of Vienne, and St John Baptist dei Rossi.

EVENTS

878 The Saxon King Alfred defeated the Danes at Edington; under the peace of Wedmore, their leader, Guthrum, was baptised as a Christian. **1169** 'The First Conquerors' landed in Ireland; they were Normans from Wales enlisted by Dermot MacMurrough to recover his kingdom of Leinster. **1430** Burgundian troops captured Joan of Arc and delivered her to the English. **1568** William of Orange with German mercenaries defeated a Spanish force under Count Aremberg at Heiligerlee; this action marked the beginning proper of the Revolt of the Netherlands. **1618** The Defenestration of Prague, when the Regents, Martinitz and Slawata, were overthrown by the Bohemian rebels, began the Thirty Years' War. **1926** France proclaimed the Lebanon a republic.

BIRTHS

Tamerlane the Great, Mongol leader, **1335**; Elias Ashmole, English antiquarian, **1617**; Carl von Linné (Linnaeus), Swedish botanist, **1707**; William Hunter, Scottish anatomist and obstetrician, **1718**; Friedrich Mesmer, Austrian physician, **1733**; Otto Lilienthal, German aviator, **1848**; Edmund Rubbra, English composer, **1901**; Hugh Casson, British architect, **1910**; Joan Collins, English actress, **1933**.

DEATHS

Richard of Wallingford, Abbot of St Albans, **1335**; Girolamo Savonarola, Florentine priest, burned at the stake, **1498**; William Kidd, Scottish pirate, hanged, **1701**; Leopold von Ranke, German historian, **1886**; Henrik Ibsen, Norwegian playwright, **1906**.

'English is no longer the language of England alone.
It is above all and in the eyes of the world the language of America.'
Georges Pompidou, reported on 23 May 1971

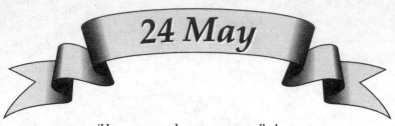

24 May

'How many roads must a man walk down
Before you can call him a man? ...
The answer, my friend, is blowin' in the wind,
The answer is blowin' in the wind.'
Bob Dylan

Feast day of St David of Scotland, St Vincent of Lerins, Saints Donatian and Rogation, and St Nicetas of Pereaslav.

EVENTS

1153 Malcolm IV acceded to the Scottish throne. **1530** A list of heretical books was drawn up in London; Tyndale's Bible was burnt. **1726** Voltaire landed in England on his liberation from the Bastille (he returned to France 1729). **1726** The first Circulating Library was opened by Allan Ramsay in Edinburgh. **1862** Westminster Bridge across the River Thames in London was opened. **1941** The British battleship HMS *Hood* was sunk by the *Bismarck* off Greenland. **1948** The USSR stopped road and rail traffic between Berlin and the West, forcing Western powers to organise airlifts.

BIRTHS

King Philip III of France, **1245**; William Byrd, English composer, **1543**; William Gilbert, English physician and early researcher into magnetism, **1540**; Jean Paul Marat, French revolutionary, **1743**; Queen Victoria, **1819**; Joseph Rowntree, social reformer and industrialist, **1836**; Arthur Wing Pinero, English playwright, **1855**; J C Smuts, South African soldier and politician, **1870**; Bob Dylan, US singer and songwriter, **1941**.

DEATHS

Nicolaus Copernicus, Polish astronomer, **1543**; Robert Cecil, Earl of Salisbury, English politician, **1612**; Jonathan Wild, English criminal, hanged, **1725**; John Dulles, US politician, **1959**; 'Duke' Ellington, US jazz composer and musician, **1974**; Hermione Gingold, English actress, **1987**.

'When it sounds good it *is* good.'
'Duke' Ellington

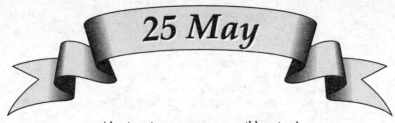

25 May

'Art is as important as council housing.'
Illtyd Harrington, reported on 25 May 1975

Feast day of St Madeleine Barat, St Gregory VII, pope, St Mary Magdalen de Pazzi, St Urban, St Zenobius, St Leo of Mantenay, St Dionysius of Milan, St Gennadius of Astorga, and St Bede.

EVENTS

1234 The Mongols took Kaifeng and destroyed the Chin dynasty. **1524** Henry VIII and Charles V formed a new league to support the Duke of Bourbon in a fresh attack on France. **1657** New Humble Petition and Advice created a new House of Lords, and increased Cromwell's power. **1657** Louis XIV put forward his name as a candidate for the Holy Roman Empire. **1659** Richard Cromwell resigned; the Rump Parliament re-established the Commonwealth. **1694** The ministry in England was remodelled when William III dismissed Tories, except Godolphin and Danby, and introduced Whig Junta of Somers, Russell, Montague, and Wharton. **1911** Porfirio Diaz resigned as president of Mexico. **1914** The British House of Commons passed the Irish Home Rule bill. **1923** The independence of Transjordan under Amir Abdullah was proclaimed. **1953** Denationalisation of road transport in Britain. **1961** US President Kennedy presents an extra-ordinary state of Union message to Congress for increased funds urgently needed for US space, defence, and air programmes.

BIRTHS

John Stuart, Earl of Bute, Britain's first Scottish prime minister, **1713**; Edward George Bulwer Lytton, Lord Lytton, English novelist, **1803**; Ralph Waldo Emerson, US poet and essayist, **1803**; Jacob Burckhardt Swiss historian, **1818**; Béla Bartók, Hungarian composer, **1881**; Josip Broz Tito, Yugoslavian soldier and president, **1892**; Miles Davis, US jazz trumpeter, **1926**; Ian McKellen, English actor, **1939**.

DEATHS

Bede, English monk and historian, **735**; Georges D'Amboise, French cardinal and politician, **1510**; Gaspard Poussin, French painter, **1675**; Pedro Calderón de la Barca, Spanish playwright, **1681**; Samuel Pepys, English diarist, **1703**; Gustav Holst, English composer, **1934**.

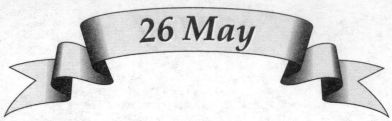

26 May

'To write one's memoirs is to speak ill of everybody except oneself.'
Marshal Henri Philippe Pétain, reported on 26 May 1946

Feast day of St Priscus, St Augustine of Canterbury, St Philip Neri, St Lambert of Venice, St Quadratus of Athens, and St Mariana of Quito.

∽ EVENTS ∽

1520 Charles V visited Henry VIII at Dover and Canterbury. **1521** The Edict of Worms imposed on Martin Luther the ban of the Empire. **1538** Jean Calvin was expelled from Geneva and settled in Strasbourg. **1659** Aurangzeb formally became Mogul Emperor. **1798** Income tax was introduced in Britain, as a tax of 10% on all incomes over £200. **1805** Napoleon was crowned King of Italy in Milan Cathedral. **1834** Sikhs captured Peshawar. **1846** Robert Peel repealed the Corn Laws (royal assent given 26 June), splitting the Conservative Party. **1865** The surrender of the last Confederate army at Shreveport, near New Orleans, ended the American Civil War. **1924** Calvin Coolidge signed a bill limiting immigration into the USA and entirely excluding the Japanese.

∽ BIRTHS ∽

Charles of Orleans, French poet, **1391**; Henry Vane the younger, English politician, **1613**; William Petty, English economist, **1623**; Lady Mary Wortley Montagu, English writer, **1689**; Edmond de Goncourt, French novelist, **1822**; A E Housman, English poet, **1859**; Princess Mary of Teck (Queen Mary, consort of George V), **1867**; Al Jolson, US singer, **1886**; John Wayne, US film actor, **1907**; Peter Cushing, British actor, **1913**.

∽ DEATHS ∽

St Augustine, first archbishop of Canterbury, **604**; Philip Neri, Italian priest, founder of the Oratory, **1595**; Charles Mayo, US surgeon, **1922**; Victor Herbert, US composer and conductor, **1924**; Lincoln Ellsworth, US scientist and polar explorer, **1951**.

'Nobody likes my acting except the public.'
John Wayne

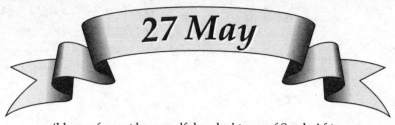
27 May

'I have often said to myself that the history of South Africa
is the one true and great romance of modern history.'
General Jan Smuts, reported on 27 May 1917

Feast day of St Julius the Veteran, St Eutropius of Orange, St Restituta of Sora, and St Melangel.

EVENTS

1063 Harold of Wessex began to conquer Wales. **1199** Pope Innocent III imposed the first direct papal taxation of Clergy. **1199** Death of Minamoto Yoritomo, first Shogun of Japan; his followers retained control of government but fought for supremacy. **1299** Peace was negotiated between Genoa and Venice, ending their war (since 1261) to control trade with the Byzantine Empire. **1719** Emperor Charles VI founded the Oriental Company in Vienna to compete with Dutch trade in the Orient. **1813** US forces occupied Fort St George, and the British abandoned the entire Niagara frontier. **1941** The German battleship *Bismarck* was sunk by the Royal Navy west of Brest.

BIRTHS

Amelia Bloomer, US feminist and dress reformer, **1818**; Julia Ward Howe, US writer, **1819**; Vincent d'Indy, French composer, **1851**; Arnold Bennett, English novelist, **1867**; John Cockcroft, English physicist, **1897**; Hubert Humphrey, US politician, **1911**; Vincent Price, US film actor, **1911**; Henry Kissinger, US politician, **1923**.

DEATHS

John Calvin, French religious reformer, **1564**; Archibald Campbell, Marquess of Argyll, Scottish Covenanter, beheaded, **1661**; Marquise de Montespan, mistress of the French King Louis XIV, **1707**; Niccolò Paganini, Italian violinist, **1840**; Robert Koch, German bacteriologist, **1910**; Jawaharlal Nehru, Indian politician, **1964**.

'Power is the ultimate aphrodisiac.'
Henry Kissinger, *Guardian* 28 Nov 1976

28 May

'Equality is a futile pursuit: equality of opportunity is a noble one.'
Ian Macleod, reported on 28 May 1969

Feast day of St Bernard of Aosta, St Ignatius of Rostov, St Senator of Milan, St William of Gellone, St Germanus of Paris, and St Justus of Urgel.

EVENTS

1358 In France the uprising known as the Jacquerie broke out - the peasants were protesting at their impoverished state after the ravages of the Hundred Years' War. **1539** Royal assent was given to an Act (the Six Articles of Religion) 'abolishing diversity of opinions' in England, after Henry VIII personally intervened in the Lords' debate to argue with the Reforming bishops. **1932** The IJselmeer was formed in the Netherlands, by the completion of a dam which enclosed the former Zuider Zee. **1956** France ceded former French settlements in India to the Indian Union. **1959** Britain announced the removal of controls on imports of many consumer goods from the dollar area, with increased import quotas of other goods. **1961** The last journey of the 'Orient Express' train, from Paris to Bucharest; it had been in operation for 78 years.

BIRTHS

King George I of Great Britain, **1660**; Joseph Guillotin, French physician and revolutionary, **1738**; William Pitt, British politician, **1759**; Thomas Moore, Irish poet, **1779**; Prosper Mérimée, French novelist, **1803**; F W Maitland, English historian, **1850**; Ian Fleming, English novelist, **1908**; Thora Hird, English actress, **1916**; Dietrich Fischer-Dieskau, German baritone, **1925**.

DEATHS

Lanfranc, Archbishop of Canterbury, **1089**; Edward Montagu, Earl of Sandwich, English admiral, **1672**; Thomas Chippendale, English cabinet-maker, **1779**; Jean Louis Rodolphe Agassiz, Swiss oceanographer and marine zoologist, **1807**; Noah Webster, US lexicographer, **1843**; Henry Thomas Buckle, English historian, **1862**; Lord John Russell, Earl Russell, British politician, **1878**; Alfred Adler, Austrian psychiatrist, **1937**.

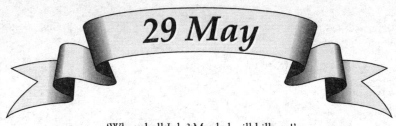

29 May

'What shall I do? My dad will kill me!'
Jade Jagger, daughter of Mick Jagger, on being
expelled from school, reported on 29 May 1988

Feast day of St Cyril of Caesarea, St Bernard of Montjoux, St Theodosia of Constantinople, St Maximinus of Trier, Saints Sisinnius, Martyrius, and Alexander, and Saints William, Stephen, Raymund, and their Companions.

∾ EVENTS ∾

862 Riurick (of Jutland) founded the first dynasty of Princes of Russia at Novgorod. **1218** The Fifth Crusade landed outside Damietta, N Egypt. **1453** Mohammed II, founder of the Ottoman empire, captured Constantinople; the Byzantine Emperor Constantine XI was killed and the Greek Empire finally extinguished. Constantinople became the Ottoman capital. **1458** Richard Neville, Earl of Warwick, defeated a Castilian fleet in the Channel. **1848** Wisconsin became a US state. **1940** The first British forces were evacuated from Dunkirk. **1947** The Indian constituent assembly outlawed 'untouchability'.

∾ BIRTHS ∾

King Charles II of Great Britain, **1630**; Louis Jean Marie Daubenton, French naturalist, **1716**; Patrick Henry, US politician, **1736**; Léon Bourgeois, French politician, **1851**; Gilbert Keith Chesterton, English novelist and critic, **1874**; Bob Hope, US actor and comedian, **1903**; John Fitzgerald Kennedy, 35th president of the USA, **1917**.

∾ DEATHS ∾

Bartholomew Diaz de Novaes, Portuguese navigator, **1500**; David Beaton, Scottish politician, **1546**; Cornelius Van Tromp, Dutch sailor, **1691**; Humphry Davy, English scientist who invented a safety lamp for miners, **1829**; John Lothrop Motley, US historian and diplomat, **1877**; W S Gilbert, English playwright and librettist, **1911**.

'Don't forget that unlike the French, unlike the British and unlike the Portuguese, we Afrikaners have no other place to go.'
Roelof Boetha, reported on 29 May 1977

30 May

'We must cultivate our garden.'
Voltaire, *Candide*

Feast day of St Hubert, St Joan of Arc, St Ferdinand, St Exuperiantius of Ravenna, St Isaac of Constantinople, St Luke Kirby, St Madelgisilus, and St Walstan.

≋ EVENTS ≋

1431 Joan of Arc was burnt as a heretic at Rouen, France. **1536** English King Henry VIII married Jane Seymour, his third wife. **1592** The Spanish defeated an English force under Sir John Norris at Cranon, Brittany. **1913** A peace treaty between Turkey and the Balkan states was signed in London. **1925** The shooting of Chinese students by municipal police in Shanghai and other incidents in Canton provoked a Chinese boycott of British goods. **1929** The British Labour Party won the general election with 287 seats. **1948** The British Citizenship Act conferred the status of British subjects on all Commonwealth citizens.

≋ BIRTHS ≋

Peter the Great, tsar of Russia, **1672**; Henry Addington, British politician, **1757**; Peter Carl Fabergé, Russian goldsmith and jeweller, **1846**; Howard Hawks, US film director, **1896**; Benny Goodman, US bandleader, **1909**.

≋ DEATHS ≋

Christopher Marlowe, English playwright, **1593**; Peter Paul Rubens, Flemish painter, **1640**; Alexander Pope, English poet and satirist, **1744**; François Boucher, French painter, **1770**; Voltaire, French author and philosopher, **1778**; Boris Pasternak, Russian novelist and poet, **1960**; Claude Rains, British-born film actor, **1967**.

'War should belong to the tragic past, to history: it should find no place on humanity's agenda for the future.'
Pope John Paul II

31 May

'O Captain! my Captain! our fearful trip is done, / The ship
has weathered every rack, the prize we sought is won.'
Walt Whitman, 'O Captain! my Captain'

Feast day of St Petronilla, Saints Cantius, Cantianus, Cantianella, and Protus,
and St Mechtildi of Edelstetten.

≫ EVENTS ≫

1287 The Genoese defeated the Venetian fleet off Acre and blockaded the coast
of Outremer. **1902** The Peace of Vereeniging ended the Boer War, in which
British casualties numbered 5,774 killed (and 16,000 deaths from disease)
against 4,000 Boers killed in action. **1916** The Battle of Jutland began, in which
Royal Navy losses exceeded those of the German fleet. **1942** Czech patriots
assassinated Gestapo leader Heydrich. **1952** In the USSR, the Volga–Don
Canal was opened. **1961** South Africa became an independent republic outside
the Commonwealth, with C R Swart as president.

≫ BIRTHS ≫

Margaret Beaufort, consort of Henry VII of England, **1443**; Matthias Corvinus,
king of Hungary, **1443**; Rudolphus Agricola, Dutch humanist, **1443**; Guilio
Alberoni, Italian cardinal and politician, **1664**; Karl August von Hardenberg,
Prussian politician, **1750**; Walt Whitman, US poet, **1819**; Francis Younghusband,
English explorer, **1863**; William Heath Robinson, English illustrator, **1872**; Don
Ameche, US film actor, **1908**; Clint Eastwood, US film actor and director, **1930**;
Terry Waite, religious adviser to the Archbishop of Canterbury, **1939**.

≫ DEATHS ≫

Jacopo Tintoretto, Italian painter, **1594**; Frederick William I of Prussia, **1740**; Jean
Cavalier, French Huguenot preacher and leader, **1740**; Joseph Haydn, Austrian
composer, **1809**; Joseph Grimaldi, English clown, **1837**; Walther Funk, German Nazi
economist, **1960**; Adolf Eichmann, Nazi leader, hanged as a war criminal, **1962**.

'Grant me paradise in this world; I'm not so sure I'll reach it in the next.'
Jacopo Tintoretto, seeking the commission to paint
the *Paradiso* at the doge's palace, Venice

1 June

'A sex symbol becomes a thing. I hate being a thing.'
Marilyn Monroe

National Day of Tunisia. Feast day of St Gwen of Brittany, St Justin, St Nicomedes, St Ronan, St Whyte, St Wistan, St Symeon of Syracuse, St Caprasius of Lérins, St Pamphilus of Caesarea, St Inigo, St Proculus the Soldier, St Proculus the Bishop, and St Theobald of Alba.

⚅ EVENTS ⚅

836 Viking raiders sacked London. **1485** Matthias of Hungary took Vienna in his conquest of Austria (from Frederick III) and made the city his capital. **1666** An English fleet under Lord Albemarle fought an inconclusive battle with the Dutch off the Dunes of Dunkirk. **1679** The Scottish Covenanters defeated Royal troops under Claverhouse at Drumclog. **1792** Kentucky became the 15th US state. **1796** Tennessee became the 16th US state. **1915** The first Zeppelin attack on London took place. **1946** Television licences were issued in Britain for the first time; they cost £2. **1957** ERNIE drew the first premium bond prizes in Britain. **1958** Iceland extended its fishery limits to 12 miles.

⚅ BIRTHS ⚅

Nicolas Carnot, French founder of thermodynamics, **1796**; Brigham Young, US Mormon leader, **1801**; Mikhail Glinka, Russian composer, **1803**; John Drinkwater, English poet, **1882**; Frank Whittle, English inventor who developed the jet engine, **1907**; Marilyn Monroe, **1926**; Morgan Freeman, US film actor, **1937**.

⚅ DEATHS ⚅

James Gillray, English caricaturist, **1815**; James Buchanan, 15th president of the USA, **1868**; Hugh Walpole, English novelist, **1941**; Leslie Howard, British film actor, **1943**; Ion Antonescu, Romanian dictator, executed, **1946**; Eric Partridge, British lexicographer, **1985**.

'I've been on a calendar, but never on time.'
Marilyn Monroe

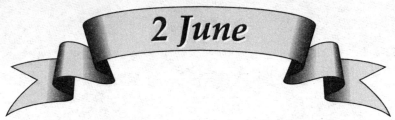

2 June

'I know I was cruel to other children because I remember stuffing their nostrils with putty, and beating a little boy with stinging nettles.'
Vita Sackville-West

National Day of Italy. Feast day of St Erasmus, St Oda, St Attalus, Saints Marcellinus and Peter, St Eugenius I, pope, St Nicholas the Pilgrim, St Stephen of Sweden, and St Pothinus and his Companions.

✎ EVENTS ✎

1619 A treaty was signed between England and Holland, regulating the trade in the East between the English and Dutch East India Companies. **1627** Charles I granted a charter of incorporation to the Guiana Company. **1627** The Duke of Buckingham sailed from Portsmouth with a fleet to aid the Huguenots in the defence of La Rochelle. **1780** The Gordon riots began in London, when Lord George Gordon headed a procession for presenting a petition to Parliament for repealing Catholic Relief act of 1778; Roman Catholic chapels were pillaged. **1793** The final overthrow of Girondins and arrest of Jacques Brissot began the Reign of Terror. **1916** The second battle of Ypres took place. **1949** Transjordan was renamed the Hashemite Kingdom of Jordan. **1953** The coronation of Queen Elizabeth II took place in Westminster Abbey.

✎ BIRTHS ✎

John Sobieski, King of Poland, **1624**; Thomas Hardy, English novelist and poet, **1840**; Edward Elgar, English composer, **1857**; Julian Huxley, English biologist, **1887**; Johnny Weissmuller, US swimmer who played Tarzan in films, **1903**; Barry Levinson, US film director, **1942**.

✎ DEATHS ✎

James Douglas, Earl of Morton, **1581**; Giuseppe Garibaldi, Italian nationalist, **1882**; Alexander Ostrovsky, Russian playwright, **1886**; Alfred Austin, English poet, **1913**; Vita Sackville-West, English writer, **1962**; Andrés Segovia, Spanish classical guitarist, **1987**; Rex Harrison, British actor, **1990**.

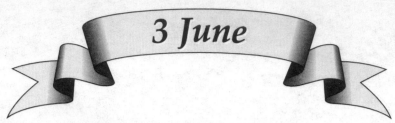

3 June

'It's often better to be in chains than to be free.'
Franz Kafka

Feast day of Genesius of Clermont, St Kevin, St Charles Lwanga, St Isaac of Cordova, St Morand, St Cecilius, St Clothilde, St Joseph Mkasa, St Lucillian and his Companions, Saints Liphardus and Urbicius, and Saints Pergentinus and Laurentinus.

EVENTS

1098 The Crusaders took Antioch. **1162** Thomas à Becket was consecrated as Archbishop of Canterbury. **1665** The English fleet defeated the Dutch at the Battle of Lowestoft. **1942** US and Japanese naval forces began the Battle of Midway, in the Pacific. **1946** King Umberto II left Italy and Alcide de Gasperi, the premier, became provisional head of state. **1959** Singapore became self-governing.

BIRTHS

William Dampier, English navigator and adventurer, **1652**; James Hutton, Scottish geologist, **1726**; Sydney Smith, English clergyman and journalist, **1771**; Richard Cobden, English economist and political reformer, **1804**; William Flinders Petrie, English archaeologist, **1853**; George V, **1865**; Wilfrid Thesiger, English explorer and writer, **1910**.

DEATHS

John Aylmer, bishop of London, **1594**; William Harvey, English physician who described the circulation of the blood, **1657**; Georges Bizet, French composer, **1875**; Johann Strauss, Austrian composer, **1899**; Franz Kafka, Austrian novelist, **1924**; Mikhail Ivanovich Kalinin, Russian politician, **1946**; Arthur Ransome, English children's writer, **1967**.

'Of course, I do have a slight advantage over the rest of you. It helps in a pinch to be able to remind your bride that you gave up a throne for her.'
Edward VIII, married on this day 1937 to Mrs Wallis Simpson

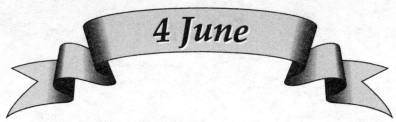

4 June

'I no more thought of style or literary excellence than the mother who rushes into the street and cries for help to save her children from a burning house, thinks of the teachings of the rhetorician or elocutionist.'
Harriet Beecher Stowe, on writing *Uncle Tom's Cabin*

Feast day of St Edfrith, St Ninnoc, St Petroc, St Metrophanes, St Francis Caracciolo, St Optatus of Milevis, St Quirinus of Siscia, and St Vincentia Gerosa.

∾ EVENTS ∾

1039 Gruffyd ap Llewelyn, King of Gwynned and Powys, defeated an English attack. **1210** King John embarked on an expedition to Ireland, enforcing his authority there. **1520** Henry VIII and Francis I met at the Field of the Cloth of Gold, between Gravelines and Ardres; on 6 June they signed a treaty confirming the marriage contract of Mary Tudor and the Dauphin and ending French interference in Scotland. **1878** A secret Anglo-Turkish agreement was made to check Russian advance in Asia Minor, by which Britain promised to defend Turkey against further attack and Britain was allowed to occupy Cyprus. **1944** The Fifth Army entered Rome. **1956** Egypt declared it would not extend the Suez Canal Company's concession after its expiry in 1968. **1959** US-owned sugar mills and plantations in Cuba were expropriated.

∾ BIRTHS ∾

François Quesnay, French economist and physician, **1694**; George III, **1738**; John Scott, later Earl of Eldon, English lawyer and politician, **1751**; Harriet Beecher Stowe, US novelist, **1811**; Garnet Wolseley, English soldier, **1833**; Christopher Cockerell, English engineer who invented the hovercraft, **1910**.

∾ DEATHS ∾

William Juxon, archbishop of Canterbury, **1663**; Giovanni Casanova, Italian adventurer, **1798**; Nassau William Senior, English economist, **1864**; Kaiser William II, **1941**; Emily Davidson, English suffragette who threw herself in front of the King's horse during the Derby, **1913**.

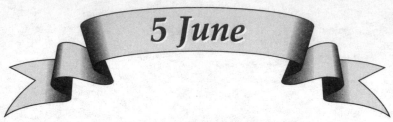

5 June

> 'But this *long run* is a misleading guide to
> current affairs. *In the long run* we are all dead.'
> **John Maynard Keynes**

National Day of Denmark. Feast Day of St Boniface, St Dorotheus of Tyre, St Tudno, and St Sanctius.

≈ EVENTS ≈

1912 US marines landed in Cuba. **1916** HMS *Hampshire* sank off the Orkneys, with Lord Kitchener aboard. **1945** The Allied Control Commission assumed control throughout Germany, which was divided into four occupation zones. **1947** US Secretary of State George Marshall called for a European Recovery Programme (Marshall Aid). **1967** The Six-Day War broke out between Israel and the Arab states. **1970** Tonga became independent within the Commonwealth. **1975** The Suez Canal was reopened after being closed for eight years.

≈ BIRTHS ≈

Nicolas Poussin, French painter, **1594**; Adam Smith, Scottish economist, **1723**; Pancho Villa, Mexican revolutionary, **1878**; John Maynard Keynes, English economist, **1883**; Federico García Lorca, Spanish playwright and poet, **1898**; Margaret Drabble, English novelist, **1939**; David Hare, British playwright, **1947**.

≈ DEATHS ≈

Orlando Gibbons, English organist and composer, **1625**; Henry Sacheverell, English political preacher, **1724**; Carl von Weber, German composer, **1826**; Stephen Crane, US poet and novelist, **1900**; Horatio, Lord Kitchener, English soldier, **1916**; Henri Gaudier-Brzeska, French artist, **1916**; Georges Feydeau, French dramatist, **1921**.

> 'The great nations have always acted like gangsters, and the
> small nations like prostitutes.'
> **Stanley Kubrick**

6 June

'I am convinced UFOs exist, because I have seen one.'
Jimmy Carter, reported on 6 June 1976

National Day of Sweden. Feast Day of St Jarlath, St Gudwal, St Ceratius, St Norbert, Saints Primus and Felician, St Claude of Besançon, St Eustorgius II of Milan, and St Philip the Deacon.

∾ EVENTS ∾

1457 Polish forces took Marienburg; the Teutonic Knights then made Königsberg their headquarters. **1636** Puritan American colonist Roger Williams, banished from Massachusetts Bay Colony, founded Providence, Rhode Island, a colony with complete religious freedom. **1664** War broke out between England and Holland in the colonies and at sea. **1797** Napoleon Bonaparte founded the Ligurian Republic in Genoa. **1820** Caroline, Princess of Wales, whom George IV wished to divorce, triumphantly entered London, demanding her recognition as Queen. **1844** The Factory Act in Britain restricted female workers to a 12-hour day; children between eight and 13 years were limited to six-and-a-half hours.

∾ BIRTHS ∾

Diego y Velasquez, Spanish painter, **1599**; Pierre Corneille, French playwright, **1606**; Henry Newbolt, English poet, **1862**; Robert Falcon Scott, English Antarctic explorer, **1868**; Thomas Mann, German novelist, **1875**; Ninette de Valois, Irish ballet dancer, **1898**; Björn Borg, Swedish tennis player, **1956**; Mike Gatting, English cricketer, **1958**.

∾ DEATHS ∾

St. Norbert of Xanten, archbishop of Magdeburg, **1134**; George Anson, English sailor and explorer, **1762**; Jeremy Bentham, English philosopher and jurist, **1832**; James Agate, English critic and essayist, **1947**; Carl Gustav Jung, Swiss psychiatrist, **1961**; Robert Kennedy, US politician, assassinated, **1968**.

'A man who has not passed through the inferno of his passions
has never overcome them.'
Carl Gustav Jung

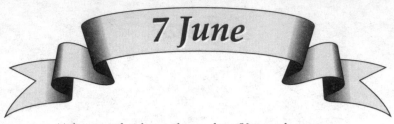

7 June

'A loving wife is better than making 50 at cricket or even
99; beyond that I will not go.'
James Barrie, reported on 7 June 1925

Feast day of St Meriasek, St Robert of Newminster, St Anthony Gianelli, St
Gottschalk, St Vulflagius, St Willibald, St Colman of Dromore, and St Paul I
of Constantinople.

EVENTS

1494 By the Treaty of Tordesillas, Spain and Portugal agreed to divide the New
World between themselves: Portugal was to have all lands east of a line north and
south drawn 370 leagues west of Cape Verde, Spain to have the rest. **1497**
English King Henry VII defeats the Cornish rebels under Lord Audley at
Blackheath. **1523** Gustavus Vasa was elected Gustav I of Sweden. **1535** John
Fisher, Bishop of Rochester, was tried for treason (he was executed on 22 June).
1672 Dutch Admiral de Ruyter was successful in action against the combined
English and French fleets in Southwold Bay. **1832** The Reform Bill became law;
over 140 seats were redistributed, and in the boroughs all antiquated forms of
franchise were eliminated and the franchise was extended to include leaseholders
paying minimum of £10 rent per annum, while in counties the 40-shilling
freehold qualification was retained and certain lease-holders acquired the vote.

BIRTHS

John Rennie, Scottish engineer, **1761**; Alexander Pushkin, Russian novelist,
playwright, and poet, **1799**; James Young Simpson, Scottish obstetrician who
pioneered the use of anaesthetics, **1811**; Pietro Annigoni, Italian painter, **1910**;
Paul Gauguin, French painter, **1848**; James Ivory, US film director, **1928**.

DEATHS

Robert I 'the Bruce', king of Scotland, **1329**; David Cox, English painter, 1859;
Jean Harlow, US film actress, **1937**; Dorothy Parker, US writer, **1967**; E M
Forster, English novelist, **1970**; Henry Miller, US novelist, **1980**.

'One more drink and I'd have been under the host.'
Dorothy Parker

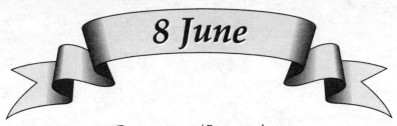

8 June

'Razors pain you / Rivers are damp
Acid stains you / And drugs cause cramp
Guns aren't lawful / Nooses give
Gas smells awful, / You might as well live.'
Dorothy Parker, *Enough Rope*, 'Resumé'

Feast day of St Medard, St William of York, St Cloud of Metz, and St Maximinius of Aix.

～ EVENTS ～

1042 Harthacnut, King of England and Denmark, died; he was succeeded in England by his adopted heir, Edward the Confessor, and in Denmark by Magnus, King of Norway. **1536** The English Parliament met and settled the succession on the future children of Henry VIII by Jane Seymour; the Princesses Mary and Elizabeth were declared illegitimate. **1919** Nicaragua asked the US for protection against Costa Rica. **1934** Oswald Mosley addressed a mass meeting of the British Union of Fascists at Olympia. **1939** George VI visited the USA at the end of his tour of Canada; he was the first British monarch to do so. **1941** British and Free French Forces invaded Syria to prevent the establishment of Axis bases. **1965** US troops were authorised to engage in offensive operations in Vietnam.

～ BIRTHS ～

Giovanni Cassini, Italian astronomer, **1625**; John Smeaton, English engineer, **1724**; Robert Stevenson, English engineer, **1772**; Robert Schumann, German composer, **1810**; John Everett Millais, English painter, **1829**; Frank Lloyd Wright, US architect, **1869**.

～ DEATHS ～

Christiaan Huygens, Dutch physicist and astronomer, **1695**; Thomas Paine, English author of The Rights of Man, **1809**; Sarah Siddons, English actress, **1831**; Joseph Paxton, English architect, **1865**; 'George Sand' (Amandine Dudevant, born Dupin), French novelist, **1876**; Gerard Manley Hopkins, English poet, **1889**; Gerhart Hauptmann, German novelist and playwright, **1946**.

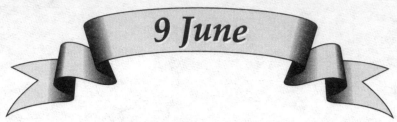

9 June

'Comedy, like sodomy, is an unnatural act.'
Marty Feldman

Feast day of St Columba, St Ephraem, St Richard of Ambria, St Vincent of Agen, and St Pelagia of Antioch.

EVENTS

1572 A new Turkish fleet put to sea against Don John of Austria to complete the capture of Cyprus. **1788** English botanist Joseph Banks founded the Africa Association for arousing interest in exploration and trade. **1885** The Treaty of Tientsin between France and China recognised the French protectorate in Annam. **1934** Cartoon character Donald Duck first appeared. **1959** The USS *George Washington* was launched, the first submarine to be armed with ballistic missiles.

BIRTHS

Peter the Great, tsar of Russia, **1672**; George Stephenson, English locomotive engineer, **1781**; Elizabeth Garrett Anderson, English physician, **1836**; Cole Porter, US composer of musicals, **1893**.

DEATHS

William Maitland of Lethington, Scottish politician, **1573**; William Lilly, English astrologer, **1681**; Charles Dickens, English novelist, **1870**; Cochise, American Apache leader, **1874**; Maxwell William Aitken, Lord Beaverbrook, Canadian-born politician and newspaper proprietor, **1964**; Sybil Thorndike, English actress, **1976**.

'They say hard work never hurt anybody,
but I figure why take the chance.'
Ronald Reagan

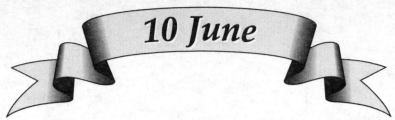

10 June

'Death is the dark backing a mirror needs if we are to see anything.'
Saul Bellow

Feast day of St Ithamar, St Bogumilus, St Landericus of Paris, and St Getulius and his Companions.

✑ EVENTS ✑

1829 The Oxford team won the first-ever Oxford and Cambridge Boat Race. **1891** L Starr Jameson became administrator of the South Africa Company's territories. **1893** Alarmed at Belgian advances in the Congo, France sent an occupying force to forestall further annexations. **1899** US Congress appointed a canal commission to report on routes through Panama. **1942** The Czech village of Lidice was destroyed and every man in it killed in reprisal for the assassination of Nazi leader Richard Heydrich. **1943** The ball-point pen was patented in the USA.

✑ BIRTHS ✑

James Francis Edward Stuart (the Old Pretender), **1688**; John Dollond, English optician, **1706**; Gustave Courbet, French painter, **1819**; Henry Morton Stanley, US journalist and explorer, **1840**; G E Buckle, English newspaper editor, **1854**; Saul Bellow, US novelist, **1915**; Prince Philip, Duke of Edinburgh, **1921**; Judy Garland, US film actress and singer, **1922**; Maurice Sendak, US illustrator, **1928**.

✑ DEATHS ✑

Luis Vaz de Camoens, Portuguese poet, **1580**; Alessandro Algardi, Italian sculptor, **1654**; Thomas Hearne, English antiquary and keeper of the Bodleian Library, **1735**; André Ampère, French physicist, **1836**; 'Pierre Loti' (Julien Viaud), French novelist, **1923**; Frederick Delius, English composer, **1934**; Spencer Tracey, US film actor, **1967**.

'There were times my pants were so thin I could sit on a dime and tell if it was heads or tails.'
Spencer Tracey

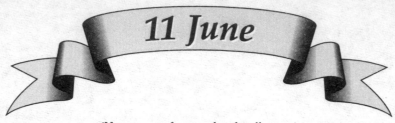

11 June

'He was not of an age, but for all time.'
Ben Jonson, of William Shakespeare

Feast day of St Barnabas, Saints Felix and Fortunatus, and St Parisio.

EVENTS

1509 Henry VIII married Catherine of Aragon, his first wife. **1727** George I became king of Great Britain. **1891** At an Anglo-Portuguese convention on territories north and south of Zambesi, Portugal assigned Barotseland to Britain; Nyasaland was subsequently proclaimed a British Protectorate. **1895** Britain annexed Togoland to block Transvaal's access to the sea. **1955** US President Eisenhower proposed financial and technical aid to all non-Communist countries to develop atomic energy. **1963** Constantine Karamanlis, the Greek premier, resigned in protest against King Paul's state visit to Britain. **1964** Greece rejected direct talks with Turkey over Cyprus.

BIRTHS

Barnabe Googe, English poet, **1540**; Ben Jonson, English playwright, **1572**; John Constable, English painter, **1776**; Millicent Garrett Fawcett, English suffragette, **1847**; Mrs Humphrey Ward (Mary Augusta Arnold), English novelist, **1851**; Jacques Cousteau, French oceanographer, **1910**; Athol Fugard, South African dramatist and director, **1932**.

DEATHS

Kenelm Digby, English writer and diplomat, **1665**; Louis, Duc de Vendôme, French soldier, **1712**; John Franklin, English Arctic explorer, **1847**; Clemens, Prince Metternich, Austrian politician, **1859**; Frank Brangwyn, British painter, **1956**; Alexander Kerensky, Russian politician, **1970**; John Wayne, US film actor, **1979**.

'The notes I handle no better than many pianists. But the pauses between the notes - ah, that is where the art resides.'
Artur Schnabel

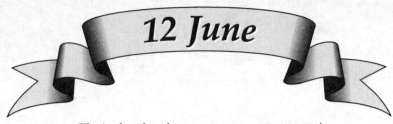
12 June

'That's what show business is - sincere insincerity.'
Benny Hill, reported on 12 June 1977

National Day of the Philippines. Feast day of St Basilides, St Eskil, St Leo II, St Odulf, St Onuphrius, St Ternan, St Peter of Mount Athos, St Antonia, St John of Sahagun, and St Paula Frassinetti.

≈ EVENTS ≈

1088 William II suppressed a revolt in England led by Odo of Bayeux, Bishop of Rochester, who was supporting Robert Curthose. **1667** The Dutch fleet under Admiral de Ruyter burned Sheerness, sailed up the River Medway, raided Chatham dockyard, and escaped with the royal barge, the *Royal Charles*; the nadir of English naval power. **1683** The Rye House Plot, to assassinate King Charles II and his brother James, Duke of York, was discovered. **1901** A Cuban convention making the country virtually a protectorate of the US was incorporated in the Cuban constitution as a condition of the withdrawal of US troops. **1934** Political parties banned in Bulgaria. **1964** Nelson Mandela and seven others were sentenced to life imprisonment for acts of sabotage in the Rivonia trial, Pretoria.

≈ BIRTHS ≈

Harriet Martineau, English writer, **1802**; Charles Kingsley, English novelist, **1819**; Anthony Eden, Viscount Avon, British politician, **1897**; George Bush, 41st president of the USA, **1924**; Anne Frank, Jewish Dutch diarist, **1929**.

≈ DEATHS ≈

James, Duke of Berwick, English-born French general, **1734**; William Collins, English poet, **1759**; Thomas Arnold, English scholar and head of Rugby School, **1842**; John Ireland, English composer, **1962**; Billy Butlin, English holiday-camp entrepreneur, **1980**; Marie Rambert, British ballet dancer and teacher, **1982**.

'Unhappiness is best defined as the difference between our
talents and our expectations.'
Edward de Bono, reported on 12 June 1977

13 June

'Photography is truth. The cinema is truth 24 times per second.'
Jean-Luc Godard

Feast day of St Antony of Padua, St Felicula, St Aquilina, and St Triphyllius.

⧉ EVENTS ⧉

1849 Communist riots in Paris were easily defeated and led to repressive legislation. **1866** The US 14th Amendment incorporated the Civil Rights Act and gave states the choice of Negro enfranchisement or reduced representation in Congress. **1900** The Boxer Rebellion began in China against Europeans. **1942** British forces lost 230 tanks in desert fighting. **1944** The first flying bomb was dropped on London. **1956** The last British troops left the Suez Canal base. **1961** Austria refused an application by Archduke Otto of Habsburg to return as a private individual.

⧉ BIRTHS ⧉

Richard Barnfield, English poet, **1574**; Thomas Arnold, English scholar, head of Rugby school, **1795**; James Clerk Maxwell, Scottish physicist, **1831**; William Butler Yeats, Irish poet, **1865**; Peter Scudamore, British jockey, **1958**.

⧉ DEATHS ⧉

Alexander the Great, 323 BC, St Antonio of Padua, **1231**; Arcangelo Corelli, Italian composer, **1713**; Henry Seagrave, British racing driver, **1930**; Jesse Boot, English pharmacist, drug manufacturer, and philanthropist, **1931**; Benny Goodman, US bandleader, **1986**.

'It is always good to remember that people find it easier to
name ten artists from any century than ten politicians.'
John Heath-Stubbs

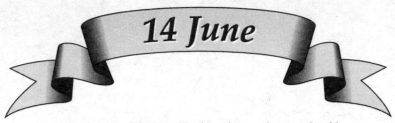

14 June

'From the age of thirteen I had revelations from our Lord by
a voice which told me how to behave.'
Joan of Arc

Feast day of St Dogmael, Saints Valerius and Rufinus, and St Methodius I of
Constantinople.

✺ EVENTS ✺

1380 In the Peasants' Revolt, the rebels occupying London killed Archbishop
Sudbury, the Chancellor, and Robert Hales, the Treasurer. **1404** Glendower, having
won control of Wales, assumes the title of Prince of Wales and holds a parliament.
1645 In the English Civil War, Oliver Cromwell defeated the Royalists at the
Battle of Naseby, Northamptonshire. **1800** Napoleon Bonaparte defeated an
Austrian army at the Battle of Marengo and reconquers Italy. **1940** In World War
II, German forces entered Paris. **1960** French President de Gaulle renewed his offer
to the Algerian provisional government to negotiate a cease-fire, to which Front de
la Libération Nationale agreed, but rejected subsequent French conditions. **1962**
The European Space Research Organisation was established at Paris.

✺ BIRTHS ✺

Charles Augustin Coulomb, French physicist, **1736**; Henry Keppel, British admiral,
1809; Bernard Bosanquet, English philosopher, **1848**; Che Guevara, Argentinian
communist revolutionary, **1928**; Steffi Graf, German tennis player, **1969**.

✺ DEATHS ✺

Henry Vane the younger, English politician, executed after the Restoration for
his parliamentarian activities, **1662**; Edward Fitzgerald, English poet and
translator, **1883**; Jerome Klapka Jerome, English novelist, **1927**; Gilbert Keith
Chesterton, English author, **1936**; John Logie Baird, Scottish inventor who
developed television, **1946**; Jorge Luis Borges, Argentinian author, **1986**;
Vincent Hamlin, US cartoonist, **1993**.

'The road is a brutal and unneeded monster.'
Carlo Ripa di Meana, (EC environment commissioner)
on a proposed extension

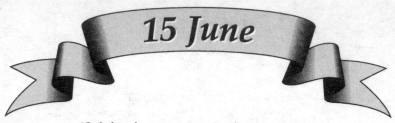
15 June

Official birthday of Queen Elizabeth II. Feast day of St Trillo, St Vitus and his
Companions, St Bardo, St Aleydia, St Germaine Cousin of Pibrac, St Hesychius
of Durostorum, St Landelinus, St Edburga of Winchester, St Tatian Dulas, and
St Orsiesus.

EVENTS

1520 Pope Leo X excommunicated Martin Luther by the bull Exsurge. **1658**
The Mogul emperor Aurangzeb imprisoned his father the Shah, after winning a
battle at Samgarh. **1672** The Sluices were opened in Holland to save
Amsterdam from the French. **1836** Arkansas became the 25th state of the USA.
1855 Stamp duty on British newspapers was abolished. **1869** Celluloid was
patented in the USA. **1954** The Convention People's Party, led by Kwame
Nkrumah, won the Gold Coast elections. **1977** Spain had its first general
elections since 1936.

BIRTHS

Edward (the Black Prince), **1330**; St Francesco de Paolo, **1416**; Joannes
Argyropoulos, Greek scholar, **1416**; Thomas Randolph, English poet and
playwright, **1605**; Edvard Grieg, Norwegian composer, **1843**; Richard Baker,
English broadcaster, **1925**.

DEATHS

Wat Tyler, English rebel leader, **1381**; Philip the Good, Duke of Burgundy,
1467; Marguerite De Launay, Baronne Staal, French writer, **1750**; James Knox
Polk, 11th president of the USA, **1849**; Evelyn Underhill, English poet and
mystic, **1941**.

'I'm surprised that a government organization
could do it that quickly.'
Jimmy Carter, on the building of the Great Pyramid

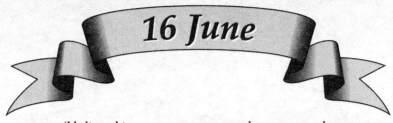
16 June

'I believe this government cannot endure permanently,
half slave and half free.'
Abraham Lincoln

Feast day of St Cyricus, St Ismael, St Aurelian, St John Francis Regis, Saints Cyr
and Julitta, St Benno of Meissen, St Lutgarde, Saints Ferreolus and Ferrutio, and
St Tychon of Amathus.

➤ EVENTS ➤

1586 Mary Queen of Scots recognised Philip II of Spain as her heir. **1745**
British troops took Cape Breton Island and subsequently Louisburg, at the
mouth of the St Lawrence River. **1779** Spain declared war on Britain (after
France had undertaken to assist in the recovery of Gibraltar and Florida), and
the siege of Gibraltar began. **1836** The formation of the London Working Men's
Association began the Chartist Movement. **1871** The University Test Acts
allowed students to enter Oxford and Cambridge without religious tests. **1972**
Burglars were caught breaking into the Democratic Party headquarters in the
Watergate Building, Washington DC, USA. **1977** Leonid Brezhnev became
president of the USSR.

➤ BIRTHS ➤

John Cheke, English classical scholar, **1514**; King Gustav V of Sweden, **1858**;
Stan Laurel, English-born US film comedian, **1890**; Enoch Powell, British
politician, **1912**; Giacomo Agostini, Italian motorcycle champion, **1942**.

➤ DEATHS ➤

Roger van der Weyden, Flemish painter, **1464**; John Churchill, Duke of
Marlborough, English general, **1722**; Guilio Alberoni, Italian-born Spanish
politician and cardinal, **1752**; Elmer Ambrose Sperry, US inventor, **1930**;
Margaret Bondfield, British politician and trade-unionist, **1953**.

'Live as long as you may, the first 20 years
are the longest half of your life.'
Robert Southey

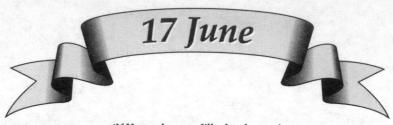

17 June

'If Kennedy runs, I'll whip his ass.'
Jimmy Carter, reported on 17 June 1979

National day of Iceland. Feast day of St Moling, St Adulf, St Nectan, St Botulf, St Alban, St Avitus, St Bessarion, St Hypatius, St Rainerius of Pisa, St Emily de Vialai, St Hervé, Saints Nicander and Marcian, and Saints Teresa and Sanchia of Portugal.

≈ EVENTS ≈

1128 Henry I's daughter, Matilda, widow of Henry V, married Geoffrey Plantagenet of Anjou; she was recognised in England as her father's heir. **1579** Francis Drake proclaimed England's sovereignty over New Albion (California). **1617** James I met his Scottish Parliament. His proposal that the Scottish lords should surrender to the Crown their hereditable jurisdictions met with vigorous opposition, but the five Articles of Religion, for introducing Anglican principles to Scottish worship were endorsed. **1775** In the War of American Independence, British troops won a victory at Bunker Hill. **1940** Russian troops occupied the Baltic states.

≈ BIRTHS ≈

Edward I, **1239**; Pedro Calderón de la Barca, Spanish playwright, **1600**; Charles XII of Sweden, **1682**; John Wesley, English evangelist, **1703**; Charles François Gounod, French composer, **1818**; William Crookes, English chemist, **1832**; Igor Stravinsky, Russian composer, **1882**.

≈ DEATHS ≈

John Sobieski, king of Poland, **1696**; Joseph Addison, English essayist and poet, **1719**; Claude, Duc de Villars, French soldier, **1734**; Prosper Jolyot de Crébillon, French playwright, **1762**; Edward Burne-Jones, English painter, **1898**; Annie S Swan (Mrs Burnett Smith), Scottish novelist, **1943**; Imre Nagy, Hungarian prime minister, executed, **1958**.

'Don't fire until you see the whites of their eyes.'
William Prescott, (American revolutionary)
at the battle of Bunker Hill, 1775

18 June

'Sorrow is so easy to express and yet so hard to tell.'
Joni Mitchell

Feast day of Saints Mark and Marcellian, St Amandus of Bordeaux, St Eliisabeth of Schönau, and St Gregory Barbarigo.

EVENTS

860 Vikings from Russia were repulsed in an attack on Constantinople. **1429** The French, led by Joan of Arc, defeated the English at the Battle of Patay. **1633** Charles I was crowned King of Scotland at Edinburgh. **1815** The Duke of Wellington and Gebhard von Blücher defeated Napoleon at the Battle of Waterloo. **1928** US aviator Amelia Earhart became the first woman to fly across the Atlantic. **1953** A republic was proclaimed in Egypt, with General M Neguib as president.

BIRTHS

Robert Stewart, later Viscount Castlereagh, Irish politician, **1769**; Edouard Daladier, French politician, **1884**; Nikolaus Horthy de Nagybánya, Hungarian politician, **1868**; George Mallory, English mountaineer, **1886**; Ian Carmichael, English actor, **1920**; Isabella Rosselini, Italian film actress, **1952**.

DEATHS

John Hampden, English patriot and politician, **1643**; Andrew Jackson, 7th president of the USA, **1845**; George Grote, English historian and politician, **1871**; Samuel Butler, English novelist, **1902**; Roald Amundsen, Norwegian polar explorer, lost this day in the Arctic, **1928**; Maxim Gorky, Russian author, **1936**.

'No one can make you feel inferior without your consent.'
Eleanor Roosevelt

19 June

'You don't have power if you surrender all your principles - you have office.'
Ron Todd, reported on 19 June 1988

Feast day of Saints Gervase and Protase, St Juliana Falconieri, St Romuald, St Boniface of Querfurt, St Deodatus of Nevers, and St Odo of Cambrai.

EVENTS

1464 An ordinance of Louis XI in France created the poste, organising relays of horses on the main roads for the king's business. **1754** The Anglo-French war broke out in North America when a force under George Washington skirmished with French troops near Fort Duquesne. **1769** Hyder Ali of Mysore compelled the British at Madras to sign a treaty of mutual assistance. **1809** Curwen's Act was passed in Britain, to prevent the sale of Parliamentary seats, thus decreasing the number of seats which the British government can manipulate for its regular supporters. **1829** Robert Peel's Act was passed, to establish a new police force in London and its suburbs. **1867** Emperor Maximilian was executed in Mexico. **1917** The British royal family renounced German names and titles, having adopted the name of Windsor. **1965** Ben Bella, President of Algeria, was deposed; Houari Boumédienne headed a revolutionary council.

BIRTHS

James VI of Scotland and I of England, **1566**; Thomas Fuller, English antiquarian and clergyman, **1608**; Blaise Pascal, French mathematician, **1623**; Félicité Robert de Lamennais, French writer, **1783**; Douglas, Earl Haig, British field-marshal, **1861**; Ernst Chain, German-born British bacteriologist who developed penicillin, **1906**; Salman Rushdie, British novelist, **1947**.

DEATHS

Alberico Gentili, Italian political writer, **1608**; William Sherlock, English prelate, **1707**; Ambrose Philips, English poet, **1749**; Joseph Banks, English botanist, **1820**; John Dalberg, Lord Acton, English historian, **1902**; J M Barrie, Scottish author of *Peter Pan*, **1937**.

'Some of my plays peter out, and some pan out.'
J M Barrie

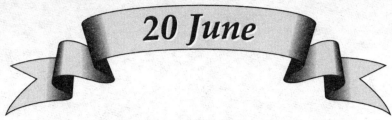

20 June

'I'll wager you that in ten years it will be fashionable again to be a virgin.'
Barbara Cartland, reported on 20 June 1976

Feast day of Edward the Martyr, St Alban, St Govan, St John of Matera, St Silverius, pope, St Bain, and St Adalbert of Magdeburg.

∞ EVENTS ∞

840 Vikings sailed up the Seine as far as Rouen, for the first time. **1530** The Diet of Augsburg met in the presence of Charles V, who was determined to exterminate heresy; Philip Melanchthon stated the Lutheran case, since Martin Luther was under the ban of the Empire. **1756** Over 140 British subjects were imprisoned in a cell ('The Black Hole of Calcutta'); only 23 came out alive. **1789** In France, the third estate took the Tennis Court oath, undertaking not to depart until a constitution was drawn up. **1791** Louis XVI attempted to leave France, but was turned back at Varennes and taken to Paris. **1837** On the death of William IV, Queen Victoria succeeded to the British throne. **1837** Hanover was automatically separated from Britain, as Salic Law forbids female succession, and the throne was taken by Ernest Augustus, Duke of Cumberland, the eldest surviving son of George III. **1837** Natal Republic was founded by Dutch settlers and a Constitution was proclaimed.

∞ BIRTHS ∞

Adam Ferguson, Scottish philosopher and historian, **1723**; John Costello, Irish politician, **1891**; Jacques Offenbach, German-born French composer, **1819**; Catherine Cookson, English novelist, **1906**; Errol Flynn, Australian-born US film actor, **1909**; Stephen Frears, English film director, **1941**.

∞ DEATHS ∞

Willem Barents, Dutch explorer, **1597**; Emmanuel Joseph Sieyès, French revolutionary leader, **1836**; William IV, **1837**; Nikolai Rimsky-Korsakov, Russian composer, **1908**; Pancho Villa, Mexican revolutionary leader, assassinated, **1923**; Bernard Baruch, US financier, **1965**.

'Whenever books are burned men also in the end are burned.'
Heinrich Heine

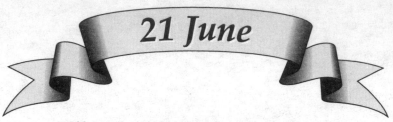

21 June

'I like men to behave like men - strong and childish.'
Françoise Sagan

Feast day of St Aloysius Gonzaga, St Leufred, St Mewan, St Engelmund, St John Rigby, St Eusebius of Samosata, and St Leutfridus.

〜 EVENTS 〜

1661 The Peace of Kardis was signed between Russia and Sweden, ending the northern war; Russia abandoned all claims to Livonia. **1788** The US constitution came into force, when ratified by the 9th state, New Hampshire. **1798** British General Gerard Lake defeated Irish rebels at Vinegar Hill and entered Wexford, ending the Irish Rebellion. **1813** The Duke of Wellington completely routed the French at Vittoria, forcing the Spanish king, Napoleon's brother Joseph, to return to France. **1827** Robert Peel reformed English criminal law, by reducing the number of capital offences, abolishing the immunity of the clergy from arrest in cases of felony, and by defining the law of offences against property in a simplified form. **1887** Queen Victoria's Golden Jubilee. **1887** Britain annexed Zululand, blocking the attempt of Transvaal to gain communication with the coast. **1919** The German fleet was scuttled in Scapa Flow, in the Orkneys. **1942** German forces under Field-Marshal Rommel captured Tobruk.

〜 BIRTHS 〜

Increase Mather, American clergyman and president of Harvard, **1639**; William Stubbs, English historian, **1825**; Claude Auchinleck, British field-marshal, **1884**; Jean-Paul Sartre, French philosopher, novelist, and playwright, **1905**; Jane Russell, US film actress, **1920**; Françoise Sagan, French novelist, **1935**.

〜 DEATHS 〜

Edward III, **1377**; John Skelton, English poet, **1529**; Sebastiano del Piombo, Italian painter, **1547**; John Smith, Virginian colonist, **1631**; Inigo Jones, English architect and stage designer, **1652**; Lord William Russell, English politician, **1683**; Alexius Petrovich, son of Peter the Great, died in prison, **1718**; Charles, Viscount Townshend, English politician, **1738**; George Hepplewhite, English cabinet-maker, **1786**; Friedrich Froebel, German educationalist, **1852**; Jean-Edouard Vuillard, French painter, **1940**.

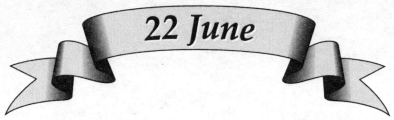

22 June

'I'd like to see the government get out of war altogether and
leave the whole field to private industry.'
Joseph Heller

Feast day of St Acacius, Saints John Fisher and Thomas More, St Paulinus of
Nola, St Nicetas of Remesiana, and St Eberhard of Salzburg.

❧ EVENTS ❧

1377 Richard II became king of England. **1671** Turkey declared war on Poland.
1679 The Duke of Monmouth subdued an insurrection of Scottish Covenanters
at Bothwell Bridge. **1826** The Pan-American Congress met in Panama under
the influence of Simon Bolivar in an unsuccessful effort to unite the American
Republics. **1894** Dahomey was proclaimed a French Colony. **1907** The
Northern Line was opened on the London Underground.

❧ BIRTHS ❧

André-Hercule de Fleury, French cardinal, **1653**; Jean Chardin, French painter,
1699; Jacques Delille, French poet, **1738**; Giuseppe Mazzini, Italian patriot,
1805; H Rider Haggard, English novelist, **1856**; John Hunt, English
mountaineer, **1910**; Peter Pears, English tenor, **1910**; Prunella Scales, English
actress, **1932**; Meryl Streep, US film actress, **1949**.

❧ DEATHS ❧

Roger I, king of Sicily, **1101**; Niccolò Machiavelli, Italian politician and
diplomat, **1527**; Jane Shore, mistress of Edward IV, **1527**; St John Fisher, bishop
of Rochester, beheaded, **1535**; Josiah Child, English merchant, **1699**; Walter de
la Mare, English author, **1956**; Fred Astaire, US dancer and film actor, **1987**.

'Even stones have a love, a love that seeks the ground.'
Meister Eckhart

23 June

'I submit to you that if a man hasn't discovered something he
will die for, he isn't fit to live.'
Martin Luther King, speech 23 June 1963

National Day of Luxembourg. Feast day of St Cyneburg, St Etheldreda, St Agrippina, St Lietbertus, St Joseph Cafasso, and St Thomas Garnet.

EVENTS

1611 English navigator Henry Hudson and eight others were cast adrift by mutineers; the mutineers returned to England, but Hudson and his companions were never seen again. **1757** British troops under Robert Clive captured Plassey, in Bengal, and recovered Calcutta. **1934** Saudi Arabia and the Yemen signed a peace agreement after a war of six weeks. **1935** British Foreign Secretary Anthony Eden offered Benito Mussolini concessions over Abyssinia, which he rejected. **1951** Guy Burgess and Donald Maclean, 'missing diplomats', fled to the USSR. **1952** The US Air Force bombed hydroelectric plants in North Korea.

BIRTHS

John Banér, Swedish general, **1596**; Giovanni Battista Vico, Italian philosopher, **1668**; Josephine de Beauharnais, wife of Napoleon, **1763**; Anna Akhmatova, Russian poet, **1889**; Jean Anouilh, French playwright, **1910**; John Habgood, archbishop of York, **1927**

DEATHS

Vespasian, Roman emperor, AD **79**; Pedro de Mendoza, Spanish explorer, **1537**; John Aubrey, English antiquary, **1697**; Hester Lucy Stanhope, English traveller, **1839**; Cecil Sharp, English collector of folk songs, **1924**.

'If you feel that you have both feet planted on the ground
then the university has failed you.'
Robert Cohen, *Time* 23 June 1961

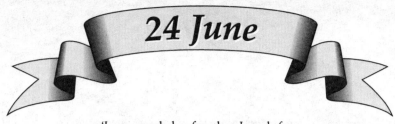

24 June

'I am scarcely less free than I was before,
for have I not been a prisoner all my life?'
Alexander II, tsar of Russia, reported on 24 June 1917

Feast day of St John the Baptist, St Bartholomew of Farne, St Simplicius of Autun, and St Ralph of Bourges.

✎ EVENTS ✎

1245 Pope Innocent sent John de Plano Carpinis, a friar minor, to the court of the Great Khan, at Karakorum; this embassy led to the establishment of Christian missions in China until c. 1368. **1277** English King Edward I began his first Welsh campaign following Llewelyn's refusal to do homage. **1314** Robert the Bruce defeated Edward II at Bannockburn and so completed his expulsion of the English from Scotland. **1535** Charles V leads an expedition to conquer Tunis from Barbarossa, with a fleet commanded by Andrea Doria. Charles restored the Bey, Mulai Hassan (deposed by the Turks in 1534) and completed the Spanish conquest of the North African coast (begun in 1494). **1559** The Elizabethan Prayer Book was first used. **1812** Napoleon crossed the River Niemen and entered Russian territory. **1917** The Russian Black Sea fleet mutinied at Sebastopol. **1956** Colonel Nasser was elected President of Egypt.

✎ BIRTHS ✎

Theodore Beza, French religious reformer, **1519**; Robert Dudley, Earl of Leicester, English explorer, **1532**; St John of the Cross (Juan de Yepez y Alvarez), **1542**; John Churchill, Duke of Marlborough, **1650**; Horatio, Lord Kitchener, British soldier, **1850**; William Penney. British physicist, **1909**; Juan Fangio, Argentinian racing driver, **1911**; Fred Hoyle, English astronomer, **1915**; Claude Chabrol, French film director, **1930**.

✎ DEATHS ✎

Ferdinand I, king of Castile and Leon, **1065**; Lucrezia Borgia, duchess of Ferrara, **1519**; John Partridge, English astrologer, **1715**; Stephen Grover Cleveland, 22nd and 24th president of the USA, **1908**; Rex Warner, British novelist, **1986**.

25 June

'BIG BROTHER IS WATCHING YOU.'
George Orwell

Feast day of St Adalbert, St Febronia, St Maximus of Turin, St Eurosia, St Gohard, St Gallicanus, St Prosper of Reggio, St Prosper of Aquitaine, St Moloc, St Thea, and St William of Vercelli.

EVENTS

1524 The Peasants' Revolt in southern Germany began at Stühlingen on the estates of Count von Lupfen. The rebels demanded the abolition of enclosures and feudal services. **1646** The surrender of Oxford to the Roundheads virtually signified the end of the English Civil War. **1788** Virginia became the 10th state of the USA. **1867** The first patent for barbed wire was taken out in Ohio, USA. **1876** US soldier George Custer and his 264 men were killed by Sioux Indians at the Battle of the Little Big Horn, Montana. **1975** Mozambique achieved independence from Portugal.

BIRTHS

John Horne Tooke, English politician, **1736**; Tsar Nicholas I **1796**; Lord Louis Mountbatten of Burma, **1900**; George Orwell, English essayist and novelist, **1903**; Sidney Lumet, US film director, **1924**.

DEATHS

Anthony Woodville, 2nd Earl Rivers, English politician, executed, **1183**; John Marston, English playwright, **1634**; George Custer, US soldier, **1876**; Margaret Oliphant, English novelist, **1897**; Laurence Alma-Tadema, English painter, **1912**; Tony Hancock, English comedian, **1968**.

'After all, science is essentially international, and it is
only through lack of historical sense that national qualities
have been attributed to it.'
Marie Curie

26 June

'Life is too short to stuff a mushroom.'
Shirley Conran

Feast day of Saints Salvius and Superius, Saints John and Paul, St Anthelmus, bishop, St Maxentius, and St Vigilius of Trent.

EVENTS

1483 Richard, Duke of Gloucester, began to rule as Richard III, having deposed his nephew, Edward V; the latter and his brother, Richard, Duke of York, were soon afterwards murdered in the Tower of London. **1519** Martin Luther's public disputation with Johann Eck on doctrine began at Leipzig. **1849** The British Navigation Acts were finally repealed. **1937** Spanish rebels took Santander. **1937** The Duke of Windsor married Mrs Wallis Simpson in France. **1960** Madagascar was proclaimed independent as the Malagasy Republic. **1960** British Somaliland became independent; it joined Somalia on 27 June. **1962** The Portuguese in Mozambique required Indian nationals to leave within three months of release from internment camps.

BIRTHS

Philip Doddridge, English Nonconformist, **1702**; William Thomson, Lord Kelvin, English physicist, **1824**; Pearl S Buck, US novelist, **1892**; Peter Lorre, US film actor, **1904**; Laurie Lee, English poet and author, **1914**; Claudio Abbado, Italian conductor, **1933**.

DEATHS

Francisco Pizarro, Spanish explorer who conquered Peru, assassinated, **1541**; Richard Fanshawe, English scholar and diplomat, **1666**; Ralph Cudworth, English philosopher, **1688**; Gilbert White, English clergyman and naturalist, **1793**; Joseph-Michel Montgolfier, French balloonist, **1810**; Ford Madox Ford, English novelist and poet, **1939**.

'Children have never been very good at listening to their elders, but they have never failed to imitate them.'
James Baldwin

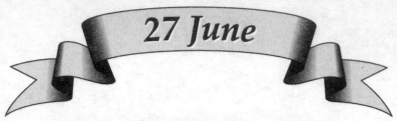
27 June

'I wasn't happy when the umpire told the spectators to be quiet. That only encourages them to make more noise.'
John McEnroe, reported on 27 June 1982

Feast day of St Cyril of Alexandria, St Zoilus, St Samson of Constantinople, St George Mtasmindeli, the Martyrs of Arras, St John of Chinon, and St Ladislas, King of Hungary.

✑ EVENTS ✑

1771 Russia completed its conquest of the Crimea. **1795** A British force landed at Quiberon to aid the revolt in Brittany. **1795** French forces recaptured St Lucia. **1801** Cairo fell to English forces. **1932** A Constitution was proclaimed in Siam. **1940** The USSR invaded Romania on the refusal of King Carol to cede Bessarabia and Bukovina; Romania appealed for German aid in vain. **1941** Hungary declared war on Russia. **1944** Allied forces took Cherbourg.

✑ BIRTHS ✑

Louis XII, king of France, **1462**; Charles Stewart Parnell, Irish nationalist leader, **1846**; John Monash, Australian civil engineer, **1865**; Helen Keller, US author and teacher, **1880**.

✑ DEATHS ✑

Giorgio Vasari, Italian painter and art historian, **1571**; Nathaniel Bailey, English lexicographer, **1742**; Samuel Hood, British admiral, **1816**; James Smithson, English scientist, **1829**; Joseph Smith, founder of the Mormons, **1844**; Malcolm Lowry, British novelist, **1957**; Mohammed Reza Pahlavi, former Shah of Iran, **1980**.

'Science may have found a cure for most evils; but it has found no remedy for the worst of them all - the apathy of human beings.'
Helen Adams Keller

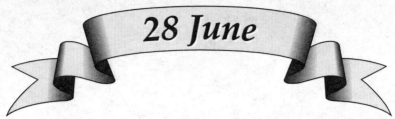

28 June

'All the world over, I will back the masses against the classes.'
William Gladstone

Feast day of St Austell, Saints Potamiaena and Basilides, St Irenaeus, St Heimrad, St John Southworth, Saints Sergius and Germanus of Valaam, and St Paul, pope.

⤳ EVENTS ⤳

1519 Charles I of Spain, Sicily and Sardinia, was elected Holy Roman Emperor as Charles V. **1645** In the English Civil War, the Royalists lost Carlisle. **1895** Union of Nicaragua, Honduras and El Salvador (ended in 1898 by El Salvador's opposition). **1914** Archduke Francis Ferdinand of Austria and his wife were assassinated at Sarajevo by Gavrilo Princip, a Bosnian revolutionary. **1919** Britain and the USA guaranteed France in event of an unprovoked German attack, which the USA later refused to ratify. **1948** Yugoslavia was expelled from Cominform for hostility to the USSR. **1950** North Korean forces captured Seoul. **1956** Sydney Silverman's bill for abolition of death penalty passed the Commons; it was defeated in the Lords, 10 July. **1956** Labour riots at Poznan, Poland, were put down with heavy loss of life.

⤳ BIRTHS ⤳

Sigismund of Luxembourg, Holy Roman Emperor, **1368**; Henry VIII, **1491**; Jean-Jacques Rousseau, French philosopher and writer, **1712**; Étienne-François, Duc de Choiseul, French politician, 1719; Luigi Pirandello, Italian playwright, **1867**; Harold Evans, British newspaper editor, **1929**.

⤳ DEATHS ⤳

Paul I, pope, **767**; Jean de Rotrou, French playwright, **1650**; James Madison, 4th president of the USA, **1836**; Robert Burke, Irish explorer of Australia, **1861**; Alfred Noyes, English poet, **1958**; Lord Raglan, British soldier, **1855**; Franz Ferdinand, heir to the Austrian throne, assassinated, **1914**; Boris Christoff, Bulgarian operatic bass, **1993**.

29 June

'Too often the strong silent man is silent only because he does not know what to say and is reputed strong only because he has remained silent.'
Winston Churchill, reported on 29 June 1924

Feast day of St Peter, St Paul, St Elwin, Saints Judith and Salome, and St Cassius of Narni.

EVENTS

1613 The Globe Theatre was destroyed by fire. **1880** France annexed Tahiti. **1943** US forces landed in New Guinea. **1945** Czechoslovakia ceded Ruthenia to the USSR. **1949** The USA completed its withdrawal of occupying forces from South Korea. **1949** British dock strike. **1949** The South African Citizenship Act suspended the automatic granting of citizenship to Commonwealth immigrants after five years, and imposed a ban on mixed marriages between Europeans and non-Europeans – the beginning of the Apartheid programme. **1954** Following the meeting of President Eisenhower and Winston Churchill in Washington the Potomac Charter, or six-point declaration of western policy, is issued.

BIRTHS

Peter Paul Rubens, English painter, **1577**; Giacomo Leopardi, Italian poet, **1798**; George Ellery Hale, US astronomer, **1868**; Antoine de Saint-Exupéry, French author and aviator, **1900**; Nelson Eddy, US singer and film actor, **1901**; Prince Bernhard of the Netherlands, **1911**.

DEATHS

Margaret, Countess of Richmond (The Lady Margaret), **1509**; Elizabeth Barrett Browning, English poet, **1861**; T H Huxley, English biologist, **1895**; Albert Sorel, French historian, **1906**; Paul Klee, Swiss painter, **1940**; Ignaz Jan Paderewski, Polish pianist, composer, and politician, **1941**; Jayne Mansfield, US film actress, **1967**.

'The goal was scored a little bit by the hand of God, another bit by the head of Maradona.'
Diego Maradona, reported on 29 June 1986

30 June

'Marx only became so influential because Lenin studied him.'
Aldous Huxley, reported on 30 June 1935

Feast day of St Theobald of Provins, the Martyrs of Rome, St Emma, St Bertrand of Le Mans, St Erentrude, and St Martial of Limoges.

EVENTS

1574 William of Orange persuaded the Estates of Holland to open the dykes to hinder the Spanish siege of Leyden. **1596** English expedition under Lord Howard of Effingham and the Earl of Essex sacked Cadiz, ravaged the Spanish coast, and captured much booty. Philip II was thus prevented from sending an Armada against England. **1782** Spain completed its conquest of Florida. **1797** The Nore mutiny was suppressed. **1846** The Mormons under Brigham Young left Nauvoo City on trail for the Great Salt Lake. **1934** A Nazi purge took place in Germany with summary executions of Kurt von Schleicher, Ernst Roehm and other party leaders for an alleged plot against Hitler. **1965** An India-Pakistan cease-fire was signed.

BIRTHS

Philip the Good, Duke of Burgundy, **1396**; Charles VIII, king of France, **1469**; Paul François Nicolas Barras, French politician, **1755**; Georges Duhamel, French novelist and poet, **1884**; Stanley Spencer, English painter, **1891**; Harold Laski, English politician, **1893**.

DEATHS

Montezuma II, Aztec ruler, assassinated, **1520**; Johann Reuchlin, German humanist and Hebrew scholar, **1522**; Willem Barents, Dutch explorer, **1597**; William Oughtred, English mathematician, **1660**; Nancy Mitford, English author, **1973**; Lillian Hellman, US playwright, **1984**.

'I have too much respect for the idea of God to make it responsible for such an absurd world.'
Georges Duhamel

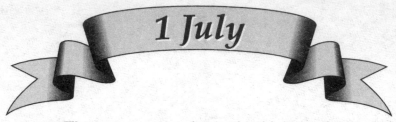
1 July

'We cannot tear out a single page of our life, but we can throw the whole book in the fire.'
George Sand

National Day of Canada. Feast day of St Gall of Clermont, Saints Aaron and Julius, St Eparchius or Cybard, St Oliver Plunket, St Carilephus or Calais, St Thierry or Theodoric of Mont d'Or, St Servanus or Serf, St Simeon Salus, and St Shenute.

EVENTS

1690 At the Battle of the Boyne, William III of England defeated the Jacobites under James II. **1751** The first volume of Diderot's *Encyclopédie* was published in Paris. **1838** Charles Darwin presented a paper to the Linnaean Society in London, on his theory of the evolution of species. **1863** The Battle of Gettysburg, in the American Civil War, began. **1916** The first Battle of the Somme began; more than 21,000 men were killed on the battle's first day. **1937** The telephone emergency service, 999, became operational in Britain. **1940** Guernsey was occupied by German forces. **1990** A state treaty establishing a unified economy and monetary system for East and West Germany went into effect. **1991** The Warsaw Pact, the last vestige of the Cold War-era Soviet bloc, was formally disbanded.

BIRTHS

George Sand, French novelist, **1804**; Louis Blériot, French aviator, **1872**; Charles Laughton, English film actor, **1899**; Olivia de Havilland, US film actress, **1916**; HRH the Princess of Wales, **1961**; Carl Lewis, US athlete, **1961**.

DEATHS

Charles Goodyear, US inventor, **1860**; Allan Pinkerton, US founder of the Detective Agency, **1884**; Harriet Beecher Stowe, US author, **1896**; Erik Satie, French composer, **1925**; Juan Perón, Argentinian politician, **1974**.

'Peace is indivisible.'
Maxim Litvinov

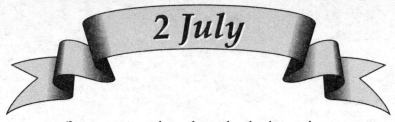

2 July

'I cannot get in and out of aircraft toilets but on three-
and-a-half-hour flights I can hold out.'
Luciano Pavarotti, reported on 2 July 1987

Feast day of Saints Processus and Martinian, St Monegundis, and St Otto of
Bamberg.

EVENTS

1644 Oliver Cromwell defeated Prince Rupert at theBattle of Marston Moor, his
first victory over the Royalists in the English Civil War. **1865** At a revivalist
meeting at Whitechapel, London, William Booth formed the Salvation Army.
1900 The 2nd Olympic Games opened in Paris. **1940** The Vichy Government
was set up in France, headed by Henri Pétain. **1956** Elvis Presley recorded
'Hound Dog' and 'Don't Be Cruel' in New York. **1964** President Johnson signed
the US Civil Rights Bill prohibiting racial discrimination. **1990** Over a
thousand Muslim pilgrims were killed when a stampede occurred in a pedestrian
tunnel leading to the holy city of Mecca.

BIRTHS

Thomas Cranmer, archbishop of Canterbury, **1489**; Christoph Gluçk, German
composer, **1714**; William Henry Bragg, English physicist, **1862**; Hermann
Hesse, German poet and novelist, **1877**; David Owen, British politician, **1938**;
Kenneth Clarke, British politician, **1940**.

DEATHS

Nostradamus, French physician and astrologer, **1566**; Jean Jacques Rousseau,
French philosopher and writer, **1778**; Amelia Earhart, US aviator, disappeared
over the Pacific, **1937**; Ernest Hemingway, US novelist, **1961**; Betty Grable, US
film actress, **1973**; Vladimir Nabokov, Russian novelist, **1977**.

'There are times in politics when you should say "never". '
David Owen

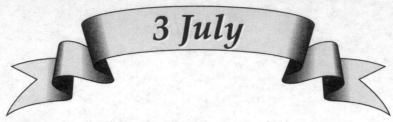

3 July

'Shyness is just egotism out of its depth.'
Penelope Keith, reported on 3 July 1988

Feast day of St Thomas the Apostle, St Anatolius of Constantinople, Saints Irenaeus and Mustiola, St Leo II, pope, St Anatolius of Laodicea, St Rumold or Rombaut, St Bernardino Realino, and St Helidorus of Altino.

EVENTS

1608 French explorer Samuel Champlain founded Québec. **1863** The Union forces, under General Meade, defeated the Confederates at the Battle of Gettysburg. **1905** In Odessa, over 6,000 people were killed by Russian troops to restore order during a general strike. **1954** Nearly nine years after the end of the World War II, food rationing in Britain finally ended. **1962** Following a referendum, France proclaimed Algeria independent. **1976** An Israeli commando force rescued 103 hostages from a hijacked aircraft, who were being held at Entebbe airport, Uganda. **1988** The USS *Vincennes*, patrolling the Gulf during the Iran–Iraq conflict, mistook an Iranian civil airliner for a bomber and shot it down, killing all 290 people on board.

BIRTHS

Robert Adam, Scottish architect and designer, **1728**; Leoš Janáček, Czech composer, **1854**; Franz Kafka, Czech writer, **1883**; Ken Russell, British film director, **1927**; Tom Stoppard, British dramatist, **1937**; Richard Hadlee, New Zealand cricketer, **1951**.

DEATHS

Marie de' Medici, Queen of France, **1642**; Theodor Herzl, Austrian Zionist leader, **1904**; Joel Chandler Harris, US author, **1908**; Brian Jones, English rock guitarist, **1961**; Jim Morrison, US singer, **1971**; Rudy Vallee, US singer, **1986**; Joe De Rita, US comedian, **1993**.

'There are no unemployed either in Russia or in Dartmoor
jail, and for the same reason.'
Philip Snowden, reported on 3 July 1932

4 July

'We hold these truths to be self-evident, that all men are created equal, that they are endowed by their creator with certain unalienable rights, that among these are life, liberty and the pursuit of happiness.'
American Declaration of Independence, 1776

Independence Day in the USA. Feast day of The Martyrs of Dorchester, St Andrew of Crete, St Elizabeth of Portugal, St Ulric of Augsburg, St Bertha of Blangy, and St Odo of Canterbury.

∾ EVENTS ∾

1776 The American Declaration of Independence was adopted. **1829** Britain's first regular scheduled bus service began running, between Marylebone Road and the Bank of England, in London. **1848** The Communist Manifesto was published by Karl Marx and Friedrich Engels. **1946** The Philippine Islands were given independence by the USA. **1968** Alec Rose landed at Portsmouth in *Lively Lady*, having sailed single-handed around the world. **1991** Colombia's President Cesar Gaviria Trujillo lifted state of siege that had been in effect since 1984.

∾ BIRTHS ∾

Nathaniel Hawthorne, US author, **1804**; Giuseppe Garibaldi, Italian soldier and patriot, **1807**; Gertrude Lawrence, English actress, **1898**; Louis Armstrong, US jazz trumpeter and singer, **1900**; Neil Simon, US dramatist, **1927**; Gina Lollobrigida, Italian film actress, **1927**.

∾ DEATHS ∾

Samuel Richardson, English novelist, **1761**; Thomas Jefferson, 3rd US president, **1826**; John Adams, 2nd US president, **1826**; James Monroe, 5th US president, **1831**; Marie Curie, Polish scientist, **1934**; Suzanne Lenglen, French tennis player, **1939**.

'If this is the way Queen Victoria treats her prisoners,
she doesn't deserve to have any.'
Oscar Wilde, upon being kept waiting for transport to prison

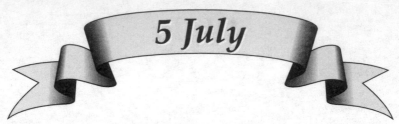

5 July

'Making money ain't nothing exciting to me. You might be able to buy a little better booze than the wino on the corner. But you get sick just like the next cat and when you die you're just as graveyard dead.'
Louis Armstrong, reported on 5 July 1970

National Day of Venezuela. Feast day of St Antony-Mary Zaccaria, and St Athanasius the Athonite.

EVENTS

1791 George Hammond was appointed the first British ambassador to the USA. **1946** A swimsuit designed by Louis Reard, called 'bikini', was first modelled at a Paris fashion show. **1948** Britain's National Health Service came into operation. **1965** Maria Callas, at the age of 41, gave her last stage performance singing Tosca at Covent Garden, London. **1967** Israel annexed Gaza. **1969** The Rolling Stones gave a free concert in Hyde Park two days after the death of guitarist Brian Jones; it was attended by 250,000 people. **1980** Bjorn Borg won the Wimbledon singles championship for a record fifth consecutive time. **1989** Convicted for his involvement in the Iran-Contra affair, US Army Colonel Oliver North was fined $150,000 and given a suspended sentence.

BIRTHS

Sarah Siddons, English actress, **1755**; Cecil Rhodes, South African statesman, **1853**; Dwight Davis, US statesman, **1879**; Jean Cocteau, French poet, novelist, artist, and film director, **1889**; Georges Pompidou, French statesman, **1911**; Elizabeth Emanuel, English dress designer, **1953**.

DEATHS

Thomas Stamford Raffles, British colonial administrator, **1826**; Austen Henry Layard, British archaeologist, **1894**; Georges Bernanos, French author, **1948**; Thomas Joseph Mboya, Kenyan statesman, **1969**; Walter Adolph Gropius, US architect, **1969**; Georgette Heyer, English novelist, **1974**.

'Life is a horizontal fall.'
Jean Cocteau

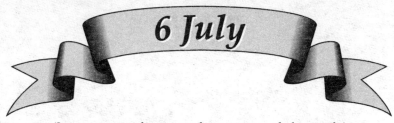

6 July

'I am not prepared to accept the economics of a housewife.'
Jacques Chirac, referring to Margaret Thatcher,
reported on 6 July 1987

National day of Malawi. Feast day of St Romulus of Fiesole, St Dominica, St Mary Goretti, St Goar, St Modwenna, St Godeleva, St Sexburga, and St Sisoes.

❧ EVENTS ❧

1535 Sir Thomas More was beheaded on London's Tower Hill for treason. **1553** Mary I acceded to the throne, becoming the first queen to rule England in her own right. **1685** James II defeated the Duke of Monmouth, claimant to the throne, at the Battle of Sedgemoor, the last battle to be fought on English soil. **1892** Britain's first non-white MP was elected – Dadabhai Naoraji won the Central Finsbury seat. **1928** The first all-talking feature film, *Lights of New York*, was presented at the Strand Theatre in New York City. **1965** The Beatles' film *A Hard Day's Night* was premiered in London, with royal attendance. **1988** An explosion aboard the North Sea oil rig Piper Alpha resulted in the loss of 166 lives.

❧ BIRTHS ❧

Nicholas I, Tsar of Russia, **1796**; Bill Haley, US rock musician, **1925**; Janet Leigh, US film actress, **1927**; Dalai Lama, Tibetan spiritual leader, **1935**; Vladimir Ashkenazy, Russian pianist, **1937**; Sylvester Stallone, US film actor, **1946**.

❧ DEATHS ❧

Guy de Maupassant, French writer, **1893**; Kenneth Grahame, Scottish children's author, **1932**; Aneurin Bevan, British statesman, **1960**; William Faulkner, US novelist, **1962**; Louis Armstrong, US jazz musician, **1971**; Otto Klemperer, German conductor, **1973**; John Bolton, English astronomer, **1993**.

'Musicians don't retire; they stop when there's no more music in them.'
Louis Armstrong

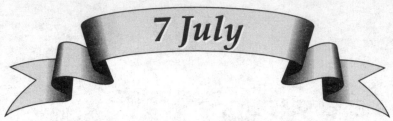
7 July

'Where there is no imagination there is no horror.'
Sir Arthur Conan Doyle

Feast day of St Hedda of Winchester, Saints Ethelburga, Ercongota and Sethrida, St Palladius, Saints Cyril and Methodius, St Pantaenus, and St Felix of Nantes.

≈ EVENTS ≈

1853 US naval officer Commodore Matthew Perry arrived in Japan, and persuaded her to open trade contacts with the West. **1927** Christopher Stone became the first 'disc jockey' on British radio when he presented his 'Record Round-up' from Savoy Hill. **1929** The Vatican City State, with the pope as its sovereign, came into being through the Lateran Treaty. **1982** Queen Elizabeth II was woken by a strange man sitting on her bed in Buckingham Palace; the presence of the intruder, who merely asked her for a cigarette, raised concerns about Palace security. **1985** The unseeded 17-year-old Boris Becker became the youngest ever men's singles champion at Wimbledon. **1990** Martina Navratilova won a record ninth Wimbledon singles title.

≈ BIRTHS ≈

Marc Chagall, Russian painter and designer, **1887**; George Cukor, US film director, **1899**; Vittorio de Sica, Italian film director, **1901**; Pierre Cardin, French fashion designer, **1922**; Ringo Starr, English drummer, **1940**; Tony Jacklin, English golfer, **1944**.

≈ DEATHS ≈

King Edward I, **1307**; Giacomo da Vignola, Italian architect, **1573**; R B Sheridan, English dramatist, **1816**; Georg Ohm, German physicist, **1854**; Arthur Conan Doyle, British author, **1930**; Flora Robson, British actress, **1984**.

'Faith is under the left nipple.'
Martin Luther

8 July

'By yesterday morning British troops were patrolling the streets of Belfast.
I fear that once Catholics and Protestants get used to our presence they will
hate us more than they hate each other.'
Richard Crossman

Feast day of St Adrian III, pope, St Raymund of Toulouse, Saints Aquila and Prisca or Priscilla, St Kilian and his Companions, St Sunniva and her Companions, St Withburga, St Grimbald, and St Procopius of Caesarea.

☞ EVENTS ☜

1497 Portuguese navigator Vasco da Gama left Lisbon for a voyage on which he discovered the Cape route to India. **1709** Charles XII of Sweden was defeated by Peter the Great's army at the Battle of Poltava, crushing Sweden's territorial ambitions. **1884** The National Society for Prevention of Cruelty to Children (NSPCC) was founded in London. **1907** Ziegfeld's Follies opened for the first time, on Broadway. **1943** Jean Moulin, the French Resistance leader known as 'Max', was executed by the Gestapo. **1978** Reinhold Messner and Peter Habeler became the first to climb Everest entirely without oxygen. **1991** Iraq admitted to the UN that it had been conducting clandestine programs to produce enriched uranium, a key element in nuclear weapons.

☞ BIRTHS ☜

Jean de la Fontaine, French writer, **1621**; Joseph Chamberlain, British statesman, **1836**; John D Rockefeller, US millionaire, **1839**; Arthur Evans, English archaeologist, **1851**; Percy Grainger, Australian composer, **1882**; Billy Eckstine, US singer, **1915**.

☞ DEATHS ☜

Percy Bysshe Shelley, English poet, **1822**; Anthony Hope, British novelist, **1933**; Henry Havelock Ellis, English physician and author, **1939**; Vivien Leigh, English film actress, **1967**; Michael Wilding, English film actor, **1979**; Judith Chrisholm, British aviator, **1988**; Fred Weick, US aeronautical engineer, **1993**.

'The day of small nations has long passed away. The day of Empires has come.'
Joseph Chamberlain, speech

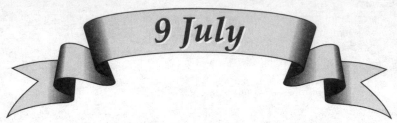

9 July

'Riots are the language of the unheard.'
Martin Luther King, reported on 9 July 1969

National Day of Argentina. Feast day of St Veronica de Julianis, St Nicholas Pieck and his Companions, St Everild, and the Martyrs of Gorcum.

EVENTS

1810 Napoleon annexed Holland, making his brother, Louis, its king. **1816** Argentina declared independence from Spain at the Congress of Tucuman. **1877** The first Wimbledon Lawn Tennis championship was held at its original site at Worple Road. **1922** Johnny Weissmuller, aged 18, swam the 100m in under a minute (58.6 sec). **1938** In anticipation of World War II, 35 million gas masks were issued to Britain's civilian population. **1979** In Nicaragua, General Somoza was overthrown by the Sandinista rebels. **1984** Lightning struck York Minster Cathedral and set the roof on fire, destroying the south transept. **1991** The International Olympic Committee lifted a 21-year-old boycott on South Africa.

BIRTHS

Elias Howe, US inventor, **1819**; Bruce Bairnsfather, British cartoonist, **1888**; Barbara Cartland, English novelist, **1901**; Edward Heath, British politician, **1916**; Michael Williams, British actor, **1935**; David Hockney, English painter, **1937**.

DEATHS

Jan van Eyck, Flemish painter, **1440**; Edmund Burke, British statesman, **1797**; Zachary Taylor, 12th US president, **1850**; King Camp Gilette, US safety-razor inventor, **1932**; Randall Thompson, US composer, **1984**.

'The greater the power, the more dangerous the abuse.'
Edmund Burke

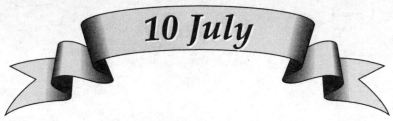
10 July

'Drama is life with the dull bits cut out.'
Alfred Hitchcock, reported on 10 July 1960

Feast day of St Felicity, The Seven Brothers, St Amelberga, and Saints Rufina and Secunda.

✒ EVENTS ✒

1460 In the Wars of the Roses, the Yorkists defeated the Lancastrians and captured Henry VI at the Battle of Northampton. **1553** Following the death of Edward VI, Lady Jane Grey was proclaimed Queen of England. **1900** The Paris underground railway, the Metro, was opened. **1958** Britain's first parking meters were installed, in Mayfair, London. **1962** The US communications satellite *Telstar* was launched, bringing Europe the first live television from the USA. **1976** Seveso, in northern Italy, was covered by a cloud of toxic weedkiller leaked from a chemicals factory; crops and 40,000 animals died. **1985** The Greenpeace campaign ship *Rainbow Warrior* sank in Auckland, New Zealand, after two explosions tore its hull.

✒ BIRTHS ✒

John Calvin, French religious reformer, **1509**; Camille Pissarro, French painter, **1830**; Marcel Proust, French author, **1871**; Carl Orff, German composer, **1895**; Arthur Ashe, US tennis player, **1943**; Arlo Guthrie, US singer, **1947**.

✒ DEATHS ✒

Hadrian, Roman emperor, **138**; El Cid, Spanish hero, **1099**; Louis Jacques Mandé Daguerre, French photographic pioneer, **1851**; Karl Richard Lepsius, German Egyptologist, **1884**; Jelly Roll Morton, US ragtime pianist and composer, **1941**; Giorgio de Chirico, Italian painter, **1978**; Masuji Ibuse, Japanese writer, **1993**.

'It is seldom indeed that one parts on good terms, because if
one were on good terms one would not part.'
Marcel Proust, A *la recherche du temps perdu*

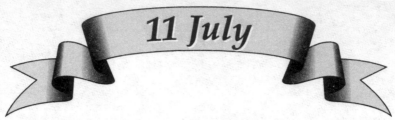

11 July

'Freedom is a bourgeois notion devised as a cloak for the
spectre of economic slavery.'
V I Lenin, reported on 11 July 1920

National Day of Mongolia. Feast day of St Benedict, St John of Bergamo, St
Drostan, St Olga, and St Hidulf.

✑ EVENTS ✑

1708 The Duke of Marlborough's forces defeated the French at the Battle of
Oudenarde, in the War of the Spanish Succession. **1776** Captain Cook sailed
from Plymouth in the *Resolution*, accompanied by the *Discovery*, on his last
expedition. **1848** London's Waterloo Station was officially opened. **1950** *Andy
Pandy*, the BBC's popular children's television programme, was first transmitted.
1975 Excavations at the tomb of Emperor Qin Shi Huangdi, near the ancient
Chinese capital of Xi'an, uncovered an army of 8,000 life-size terracotta warriors
dating to about 206 BC **1977** In Britain, *Gay News* was fined £1,000 for
publishing a poem which portrayed Jesus as homosexual. **1979** America's *Skylab
I* returned to earth after 34,981 orbits and six years in space.

✑ BIRTHS ✑

Robert the Bruce, King of Scotland, **1274**; Frederick I, King of Prussia, **1657**; John
Quincy Adams, 6th US president, **1767**; Yul Brynner, US film actor, **1915**; Peter de
Savary, British entrepreneur and yachtsman, **1944**; Leon Spinks, US boxer, **1953**.

✑ DEATHS ✑

Alfred Dreyfus, French soldier, **1935**; George Gershwin, US composer, **1937**;
Arthur John Evans, English archaeologist, **1941**; Paul Nash, English painter,
1946; Buddy DeSylva, US lyricist and film director, **1950**; Laurence Olivier,
English actor and director, **1989**.

'The attempt to build up a Communist Republic on the lines of strongly
centralised State Communism, under the iron rule of the dictatorship
of a party, is ending in a failure.'
Prince Kropotkin, reported on 11 July 1920

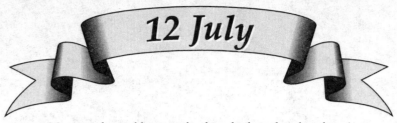

12 July

'Most people would sooner die than think: in fact they do so.'
Bertrand Russell, reported on 12 July 1925

Orangeman's Day in Northern Ireland. Feast day of St John the Iberian, St Jason, Saints Hermagoras and Fortunatus, St John Gualbert, St John Jones, St Veronica, and St Felix.

✖ EVENTS ✖

1543 Henry VIII married Catherine Parr, his sixth and last wife, at Hampton Court Palace. **1794** British admiral Horatio Nelson lost his right eye at the siege of Calvi, in Corsica. **1878** Cyprus was ceded to British administration by Turkey. **1920** US President Wilson opened the Panama Canal. **1930** Australian batsman Don Bradman scored a record 334 runs – of which a record 309 were scored in one day – against England at Leeds. **1970** Thor Heyerdahl and his crew crossed the Atlantic in 57 days, in a papyrus boat. **1991** Hitoshi Igarashi, the Japanese translator of Salman Rushdie's *Satanic Verses*, was found stabbed to death in Tokyo.

✖ BIRTHS ✖

Gaius Julius Caesar, Roman emperor, **100 BC**; Henry Thoreau, US author, **1817**; George Eastman, US photographic pioneer, **1854**; Amadeo Modigliani, Italian painter and sculptor, **1884**; Bill Cosby, US comedian and actor, **1937**; Jennifer Saunders, English comedienne and actress, **1958**.

✖ DEATHS ✖

Desiderius Erasmus, Dutch scholar, **1536**; Titus Oates, British conspirator, **1705**; Charles Stewart Rolls, British engineer and aviator, **1910**; Mazo de la Roche, Canadian novelist, **1961**; Kenneth More, British actor, **1982**.

'I still believe that, if your aim is to change the world,
journalism is a more immediate short-term weapon.'
Tom Stoppard, reported on 12 July 1981

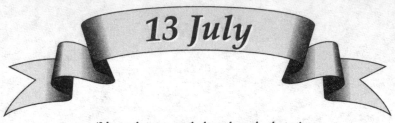

13 July

'I have done my task, let others do theirs.'
Charlotte Corday, on being interrogated for the
murder of Jean-Paul Marat

Feast day of Saints Bridget and Maura, St Henry the Emperor, St Silas or
Silvanus, St Francis Solano, and St Eugenius of Carthage.

EVENTS

1793 Jean-Paul Marat, French revolutionary leader, was stabbed to death in his
bath by Charlotte Corday. **1837** Queen Victoria became the first sovereign to
move into Buckingham Palace. **1871** The first cat show was held, organised by
Harrison Weir, at Crystal Palace, London. **1878** The Treaty of Berlin was signed,
granting Bosnia-Herzegovina to Austria-Hungary, and gaining the independence
of Romania, Serbia, and Montenegro from Turkey. **1930** The World Football
Cup was first held in Uruguay; the hosts beat the 13 other competing countries.
1985 Two simultaneous 'Live Aid' concerts, one in London and one in
Philadelphia, raised over £50 million for famine victims in Africa.

BIRTHS

John Dee, English alchemist, astrologer, and mathematician, **1527**; George
Gilbert Scott, English architect, **1811**; Sidney Webb, English social reformer,
1859; David Storey, English novelist and dramatist, **1933**; Harrison Ford, US
film actor, **1942**.

DEATHS

Richard Cromwell, Lord Protector of England, **1712**; James Bradley, English
astronomer, **1762**; Jean-Paul Marat, French revolutionary leader, **1793**; John
Charles Frémont, US explorer, **1890**; Arnold Schoenberg, Austrian composer,
1951; Seretse Khama, Botswanan politician, **1980**.

'My music is not modern. It is only badly played.'
Arnold Schoenberg

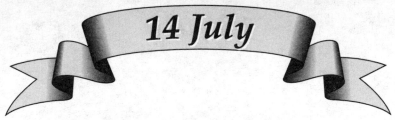

14 July

'It is far easier to make war than to make peace.'
Georges Clemenceau

National day of France (Bastille Day), and of Iraq. Feast day of St Marcellinus or Marchelm, St Camillus de Lellis, St Ulric of Zell, and St Deusdedit of Canterbury.

≋ EVENTS ≋

1789 The Bastille was stormed by the citizens of Paris and razed to the ground as the French Revolution began. **1823** During a visit to Britain, King Kamehameha II of Hawaii and his queen died of measles. **1867** Alfred Nobel demonstrated dynamite for the first time at a quarry in Redhill, Surrey. **1958** In a military coup led by General Kassem, King Faisal of Iraq was assassinated and a republic proclaimed. **1959** The USS *Long Beach*, the first nuclear warship, was launched. **1967** Abortion was legalized in Britain. **1972** Gary Glitter and the Glittermen (later called the Glitter Band) gave their first concert in Wiltshire. **1989** Over 300,000 Siberian coalminers went on strike, demanding better pay and conditions.

≋ BIRTHS ≋

Emmeline Pankhurst, English suffragette, **1858**; Isaac Bashevis Singer, Polish author, **1904**; Woody Guthrie, US folk singer, **1912**; Gerald Ford, 38th US president, **1913**; Ingmar Bergman, Swedish film director, **1918**; Bruce Oldfield, British fashion designer, **1950**.

≋ DEATHS ≋

Alfred Krupp, German industrialist, **1887**; Paul Kruger, Boer leader, **1904**; William Henry Perkin, English chemist and inventor of aniline dyes, **1907**; Grock, Swiss clown, **1959**; Adlai Stevenson, US statesman, **1965**.

'In each of us there is a little of all of us.'
Georg Lichtenberg

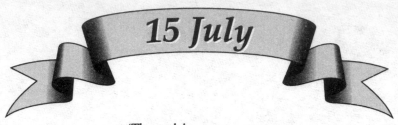

15 July

'The weak have one weapon:
the errors of those who think they are strong.'
Georges Bidault, reported on 15 July 1962

Feast day of St Swithin, St Athanasius of Naples, St Bonaventure, St Donald, St Edith of Polesworth, St Barhadbesaba, St David of Munktorp, St Vladimir of Kiev, and St Pompilio Pirrotti.

EVENTS

1099 Jerusalem was captured by the Crusaders with troops led by Godfrey and Robert of Flanders and Tancred of Normandy. **1795** The *Marseillaise*, written by Rouget de Lisle in 1792, was officially adopted as the French national anthem. **1857** During the Indian Mutiny, the second Massacre of Cawnpore (now Kanpur) took place, in which 197 English women and children were killed. **1869** Margarine was patented by Hippolyte Mège-Mouriès in Paris. **1948** Alcoholics Anonymous, in existence in the USA since 1935, was founded in London. **1965** US *Mariner* transmitted the first close-up pictures of Mars. **1990** In an ongoing campaign of violence, separatist Tamil Tigers massacred 168 Muslims in Colombo, the Sri Lankan capital.

BIRTHS

Inigo Jones, English architect, **1573**; Rembrandt, Dutch painter, **1606**; Hammond Innes, English novelist, **1913**; Iris Murdoch, Irish novelist, **1919**; Julian Bream, English guitarist, **1933**; Harrison Birtwistle, English composer, **1934**; Linda Ronstadt, US singer, **1946**.

DEATHS

General Tom Thumb, circus dwarf, **1883**; Anton Chekhov, Russian dramatist and author, **1904**; Hugo von Hofmannsthal, Austrian dramatist and poet, **1929**; John Pershing, US soldier, **1948**; Paul William Gallico, US writer, **1976**; Margaret Mary Lockwood, English film actress, **1990**.

'A diplomat is a man who can make his guests feel at home
when he wishes they were at home.'
Walter Gifford, reported on 15 July 1951

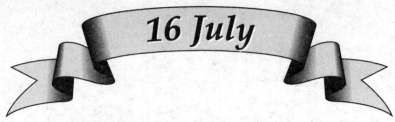
16 July

'You'd be surprised how much it costs to look this cheap.'
Dolly Parton

Feast day of St Mary Magdalen Postel, St Fulrad, St Athenogenes, St Helier, St Eustathius of Antioch, and St Reineldis.

EVENTS

622 Traditionally, the beginning of the Islamic Era, when Mohammed began his flight (the Hejira) from Mecca to Medina. **1661** Europe's first banknotes were issued, by the Bank of Stockholm. **1782** Mozart's opera *Die Entführung aus dem Serail* was first performed, in Vienna. **1918** The last tsar of Russia, Nicholas II, along with his entire family, family doctor, servants, and even the pet dog, was murdered by Bolsheviks at Ekaterinburg. **1945** The first atomic bomb developed by Robert Oppenheimer and his team at Los Alamos was exploded in New Mexico. **1965** The Mont Blanc road tunnel, linking France with Italy, was opened. **1990** An earthquake struck the main Philippine island of Luzon, killing over 1,500 people.

BIRTHS

Andrea del Sarto, Italian painter, **1486**; Joshua Reynolds, English painter, **1723**; Roald Amundsen, Norwegian polar explorer, **1872**; Barbara Stanwyck, US film actress, **1907**; Ginger Rogers, US film actress and dancer, **1911**; Margaret Court, Australian tennis player, **1942**.

DEATHS

Pope Innocent III, **1216**; Anne of Cleves, 4th wife of Henry VIII, **1557**; Josiah Spode, English potter, **1827**; Hilaire Belloc, British author, **1953**; John Phillips Marquand, US writer, **1960**; Herbert von Karajan, Austrian conductor, **1989**.

'Once: a philosopher; twice: a pervert!'
Voltaire, turning down an invitation to a second orgy

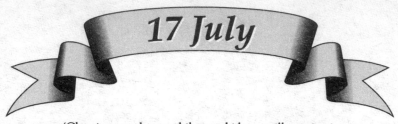

17 July

'Cleaning your house while your kids are still growing is like shoveling the walk before it stops snowing.'
Phyllis Diller

Feast day of The Seven Apostles of Bulgaria, St Clement of Okhrida and his Companions, St Leo IV, pope, St Ennodius, St Kenelm, St Speratus and his Companions, St Marcellina, and St Nerses Lampronazi.

∞ EVENTS ∞

1453 With the defeat of the English at the Battle of Castillon, the Hundred Years' War between France and England came to an end. **1841** The first issue of the humorous magazine *Punch* was published in London. **1917** The British royal family changed their name from 'House of Saxe-Coburg-Gotha' to 'House of Windsor'. **1945** The Potsdam Conference of Allied leaders Truman, Stalin, and Churchill (later replaced by Attlee) began. **1975** The US *Apollo* spacecraft and the Russian *Soyuz* craft successfully docked while in orbit. **1981** The Humber Estuary Bridge, the world's longest single-span structure, was officially opened by the Queen. **1990** Iraqi President Saddam Hussein threatened to use force against Kuwait and the United Arab Emirates, to stop them driving oil prices down by overproduction.

∞ BIRTHS ∞

Maxim Litvinov, Soviet leader, **1876**; Erle Stanley Gardner, US novelist, **1889**; James Cagney, US film actor, **1899**; Phyllis Diller, US comedienne, **1917**; Donald Sutherland, Canadian film actor, **1935**; Wayne Sleep, British dancer and choreographer, **1948**.

∞ DEATHS ∞

Adam Smith, Scottish economist, **1790**; Charlotte Corday, murderess of Marat, executed, **1793**; James McNeill Whistler, US painter, **1903**; Dragolub Mihajlovic, Serbian nationalist, executed, **1946**; Billy Holiday, US jazz singer, **1959**.

'To say of a picture, as is often said in its praise, that it shows great and earnest labor, is to say that it is incomplete and unfit for view.'
James McNeill Whistler, *The Gentle Art of Making Enemies*

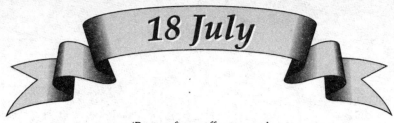

18 July

'Borrow fivers off everyone.'
Richard Branson in answer to the question: 'What
is the quickest way to become a millionaire?'

National day of Spain. Feast day of St Bruno of Segni, St Pambo, St Arnoul or
Arnulf of Metz, and St Frederick of Utrecht.

❧ EVENTS ❧

64 The great fire began in Rome and lasted for nine days. **1870** The Vatican
Council proclaimed the Dogma of Papal Infallibility in matters of faith and
morals. **1923** Under the Matrimonial Causes Bill, British women were given
equal divorce rights with men. **1925** *Mein Kampf*, Hitler's political testament,
was published. **1936** The Spanish Civil War began with an army revolt led by
Francisco Franco against the Republican government. **1955** Disneyland, the
160-acre amusement park, opened near Anaheim, California. **1984** In San
Ysidro, California, a security guard walked into a McDonalds and began shooting
randomly, killing 20 people and wounding 16.

❧ BIRTHS ❧

Gilbert White, English naturalist, **1720**; W M Thackeray, English novelist and
poet, **1811**; Nelson Mandela, South African politician, **1918**; John Glenn, US
astronaut and politician, **1921**; Richard Branson, British entrepreneur, **1950**;
Nick Faldo, English golfer, **1957**.

❧ DEATHS ❧

Michelangelo Merisi da Caravaggio, Italian painter, **1610**; Antoine Watteau,
French painter, **1721**; Peter III, Tsar of Russia, murdered, **1762**; Jane Austen,
English novelist, **1817**; Thomas Cook, British pioneer travel agent, **1892**; Jack
Hawkins, British film actor, **1973**; Jean Negulesco, Romanian-born US film
director, **1993**.

'Life resembles a novel more often than novels resemble life.'
George Sand

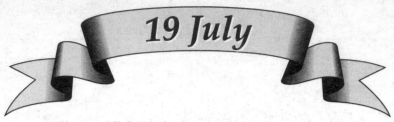

19 July

'You can tell the ideals of a nation by its advertisements.'
Norman Douglas, *South Wind*

Feast day of Saints Justa and Rufina, St Ambrose Autpert, St Macrina the Younger, St Arsenius the Great, St James of Nisibia, St Symmachus, pope, and St John Plesington.

EVENTS

1545 The *Mary Rose*, the pride of Henry VIII's battle fleet, keeled over and sank in the Solent with the loss of 700 lives. (The ship was raised 11 Oct 1982 to be taken to Portsmouth Dockyard.) **1837** Brunel's 70 m/236 ft steamship, the *Great Western*, was launched at Bristol. **1848** At a convention in Seneca Falls, New York, female rights campaigner Amelia Bloomer introduced 'bloomers' to the world. **1903** The first Tour de France cycle race was won by Maurice Garin. **1949** Laos gained independence. **1991** A major political scandal erupted in South Africa after the government admitted that it had made secret payments to the Zulu-based Inkatha Freedom Party.

BIRTHS

Samuel Colt, US inventor, **1814**; Edgar Degas, French painter, **1834**; Lizzie Borden, alleged US axe murderess, **1860**; Charles Horace Mayo, US physician, **1865**; A J Cronin, Scottish novelist, **1896**; Ilie Nastase, Romanian tennis player, **1946**.

DEATHS

Petrarch, Italian poet, **1374**; Matthew Flinders, English navigator and explorer of Australia, **1814**; Tom Hayward, English cricketer, **1939**; Syngman Rhee, Korean politician, **1965**; Clarence White, US pop guitarist, **1973**; Szymon Goldberg, Polish-born violinist and conductor, **1993**.

'I don't want to achieve immortality through my work ... I want to achieve it through not dying.'
Woody Allen

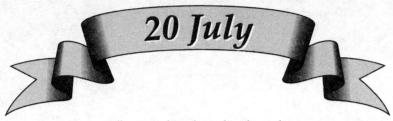
20 July

'Idleness is the refuge of weak minds.'
Earl of Chesterfield

National day of Colombia Feast day of St Margaret of Antioch, St Elias of Jerusalem, St Ansegisus, St Aurelius of Carthage, St Flavian of Antioch, St Wulmar, St Gregory Lopez, St Wilgefortis or Liberata, and St Joseph Barsabas the Just.

⇛ EVENTS ⇚

1837 London's first railway station, Euston, was opened. **1845** Charles Sturt became the first European to enter Simpson's Desert in central Australia. **1885** Professional football was legalized in Britain. **1940** In the USA, *Billboard* published the first singles-record charts. **1944** German staff officer Colonel von Stauffenberg attempted to assassinate Hitler, in Rastenburg, Germany. **1968** During a BBC radio interview, actress Jane Asher announced that her engagement to Beatle Paul McCartney was off; he was not the first to find out. **1975** After an 11-month journey, the US uncrewed *Viking 1* made a soft landing on Mars.

⇛ BIRTHS ⇚

Petrarch, Italian poet, **1304**; Alberto Santos-Dumont, Brazilian aviator, **1873**; John Reith, Scottish engineer and 1st director general of the BBC, **1889**; Edmund Hillary, New Zealand mountaineer, **1919**; Jacques Delors, French politician, **1925**; Diana Rigg, English actress, **1938**.

⇛ DEATHS ⇚

Pope Leo XIII, **1903**; Andrew Lang, Scottish historian and folklore scholar, **1912**; Guglielmo Marconi, Italian inventor, **1937**; Ian Macleod, British statesman, **1970**; Bruce Lee, US 'Chinese Western' actor, **1973**; Harry Worth, English comedian, **1989**.

'Hope is a waking dream.'
Aristotle

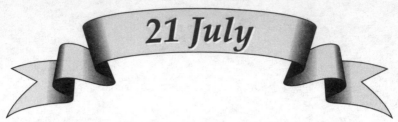

21 July

'That's one small step for man, one giant leap for all mankind.'
Neil Armstrong, reported on 21 July 1969

National day of Belgium. Feast day of St Laurence of Brindisi, St Victor of Marseilles, St Arbogastes, and St Praxedes.

EVENTS

1798 The Battle of the Pyramids took place, in which Napoleon, soon after his invasion of Egypt, defeated an army of some 60,000 Mamelukes. **1861** The Confederates defeated the Union troops in the first Battle of Bull Run, in the American Civil War. **1897** London's Tate Gallery, built on the site of the Millbank Prison, was opened. **1944** Guam, in the western Pacific, which had been under Japanese occupation since Dec 1941, was retaken by US Marines. **1960** Sirimavo Bandaranaike replaced her murdered husband as prime minister of Sri Lanka, becoming the first woman to hold this office. **1969** The lunar module *Apollo 11* landed on the Moon, and US astronauts Armstrong and Aldrin took their first exploratory walk. **1990** More than 150,000 people attended 'The Wall', a large-scale concert staged by rock performers in East Berlin to celebrate the dismantling of the Berlin Wall.

BIRTHS

Paul Julius von Reuter, German news agency founder, **1816**; Ernest Hemingway, US novelist, **1899**; Kay Starr, US singer, **1922**; Norman Jewison, canadian film director, **1926**; Jonathan Miller, English TV, film and theatre director, **1934**; Cat Stevens, English rock singer and songwriter, **1948**.

DEATHS

Robert Burns, Scottish poet, **1796**; Ellen Tracy, English actress, **1928**; George Macaulay Trevelyan, British historian, **1962**; Albert Luthuli, South African politician, **1967**; Basil Rathbone, English actor, **1967**.

'The removal of the perpetual fear of losing one's job is the greatest human problem that will have to be solved in the course of this century.'
Lord Trent, reported on 21 July 1935

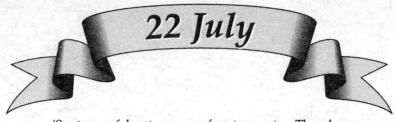

22 July

'Sex is one of the nine reasons for reincarnation. The other eight are unimportant.'
Henry Miller

National Day of Poland. Feast day of St Mary Magdalen, St Joseph of Palestine, St Philip Evans, St Vandrille or Wandregesilus, and St John Lloyd.

≈ EVENTS ≈

1812 The Duke of Wellington defeated the French in the Battle of Salamanca, in Spain. **1933** Wiley Post completed the first around the world solo aeroplane flight – the journey took 7 days, 18 hrs and 49.5 min. **1934** US bank robber and 'public enemy no 1', John Dillinger, was gunned down by an FBI squad in Chicago. **1946** Bread rationing started in Britain. **1976** The musical show *A Chorus Line* was staged in London for the first time. **1991** Prime Minister John Major unveiled the government's 'Citizen's Charter' aimed at improving public services.

≈ BIRTHS ≈

Philip I, King of Spain, **1478**; Gregor Mendel, Austrian monk and botanist, **1822**; Selman Abraham Waksman, US biochemist, **1888**; Alexander Calder, US sculptor, **1898**; Bryan Forbes, British author, director and producer, **1926**; Terence Stamp, British actor, **1938**.

≈ DEATHS ≈

Marie François Xavier Bichat, French anatomist, **1802**; Florenz Ziegfeld, US theatrical producer, **1932**; Mackenzie King, Canadian statesman, **1950**; Carl Sandburg, US poet, **1967**; Mortimer Wheeler, British archaeologist, **1976**.

'Continental people have sex life; the English have hot-water bottles.'
George Mikes

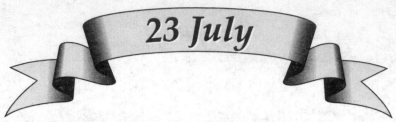

23 July

'Interpretation is the revenge of the intellect upon art.'
Susan Sontag

National Day of Ethiopia and of The United Arab Republic. Feast day of St Anne or Susanna, St John Cassian, St Romula and her Companions, St Apollinaris of Ravenna, The Three Wise Men, St Bridget of Sweden, and St Liborius.

➣ EVENTS ➣

1745 Charles Stuart, the Young Pretender, landed in the Hebrides. **1864** Dr Livingstone returned to England. **1940** The Local Defence Volunteers were renamed the Home Guard by Winston Churchill. **1952** King Farouk of Egypt was deposed by General Neguib. **1967** In the heat of the mountain stage of the Tour de France, British cyclist Tony Simpson, 29, collapsed and died. **1986** Prince Andrew married Lady Sarah Ferguson in Westminster Abbey, and was created Duke of York.

➣ BIRTHS ➣

Arthur Whitten Brown, British aviator, **1886**; Raymond Chandler, US novelist, **1888**; Haile Selassie, Ethiopian emperor, **1892**; Michael Wilding, English actor, **1912**; Richard Rogers, English architect, **1933**; Graham Gooch, English cricketer, **1953**.

➣ DEATHS ➣

Domenico Scarlatti, Italian composer, **1757**; Isaac Singer, US inventor, **1875**; Ulysses Grant, general and 18th US president, **1885**; D W Griffith, US film director, **1948**; Eddie Rickenbacker, US World War I fighter pilot, **1973**; Jahangir, Pakistani cricketer, **1988**; Raul Gardini, Italian businessman, **1993**.

'What are the thoughts of the canvas on which a masterpiece is being painted? "I am being soiled, brutally treated and concealed from view." Thus men grumble at their destiny, however fair.'
Jean Cocteau, *Cock and Harlequin*

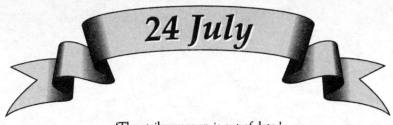
24 July

'The strike weapon is out of date.'
Joseph Jones, Yorkshire miners' leader,
reported on 24 July 1938

Feast day of St Christina the Astonishing, St Boris or Romanus, St Declan, St Christina of Bolsena, St Lewinna, and St Gleb or David.

EVENTS

1534 Jacques Cartier landed at Gaspé in Canada and claimed the territory for France. **1704** Admiral Sir George Rooke captured Gibraltar from the Spaniards. **1824** The result of the world's first public opinion poll, on voters' intentions in the 1824 US Presidential election, was published in the *Harrisburg Pennsylvanian*. **1851** The window tax in Britain was abolished. **1925** A six-year-old girl became the first patient to be successfully treated with insulin, at Guy's Hospital, London. **1990** A Catholic nun and three policemen were killed by an IRA landmine hidden at the side of a road in County Armagh.

BIRTHS

Simón Bolívar, South American liberator, **1783**; Alexandre Dumas *Père*, French author, **1802**; Frank Wedekind, German dramatist, **1864**; Emelia Earhart, US aviator, **1898**; Peter Yates, British film director, **1919**; Lynda Carter, US actress and singer, **1951**.

DEATHS

Martin van Buren, 8th US president, **1862**; Matthew Webb, English swimmer, **1883**; Sacha Guitry, French actor and dramatist, **1957**; Constance Bennett, US film actress, **1965**; James Chadwick, English physicist, **1974**; Peter Sellers, English actor, **1980**.

'The most important thing in the Olympic Games is not winning
but taking part ... The essential thing in life is not
conquering but fighting well.'
Pierre de Coubertin, speech on this day 1908

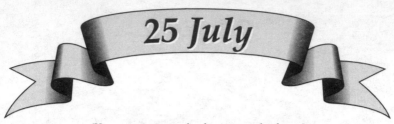
25 July

'You cannot control a free society by force.'
Robert Mark, police commissioner

Feast day of St Christopher, Saints Thea, Valentina and Paul, St James the Greater, and St Magnericus.

☞ EVENTS ☜

1139 Alfonso I of Portugal defeated the Moors at Ourique. **1581** A confederation of the northern provinces of the Netherlands proclaimed their independence from Spain. **1909** French aviator Louis Blériot made the first Channel crossing in an aeroplane, which he had designed. **1917** Margaretha Zelle, the Dutch spy known as Mata Hari, was sentenced to death. **1943** Benito Mussolini was forced to resign as Dictator of Italy, bringing an end to the Fascist regime. **1948** Bread rationing in Britain ended. **1952** The European Coal and Steel Community, established by the treaty of Paris **1951**, was ratified. **1978** The first test-tube baby in Britain was born – Louise Joy Brown, at Oldham General Hospital, Lancashire.

☞ BIRTHS ☜

Arthur James Balfour, British statesman, **1848**; Walter Brennan, US film actor, **1894**; Johnny 'Rabbit' Hodges, US jazz saxophonist, **1907**; Annie Ross, British singer, **1930**; Colin Renfrew, British archaeologist, **1937**; Steve Goodman, US songwriter, **1948**.

☞ DEATHS ☜

Flavius Valerius Constantinus, Roman emperor, **306**; Samuel Taylor Coleridge, English poet, **1834**; Charles Macintosh, Scottish chemist and inventor, **1843**; Henry Mayhew, British social investigator and founder of *Punch*, **1887**; Engelbert Dolfuss, Austrian statesman, **1934**.

'If you are lucky enough to have lived in Paris as a young man, then wherever you go for the rest of your life, it stays with you, for Paris is a moveable feast.'
Ernest Hemingway

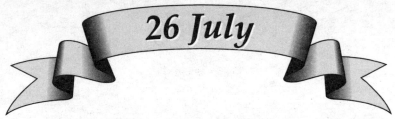

26 July

'When a stupid man is doing something he is ashamed of, he
always declares that it is his duty.'
George Bernard Shaw

National Day of Liberia. Feast day of St Anne, St Simeon the Armenian, St
Joachim, and St Bartholomea Capitanio.

❦ EVENTS ❦

1745 The first recorded women's cricket match was played near Guildford, Surrey,
between teams from Hambledon and Bramley. **1847** Liberia became the first
African colony to secure independence. **1908** The US Federal Bureau of
Investigation, concerned in particular with internal security, was founded. **1945**
The Labour Party won a landslide victory in Britain's General Election. **1956**
President Nasser of Egypt nationalized the Suez Canal which led to confrontation
with Britain, France, and Israel. **1958** Debutantes were presented at the British
Royal Court for the last time. **1987** Cyclist Steve Roche became the first Irishman,
and only the second non-continental European, to win the Tour de France.

❦ BIRTHS ❦

George Bernard Shaw, Irish dramatist, **1856**; Carl Jung, Swiss psychologist, **1875**;
Aldous Huxley, English novelist, **1894**; Stanley Kubrick, US film director, **1928**;
Mick Jagger, British rock singer, **1943**; Vitas Gerulaitis, US tennis player, **1954**.

❦ DEATHS ❦

Samuel Houston, US general and president of the Republic of Texas, **1863**;
George Borrow, English writer, **1881**; Eva Perón, Argentinian populist leader,
1952; Charles Clore, English financier, **1979**; Averell Harriman, US statesman
and diplomat, **1986**.

'It is uncertain whether the development and spread of
electronic and computer technology will increase the spread of
literacy or diminish the need for it and result in an oral
culture overwhelming the present written one.'
Eugene Radwin, US educationalist

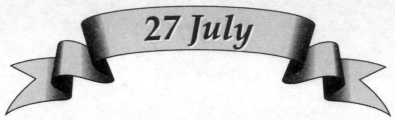
27 July

'I don't want to have anything to do with Mrs Thatcher.'
Robert Maxwell, reported on 27 July 1986

Feast day of The Seven Sleepers of Ephesus, St Theobald of Marly, The Martyrs of Salsette, Saints Aurelia, Natalia and their Companions, and St Pantaleon.

≋ EVENTS ≋

1694 The Bank of England was founded by act of Parliament. **1866** The *Great Eastern* arrived at Heart's Content in Newfoundland, having successfully laid the transatlantic telegraph cable. **1942** The Battle of El Alamein ended after 17 days, with the British having prevented the German and Italian advance into Egypt. **1953** The Korean armistice was signed at Panmujom, ending three years of war. **1985** Ugandan President Milton Obote was overthrown for a second time, this time by a coup led by Brigadier Tito Okello. **1988** British pole-vault record holder Jeff Gutteridge was banned for life by the British Amateur Athletic Board for taking steroids.

≋ BIRTHS ≋

Alexandre Dumas *fils*, French dramatist, **1824**; Hilaire Belloc, English poet and author, **1870**; Anton Dolin, British dancer and choreographer, **1904**; Bobbie Gentry, US singer, **1942**; Alan Border, Australian cricketer, **1955**; Christopher Dean, British ice skater, **1958**.

≋ DEATHS ≋

John Dalton, English physicist and chemist, **1844**; William Matthew Flinders Petrie, English Egyptologist, **1942**; Gertude Stein, US novelist and poet, **1946**; Mohammad Reza Pahlavi, Shah of Iran, **1980**; James Mason, English actor, **1984**; Osbert Lancaster, British writer and artist, **1986**.

'I've been thrown out of better places than this.'
Peter Langan, restaurateur, after a misunderstanding
at the Savoy Hotel, reported on 27 July 1986

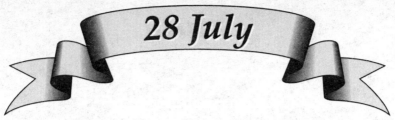
28 July

'Every country gets the government it deserves.'
Joseph de Maistre

National Day of Peru. Feast day of Saints Nazarius and Celsus, St Botvid, and St Samson of Dol.

⚘ EVENTS ⚘

1786 The first potato arrived in Britain, brought from Colombia by Sir Thomas Harriot. **1794** Maximilien Robespierre and 19 other French Revolutionaries went to the guillotine. **1821** San Martin and his forces liberated Peru and proclaimed its independence from Spain. **1858** Fingerprints were first used as a means of identification by William Herschel, who later established a fingerprint register. **1868** The 14th Amendment to the US Constitution, dealing with citizens' rights of all races, was ratified. **1914** Austria-Hungary declared war on Serbia, beginning World War I. **1976** The Tian Shan area of China was struck by an earthquake which caused over 800,000 deaths.

⚘ BIRTHS ⚘

Gerard Manley Hopkins, English poet, **1844**; Beatrix Potter, English author and illustrator, **1866**; Marcel Duchamp, French painter, **1887**; Rudy Vallee, US singer, **1901**; Garfield Sobers, West Indian cricketer, **1936**; Riccardo Muti, Italian conductor.

⚘ DEATHS ⚘

Thomas Cromwell, Chancellor to King Henry VIII, executed, **1540**; Cyrano de Bergerac, French poet and soldier, **1655**; Antonio Vivaldi, Italian composer, **1741**; Johann Sebastian Bach, German composer, **1750**; Nathan Mayer Rothschild, British banker, **1836**; Otto Hahn, German nuclear physicist, **1944**.

'In anything it is a mistake to think one can perform an action or behave in a certain way once and no more. What one does, one will do again, indeed has probably already done in the distant past.'
Cesare Pavese

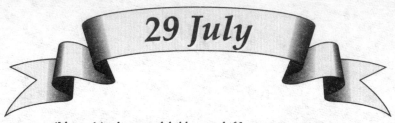
29 July

'I have 14 other grandchildren and if I pay one penny now, then I'll have 14 kidnapped grandchildren.'
Paul Getty, reported on 29 July 1973

Feast day of St Martha, Saints Beatrice and Simplicius, Saints Faustinus and Beatrice, St Felix, antipope, St William of Saint-Brieuc, St Lupus of Troyes, and St Olav, King of Norway.

EVENTS

1588 The Spanish Armada was defeated by the English fleet under Howard and Drake, off Plymouth. **1900** King Umberto I of Italy was assassinated by an anarchist and succeeded by Victor Emmanuel. **1948** The 14th Olympic Games opened in London – the first in 12 years, due to World War II. **1949** The first regular televised weather forecast was broadcast by the BBC. **1968** Pope Paul VI reaffirmed the Church's traditional teaching on (and condemnation of) birth control. **1981** The Prince of Wales married Lady Diana Spencer at London's St Paul's Cathedral; the televised ceremony was watched by over 700 million viewers around the world.

BIRTHS

Alexis de Tocqueville, French historian and politician **1805**; Booth Tarkington, US author, **1869**; Benito Mussolini, Italian leader, **1883**; Sigmund Romberg, US composer, **1887**; Dag Hammarskjöld, Swedish UN secretary-general, **1905**; Mikis Theodorakis, Greek composer, **1925**.

DEATHS

Robert Schumann, German composer, **1833**; Vincent van Gogh, Dutch painter, **1890**; John Barbirolli, English conductor, **1970**; Raymond Massey, Canadian actor, **1983**; David Niven, British film actor, **1983**; Luis Buñuel, Spanish film director, **1983**.

'I invented my life by taking for granted that everything I did not like would have an opposite, which I would like.'
Coco Chanel

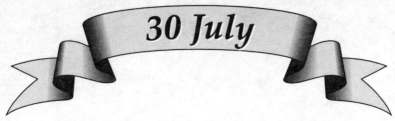

30 July

'I have come to regard the law courts not as a cathedral but rather as a casino.'
Richard Ingrams

Feast day of St Julitta of Caesarea, St Tatwin, Archbishop of Canterbury, Saints Abdon and Sennen, and St Peter Chrysologus.

☙ EVENTS ❧

1793 Toronto (known as York until 1834) was founded by General John Simcoe. **1935** 'Penguin' paperback books, founded by Allen Lane, went on sale in Britain. **1948** The world's first radar station was opened, to assist shipping at the port of Liverpool. **1963** Kim Philby, British intelligence officer from 1940 and Soviet agent from 1933, fled to the USSR. **1966** England won the Football World Cup in London, beating West Germany 4–2. **1990** Ian Gow, Conservative MP for Eastbourne, a close friend and personal advisor to Prime Minister Thatcher, was killed by a car bomb at his home.

☙ BIRTHS ❧

Giorgio Vasari, Italian painter, architect, and writer, **1511**; Emily Brontë, English novelist, **1818**; Henry Ford, US car manufacturer, **1863**; Henry Moore, English sculptor, **1898**; Daley Thompson, British athlete, **1958**; Kate Bush, English singer, **1958**.

☙ DEATHS ❧

William Penn, English Quaker leader, **1718**; Thomas Grey, English poet, **1771**; Denis Diderot, French encyclopedist, **1784**; Otto von Bismarck, German politician, **1898**; Lynn Fontanne, US actress, **1983**; Howard Dietz, US lyricist, **1983**.

'It is salutary to remember that the Hiroshima explosion of 1945 is widely known in Japan as the "Christian Bomb".'
The Very Reverend Lord Macleod of Fuinary
reported on 30 July 1978

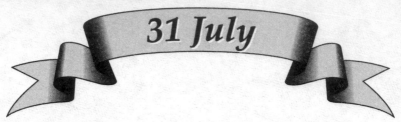
31 July

'All politicians have vanity. Some wear it more gently than others.'
David Steele

Feast day of St Ignatius of Loyola, St Justin de Jacobis, St Neot, and St Helen of Skövde.

⚞ EVENTS ⚟

1498 Columbus arrrived at Trinidad on his third voyage. **1919** The Weimar Republic was established in post-war Germany. **1910** Dr Crippen was arrested aboard the SS *Montrose* as it was docking at Quebec; charged with the murder of his wife, he was the first criminal to be caught by the use of radio. **1954** Mount Godwin-Austin (K2) in the Himalayas was first climbed by an Italian expedition, led by Ardito Desio. **1965** Cigarette advertising on British television was banned. **1971** US astronauts David Scott and James Irwin entered their Lunar Roving Vehicle and went for a ride on the Moon. **1991** At a superpower summit in Moscow, Presidents Bush and Gorbachev signed the Strategic Arms Reduction Treaty (START), and announced that they would be co-sponsoring a Middle East peace conference.

⚞ BIRTHS ⚟

John Ericsson, US naval engineer, **1803**; Milton Friedman, US economist, **1912**; Peter Nichols, English dramatist, **1927**; Lynne Reid Banks, English author, **1929**; Geraldine Chaplin, US film actress, **1944**; Evonne Cawley, Australian tennis player, **1951**.

⚞ DEATHS ⚟

Ignatius of Loyola, Spanish founder of the Jesuits, **1556**; Andrew Jackson, 17th US president, **1875**; Franz Liszt, Hungarian composer, **1886**; Hedley Verity, English cricketer, **1943**; Jim Reeves, US country singer, **1964**; Leonard Cheshire, British pilot and philanthropist, **1992**; King Baudouin I of the Belgians, **1993**.

'The wrong sort of people are always in power because they would not be in power if they were not the wrong sort of people.'
Jon Wynne-Tyson

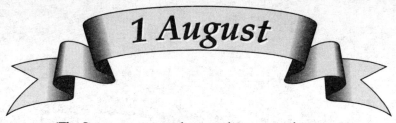
1 August

'The Swiss are not a people so much as a neat, clean, quite
solvent business.'
William Faulkner, *Intruder in the Dust*

National Day of Switzerland. Feast day of Saints Pistis, Elpis, and Agape (Faith,
Hope, and Charity), St Peter Julian Eymard, St Ethelwold of Winchester, St
Almedha or Aled, St Alphonse Liguori, and The Holy Macabees.

EVENTS

1498 Christopher Columbus reached the American mainland, and named it
Santa Isla, believing it to be an island. **1714** George Louis, Elector of Hanover,
was proclaimed King George I of Great Britain. **1774** English chemist Joseph
Priestley identified oxygen, which he called 'a new species of air'. **1778** The first
savings bank was opened, in Hamburg, Germany. **1793** The kilogram was introduced in France as the first metric weight. **1798** The English under Nelson
destroyed the French fleet at the Battle of the Nile, in Aboukir Bay. **1834**
Slavery was abolished throughout the British Empire. **1936** The XIth Olympics,
the last for 12 years, opened in Berlin. **1975** Thirty-five nations, including the
USA and the USSR, signed the Helsinki Agreement on cooperation in human
rights and other global issues.

BIRTHS

Claudius, Roman emperor, **10 BC**; Jean Baptiste de Lamarck, French zoologist,
1744; Richard Henry Dana, US novelist, **1815**; Herman Melville, US novelist,
1819; Jack Kramer, US tennis champion, **1921**; Yves Saint-Laurent, French
couturier, **1936**.

DEATHS

Louis VI, King of France, **1137**; Queen Anne, **1714**; Robert Morrison, English
missionary and translator, **1834**; Theodore Roethke, US poet, **1963**; Walter
Ulbricht, East German politician, **1973**; John Ogdon, English concert pianist,
1989; Alfred Manessier, French painter, **1993**.

'I used to get on great with journalists until I married Paul.'
Linda McCartney

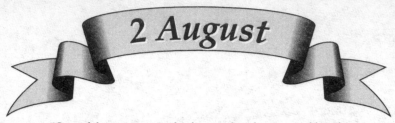
2 August

'One of the reasons people cling to their hates so stubbornly
is because they seem to sense once hate is gone that they will
be forced to deal with pain.'
James Baldwin, *Notes of a Native Son*

Feast day of St Theodota and her Three Sons, St Eusebius of Vercelli, St
Plegmund, St Stephen I, pope, St Syagrius of Autun, and St Sidwell or Sativola.

EVENTS

1718 Britain, France, Austria, and Holland concluded the Quadruple Alliance
against Spain, in an attempt to prevent Spain from annexing Sardinia and Sicily.
1858 The rule of the East India Company, which was established throughout
India, was transferred to the British government. **1875** Britain's first roller skating rink was opened to the public, in Belgravia, London. **1894** Death duties,
now known as inheritance tax, were introduced in Britain. **1945** The Potsdam
Conference, establishing the initial post war treatment of Germany and
demanding unconditional Japanese surrender, ended. **1980** Right-wing terrorists
exploded a bomb in the crowded Bologna Railway Station, northern Italy,
killing 84 people. **1990** Iraq invaded and annexed Kuwait, precipitating an
international crisis.

BIRTHS

John Tyndall, Irish physicist, **1820**; Ethel M Dell, British novelist, **1881**; Arthur
Bliss, English composer, **1891**; Myrna Loy, US film actress, **1905**; James
Baldwin, US writer, **1924**; Peter O'Toole, Irish actor, **1932**; Sammy McIlroy,
Irish footballer, **1954**.

DEATHS

Thomas Gainsborough, English painter, **1788**; Jacques Étienne Montgolfier,
French balloonist, **1799**; Enrico Caruso, Italian tenor, **1921**; **1923**; Louis
Blériot, French aviator, **1936**; Fritz Lang, Austrian film director, **1976**; Carlos
Chavez, Mexican composer, **1978**.

'The root function of language is to control the universe by describing it.'
James Baldwin, *Notes of a Native Son*

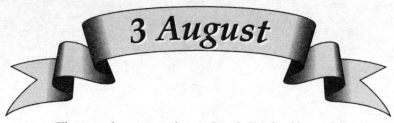
3 August

'There are three groups that no British PM should provoke:
the Vatican, the Treasury, and the miners.'
Stanley Baldwin, Attr.

Feast day of St Walthen or Waltheof, St Germanus of Auxerre, and St Thomas of Hales or Dover.

〜 EVENTS 〜

1492 Christopher Columbus left Palos de la Frontera in Andalusia, Spain, on his first voyage of discovery. **1778** La Scala opera house opened in Milan, Italy. **1858** Lake Victoria, the source of the Nile, was discovered by the English explorer John Speke. **1904** A British expedition, led by Col Francis E Younghusband, became the first westerners to enter the 'Forbidden City' of Lhasa, Tibet. **1914** Germany declared war on France. **1914** The first ships passed through the completed Panama Canal. **1940** Latvia was incorporated into the USSR as a constituent republic. **1958** The USS *Nautilus*, the first nuclear submarine, passed under the North Pole. **1963** The Beatles played The Cavern in their home town, Liverpool, for the last time.

〜 BIRTHS 〜

Joseph Paxton, English architect, **1801**; Stanley Baldwin, British statesman, **1867**; King Haakon VII of Norway, **1872**; Rupert Brooke, English poet, **1887**; Tony Bennett, US singer, **1926**; Martin Sheen, US actor, **1940**; Osvaldo Ardiles, Argentine footballer, **1953**.

〜 DEATHS 〜

James II, King of Scotland, **1460**; Richard Arkwright, English inventor, **1792**; Roger Casement, Irish nationalist, **1916**; Joseph Conrad, British novelist, **1924**; Colette, French novelist, **1954**; Lenny Bruce, US comedian, **1966**.

'If I should die, think only this of me:
that there's some corner of a foreign field
that is for ever England.'
Rupert Brooke, 'The Soldier'

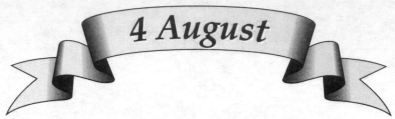

4 August

'We're more popular than Jesus Christ now. I don't know which
will go first. Rock 'n' roll or Christianity.'
John Lennon, *The Beatles' Illustrated Lyrics*

Feast day of St Molua or Lughaidh, St Ia, St Sezni, and St John Baptist Vianney.

☙ EVENTS ☙

1265 The Battle of Evesham took place, in which Simon de Montfort was
defeated by Royalist forces led by the future King Edward I, during the Barons'
War. **1578** The Portuguese were defeated by the Berbers at the Battle of
Alcazarquivir. **1870** The British Red Cross Society was founded. **1914** Britain
declared war on Germany after the Germans had violated the Treaty of London,
and World War I began. **1918** The Second Battle of the Marne ended. **1940**
Italy invaded Kenya, the Sudan, and British Somaliland. **1966** In a US radio
interview, John Lennon claimed that the Beatles were probably more popular
than Jesus Christ; Beatles records were consequently banned in many US states
and in South Africa.

☙ BIRTHS ☙

Percy Bysshe Shelley, English poet, **1792**; William Henry Hudson, British writer
and naturalist, **1841**; Knut Hamsun, Norwegian novelist, **1859**; HM Queen
Elizabeth, the Queen Mother, **1900**; Osbert Lancaster, English cartoonist and
writer, **1908**; Peter Squires, English rugby player, **1951**.

☙ DEATHS ☙

Henry I, King of France, **1060**; Hans Christian Andersen, Danish fairy tale
writer, **1875**; James Cruze, US film director, **1942**; Edgar Adrian, British
physiologist, **1977**; Pola Negri, German silent-film actress, **1987**.

'That orbed maiden, with white fire laiden,
Whom mortals call the Moon.'
P B Shelley, 'The Cloud'

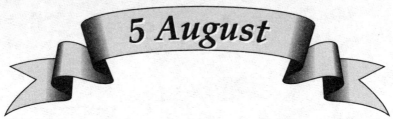
5 August

'I cannot and will not give my undertaking at a time when I, and you, the people, are not free. Your freedom and mine cannot be separated.'
Nelson Mandela, message read by his daughter to a rally in Soweto 10 Feb 1985

Feast day of St Afra, St Nonna, and Saints Addai and Mari.

☞ EVENTS ☜

1583 English soldier and navigator Humphrey Gilbert claimed Newfoundland for Elizabeth I. **1858** The first transatlantic cable was opened when Queen Victoria exchanged greetings with US President Buchanan. **1891** The first American Express traveller's cheque was cashed. **1914** The first electrical traffic lights were installed, in Cleveland, Ohio. **1924** The Turkish government abolished polygamy. **1960** Upper Volta (now Burkina Faso) achieved full independence from France. **1962** ANC leader Nelson Mandela was arrested and given a life sentence on charges of attempting to overthrow the South African government. **1963** The Test Ban Agreement was signed by the USA, the USSR, and the UK, contracting to test nuclear weapons only underground.

☞ BIRTHS ☜

Niels Henrik Abel, Norwegian mathematician, **1802**; Guy de Maupassant, French author, **1850**; John Huston, US film director, **1906**; Joan Hickson, English actress, **1906**; Neil Armstrong, US astronaut, **1930**; Bob Geldof, Irish musician, **1951**.

☞ DEATHS ☜

Thomas Newcomen, English inventor, **1729**; Frederick North, British politician, **1792**; Alexis Benoît Soyer, French chef and writer, **1858**; Friedrich Engels, German political writer, **1895**; Marilyn Monroe, US film actress, **1962**; Richard Burton, Welsh actor, **1984**; Eugen Suchon, Slovakian composer, **1993**.

'You have these men, these priests, who, if they are to be believed, have never had sex in their lives, and they are telling the rest of the world how to have sex. It's tragic.'
Clare Short

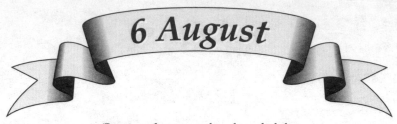

6 August

'Rest in soft peace and say here doth lie
Ben Jonson his best piece of poetry.'
Ben Jonson, epitaph for his son 1616

The national day of Bolivia. Feast of the Transfiguration and Feast day of Saints Justus and Pastor, and St Hormisdas, pope.

❧ EVENTS ❧

939 The Spanish defeated the Moors at the Battle of Salamanca. **1806** The Holy Roman Empire came to an end when Francis II renounced the crown, becoming Francis I, Emperor of Austria. **1889** The Savoy Hotel, in London, opened. **1890** William Kemmler, a murderer, became the first to be executed in the electric chair, in Auburn Prison, New York. **1926** US swimmer Gertrude Ederle became the first woman to swim the English Channel, in 14 hr 34 min. **1945** An atomic bomb was dropped on the Japanese city of Hiroshima from a US Boeing B29 bomber. **1962** Jamaica became independent after being a British colony for 300 years. **1988** Russian ballerina Natalia Makarova danced again with the Kirov Ballet in London, 18 years after she defected to the West.

❧ BIRTHS ❧

Daniel O'Connell, Irish politician, **1775**; Alfred Tennyson, English poet, **1809**; Paul Claudel, French poet, **1868**; Alexander Fleming, Scottish bacteriologist, **1881**; Robert Mitchum, US film actor, **1917**; Chris Bonington, British mountaineer, **1934**.

❧ DEATHS ❧

Anne Hathaway, wife of William Shakespeare, **1623**; Ben Jonson, English playwright, **1637**; Diego Velázquez, Spanish painter, **1660**; Fulgencio Batista y Zaldivar, Cuban dictator, **1973**; Pope Paul VI, **1978**.

'I am become death, the destroyer of worlds.'
Robert J Oppenheimer, nuclear physicist, quoting Vishnu

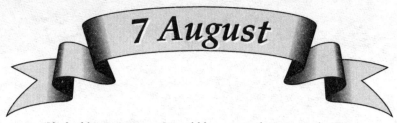

7 August

'If a had been a woman I would be constantly pregnant because
I simply cannot say no.'
Robert Maxwell, reported on 7 Aug 1988

Feast day of St Donatus of Arezzo, St Victricius, Saints Agapitus, Sixtus II and
Felicissimus, St Dogmetius the Persian, St Albert of Trapani, St Claudia, and St
Cajetan or Gaetano.

≈ EVENTS ≈

1711 The first race meeting was held at Ascot, established by Queen Anne.
1830 Louis Philippe was proclaimed 'Citizen King' (Philippe Egalité), for his
support of the **1792** Revolution. **1840** The employment of climbing boys as
chimney sweeps was prohibited by an Act of Parliament. **1858** Queen Victoria
chose Ottawa as the capital of the Dominion of Canada. **1913** In Britain's first
aviation tragedy, US airman 'Colonel' Samuel Cody was killed when his aircraft
crashed at Farnborough. **1926** Britain's first motor racing Grand Prix was held
at Brooklands; the winning car averaged 71.61 mph. **1942** Guadalcanal, in the
southern Solomon Islands, was assaulted by the US Marines in one of the most
costly campaigns of World War II. **1960** The Ivory Coast (Côte d'Ivoire)
achieved independence from France.

≈ BIRTHS ≈

Mata Hari (Margaretha Geertruide Zelle), Dutch courtesan, dancer, and
probable spy, **1876**; Louis Leakey, British archaeologist, **1903**; Ralph Bunche,
US diplomat, **1904**; Greg Chappell, Australian cricketer, **1948**; Alexei Sayle,
British comedian, **1952**.

≈ DEATHS ≈

Robert Blake, British admiral, **1657**; Bix Beiderbecke, US jazz musician and
composer, **1931**; Konstantin Stanislavsky, Russian theatre director, **1938**;
Rabindranath Tagore, Indian writer, **1941**; Oliver Hardy, US film comedian, **1957**.

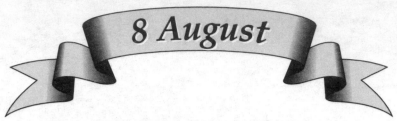

8 August

'When the President does it, that means that it is not illegal.'
Richard Nixon, in David Frost's *I gave them a sword*

Feast day of St Dominic, Saints Cyriacus, Largus, and Smaragdus, St Hormidas the Martyr, and The Fourteen Holy Helpers.

EVENTS

117 Hadrian became emperor of Rome following the death of his father Trajan. **1786** Mont Blanc, Europe's tallest peak, was climbed for the first time; Swiss scientist Horace Saussure had offered a prize for the accomplishment of this feat. **1940** The Battle of Britain, which would continue into the following Oct, began. **1945** The USSR declared war on Germany. **1963** The Great Train Robbery, in which over £2.5 million was stolen, took place near Bletchley, Buckinghamshire. **1974** Richard Nixon became the first US president to resign from office in face of threats to impeach him for his implication in the Watergate scandal. **1988** The luckiest day of the decade, according to the Chinese, because the date – 8.8.88 – is a palindrome. **1991** Islamic Jihad released John McCarthy, a British journalist who had been held hostage since April 1986.

BIRTHS

Godfrey Kneller, German-born painter, **1646**; Ernest O Lawrence, US physicist, **1901**; Dino De Laurentiis, Italian film producer, **1919**; Esther Williams, US swimmer and film actress, **1923**; Dustin Hoffman, US film actor, **1937**; Nigel Mansell, British racing driver, **1953**.

DEATHS

Girolamo Fracastoro, Italian physician and writer, **1553**; James Tissot, French painter, **1902**; Frank Winfield Woolworth, US chainstore founder, **1919**; James Gould Cozzens, US novelist, **1978**; Louise Brooks, US actress, **1985**.

'The people would be just as noisy if they were going to see me hanged.'
Oliver Cromwell, referring to a cheering crowd

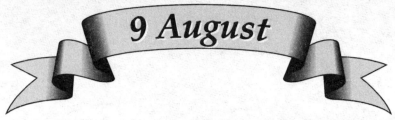

9 August

'Deprivation is for me what daffodils were for Wordsworth.'
Philip Larkin, *Required Writing*

Feast day of St Oswald of Northumbria, Saints Nathy and Felim, St Romanus, and St Emygius.

≈ EVENTS ≈

1842 The frontier between Canada and the USA was defined by the Webster–Ashburton treaty, signed by the USA and Britain. **1870** The British Parliament passed The Married Women's Property Act, improving the situation of the nation's wives. **1902** Following a six-week delay due to an emergency appendectomy, Edward VII was crowned king in Westminster Abbey. **1912** An earthquake struck Turkey, in the area of Istanbul, killing 6,000 people and rendering 40,000 homeless. **1945** The second atom bomb of World War II was dropped on the Japanese city of Nagasaki. **1965** Singapore gained independence. **1974** Succeeding Richard Nixon, Gerald Ford was sworn in as the 38th president of the USA. **1979** Britain's first nudist beach was established in Brighton.

≈ BIRTHS ≈

Izaak Walton, English author, **1593**; Thomas Telford, Scottish civil engineer, **1757**; Leonid Nikolayevich Andreyev, Russian author, **1871**; Léonide Massine, Russian dancer and choreographer, **1869**; Philip Larkin, English poet, **1922**; Rod Laver, Australian tennis player, **1938**.

≈ DEATHS ≈

Maarten Harpertszoon Tromp, Dutch admiral, **1653**; Ruggiero Leoncavallo, Italian composer, **1919**; Hermann Hesse, German author, **1962**; Joe Orton, English playwright, **1967**; Dmitri Shostakovich, Russian composer, **1975**.

'If you hate a person, you hate something in him that is part of yourself. What isn't part of ourselves doesn't disturb us.'
Hermann Hesse, *Demian*

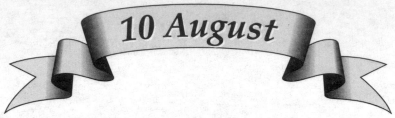

10 August

'The American system of rugged individualism.'
Herbert Clark Hoover

National Day of Ecuador. Feast day of St Laurence of Rome.

EVENTS

1675 King Charles II laid the foundation stone of the Royal Observatory, Greenwich. **1787** Wolfgang Amadeus Mozart completed his popular *Eine Kleine Nachtmusik* (*A Little Night Music*). **1846** The Smithsonian Institution was established in Washington DC, to foster scientific research. **1889** The screw bottle top was patented by Dan Rylands of Hope Glass Works, Yorkshire. **1895** The first Promenade Concert was held at the Queen's Hall, London, conducted by Henry Wood. **1904** In the Russo-Japanese War, Japan inflicted heavy losses on the Russian fleet at the Battle of the Yellow Sea, off Port Arthur. **1911** British MPs voted to receive salaries for the first time. **1966** *Orbiter I*, the first US lunar satellite, was launched.

BIRTHS

Charles James Napier, British general, **1782**; Camillo Benso, Count Cavour, Italian nationalist politician, **1810**; Herbert Hoover, 31st US president, **1874**; Eddie Fisher, US singer, **1928**; Anita Lonsborough Porter, English swimmer, **1941**.

DEATHS

Allan Ramsay, Scottish portrait painter, **1784**; Edward William Lane, English traveller and translator, **1876**; Otto Lillienthal, German aviator, **1896**.

'The easiest kind of relationship for me is with ten thousand
people. The hardest is with one.'
Joan Baez

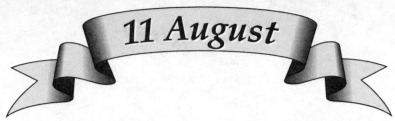
11 August

'Throughout the war, Japan caused trouble, especially to
Asian countries. It is important to acknowledge facts frankly.'
Tsutomu Hata, Japanese prime minister

Feast day of St Attracta or Araght, St Clare of Assisi, St Tiburtius, St Susanna,
St Equitius, St Alexander of Comana, St Lelia, St Blane, St Gerard of Gallinaro,
and St Gery or Gaugericus.

⚜ EVENTS ⚜

1576 English navigator Martin Frobisher, on his search for the Northwest
Passage, entered the bay in Canada now named after him. **1810** Severe earthquakes struck the Azores, causing the village of São Miguel to sink. **1877**
Phobos and Deimos, the satellites or 'moons' of Mars, were discovered by US
astronomer Asaph Hall. **1941** President Roosevelt and Winston Churchill
signed the Atlantic Charter, largely to demonstrate public solidarity between the
Allies. **1952** King Talal of Jordan was deposed because of mental illness, and his
son, Crown Prince Hussein, succeeded to the throne. **1960** Chad gained its
independence from France. **1963** Canton was entered by Chinese General
Chiang Kai-shek and his supporters.

⚜ BIRTHS ⚜

Jean Victor Marie Moreau, French General, **1772**; Charlotte Mary Yonge,
English novelist, **1823**; Hugh MacDiarmid, Scottish poet, **1892**; Enid Blyton,
English author, **1897**; Alun Hoddinott, Welsh composer, **1929**; Anna Massey,
English actress, **1937**.

⚜ DEATHS ⚜

Hans Memling, Flemish painter, **1495**; John Henry Newman, English Roman
Catholic theologian, **1890**; Andrew Carnegie, US industrialist and
philanthropist, **1919**; Jackson Pollock, US painter, **1956**.

'Abstract painting is abstract. It confronts you. There was a reviewer a while
back who wrote that my pictures didn't have any beginning or any end. He
didn't mean it as a compliment, but it was. It was a fine compliment.'
Jackson Pollock

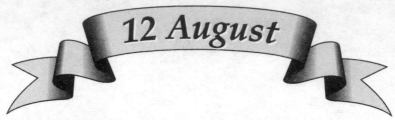

12 August

'The English is rather a hissing than a harsh language, and
perhaps this was the characteristic to which Charles V alluded
when he said it was fit to speak to birds in.'
Robert Southey, *Letters from England, by Don Manuel Alvarez Espriella*

Feast day of St Porcarius and his Companions, St Jambert, Archbishop of
Canterbury, St Euplus, and St Murtagh or Muredach.

⤳ EVENTS ⤳

1687 The Austro-Hungarians defeated the Turks at the Battle of Mohács, in
Hungary, effectively ending Turkish expansion into Europe. **1812** In the
Peninsular War, the Duke of Wellington's troops entered Madrid. **1851** The US
schooner *America* won a race around the Isle of Wight, giving rise to the later
America's Cup trophy. **1883** The quagga in Amsterdam Zoo died, the last of this
species in the world. **1898** Spain and the USA concluded an armistice over Cuba
and other possessions. **1944** PLUTO ('pipe line under the ocean') began operating
beneath the English Channel, supplying petrol to Allied forces in France. **1969**
The world's first communications satellite was launched – *America's Echo*. **1991**
England defeated the West Indies in the fifth Test Match at the Oval, to draw the
summer series 2 – 2.

⤳ BIRTHS ⤳

Thomas Bewick, British wood engraver, **1753**; King George IV, **1762**; Robert
Southey, English poet, **1774**; Cecil B De Mille, US film director and producer,
1881; George Hamilton, US film actor, **1939**; Mark Knopfler, rock guitarist, **1949**.

⤳ DEATHS ⤳

Giovanni Gabrieli, Italian composer, **1612**; William Blake, English poet, **1827**;
George Stephenson, English engineer, **1848**; Thomas Mann, German novelist,
1955; Ian Fleming, English novelist, **1964**; Henry Fonda, US film actor, **1982**.

'To make your children capable of honesty is the beginning of education.'
John Ruskin

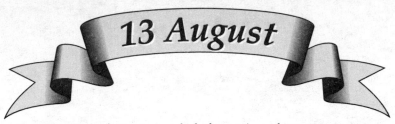

13 August

'A revolution is not a bed of roses. A revolution is a
struggle to the death between the future and the past.'
Fidel Castro, speech given on the second anniversary of the revolution

Feast day of St Simplician of Milan, St Radegund, St Wigbert, St Pontian, pope,
St Benildus, St Hippolytus of Rome, St Narses Klaietus, St Cassian of Imola, and
St Maximus the Confessor.

✌ EVENTS ✌

1521 Spanish conquistador Hernándo Cortés recaptured Tenochtitlán (Mexico
City), and overthrew the Aztec empire. **1705** The Battle of Blenheim took place
in southern Germany, in which the Anglo-Austrian army inflicted a decisive
defeat on the French armies. **1814** The Cape of Good Hope Province became a
British colony when it was ceded by the Dutch (sold for £6 million). **1868**
Earthquakes killed over 25,000 people and destroyed four cities in Peru and
Ecuador. **1923** Kemal Atatürk was elected the first president of Turkey. **1961**
The border between East and West Berlin was sealed off by East Germany with
the closure of the Brandenburg Gate to stop the exodus to the West. **1964** The
last hangings in Britain took place; two murderers were executed at Liverpool
and Manchester. **1972** The last US troops left Vietnam. **1991** Prosecutors
announced the discovery of one of the largest bank frauds in Japan's history,
involving $2.5 billion in fraudulently obtained loans.

✌ BIRTHS ✌

Queen Adelaide, consort of William IV, **1756**; John Baird, Scottish television
pioneer, **1888**; Alfred Hitchcock, English film director, **1899**; Basil Spence,
British architect, **1907**; Ben Hogan, US golfer, **1912**; Fidel Castro, Cuban
leader, **1927**.

✌ DEATHS ✌

René Laënnec, French physician, **1826**; Eugéne Delacroix, French painter,
1863; John Everett Millais, British painter, **1896**; Florence Nightingale, English
nurse, **1910**; H G Wells, English writer, **1946**; Henry Williamson, English
author, **1977**.

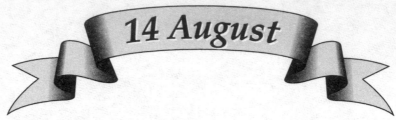

14 August

'All one's inventions are true, you can be sure of that.
Poetry is as exact a science as geometry.'
Gustave Flaubert

Feast day of St Marcellus of Apamea, St Fachanan, St Athanasia of Aegina, St Eusebius of Rome, and St Maximilian Kolbe.

≈ EVENTS ≈

1678 The French repulsed William of Orange at the Battle of Mons, in Belgium. **1880** Cologne Cathedral was completed; it had been started in the 13th century. **1882** Cetewayo, King of Zululand, South Africa, was received by Queen Victoria. **1893** France became the first country to introduce vehicle registration plates. **1900** The Boxer Rebellion was ended and Beijing captured by an international punitive force. **1947** Pakistan became an independent dominion. **1969** The first British troops were deployed in Northern Ireland to restore order. **1986** Pakistani politician Benazir Bhutto was arrested by President Zia and detained in prison for 30 days.

≈ BIRTHS ≈

Samuel Wesley, English organist and composer, **1810**; John Galsworthy, English novelist and playwright, **1867**; Fred Davis, English snooker player, **1913**; Frederic Raphael, English novelist, **1931**; Sarah Brightman, English soprano and actress, **1961**.

≈ DEATHS ≈

Augustus Toplady, British priest and hymn-writer, **1778**; Alfred Harmsworth, British newspaper proprietor, **1922**; William Randolph Hearst, US newspaper proprietor, **1951**; Bertolt Brecht, German writer, **1956**; J B Priestley, English novelist and playwright, **1984**.

'Always design a thing by considering it in its larger
context - a chair in a room, a room in a house, a house in an
environment, an environment in a city plan.'
Eero Saarinen

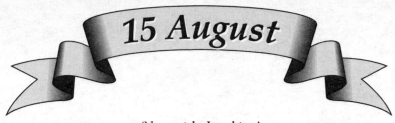

15 August

'Not tonight Josephine.'
Napoleon Bonaparte, Attr.

Feast day of The Assumption of the Virgin Mary, St Tarsicius, and St Arnulf of Soissons.

EVENTS

1543 The Jesuit order (Society of Jesus) was founded by Ignatius de Loyola in Paris, with the aims of protecting Catholicism against the Reformation and carrying out missionary work. **1843** The Tivoli Pleasure Gardens were opened in Copenhagen. **1947** India gained independence. **1948** The republic of South Korea was proclaimed. **1965** The National Guard was called in to quell race riots in Watts, Los Angeles, which left 28 dead and 676 injured. **1969** The Woodstock Music and Arts Fair began on a dairy farm in upstate New York. In the three days it lasted, 400,000 attended, two children were born, and three people died. **1987** Caning was officially banned in British schools (excluding independent schools).

BIRTHS

Napoleon Bonaparte, French emperor, **1769**; Sir Walter Scott, Scottish novelist, **1771**; Thomas De Quincey, English writer, **1785**; T E Lawrence, English soldier and writer, **1888**; Robert Bolt, British dramatist, **1924**; Princess Anne, the Princess Royal, **1950**.

DEATHS

Macbeth, King of Scotland, **1057**; Joseph Joachim, Hungarian violinist and composer, **1907**; Will Rogers, US humorist, **1935**; Wiley Post, US aviator, **1935**; Paul Signac, French painter, **1935**; René Magritte, Belgian painter, **1967**.

'Whereas it previously took as long as five years to make a detailed survey of just 40 galaxies, I can now knock off two dozen a day.'
Tony Redhead, US astronomer

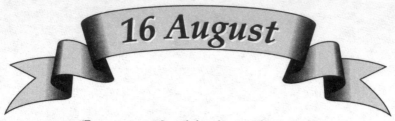

16 August

'Every morning I read the obits in *The Times*. If
I'm not there, I carry on.'
William Douglas-Hume, reported on 16 Aug 1987

Feast day of St Stephen of Hungary, St Armel, and St Arsacius.

EVENTS

1513 King Henry VIII and his troops defeated the French in the Battle of the Spurs, at Guinigatte, NW France. **1743** The earliest prize-ring code of boxing rules was formulated in England by the champion pugilist Jack Broughton. **1819** The Peterloo massacre took place in Manchester when militia opened fire on a crowd gathered to hear discussion of reform, killing 11 people. **1897** Endowed by the sugar merchant Henry Tate, the Tate Gallery, in London, was opened. **1934** US explorer Charles Beebe and engineer Otis Barton made a record-breaking dive to 923 m/3028 ft in their bathysphere (a spherical diving vessel) near Bermuda. **1960** Cyprus became an independent republic, with Archbishop Makarios as president. **1974** Turkish forces called a cease-fire in Cyprus, after having taken control of the northern part of the island.

BIRTHS

Arthur Cayley, British mathematician, **1821**; Johan Siegwald Dahl, Norwegian painter, **1827**; Menachem Begin, Israeli statesman, **1913**; Ted Hughes, English poet, **1930**; Jeff Thomson, Australian cricketer, **1950**; Madonna, US rock singer, **1958**.

DEATHS

Joe Miller, English comedian, **1738**; Robert Wilhelm Bunsen, German chemist and inventor, **1899**; Umberto Boccioni, Italian sculptor, **1916**; Margaret Mitchell, US novelist, **1949**; Bela Lugosi, US film actor, **1956**; Elvis Presley, US rock singer, **1977**; Irene Sharaff, US film-set and costume designer, **1993**; Alison Smithson, English architect, **1993**; Stewart Granger, English-born US actor, **1993**.

'I can throw a fit, I'm master at it.'
Madonna

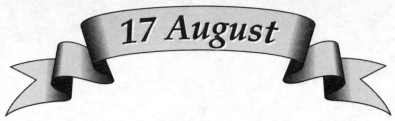
17 August

'Is that a gun in your pocket or are you just glad to see me?'
Mae West, *Peel me a grape*

National day of Indonesia. Feast day of St Joan Delanoue, St Mamas, St Liberatus of Capua, St Rock or Roch, St Clare of Montefalco, St Hyacinth, and St Eusebius, pope.

EVENTS

1833 The Canadian *Royal William*, the first steamship to cross the Atlantic entirely under power, set off from Nova Scotia. **1836** Under the Registration Act, the registration of births, deaths, and marriages was introduced in Britain. **1876** The first performance of Wagner's opera *Götterdämmerung* was given in Bayreuth, Germany. **1896** Gold was discovered at Bonanza Creek in Canada's Yukon Territory, leading to the great gold rush of 1898. **1976** Earthquakes and tidal waves in the Philippines resulted in the deaths of over 6,000 people. **1989** Electronic tagging was used for the first time in Britain, on Richard Hart, accused of theft.

BIRTHS

Davy Crockett, US frontiersman, **1786**; Mae West, US film actress, **1892**; George Melly, English jazz singer, **1926**; V S Naipaul, English novelist, **1932**; Robert De Niro, US film actor, **1943**; Alan Minter, middleweight boxer, **1951**; Robin Cousins, ice skater, **1957**.

DEATHS

Frederick II (the Great), King of Prussia, **1786**; Honoré de Balzac, French novelist, **1850**; Fernand Léger, French painter, **1955**; Ludwig Mies van der Rohe, US architect, **1973**; Ira Gershwin, US lyricist, **1983**; Mohammad Zia ul-Haq, Pakistani general, **1988**.

'The bonds social, economic, industrial and commercial, which are always drawing North and South Ireland together, will prove too powerful for the bigots and revolutionaries.'
J R Devlin, reported on 17 Aug 1924

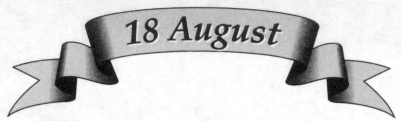

18 August

'There is scarcely any book so bad that nothing can be learnt from it.'
Enoch Powell, reported on 18 Aug 1985

Feast day of St Helena, Saints Florus and Laurus, St Agapitus, St Alipius, and St Beatrice or Brites da Silva.

EVENTS

1759 The British, under Admiral ('Old Dreadnought') Boscawen, defeated the French fleet at the Battle of Lagos Bay. **1812** Napoleon's forces defeated the Russians at the Battle of Smolensk. **1866** The Treaty of Alliance forming the North German Confederation, under the leadership of Prussia, was signed. **1941** Britain's National Fire Service was established. **1960** The first oral contraceptive was marketed by the Searle Drug Company in the USA. **1964** South Africa was banned from participating in the Olympics because of its racial policies. **1967** The town of Long Beach, in California, purchased the liner *Queen Mary*.

BIRTHS

Antonio Salieri, Italian composer, **1750**; Franz Josef I, Austro-Hungarian emperor, **1830**; Moura Lympany, English concert pianist, **1916**; Shelley Winters, US film actress, **1922**; Roman Polanski, Polish film director, **1933**; Robert Redford, US film actor, **1937**.

DEATHS

Genghis Khan, **1227**; Guido Reni, Italian painter, **1642**; André Jacques Garnerin, French balloonist, **1823**; William Henry Hudson, US writer, **1922**; Anita Loos, US writer, **1981**; Nikolaus Pevsner, architectural historian, **1983**.

'I did a picture in England one winter and it was so cold I
almost got married.'
Shelley Winters

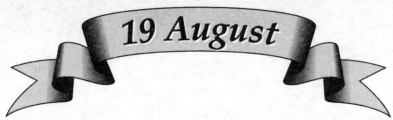
19 August

'I never forget a face but in your case I'll be glad to make an exception.'
Groucho Marx, in Leo Rosten's *People I have loved, known or admired*

Feast day of St Mocha, Saints Agapius and Timothy, St Sebald, St Thecla, St Andrew the Tribune, St Sixtus III, St Berulf of Bobbio, St Louis of Anjou, St John Eudes, and St Credan of Evesham.

EVENTS

1274 The coronation of Edward I took place. **1796** France and Spain formed an alliance against Britain. **1897** Electric-powered cabs appeared in London; they proved to be uneconomical and were withdrawn in 1900. **1934** A plebiscite was held in Germany giving sole power to Adolf Hitler, the Führer. **1942** British and Canadian troops raided the port of Dieppe, resulting in heavy casualties for the attacking force. **1989** Poland became the first eastern European country to end one-party rule, when a coalition government was formed with Tadeuz Mazowiecki as prime minister.

BIRTHS

John Dryden, English poet, **1631**; John Flamsteed, first Astronomer Royal, **1646**; James Nasmyth, Scottish inventor, **1808**; Gabrielle (Coco) Chanel, French couturier, **1883**; Ogden Nash, US humorist, **1902**; Bill Clinton, 42nd US president, **1945**.

DEATHS

Augustus, 1st Roman emperor, **14**; Blaise Pascal, French philosopher and mathematician, **1662**; Sergei Pavlovich Diaghilev, Russian choreographer, **1929**; Federico García Lorca, Spanish poet and playwright, **1936**; 'Groucho' Marx, US comedian, **1977**; Frederick Ashton, British choreographer, **1988**.

'If you want people to think well of you, do not speak well of yourself.'
Blaise Pascal

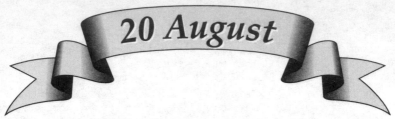

20 August

'Never in the field of conflict was so much owed by so many to so few.'
Winston Churchill, speech

Feast day of St Rognwald or Ronald, St Bernard of Clairvaux, St Amator or Amadour, St Philibert, and St Oswin.

EVENTS

1710 The French were defeated by the Austrians at the Battle of Saragossa. **1914** German forces occupied Brussels. **1924** Although considered the likely winner, British sprinter Eric Liddel refused to run in the 100m heats at the Paris Olympics because it fell on a Sunday. **1956** Calder Hall nuclear power plant, Britain's first nuclear power station, began operating. **1960** Senegal gained independence from France. **1968** Russian troops invaded Czechoslovakia. **1977** The US *Voyager I* spacecraft was launched on its journey via Jupiter and Saturn to become the first artificial object to leave the solar system.

BIRTHS

Thomas Corneille, French playwright, **1625**; Benjamin Harrison, 23rd US president, **1833**; Raymond Poincaré, French statesman, **1860**; H P Lovecraft, US writer, **1890**; Jack Teagarden, US jazz trombonist, **1905**; Jim Reeves, US country singer, **1924**.

DEATHS

Friedrich Wilhelm Joseph von Schelling, German philosopher, **1854**; Adolphe William Bouguereau, French painter, **1905**; William Booth, founder of the Salvation Army, **1912**; Paul Ehrlich, German biochemist, **1915**; Leon Trotsky, Russian politician, **1940**.

'To be successful, keep looking tanned, live in an elegant building
(even if you're in the cellar), be seen in smart restaurants
(even if you nurse one drink) and if you borrow, borrow big.'
Aristotle Onassis, reported on 20 Aug 1972

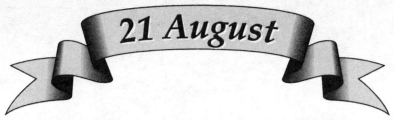
21 August

'If sunbeams were weapons of war we would have had solar
energy long ago.'
Sir George Porter, reported on 21 Aug 1973

Feast day of St Pius X, pope, St Abraham of Smolensk, St Sidonius Apollinaris,
Saints Bonosus and Maximian, and Saints Cisellus and Camerinus.

EVENTS

1808 The French forces, under General Junot, were defeated by Wellington at
the Battle of Vimiero. **1901** The Cadillac Motor Company was formed in
Detroit, Michigan, USA, named after the French explorer, Antoine Cadillac.
1911 Leonardo da Vinci's painting, the *Mona Lisa*, was stolen from the Louvre
in Paris – it was recovered two years later. **1939** Civil Defence, to mitigate the
effects of enemy attack, was started in Britain. **1959** Hawaii became the 50th of
the United States. **1991** An attempted coup d'état in the USSR failed; faced
with international condemnation and popular protests led by Boris Yeltsin, the
junta stepped down and Gorbachev was reinstated.

BIRTHS

William Murdock, Scottish inventor, **1754**; King William IV, **1765**; Aubrey
Beardsley, English illustrator, **1872**; Count Basie, US jazz pianist and bandleader,
1904; HRH Princess Margaret, **1930**; Janet Baker, English mezzo-soprano, **1933**.

DEATHS

Richard Crashaw, English poet, **1649**; Aston Webb, English architect, **1930**;
Leonard Constant Lambert, English composer, **1951**; Jacob Epstein, British
sculptor, **1959**; Benigno Aquino, Philippine politician, **1983**; Tatiana Troyanos,
US operatic mezzo-soprano, **1993**.

'There is on the Tory side some apprehension about having an
overeducated public. We have I think the worst-educated
working class in western Europe. The standard of proletarian education,
if one may use that snobbish word, is lamentable.'
Arnold Goodman

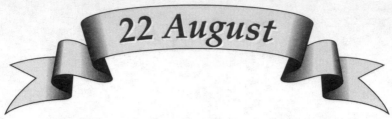
22 August

'It serves me right for putting all my eggs in one bastard.'
Dorothy Parker, on entering hospital for an abortion

Feast day of St Timothy, St Andrew of Fiesole, St Sigfrid of Wearmouth, and St John Kemble.

✿ EVENTS ✿

1642 The English Civil War began, between the supporters of Charles I and of Parliament, when the king raised his standard at Nottingham. **1788** The British settlement in Sierra Leone was founded, the purpose of which was to secure a home in Africa for freed slaves from England. **1846** New Mexico was annexed by the USA. **1864** The International Red Cross was founded by the Geneva Convention to assist the wounded and prisoners of war. **1910** Korea was annexed by Japan. **1985** Following an aborted take-off, a British Airtours Boeing 737 burst into flames on the runway at Manchester Airport; 55 persons were killed.

✿ BIRTHS ✿

Claude Debussy, French composer, **1862**; Jacques Lipchitz, US sculptor and painter, **1891**; Dorothy Parker, US humorist and writer, **1893**; Henri Cartier-Bresson, French photographer, **1908**; Ray Bradbury, US writer, **1920**; Karlheinz Stockhausen, German composer, **1928**

✿ DEATHS ✿

Jean Honoré Fragonard, French painter, **1806**; Michael Collins, Irish nationalist, **1922**; Oliver Lodge, English physicist, **1940**; Michael Fokine, Russian dancer and choreographer, **1942**; William Richard Morris, British car manufacturer, **1963**.

'I won't be photographed. They only push a button.'
Henri Cartier-Bresson

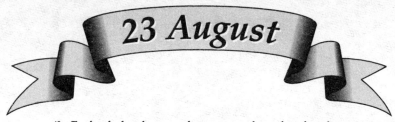
23 August

'In England, they have made pop music legendary, but they
hold it in contempt.'
Bono Vox, singer/songwriter

The national day of Romania. Feast day of St Rose of Lima, Saints Asterius and
Claudius, St Tydfil, St Philip Benizi, and St Eugene or Eoghan of Ardstraw.

✎ EVENTS ✎

1813 The French were driven back by the Prussians under General von Bülow
at the Battle of Grossbeeren. **1839** Hong Kong was taken by the British. **1914**
The British Expeditionary Force fought its first battle at Mons, in World War I.
1921 Faisal I was crowned as King of Iraq. **1927** Nicola Sacco and Bartolomeo
Vanzetti, two Italo-American anarchists, were falsely accused of robbery and
murder, and were sent to the electric chair. **1939** The USSR and Germany
signed a non-aggression pact which, although short-lived, eased the way for
Hitler's invasion of Poland. **1940** The Blitz began as German bombers began an
all-night raid on London. **1948** The World Council of Churches was founded.

✎ BIRTHS ✎

Louis XVI, King of France, **1754**; Edgar Lee Masters, US poet and novelist,
1869; Gene Kelly, US dancer and singer, **1912**; Peter Thomson, Australian
golfer, **1929**; Willy Russell, English playwright, **1947**; Keith Moon, British rock
drummer, **1947**.

✎ DEATHS ✎

William Wallace, Scottish patriot, **1305**; Charles Auguste de Coulomb, French
physicist, **1806**; Rudolph Valentino, Italian-born film actor, **1926**; Oscar
Hammerstein II, US lyricist, **1960**; Didier Peroni, French racing driver, **1987**.

'Vice is nice
But a little virtue
Won't hurt you.'
Felicia Lamport

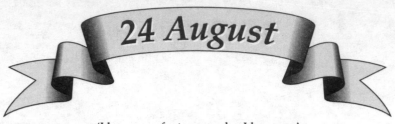
24 August

'I have a confession to make: I love cars.'
Robert Key, UK minister of transport

———

Feast day of St Bartholomew, The Martyrs of Utica, and St Audenoeus or Ouen.

≋ EVENTS ≋

AD 79 Mount Vesuvius erupted and buried the cities of Pompeii and Herculaneum in hot volcanic ash. 410 The Visigoths, led by Alaric, sacked Rome. 1572 Charles IX ordered the massacre of the Huguenots throughout France; in Paris thousands were killed in what became known as the Massacre of St Bartholomew. 1704 The French were defeated by the English and Dutch fleets at the Battle of Malaga. 1814 British forces captured Washington DC and set the White House on fire. 1921 The Turkish army, led by Mustafa Kemal, drove back the Greeks at the Battle of the Sakkaria River. 1959 The *Manchester Guardian* was renamed the *Guardian*.

≋ BIRTHS ≋

George Stubbs, English painter, 1724; William Wilberforce, English philanthropist, 1759; Max Beerbohm, English writer and caricaturist, 1872; Graham Sutherland, English painter, 1903; Charles Causley, English poet, 1917; Stephen Fry, English actor and writer, 1957.

≋ DEATHS ≋

Pliny the Elder, Roman naturalist and writer, 79; Alaric I, King of the Visigoths, 410; Thomas Blood, Irish adventurer, 1680; Thomas Chatterton, English poet, 1770; Nicolas Léonard Sadi Carnot, French physicist, 1832; Ronald Knox, British theologian, 1957.

———

'The whole thing is like finding a frog in a coffee jar.'
Stephen Fry, on sex

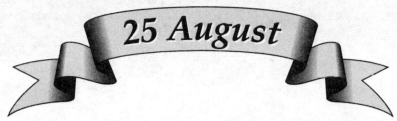

25 August

'I'd like to see new laws passed to fine soccer hooligans anything from £50 to £100. I'd have no hesitation either in putting these thugs in prison.'
Don Revie, reported on 25 Aug 1974

National Day of Uruguay. Feast Day of St Ebba, St Genesius the Comedian, St Gregory of Utrecht, St Louis IX, King of France, St Mennas of Constantinople, and St Patricia.

EVENTS

325 The Council of Nicaea set the rules for the computation of Easter. **1830** A revolution against the Netherlands union erupted in Brussels. **1914** Louvain was sacked by the Germans. **1919** The first daily scheduled flights started between London and Paris. **1931** Ramsay MacDonald formed a National Government. **1940** The RAF made the first air raid on Berlin. **1944** The Allies liberated Paris. **1960** The XVIIth Olympic Games opened in Rome. **1989** The US space probe *Voyager* reached Neptune; pictures of Triton, its moon, revealed the existence of two additional moons.

BIRTHS

Ivan IV ('The Terrible'), Tsar of Russia, **1530**; Allan Pinkerton, founder of the US detective agency, **1819**; Leonard Bernstein, US conductor and composer, **1918**; Sean Connery, Scottish actor, **1930**; Martin Amis, English novelist, **1949**.

DEATHS

Jan Vermeer, Dutch painter, **1691**; David Hume, Scottish philosopher, **1776**; William Herschel, English astronomer, **1822**; Michael Faraday, English chemist and physicist, **1867**; Friedrich Wilhelm Nietzsche, German philosopher, **1900**; Truman Capote, US author, **1984**.

'God is dead.'
F W Nietzsche

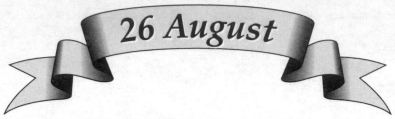

26 August

'Veni, vidi, vici. (I came, I saw, I conquered).'
Julius Caesar

Feast Day of St Bergwine, archbishop of Canterbury, St John Wall, St Mary Desmaisieres, St Pandonia, and St Teresa Jornet Ihars.

EVENTS

55 BC Julius Caesar landed in Britain. **1346** King Edward III, aided by the Black Prince, his son, defeated the French at the Battle of Crécy. **1789** The French Assembly adopted the Declaration of the Rights of Man. **1846** Mendelssohn's oratorio *Elijah* was first performed, Birmingham Festival. **1883** Krakatoa, the island volcano, began erupting, killing thousands. **1920** Women in the USA were granted the right to vote. **1936** The Anglo-Egyptian alliance was signed. **1952** The USSR announced that it had successfully tested the ICBM (Intercontinental Ballistic Missile). **1972** The XXth Olympic Games opened in Munich. **1978** Cardinal Albino Luciani was elected Pope John Paul I.

BIRTHS

Sir Robert Walpole, English statesman, **1676**; Prince Albert, Consort to Queen Victoria, **1819**; Lee De Forest, US physicist, **1873**; Jules Romains, French novelist, playwright and poet, **1885**; Christopher Isherwood, English novelist, **1904**.

DEATHS

Frans Hals, Dutch painter, **1666**; Anton van Leeuwenhoek, Dutch naturalist and microscopist, Louis Philippe, 'Citizen King' of France, **1850**; Charles Lindbergh, US pioneer aviator, **1974**; Charles Boyer, French actor, **1978**.

'We discover in ourselves what others hide from us, and we recognise in others what we hide from ourselves.'
Marquis de Vauvenargues, *Reflections and Maxims*

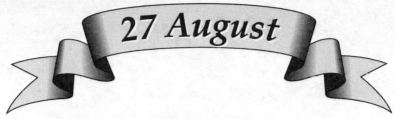
27 August

'What you do not want done to yourself do not do to others.'
Confucius

Feast Day of St Caesarius of Arles, St David Lewis, Little St Hugh, St Monica, St Margaret the Barefooted, St Marcellus of Tomi, and St Poemen.

EVENTS

1784 The first balloon ascent was made in Britain by James Tytler at Edinburgh. **1813** Napoleon defeated the Austrians at the Battle of Dresden. **1816** Algiers, then a refuge for Barbary pirates, was bombarded by Lord Exmouth. **1859** Edwin Drake was the first in the USA to strike oil – at Titusville, Pennsylvania. **1913** A Russian pilot, Lieutenant Peter Nesterov, became the first to perform the loop-the-loop. **1928** The anti-war Kellogg-Briand Pact was signed by 15 nations. **1939** The first jet-propelled aircraft, the Heinkel 178, made its first flight. **1958** The USSR launched *Sputnik 3*, carrying two dogs. **1987** At about 30,000 feet above the USA, the amorous behaviour of a just-married couple caused the pilot of a jet-liner on a coast-to-coast flight to land in Houston; the couple faced a maximum of one year in prison.

BIRTHS

Confucius, Chinese philosopher, **551 BC**; Georg Wilhelm Friedrich Hegel, German philosopher, **1770**; Samuel Goldwyn, US film magnate, **1882**; Lyndon B Johnson, 36th US President, **1908**; Donald Bradman, Australian cricketer, **1908**; Lester Young, US jazz saxophonist, **1909**; Mother Teresa, Albanian-born Indian missionary, **1910**.

DEATHS

Titian, Italian painter, **1576**; James Thomson, Scottish poet, **1748**; Louis Botha, South African statesman, **1919**; Le Corbusier, Swiss architect, **1965**; Haile Selassie, deposed Emperor of Ethiopia, **1975**; Earl Mountbatten of Burma, murdered by the IRA, **1979**.

'I think I was lucky - I was loved but not brought up.'
Björk Gudmundsdottir, Icelandic singer

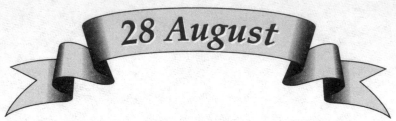

28 August

'You know you can only perceive real beauty in a person as they get older.'
Anouk Aimée, reported on 28 Aug 1988

Feast Day of St Augustine of Hippo, St Alexander of Constantinople, St Edmund Arrowsmith, St Julian of Brioude, and St Moses of Abyssinia.

✎ EVENTS ✎

1640 The Indian War in New England ended with the surrender of the Indians. **1849** Venice was taken by the Austrians after a siege. **1850** The Channel telegraph cable was laid between Dover and Cap Gris Nez. **1914** The Battle of Heligoland Bight, the first major naval battle of World War I, was fought. **1933** For the first time, a BBC-broadcasted appeal was used by the police in tracking down a wanted man. **1945** US forces under General George Marshall landed in Japan. **1963** The massive (200,000 people) civil rights march from the South ended in Washington DC where Martin Luther King delivered his famous 'I have a dream' speech. **1988** The Yan Hee Polyclinic in Bangkok, Thailand, reported on a new slimming technique – overweight Thais were suppressing their appetites by sticking lettuce seeds in their ears and pressing them in ten times before meals.

✎ BIRTHS ✎

Johann Wolfgang Goethe, German poet, novelist and dramatist, **1749**; Edward Burne-Jones, British painter, **1833**; Liam O'Flaherty, Irish novelist, **1896**; Godfrey Hounsfield, British inventor of the EMI-scanner, **1919**; Ben Gazzara, US film actor, **1930**.

✎ DEATHS ✎

Hugo Grotius, Dutch jurist and politician, **1645**; William Smith, British geologist, **1839**; Leigh Hunt, critic and poet, **1859**; Ernest Orlando Lawrence, US physicist, **1958**; Prince William of Gloucester, killed in an air crash, **1972**, John Huston, US film director, **1988**.

'I have a dream that my four little children will one day live in a
nation where they will not be judged by the colour of their skin
but by the content of their character.'
Martin Luther King

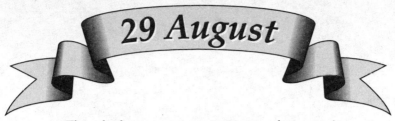

29 August

'The only alternative to co-existence is co-destruction.'
Pandit Nehru, reported on 29 Aug 1954

Feast Day of St Sabina of Rome, St Edwold of Cerne, and St Medericus or Merry.

❧ EVENTS ❧

1526 The Hungarians were defeated by the Turks at the Battle of Mohacs. **1831** Michael Faraday successfully demonstrated the first electrical transformer at the Royal Institute, London. **1835** The city of Melbourne, Australia, was founded. **1842** The Treaty of Nanking was signed between the British and the Chinese, ending the Opium War, and leasing the Hong Kong territories to Britain. **1848** The Boers were defeated by the British army at Boomplatz. **1882** Australia defeated England at cricket for the first time; the *Sporting Times* published an 'obituary' for English cricket. **1895** The Rugby League (called the 'Northern Union' until 1922) was formed from 21 clubs in the North of England. **1904** The third Olympic Games opened at St Louis, Missouri. **1953** The USSR exploded a hydrogen bomb. **1966** At Candlestick Park, San Francisco, the Beatles played their last live concert. **1991** The Supreme Soviet voted to suspend formally all activities of the Communist Party.

❧ BIRTHS ❧

John Locke, English philosopher, **1632**; Jean Auguste Dominique Ingres, French painter, **1780**; Ingrid Bergman, Swedish actress, **1915**; Charlie Parker, US jazz saxophonist, **1920**; Richard Attenborough, English actor and director, **1923**; Richard Gere, US actor, **1949**; Michael Jackson, US pop singer, **1958**.

❧ DEATHS ❧

Brigham Young, US Mormon leader, **1877**; Cesare Pavese, Italian novelist, **1950**; Éamon de Valera, Irish nationalist politician, **1975**; Ingrid Bergman, Swedish actress, **1982**; Lee Marvin, US actor, **1987**.

'In Casablanca there was often nothing in my face. But the audience put into my face what they thought I was giving.'
Ingrid Bergman, *My Story*

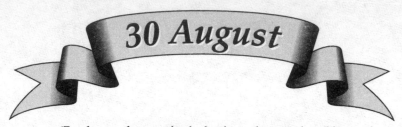
30 August

'For the past few months she has been charging about like
some bargain-basement Boadicea.'
Denis Healey, referring to Margaret Thatcher, reported on 7 Nov 1982

Feast Day of Saints Felix and Audauctus, St Fantinus, St Pammachius, St Margaret Ward, and St Ruan or Rumon.

❧ EVENTS ❧

1762 The French defeated Frederick II, King of Prussia, at Johannesburg. **1860** The first British tramway, operated by the Birkenhead Street Railway, was inaugurated by an American, George Francis Train. **1862** 'Stonewall' Jackson led the Confederates to victory at the second Battle of Bull Run, in Virginia, during the American Civil War. **1881** The first stereo system, for a telephonic broadcasting service, was patented in Germany by Clement Adler. **1901** Hubert Cecil Booth patented the vacuum cleaner. **1916** Paul von Hindenburg became Chief of the General Staff of Germany. **1939** In anticipation of German bombing, the great evacuation of children from British cities began, four days before the outbreak of World War II. **1941** The seige of Leningrad by German forces began (ended in Jan 1943). **1963** To reduce the risk of accidental nuclear war, the 'Hotline' between the US President and the Soviet Premier was established.

❧ BIRTHS ❧

Jacques Louis David, French painter, **1748**; Mary Wollstonecraft Shelley, English writer, **1797**; Ernest Rutherford, New Zealand physicist, **1871**; Raymond Massey, Canadian film actor, **1896**; Fred MacMurray, US film actor, **1908**; Denis Healey, British politician, **1917**; Jean Claude Killy, French ski champion, **1943**.

❧ DEATHS ❧

Cleopatra, queen of Egypt, **30 BC**; Louis XI, King of France, **1483**; John Ross, Scottish explorer, **1856**; Georges Sorel, French socialist philosopher, **1922**; J(oseph) J(ohn) Thomson, English physicist, **1940**.

'I used to be Snow White ... but I drifted.'
Mae West

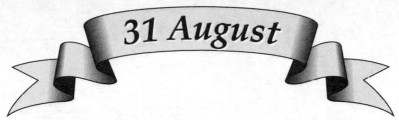

31 August

'Writers often do not know what they are writing. A lot of the depth of
the book comes from what is going on underground without his
[the author's] knowledge.'
V S Naipaul

National Day of Malaysia, and of Trinidad and Tobago. Feast Day of St Paulinus
of Trier, St Aidan of Lindisfarne, St Raymond Nonnatus, and The Servite
Martyrs of Prague.

EVENTS

1422 Henry VI, aged nine months, acceded as King. **1888** The body of Mary
Ann 'Polly' Nichols, the first victim of Jack the Ripper, was found mutilated in
Buck's Row. **1900** Coca Cola first went on sale in Britain. **1928** The
Brecht–Weill musical *The Threepenny Opera* was first performed, in Berlin. **1942**
The German offensive was halted by the British at the Battle of Alam al-Halfa,
marking the turning-point in the North African Campaign. **1957** Malaya, later
Malaysia, became independent. **1972** US swimmer Mark Spitz won five of the
seven gold medals he achieved in total at the Munich Olympics. **1983** The
USSR shot down a South Korean airliner, killing 269 people aboard. **1984** A
tropical storm hit the Philippines, killing over 1,000 people. **1989** Buckingham
Palace issued a brief statement stating that the Princess Royal, Princess Anne,
was separating from her husband, Captain Mark Phillips.

BIRTHS

Caligula, Roman emperor, **12**; Jahangir, Mogul emperor, **1569**; Maria
Montessori, Italian educationalist, **1870**; Fredric March, US actor, **1897**;
Bernard Lovell, British astronomer, **1913**; James Coburn, US film actor, **1928**;
Van Morrison, Irish rock vocalist, **1945**; Edwin Moses, US athlete, **1955**.

DEATHS

King Henry V, **1422**; John Bunyan, English author, **1688**; Charles Pierre
Baudelaire, French poet, **1867**; Georges Braque, French painter, **1963**; Rocky
Marciano, US heavyweight boxer, **1969**; John Ford, US film director, **1973**;
Henry Moore, British sculptor, **1986**.

1 September

'Thank God kids never mean well.'
Lily Tomlin

National Day of Libya. Feast Day of St Fiacre, St Giles or Aegidiu,
St Lupus or Leu of Sens, St Sebe, St Priscus of Capua, and St Verena.

≈ EVENTS ≈

AD 70 The destruction of Jerusalem under Titus took place. 1853 The world's
first triangular postage stamps were issued by the Cape of Good Hope. 1870
The siege of Metz (Franco-German War) started. 1886 The Severn Tunnel
was opened for goods traffic. 1920 The state of Lebanon was created by the
French. 1923 Nearly 200,000 people were killed in earthquakes in Tokyo and
Yokohama. 1928 Albania was declared a kingdom, with Zog I as king. 1933
The Shape of Things to Come, the classic science fiction novel by H G Wells,
was published. 1939 Germany invaded Poland, starting World War II. 1969
Colonel Khaddhafi seized power in Libya, after overthrowing King Idris I.
1972 Bobby Fischer beat Boris Spassky at Reykjavik, becoming the first US
world chess champion.

≈ BIRTHS ≈

Engelbert Humperdinck, German composer, 1854; Roger David Casement, Irish
nationalist, 1864; Edgar Rice Burroughs, US novelist, 1875; Francis Aston,
English physicist, 1877; Rocky Marciano, US heavyweight boxer, 1923; Lily
Tomlin, US comedienne, 1939; Leonard Slatkin, US conductor, 1954.

≈ DEATHS ≈

Pope Adrian IV, the only English pope, 1159; Jacques Cartier, French explorer,
1557; Louis XIV, the 'Sun King' of France, 1715; Richard Westmacott, British
sculptor, 1856; Siegfried Sassoon, English writer, 1967; François Mauriac,
French novelist, 1970.

'Let us be wary of ready-made ideas about courage and cowardice:
the same burden weighs infinitely more heavily on
some shoulders than others.'
François Mauriac

2 September

'Too much democracy leads to homosexuality, moral decay, and single-parent families.'
Mahathir bin Mohamed, Malaysian prime minister

Feast day of St William of Roskilde, The Martyrs of September 1792, St Agricolus, St Antoninus of Pamiers, St Brocard, and St Castor of Apt.

≈ EVENTS ≈

31 BC Emperor Augustus (Octavian) defeated Antony at the Battle of Actium. **1666** The Great Fire of London started; it destroyed 13,000 buildings in four days. **1752** The Julian calendar was used in Britain and the Colonies 'officially' for the last time; as in the rest of Europe, the following day became 14 Sept in the Gregorian calendar. **1898** The British, led by Lord Kitchener, defeated the Sudanese at the Battle of Omdurman and re-occupied Khartoum, the capital. **1906** Roald Amundsen completed his sailing round Canada's Northwest Passage. **1923** The Irish Free State held its first elections. **1939** Under the National Service Bill, men aged 19–41 were conscripted in Britain. **1958** China's first television station opened in Beijing. **1987** The CD-video, combining digital sound with high-definition video, was launched by Philips.

≈ BIRTHS ≈

John Howard, English philanthropist, **1726**; Giovanni Verga, Italian novelist and dramatist, **1840**; Wilhelm Ostwald, German chemist, **1853**; Frederick Soddy, English physical chemist, **1877**; Michael Hastings, English dramatist, **1938**; Jimmy Connors, US tennis player, **1952**.

≈ DEATHS ≈

José Ribera ('Lo Spagnoletto'), Spanish painter, **1652**; Thomas Telford, Scottish civil engineer, **1834**; Henri Rousseau, French painter, **1910**; Pierre de Coubertin, founder of the modern Olympics, **1937**; J R R Tolkein, English writer, **1973**.

'There is no such thing as a great talent without great will-power.'
Honoré de Balzac, *La Muse du Département*

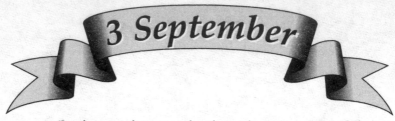
3 September

'It is better to die on your feet than to live on your knees.'
Dolores Ibarruri

Feast Day of St Simeon Stylites the Younger, St Phoebe, St Remaclus, St Aigulf or Ayoul of Lerins, St Gregory the Great, St Cuthburga, St Hildelitha, and St Macanisius.

EVENTS

1650 Cromwell defeated the Scots at the second Battle of Dunbar. **1651** The Royalist troops under Charles II were defeated by Oliver Cromwell at the second Battle of Worcester. **1783** Britain recognised US independence with the signing of a treaty in Paris. **1916** The first Zeppelin was shot down over England. **1930** Santo Domingo, in the Dominican Republic, was destroyed by a hurricane which killed 5,000 people. **1935** Malcolm Campbell reached a new world land speed record of 301.13 mph in *Bluebird* on Bonneville Salt Flats, Utah. **1939** Britain, New Zealand, Australia, and France declared war on Germany. **1943** The Allies landed at Salerno, on mainland Italy, and the Italian government surrendered. **1967** Sweden changed from driving on the left to the right. **1976** The US spacecraft *Viking 2* landed on Mars and began sending pictures of the red planet to earth.

BIRTHS

Joseph Wright, British painter, 1734; Louis Henry Sullivan, US architect, 1856; Jean-Léon Jaurès, French socialist politician, 1859; Macfarlane Burnet, Australian immunologist, 1899; Alan Ladd, US actor, 1913; Brian Lochore, New Zealand rugby player, 1940.

DEATHS

Oliver Cromwell, Lord Protector, 1658; Ivan Sergeyevich Turgenev, Russian dramatist, 1883; e e cummings, poet, US 1962; Frederick Louis MacNiece, British poet, 1963; Ho Chi Minh, president of North Vietnam, 1969; Frank Capra, US film director, 1991; David Brown, English engineer and industrialist, 1993.

'What's gone and what's past help
Should be past grief.'
William Shakespeare

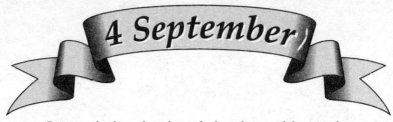

4 September

'Poor people always lean forward when they speak because they want people to listen to them. Rich people can sit back.'
Michael Caine, reported on 4 Sept 1966

Feast Day of St Rosalio, St Rose of Viterbo, Saints Marcellus and Valerian, St Marinus of San Marino, St Boniface I, pope, St Ultan of Ardbraccan, and St Ida of Herzfeld.

EVENTS

1260 The Battle of Montaperti, between the rival Guelphs and Ghibellines, was fought in Central Italy. **1870** Emperor Napoleon III, Bonaparte's nephew, was deposed and the Third Republic was proclaimed. **1886** Geronimo, the Apache chief, surrendered to the US army. **1909** The first Boy Scout rally was held at Crystal Palace, near London. **1940** The US Columbia Broadcasting System gave a demonstration of colour TV on station W2XAB. **1944** The Allies liberated Antwerp, Belgium. **1970** Natalia Makarova, of the Kirov Ballet, defected to the West. **1985** The wreck of the *Titanic* on the Atlantic seaboard was photographed by remote control. **1988** British Customs officials thwarted the first known attempt by persons to smuggle drugs into Britain from Holland using a helicopter.

BIRTHS

Vicomte François René de Chateaubriand, French author, **1768**; Anton Bruckner, Austrian composer, **1824**; Antonin Artaud, French dramatist and director, **1896**; Mary Renault, English novelist, **1905**; Dawn Fraser, Australian swimmer, **1937**; Tom Watson, US golfer, **1949**.

DEATHS

Charles Townshend, British politician, **1767**; James Wyatt, English architect, **1813**; Robert Schuman, French statesman, **1963**; Albert Schweitzer, French organist and missionary surgeon, **1965**; Georges Simenon, Belgian crime writer, **1989**.

'The original writer is not he who refrains from imitating others, but he who can be imitated by none.'
François de Chateaubriand

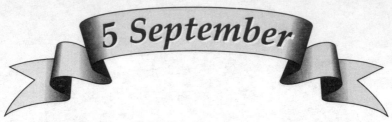

5 September

'Men are not allowed to think freely about chemistry and biology, why should they be allowed to think freely about political philosophy?'
Auguste Comte

Feast Day of Saints Urban and Theodore and their Companions, St Laurence Giustiniani, St Bertinus, and St Genebald of Laon.

≈ EVENTS ≈

1774 The first Continental Congress in America opened at Philadelphia. **1800** French troops surrendered Malta to the British, following Nelson's naval blockade. **1914** The first Battle of the Marne, during World War I, began. **1922** US aviator James Doolittle made the first US coast-to-coast flight in 21 hrs, 19 min. **1963** Christine Keeler, one of the women involved in the Profumo scandal, was arrested and charged with perjury. **1972** At the Olympic Games in Munich, terrorists of the Black September group seized Israeli athletes as hostages; nine of the Israelis, four of the terrorists, and one German policeman were killed. **1980** The world's longest road tunnel, the St Gotthard, was opened running 16km/10mi from Goschenen to Airolo, Switzerland. **1988** *No Sex Please – We're British*, the longest running comedy, closed (after 6,671 performances over 16 years).

≈ BIRTHS ≈

Louis VIII, King of France, 1187; Louis XIV, the 'Sun King' of France, 1638; Giacomo Meyerbeer, German composer, 1791; Victorien Sardou, French dramatist, 1831; Arthur Koestler, Hungarian author, 1905; Raquel Welch, US actress, 1940; Freddy Mercury, British pop singer, 1946.

≈ DEATHS ≈

Pieter Brueghel the Elder, Flemish painter, 1569; Auguste Comte, French philosopher, 1857; Charles Péguy, French poet, 1914; Josh White, US blues singer, 1969; Douglas Bader, British fighter pilot, 1962.

'A writer's ambition should be to trade a hundred contemporary readers for ten readers in ten years' time and for one reader in a hundred years' time.'
Arthur Koestler

6 September

'Photography is going to marry Miss Wireless, and heaven help everybody when they get married. Life will be very complicated.'
Marcus Adams, photographer, reported on 6 Sept 1925

Feast Day of St Eleutherius of Spoleto, St Cagnoald or Chainoaldus, and Saints Donatian, Laetus, and Others.

EVENTS

1522 Ferdinand Magellan's 17 surviving crew members reached the Spanish coast aboard the *Vittoria*, having completed the first circumnavigation of the world. **1852** Britain's first free lending library opened in Manchester. **1880** The first cricket test match in England was played between England and Australia at the Oval, London. **1901** US President William McKinley was shot and fatally wounded by an anarchist. **1941** Nazi Germany made the wearing of the yellow Star of David badges compulsory for all its Jewish citizens. **1965** India invaded West Pakistan. **1975** A massive earthquake centred on Lice, Turkey, caused nearly 3,000 deaths. **1989** Due to a computer error, 41,000 Parisians received letters charging them with murder, extortion, and organised prostitution instead of traffic violations.

BIRTHS

Marquis de Lafayette, French soldier and statesman, **1757**; John Dalton, British chemist, **1766**; Jane Addams, US sociologist, **1860**; Edward Appleton, British physicist, **1892**; Britt Ekland, Swedish film actress, **1943**; Roger Waters, English bassist, **1947**.

DEATHS

Suleiman I, sultan of Turkey, **1566**; Jean-Baptiste Colbert, French politician, **1683**; Gertrude Lawrence, English actress and singer, **1952**; Hendrik Verwoerd, South African prime minister, assassinated, **1966**.

'I am a businessman, not a moralist. Porn is in the eye of the beholder.'
Andrew Cameron, proprietor, United Newspapers,
reported on 6 Sept 1987

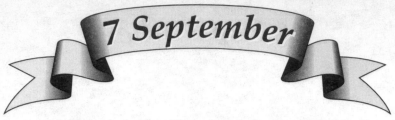
7 September

'A man travels the world in search of what he needs and
returns home to find it.'
George Moore

National Day of Brazil. Feast Day of St Anastasius the Fuller, St Cloud or
Clodoald, Saints Alcmund and Tilbert, St Grimonia, St Regina or Reine of
Alize, St Sozon, and St John of Nicomedia.

EVENTS

1812 The Russians were defeated by Napoleon's forces at the Battle of
Borodino, 70 mi west of Moscow. **1838** Grace Darling and her father rescued the
crew of the *Forfarshire*, a steamer wrecked off the Northumberland coast; she
subsequently became a national heroine. **1901** The Peace of Peking was signed,
ending the Boxer Rebellion in China. **1904** Francis Younghusband led a British
expedition to Tibet, where a treaty was signed with the Dalai Lama. **1973** Jackie
Stewart became world champion racing driver for the third consecutive year.
1986 Bishop Desmond Tutu was appointed Archbishop of Capetown, the first
black head of South African Anglicans. **1991** Peace talks on the Yugoslav civil
war opened in The Hague, the Netherlands, under EC sponsorship.

BIRTHS

Queen Elizabeth I, **1533**, John McDougall Stuart, Australian explorer, **1815**;
Elia Kazan, US stage and film director, **1909**; Anthony Quayle, English actor,
1913; Peter Lawford, English actor, **1923**; Sonny Rollins, US saxophonist,
1929; Buddy Holly, US rock singer, **1936**.

DEATHS

Catherine Parr, 6th wife of Henry VIII, **1548**; Armand Sully-Prudhomme, French
poet, **1907**; William Hunt, British painter, **1910**; Keith Moon, English rock
drummer, **1978**; Christy Brown, Irish novelist, **1981**; Liam O'Flaherty, Irish
novelist, **1984**.

'Those who have some means think that the most important
thing in the world is love. The poor know that it is money.'
Gerald Brenan, *Thoughts in a Dry Season*

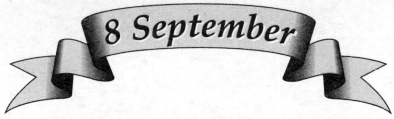

8 September

'If you press me to say why I loved him, I feel that it can only be
expressed by replying "Because it was him; because it was me" .'
Michel Eyquem de Montaigne

Feast Day of St Corbinian, St Disibod, St Eusebius, Saints Adrian and Natalia,
St Kingsmark or Cynfarch Oer, St Sergius I, pope, St Zeno, St Nestabus, and St
Nestor.

EVENTS

1664 The Dutch colony of New Amsterdam was surrendered to the British who
renamed it New York in 1669. **1831** William IV was crowned King of Great
Britain. **1886** Johannesburg, South Africa, was founded after the discovery of
gold there. **1888** The first English Football league matches were played. **1900**
Parts of Texas, USA, were hit by a tornado and tidal waves, which caused over
6,000 deaths near Galveston. **1926** Germany was admitted to the League of
Nations. **1944** The first German V2 flying bombs fell on Britain. **1951** The
Treaty of Peace with Japan was signed by 49 nations in San Francisco. **1966** The
Severn Road Bridge was officially opened. **1974** US President Ford fully
pardoned Richard Nixon for his part in the Watergate affair.

BIRTHS

King Richard I (the Lion Heart), **1157**; Ludovico Ariosto, Italian poet, **1474**;
Antonin Dvořák, Czech composer, **1841**; Siegfried Sassoon, English writer,
1863; Jean-Louis Barrault, French actor and director, **1910**; Peter Sellers,
English actor and comedian, **1925**; Frankie Avalon, US singer, **1940**.

DEATHS

Francisco Gomez de Quevedo y Villegas, Spanish writer, **1645**; George
Bradshaw, British publisher of the first railway guides, **1853**; Richard Strauss,
German composer, **1949**; André Derain, French painter, **1954**; Jean Seberg, US
actress, **1979**.

'Most men make little use of their speech other than to give
evidence against their own understanding.'
Lord Halifax

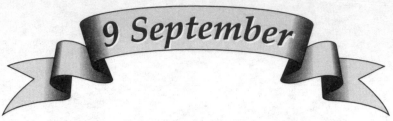

9 September

'A woman will always sacrifice herself if you give her the opportunity. It is her favourite form of self-indulgence.'
W Somerset Maugham

Feast Day of St Omer or Audomaurus, St Peter Claver, St Ciaran or Kieran of Clonmacnois, St Bettelin, St Joseph of Volokolamsk, St Gorgonius, and St Isaac or Sahak the Great.

EVENTS

1513 The Scots were defeated by the English at the Battle of Flodden Field. **1835** Local government in Britain was constituted under the British Municipal Corporations Act. **1850** California became the 31st state of the Union. **1943** Allied forces landed at Salerno, Italy. **1945** Palestinians attempted to hijack an El Al flight but were overpowered by security guards. The Israelis reluctantly handed over the failed hijackers at Heathrow, where the plane made its landing. **1971** Geoffrey Jackson, who had been kidnapped by the Tupamaros in Uruguay eight months previously, was released. **1975** Czech tennis player Martina Navratilova, aged 18, defected to the West, requesting political asylum in the USA. **1985** Massive earthquakes in Mexico left more than 4,700 dead and 30,000 injured.

BIRTHS

Cardinal Richelieu, French statesman, **1585**; Luigi Galvani, Italian physiologist, **1737**; Leo Tolstoy, Russian novelist, **1828**; James Hilton, English novelist, **1900**; Otis Redding, US singer and songwriter, **1941**; John Curry, English figure skating champion, **1949**.

DEATHS

King William I (the Conqueror), **1087**; James IV, King of Scotland, **1513**; Giambattista Piranesi, Italian architect, **1778**; Stéphane Mallarmé, French poet, **1898**; Henri Toulouse-Lautrec, French painter, **1901**; Mao Zedong, Chinese leader, **1976**.

'Political power grows out of the barrel of a gun.'
Mao Zedong

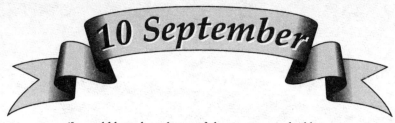
10 September

'It would have been better if the experiment had been conducted in a small country to make it clear that it was a utopian idea, although a beautiful idea.'
Boris Yeltsin

Feast Day of St Theodard of Maestricht, St Salvius or Salvy of Albi, St Ambrose Barlow, St Aubert of Avranches, Saints Menodora, Metrodora and Nymphodora, St Finian of Moville, St Nemesian, St Nicholas of Tolentino, and St Pulcheria.

❧ EVENTS ❧

1721 The Peace of Nystad was concluded between Russia and Sweden. **1823** Simón Bolívar, known as The Liberator, became the dictator of Peru. **1894** George Smith, a London cab driver, became the first person to be convicted for drunken driving; he was fined 20s (£1). **1919** The Treaty of Saint-Germain was signed; the new boundaries it set brought about the end of the Austrian Empire. **1942** In a single raid, the RAF dropped 100,000 bombs on Dusseldorf. **1945** Former Norwegian Premier Vidkun Quisling, who had collaborated with the Germans during World War II, was sentenced to death. **1981** Picasso's *Guernica* was returned to Spain after 40 years in US custodianship; the artist had refused to show the painting in Spain before the restoration of democracy. **1989** Hungary opened its border to the West allowing thousands of East Germans to leave, much to the anger of the East German government.

❧ BIRTHS ❧

Giovanni Tiepolo, Italian painter, **1727**; John Soane, English architect, **1753**; Mungo Park, Scottish explorer, **1771**; Franz Werfel, Austrian novelist and poet, **1890**; Robert Wise, US film director, **1914**; Arnold Palmer, US golfer, **1929**; José Feliciano, US singer, **1945**.

❧ DEATHS ❧

Louis IV, King of France, **954**; Mary Wollstonecraft, British feminist, **1797**; Huey Long, US politician, assassinated, **1935**; Charles Cruft, British dog expert, **1938**; Balthazar Johannes Vorster, South African Nationalist politician, **1983**.

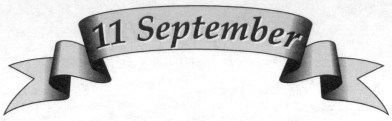

'I'm not defying anybody. I'm obeying God.'
Desmond Tutu, reported on 11 Sept 1988

Feast Day of St Theodora of Alexandria, St Peter of Chavanon, Saints Protus and Hyacinth, St Deiniol, St Patiens of Lyon, and St Paphnutius.

EVENTS

1709 The Duke of Marlborough and Prince Eugene of Austria defeated the French, under Marshal Villars, at the Battle of Malplaquet. **1777** American troops led by George Washington were defeated by the British at the Battle of Brandywine Creek, in the American War of Independence. **1841** The London to Brighton commuter express train began regular service, taking just 105 minutes. **1855** In the Crimean War, Sebastopol was taken by the Allies after capitulation by the Russians. **1922** A British mandate was declared in Palestine. **1951** Stravinsky's *The Rake's Progress* was performed for the first time, in Venice; the libretto was by W H Auden. **1973** A military junta, with US support, overthrew the elected government of Chile. **1978** Georgi Markov, a Bulgarian defector, was fatally stabbed by a poisoned umbrella point wielded by a Bulgarian secret agent in London.

BIRTHS

Pierre de Ronsard, French poet, 1524; James Thomson, Scottish poet, 1700; O Henry, US short story writer, 1862; James Hopwood Jeans, British mathematician and scientist, 1877; D H Lawrence, English writer, 1885; Barry Sheene, British racing motor cyclist, 1950.

DEATHS

Giovanni Domenico Cassini, Italian-French astronomer, 1712; David Thomas Graham, Scottish chemist, 1869; Jan Christian Smuts, South African statesman, 1950; Nikita Khrushchev, Russian leader, 1971; Salvador Allende Gossens, Chilean politician, 1973; Peter Tosh, Jamaican reggae star, 1987.

'I believe that Providence has chosen me for a great work.'
Adolf Hitler, reported on 11 Sept 1932

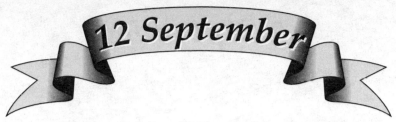
12 September

'While we may believe all men are brethren, we strongly
object to any big brother trying to push us around.'
Jack Tanner, TUC president, reported on 12 Sept 1954

Feast Day of St Guy of Anderlecht, St Ailbhe, and St Eanswida.

❧ EVENTS ❧

1609 Henry Hudson sailed the sloop *Half Moon* into New York Harbour and up
to Albany to discover the river named after him. **1878** Cleopatra's Needle, the
obelisk of Thothmes II, was erected on London's Embankment. **1910** Alice
Stebbins Wells, a former social worker, became the world's first policewoman,
appointed by the Los Angeles Police Department. **1914** The Allies were
victorious at the First Battle of Marne, in World War I. **1919** Italian writer and
nationalist Gabriele D'Annunzio led an unofficial army and seized Fiume from
Yugoslavia. **1940** The Lascaux Caves, France, containing prehistoric wall
paintings, were discovered. **1943** Benito Mussolini, imprisoned by the Allies,
was rescued by German parachutists. **1974** A military coup deposed Emperor
Haile Selassie of Ethiopia, the Lion of Judah.

❧ BIRTHS ❧

Richard Jordan Gatling, US inventor, **1818**; Herbert Henry Asquith, British
statesman, **1852**; Maurice Chevalier, French actor and entertainer, **1888**; Louis
MacNeice, British poet, **1907**; John Cleveland 'Jesse' Owens, US athlete, **1913**;
Wesley Hall, West Indies cricketer and politician, **1937**.

❧ DEATHS ❧

François Couperin, French composer, **1733**; Jean-Philippe Rameau, French
composer, **1764**; Gebhard Leberecht von Blücher, Prussian general and field-
marshal, **1819**; Peter Mark Roget, English lexicographer, **1869**; Steve Biko,
South African civil rights leader, **1977**; Anthony Perkins, US actor, **1992**.

'The most potent weapon in the hands of the aggressor is the
mind of the oppressed.'
Steve Biko

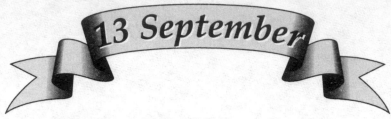

13 September

'Suicide is a real threat to health in a modern society.'
Virginia Bottomley

Feast Day of St John Chrysostom, St Maurilius of Angers, St Amatus or Amé, abbot, and St Eulogius of Alexandria.

❧ EVENTS ❧

1759 The British defeated the French at the Battle of Quebec, completing the British conquest of North America. **1788** New York became the capital of the USA (until 1789). **1845** The Knickerbocker Club, the first baseball club, was founded in New York. **1914** The first Battle of the Aisne, during World War I, began. **1942** The Germans began their attack on Stalingrad. **1943** General Chiang Kai-shek was re-elected president of the Republic of China. **1956** Little Richard recorded 'Tutti Frutti' in Los Angeles with cleaned-up lyrics. **1957** *The Mousetrap* became Britain's longest running play, reaching its 1,998th performance. **1989** Britain's biggest ever banking computer error gave customers an extra £2 billion in a period of 30 minutes; 99.3 per cent of the money was reportedly returned.

❧ BIRTHS ❧

William Betty, British boy actor, **1791**; Arnold Schoenberg, Austrian composer, **1874**; John Joseph Priestley, English author, **1894**; Claudette Colbert, French actress, **1905**; John Smith, British politician, **1938**; Jacqueline Bisset, English actress, **1944**.

❧ DEATHS ❧

Andrea Mantegna, Italian painter, **1506**; Michel Eyquem de Montaigne, French essayist, **1592**; Charles James Fox, English statesman, **1806**; Alexis-Emmanuel Chabrier, French composer, **1894**; Leopold Stokowski, US conductor, **1977**; Joe Pasternak, US film producer, **1991**.

'I do not have to forgive my enemies, I have had them all shot.'
Ramón María Narvález, on his deathbed when a
priest asked if he forgave them

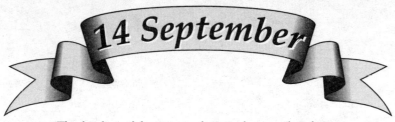
14 September

'The freedom of the press works in such a way that there is
not much freedom from it.'
Princess Grace of Monaco

Feast Day of St Maternus of Cologne and St Notburga.

≈ EVENTS ≈

1402 The English defeated the Scots at the Battle of Homildon Hill. **1759** A
Journey Through Europe, or the play of Geography, the earliest dated English board
game, went on sale, priced 8s (40p). **1812** Napoleon entered Moscow in his
disastrous invasion of Russia. **1891** The first penalty kick was taken in an
English League football game was taken by Heath of Wolverhampton Wanderers
against Accrington. **1901** Theodore Roosevelt became the 26th US president,
12 hours after the death of President McKinley, who had been shot by an
anarchist on 6 Sept. **1923** Miguel Primo de Riviera became dictator of Spain.
1959 The Soviet *Lunik II* became the first spacecraft to land on the Moon. **1991**
The South African government, the ANC, and the Inkatha Freedom Party
signed a peace accord aimed at ending the factional violence in the black
townships.

≈ BIRTHS ≈

Peter Lely, Dutch painter, **1617**; Baron von Humboldt, German traveller and
naturalist, **1769**; Jan Garrigue Masaryk, Czech statesman, **1886**; Peter Scott,
British artist and ornithologist, **1909**; Jack Hawkins, British film actor, **1910**;
Kepler Wessels, Australian cricketer, **1957**.

≈ DEATHS ≈

Dante Alighieri, Italian poet, **1321**; James Fenimore Cooper, US novelist,
1851; Augustus Pugin, English architect, **1852**; Arthur Wellesley, 1st Duke of
Wellington, English soldier and politician, **1852**; Isadora Duncan, US dancer,
1927; Princess Grace of Monaco (Grace Kelly), **1982**.

'No one who has not sat in prison knows what the State is like.'
Leo Tolstoy

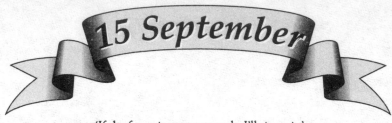
15 September

'If the fence is strong enough, I'll sit on it.'
Cyril Smith, reported on 15 Sept 1974

National day of Costa Rica. The Battle of Britain day. Feast Day of St Nicetus the Goth, St Nicomedes, St Aachard or Aichardus, St Mirin, and St Catherine of Genoa.

≈ EVENTS ≈

1784 The first ascent in a hydrogen balloon in England was made by the Italian aeronaut Vincenzo Lunardi. **1812** The Russians set fire to Moscow in order to halt the French occupation. **1830** The Manchester and Liverpool railway opened; during the ceremony, William Huskisson, MP, became the first person to be killed by a train. **1915** Military tanks, designed by Ernest Swinton, were first used by the British Army, at Flers, in the Somme offensive. **1917** Alexander Kerensky proclaimed Russia a republic. **1935** The Nuremburg laws were passed in Germany, outlawing Jews and making the swastika the country's official flag. **1964** The *Sun*, which became Britain's biggest selling newspaper, was first published. **1974** The civil war between Christians and Muslims in Beirut began. **1985** Tony Jacklin's European golf team won the Ryder Cup from the USA who had long dominated the competition.

≈ BIRTHS ≈

Trajan, Roman emperor, **53**; Titus Oates, British priest and conspirator, **1649**; William Taft, 27th US president, **1857**; Agatha Christie, English detective novelist, **1890**; Jean Renoir, French film director, **1894**; Jessye Norman, US soprano, **1945**; Freddie Mercury, British rock singer, **1946**.

≈ DEATHS ≈

Isambard Kingdom Brunel, British engineer, **1859**; John Hanning Speke, British explorer, **1864**; José Echegaray, Spanish dramatist and scientist, **1916**; Geoffrey Fisher, former Archbishop of Canterbury, **1972**; Gustav VI, King of Sweden, **1973**; Robert Penn Warren, US novelist, **1989**.

'He may be a little bad now and then - but what man isn't?'
Victoria Gotti, wife of Mafia boss John Gotti

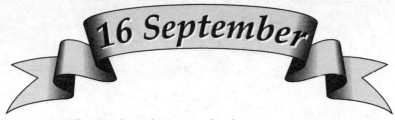

16 September

'The sexual impulse in its widest form was a very great
impulse towards the building of the Panama Canal.'
D H Lawrence, reported on 16 Sept 1923

National day of Mexico. Feast Day of St Cornelius, pope, St Cyprian, St
Ludmila, St Ninian, Saints Abundius and Abundantius, St Edith of Wilton, and
St Euphemia.

EVENTS

1847 The house in which Shakespeare was born in Stratford-upon-Avon
became the first building in Britain to be purchased for preservation. **1859**
David Livingstone discovered Lake Nyasa. **1906** The US Buick and Oldsmobile
car manufacturers merged to become General Motors. **1941** The Shah of Iran,
Reza Khan Pahlavi, abdicated. **1963** Malaysia became independent and a mob
of over 100,000 burned down the British Embassy. **1969** Biba, considered
London's trendiest store in the 'swinging 60s', opened on Kensington High
Street. **1976** The Episcopal Church in the USA approved the ordination of
women to the priesthood. **1987** For the first time in South Africa, Othello was
performed with a black actor, John Khani, playing the Moor. **1991** All Iran-
Contra charges against Oliver North were dropped.

BIRTHS

King Henry V, **1387**; Alexander Korda, British film director and producer,
1893; Lauren Bacall, US actress, **1924**; Charles Haughey, Irish politician,
1925; B B King, US blues singer, **1926**; Peter Falk, US actor, **1927**; Andy
Irvine, British rugby footballer, **1951**.

DEATHS

Tomás de Torquemada, Spanish Inquisitor-General, **1498**; Gabriel Daniel
Fahrenheit, German physicist, **1736**; Louis XVIII, King of France, **1824**; Leo
Amery, British statesman and journalist, **1955**; Walter Greenwood, English
novelist, **1974**; Maria Callas, US opera singer, **1977**.

'I think your whole life shows in your face and you should be proud of that.'
Lauren Bacall, reported on 6 March 1988

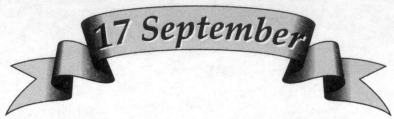
17 September

'Anyone who looks for a source of power in the transformation
of the atom is talking moonshine.'
Sir Ernest Rutherford, reported on 17 Sept 1933

Feast day of St Francis of Camporosso, St Hildegard, St Columba of Cordova,
Saints Socrates and Stephen, St Satyrus of Milan, St Theodora, St Lambert of
Maastricht, St Robert Bellarmine, and St Peter Arbues.

EVENTS

1787 The Constitution of the United States of America was signed. **1862**
General McClellan repulsed General Lee's invasion of the North at Antietam,
ending one of the decisive battles in the American Civil War. **1900** The
Commonwealth of Australia, a federation of six colonies, was proclaimed. **1908** Lt
Selfridge, on a test flight with Orville Wright, was killed when the plane crashed,
becoming the first passenger to die in an air crash. **1931** The first long-playing
record was demonstrated in New York by RCA-Victor, but the venture failed
because of the high price of the players. **1939** Poland was invaded by the USSR.
1944 The British airborne invasion of Arnhem, Holland began as part of
'Operation Market Garden'. **1991** Estonia, Latvia, Lithuania, North and South
Korea, the Marshall Islands, and Micronesia were admitted to the United Nations.

BIRTHS

Francisco Gomez de Quevado y Villegas, Spanish poet and satirist, **1580**;
William Carlos Williams, US poet, **1883**; Frederick Ashton, British
choreographer, **1906**; Stirling Moss, English racing driver, **1929**; Anne
Bancroft, US actress, **1931**; Maureen Connolly, US tennis player, **1934**.

DEATHS

Philip IV, King of Spain, **1665**; Tobias George Smollett, Scottish novelist,
1771; William Henry Fox Talbot, English photographic pioneer, **1877**; Count
Folke Bernadotte, Swedish diplomat, assassinated, **1948**; Laura Ashley, Welsh
designer and fabric retailer, **1985**.

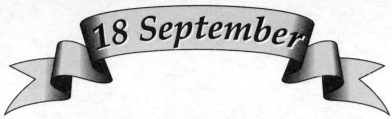

18 September

'We're born naked and the rest is drag. Mine is just more glamorous.'
Ru Paul, US drag queen

National Day of Chile. Feast Day of St John Massias, St Joseph of Cupertino, St Richardis, St Ferreolus of Limoges, St Ferreolus of Vienne, and St Methodius of Olympus.

⟨ EVENTS ⟩

1851 The *New York Times* was first published. **1879** Blackpool's famous illuminations were switched on for the first time. **1910** The Chilean revolt against Spanish rule began. **1914** The Irish Home Rule Bill went into effect. **1918** The Battle of Megiddo, in Palestine, began. **1927** CBS, the Columbia Broadcasting System, was inaugurated in the USA. **1931** Japan seized Manchuria and set up a puppet state called Manchukuo – it was returned to China in 1945 after World War II. **1934** The USSR was admitted to the League of Nations. **1939** William Joyce, whose upper-class accent earned him the nickname Lord Haw-Haw, made his first Nazi propaganda broadcast from Germany to the UK. **1981** France abolished execution by guillotine. **1991** The Yugoslav navy began a blockade of seven port cities on the Adriatic coast in Dalmatia.

⟨ BIRTHS ⟩

Dr Samuel Johnson, English writer and lexicographer, **1709**; Jean Bernard Léon Foucault, French physicist, **1819**; Greta Garbo, Swedish film actress, **1905**; Jack Cardiff, British film director, **1914**; Frankie Avalon, US singer and actor, **1939**; Peter Shilton, English footballer, **1949**.

⟨ DEATHS ⟩

Leonhard Euler, Swiss mathematician, **1783**; William Hazlitt, British essayist and critic, **1830**; Dag Hammarskjöld, Swedish UN secretary-general, **1961**; Sean O'Casey, Irish dramatist, **1964**; John Douglas Cockcroft, English nuclear physicist, **1967**; Jimi Hendrix, US rock guitarist, **1970**.

'I never said "I want to be alone." I only said "I want to be let alone." '
Greta Garbo

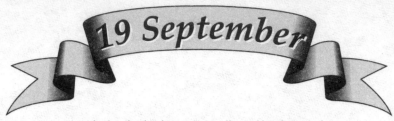

19 September

'A girl who thinks that a man will treat her better after
marriage than before is a fool.'
William Clarke Hall, reported on 19 Sept 1920

Feast Day of St Januarius of Benevento, St Peleus and his Companions, St Emily
de Rodat, St Mary of Cerevellon, St Goericus or Abbo, St Theodore of
Canterbury, St Susanna of Eleutheropolis, and St Sequanus or Seine.

EVENTS

1356 Led by Edward, the Black Prince, the English defeated the French at the
Battle of Poitiers in the Hundred Years' War. **1783** The Montgolfier brothers
sent up the first balloon with live creatures aboard; passengers included a sheep,
a rooster, and a duck. **1876** The US inventor Melville Bissell patented the first
carpet sweeper. **1893** New Zealand became the first country to grant its female
citizens the right to vote. **1945** William Joyce (Lord Haw-Haw) was sentenced
to hang for treason. **1960** A new dance craze began when Chubby Checker's
'The Twist' entered the US charts. **1960** The new traffic wardens issued the first
344 parking tickets in London. **1989** The New York Supreme Court reversed an
earlier decision to award the America's Cup to New Zealand, allowing the San
Diego Yacht Club to retain the award.

BIRTHS

Lajos Kossuth, Hungarian statesman, **1802**; George Cadbury, English chocolate
manufacturer and social reformer, **1839**; William Golding, English novelist,
1911; Jeremy Irons, English actor, **1948**; Rosemary Casals, US tennis player,
1948; Twiggy (Lesley Hornby), English model and actress, **1949**.

DEATHS

Meyer Amschel Rothschild, German banker, **1812**; James Garfield, 20th US
president, **1881**; Thomas John Barnardo, British philanthropist, **1905**; David
Low, British cartoonist, **1963**; Chester Carlson, US inventor of the xerography
photocopying process, **1968**; Roy Kinnear, English comedy actor, **1988**.

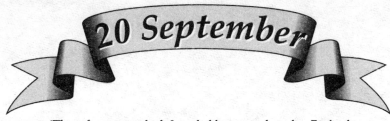

20 September

'The inference to which I am led by my study is that England
is heading rapidly toward an era of great revolutionary upheavals.'
Leon Trotsky, reported on 20 Sept 1925

Feast Day of Saints Fausta and Evilasius, St Candida of Carthage, St Vincent
Madelgarius, and Saints Theodore, Philippa, and their Companions.

～ EVENTS ～

451 The Romans defeated the Huns under Attila at Châlon-sur-Marne. **1519**
Ferdinand Magellan, with a fleet of five small ships, sailed from Seville on his
expedition around the world. **1854** The Russian army was defeated by the Allied
armies at the Battle of Alma in the Crimean War; the first six Victoria Crosses
to be awarded to the British Army were won at this battle. **1928** The Fascist
Party took over the supreme legislative body in Rome, replacing the Chamber of
Deputies. **1961** Argentinian Antonio Abertondo started the first successful
non-stop swim across the Channel and back, completed in 43 hr 5 min. **1966**
The liner *Queen Elizabeth II* (QE2) was launched at Clydebank, Scotland. **1984**
The US embassy in Beirut was attacked by a suicide bomber; explosives within
a lorry were set off, killing 40 people.

～ BIRTHS ～

Alexander the Great, **356 BC**; Henry Arthur Jones, British dramatist, **1851**;
Upton Sinclair, US novelist, **1878**; Jelly Roll Morton, US pianist and composer,
1885; John Dankworth, English bandleader and jazzman, **1927**; Sophia Loren,
Italian film actress, **1934**.

～ DEATHS ～

Robert Emmet, Irish nationalist, executed, **1803**; Jakob Karl Grimm, German
philologist, **1863**; Annie Besant, British socialist and feminist activist, **1933**; Jean
Sibelius, Finnish composer, **1957**; George Seferis, Greek poet-diplomat, **1971**.

'From Hollywood as well as Peking we have learned that power
comes down the barrel of a gun.'
Reverend Don Cupitt, reported on 20 Sept 1970

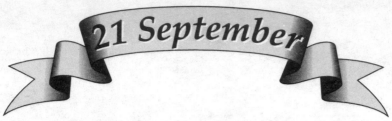

21 September

'Meanwhile, Time is flying - flying never to return.'
Virgil

National day of Malta Feast day of St Theodore of Chernigov, The Martyrs of Korea, St Michael of Chernigov, St Matthew, and St Maures of Troyes.

☞ EVENTS ☞

1529 The Turkish army under Suleiman the Magnificent was defeated at Vienna. **1745** Bonnie Prince Charles and his Jacobite army defeated the English at the Battle of Prestonpans in Scotland. **1784** *The Pennsylvania Packet and General Advertiser*, the first successful US daily newspaper, was published. **1915** Stonehenge was sold at auction to Mr C H Chubb for £6,600. Mr Chubb presented it to the nation three years later. **1917** Latvia proclaimed its independence. **1938** The Anglo-French plan to cede Sudetenland to Germany was accepted by the Czech cabinet. **1949** The Republic of Ireland beat England 2–0 at Goodison Park – England's first home defeat by a foreign football team. **1974** Over 8,000 people were killed by floods caused by hurricanes in Honduras. **1989** Hurricane Hugo struck the US coastal states of Georgia and South Carolina, causing widespread damage and loss of life.

☞ BIRTHS ☞

Girolamo Savonarola, Italian political reformer and martyr, **1452**; John Loudon McAdam, Scottish engineer, **1756**; Edmund William Gosse, English author, **1849**; H G Wells, English writer, **1866**; Larry Hagman, US actor, **1931**; Stephen King, US novelist, **1948**.

☞ DEATHS ☞

Virgil, Roman poet, **19 BC**; King Edward II, murdered, **1327**; Sir Walter Scott, Scottish novelist, **1832**; Arthur Schopenhauer, German philosopher, **1860**; Haakon VII, King of Norway, **1957**; William Plomer, South African author, **1973**; Walter Brennan, US film actor, **1974**.

'I don't know if History is tragic, but I am convinced that we must act as if it is, so that it will not be.'
Alain Minc, French economist

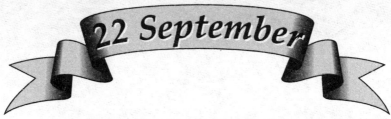

22 September

I only regret that I have but one life to lose for my country.
Nathan Hale, American revolution hero, on being hanged by the British

Feast day of St Felix II, pope, St Landus or Lô, St Bodo, St Emmeramus, St Maurice of Agaunum, St Thomas of Villanova, The Theban Legion, St Phocas the Gardener, and St Salaberga.

✐ EVENTS ✐

1735 Sir Robert Walpole became the first prime minister to occupy 10 Downing Street. **1792** France was declared a Republic. **1862** US President Lincoln issued the Emancipation Proclamation, ordering the freeing of slaves. **1869** Wagner's opera *Das Rheingold* was first performed in Munich. **1914** Three British cruisers, *Aboukir*, *Hogue*, and *Cressy*, were torpedoed and sunk by German U-boats. **1955** Argentinian leader Juan Perón was deposed in a military coup. **1955** Independent TV began operating; Britain's first commercial and first woman newsreader were transmitted. **1972** Idi Amin gave the 8,000 Asians in Uganda 48 hours to leave the country. **1980** The Solidarity movement in Poland was created, with Lech Walesa as its elected leader. **1985** A severe earthquake hit Mexico, killing 2,000 people. **1989** An IRA bomb attack on the Royal Marines School of Music killed ten and injured twelve of the bandsmen.

✐ BIRTHS ✐

Anne of Cleves, 4th wife of Henry VIII, **1515**; Michael Faraday, English chemist and physicist, **1791**; Christabel Pankhurst, English suffragette, **1880**; Erich von Stroheim, Austrian actor and film director, **1885**; John Houseman, US actor and producer, **1902**; Fay Weldon, British author, **1931**; Catherine Oxenberg, US film actress, **1961**.

✐ DEATHS ✐

Nathan Hale, American revolutionary patriot, hanged, **1776**; Axel Springer, German publisher, **1985**; Jaco Pastorius, US bass guitarist, **1987**; Louis Kentner, English pianist, **1987**; Irving Berlin, US composer, **1989**.

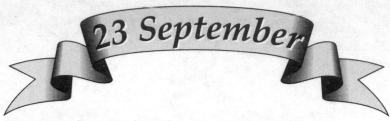

23 September

'At bottom God is nothing more than an exalted father.'
Sigmund Freud

National day of Saudi Arabia. Feast day of Saints Andrew, John, Peter and Antony, and St Adamnan or Eunan of Iona.

EVENTS

480 BC The Persians were defeated by the Greeks at the Battle of Salamis. **1779** In the American War of Independence, a French and American fleet commanded by John Paul Jones, captured the British ship Serapis in the Battle of Flamborough Head. **1803** The British under Arthur Wellesley (later Duke of Wellington) defeated Scindia and the Rajah of Berar at Assaye in India. **1846** German astronomer Johann Galle discovered the planet Neptune. **1848** Chewing gum was first commercially produced in the USA by John Curtis in his home, and was called 'State of Maine Pure Spruce Gum'. **1912** *Cohen Collects a Debt*, the first of US film producer Mack Sennet's silent Keystone Cops films, was released. **1940** The George Cross and the George Medal for civilian acts of courage were instituted. **1973** Juan Perón was re-elected President of Argentina; he had been ousted in 1955. **1974** The world's first Ceefax teletext service was begun by the BBC.

BIRTHS

Augustus, 1st Roman Emperor, **63 BC**; Ferdinand VI, King of Spain, **1713**; Mickey Rooney, US film actor, **1920**; John Coltrane, US saxophonist, **1926**; Ray Charles, US singer, **1930**; Julio Iglesias, Spanish singer, **1943**; Bruce Springsteen, US rock singer, **1949**; Jeff Squire, rugby footballer, **1951**.

DEATHS

Nicholas François Mansart, French architect, **1666**; Prosper Merimée, French novelist, **1870**; Wilkie Collins, English novelist, **1889**; Sigmund Freud, Austrian psychoanalyst, **1939**; Pablo Neruda, Chilean poet, **1973**; Bob Fosse, US director, **1987**.

'It is not enough to succeed. Others must fail.'
Gore Vidal

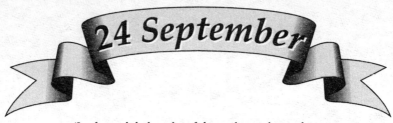

24 September

'In the real dark night of the soul it is always three
o'clock in the morning, day after day.'
F Scott Fitzgerald

Feast day of St Pacifico of San Severino, St Robert Flower of Knaresborough, St
Geremarus or Germer, and St Gerard of Csanad.

➣ EVENTS ➣

1776 The St Leger horse race was run for the first time at Doncaster. **1852**
French engineer Henri Giffaud made the first flight in a dirigible balloon, from
Paris to Trappe. **1930** Noel Coward's *Private Lives* was first staged in London.
1953 *The Robe*, the first Cinemascope film, premiered in Hollywood. **1960** The
first nuclear-powered aircraft carrier, the USS *Enterprise*, was launched at
Newport, Virginia. **1975** British mountaineers Dougal Haston and Doug Scott
became the first to reach Mt Everest's summit via the south-west face. **1980** The
Iraqis blew up the Abadan oil refinery, turning the Iran–Iraq conflict into a full
scale war. **1991** The Shiite Muslim Revolutionary Justice Organization freed
British hostage Jack Mann, kidnapped in May 1989.

➣ BIRTHS ➣

Geronimo Cardano, Italian physician and mathematician, **1501**; Horace
Walpole, 4th Earl of Orford, English writer, **1717**; F Scott Fitzgerald, US
novelist, **1896**; Howard Walter Florey, pathologist, **1898**; Svetlana Beriosova,
British ballerina, **1932**; Gerry Marsden, English rock musician, **1942**.

➣ DEATHS ➣

Pépin III (the Short), King of the Franks, **768**; Pope Innocent II, **1143**;
Paracelsus, Swiss physician, alchemist, and scientist, **1541**; Isobel Baillie,
Scottish oratorio singer, **1983**.

'India is a geographical term. It is no more a united nation
than the Equator.'
Winston Churchill

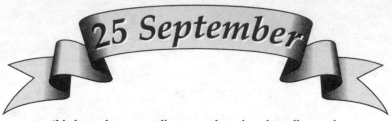
25 September

'I believe that man will not merely endure, he will prevail.
He is immortal, not because he, alone among creatures, has an
inexhaustible voice but because he has a soul, a spirit
capable of compassion and sacrifice and endurance.'
William Faulkner, speech on receiving the Nobel Prize

Feast Day of St Sergius of Radonezh, St Vincent Strambi, St Aunacharius or
Aunaire, St Albert of Jerusalem, St Firminus of Amiens, St Ceolfirth, St Fibar
or Bairre.

∾ EVENTS ∾

1066 King Harold II defeated the King of Norway, Harald Hardrada, at the
Battle of Stamford Bridge. **1513** Vasco Balboa, Spanish explorer, became the
first European to sight the Pacific Ocean after crossing the Darien isthmus. **1818**
The first blood transfusion using human blood, as opposed to earlier attempts
with animal blood, took place at Guy's Hospital in London. **1888** London's
Royal Court Theatre, in Sloane Square, opened. **1909** The French battleship
Liberté exploded in Toulon Harbour, killing 226 people. **1915** The Battle of
Loos, in World War I, began; it would continue into Oct. **1954** François
Duvalier ('Papa' Doc) was elected president of Haiti. **1972** Norway voted
against joining the EC in a referendum.

∾ BIRTHS ∾

Jean Philippe Rameau, French composer, **1683**; William Faulkner, US novelist,
1897; Mark Rothko, US painter, **1903**; Dmitri Shostakovich, Russian
composer, **1906**; Colin Davis, British conductor, **1927**; Michael Douglas, US
actor, **1944**; Christopher Reeve, US film actor, **1952**.

∾ DEATHS ∾

Samuel Butler, English writer, **1680**; Johann Strauss the Elder, Austrian
composer, **1849**; Emily Post, US writer, **1960**; Erich Maria Remarque, German
novelist, **1970**; Walter Pidgeon, US film actor, **1984**.

'All Quiet on the Western Front'
Erich Maria Remarque, title of novel

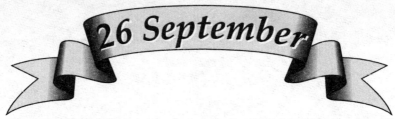
26 September

'I see decline all around me, people in sort of huddled ghettos of the poor and disadvantaged. I don't think you can find that on the same scale in other countries of the European Community, and I'm a bit ashamed that's going on in our country.'
John Smith

Feast day of Saints Cosmas and Damian, St Nilus of Rossano, St Colman of Lann Elo, St Teresa Couderc, and St John of Meda.

≫ EVENTS ≫

1687 The Parthenon in Athens was severely damaged by mortar bombs fired by the Venetian army as it besieged the Turkish-held Acropolis. **1887** German-born US Emile Berliner patented the first gramophone. **1907** New Zealand became a Dominion. **1934** The liner *Queen Mary* was launched at Clydebank, Scotland, by Queen Mary. **1953** Sugar rationing in Britain came to an end. **1955** Frozen Birds Eye fish fingers first went on sale in Britain. **1961** Bob Dylan made his debut in New York's Greenwich Village, at Gerdie's Folk City. **1983** Alan Bond's Australia II won the America's Cup, the first non-US winner for 132 years. **1984** Britain agreed to transfer full sovereignty of Hong Kong to China in 1997. **1988** Canadian sprinter Ben Johnson was stripped of his gold medal in the 100 metres at the Seoul Olympics after failing a drugs test.

≫ BIRTHS ≫

Théodore Géricault, French painter, **1791**; Ivan Petrovich Pavlov, Russian physiologist, **1849**; T S Eliot, US-born British poet and playwright, **1888**; George Gershwin, US composer, **1898**; Ian Chappell, Australian cricketer **1943**; Bryan Ferry, English rock singer, **1945**; Olivia Newton-John, English singer, **1948**.

≫ DEATHS ≫

Daniel Boone, US frontiersman, **1820**; James Keir Hardie, Scottish Labour Party pioneer, **1915**; Béla Bartók, Hungarian composer, **1945**; Alberto Moravia, Italian writer, **1990**.

'I will show you fear in a handful of dust.'
T S Eliot

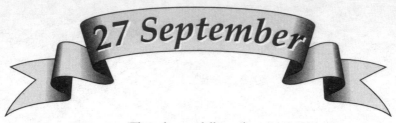

27 September

'The rules are different here.'
Florida tourism campaign

Feast day of St Elzear of Sabran, St Barrog or Barnoch, and St Vincent de Paul.

⤳ EVENTS ⤳

1821 Mexico achieved independence through the efforts of General Hubride, who declared himself Emperor Augustin I. **1826** The Stockton and Darlington Railway, the first passenger rail service, opened, with its first steam locomotive travelling at 10 mph. **1922** Constantine I, King of Greece, abdicated following the Greek defeat in Turkey. **1938** The 80,000-ton liner *Queen Elizabeth* was launched by the Queen Mother. **1939** Warsaw, the capital of Poland, surrendered to the German forces. **1968** The musical *Hair*, which took advantage of the end of British stage censorship by including a scene cast in the nude, had its first London performance.

⤳ BIRTHS ⤳

Samuel Adams, US revolutionary leader, **1722**; George Cruikshank, English caricaturist and illustrator, **1792**; Louis Botha, South African politician, **1862**; Vincent Youmans, US composer, **1898**; Alvin Stardust, rock singer, **1942**; Michele Dotrice, English actress, **1948**.

⤳ DEATHS ⤳

Ivan Alexandrovich Goncharov, Russian novelist, **1891**; Edgar Degas, French painter, **1917**; Engelbert Humperdinck, German composer, **1921**; Aristide Maillol, French painter and sculptor, **1944**; Clara Bow, US film actress, **1965**; Gracie Fields, English singer and comedian, **1979**.

'When you interviewed the Pope, did you ask him why it is
that he always wears that white outfit? '
Fidel Castro, when asked why he always wears his uniform

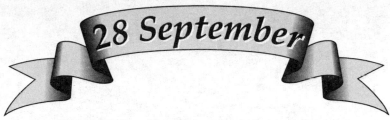
28 September

'[The chancellor is] lumbering, neanderthal, and clumsy -
Jurassic Clarke. We will make him extinct.'
Gordon Brown

Feast Day of St Eustochium of Bethlehem, St Annemund or Chamond, St Faustus of Riez, St Ferreolus of Vienne, St Lioba, St Wenceslaus of Bohemia, and St Exuperius or Soupire of Toulouse.

∞ EVENTS ∞

490 BC The Greeks defeated the Persians at the Battle of Marathon. **1745** At the Drury Lane Theatre, London, *God Save the King*, the national anthem, was sung for the first time. **1794** Britain, Russia, and Austria formed the Alliance of St Petersburg against France. **1864** The First International was founded in London, when Karl Marx proposed the formation of an International Working Men's Association. **1865** Elizabeth Garrett Anderson became the first qualified woman physician in Britain. **1894** Simon Marks and Tom Spencer opened their Penny Bazaar in Manchester, the first of what would become a nation-wide chain of stores. **1978** Pope John Paul I, pope for only 33 days, was found dead.

∞ BIRTHS ∞

Caravaggio, Italian painter, **1573**; Prosper Merimée, French writer, **1803**; Georges Clemenceau, French politician, **1841**; Peter Finch, British film actor, **1916**; Michael Soames, English dancer, **1917**; Marcello Mastroianni, Italian actor, **1924**; Brigitte Bardot, French film actress, **1934**.

∞ DEATHS ∞

Andrea del Sarto, Italian painter, **1530**; Herman Melville, US novelist, **1891**; Louis Pasteur, French chemist, **1895**; Émile Zola, French novelist, **1902**; W H Auden, English poet, **1973**; William Douglas-Home, British playwright, **1992**.

'A whale ship was my Yale College and my Harvard.'
Hermen Melville, *Moby Dick*

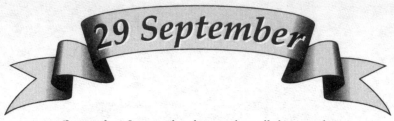

29 September

'I come from Liverpool and we used to sell slaves to the
United States, so when the Norwegians defend the killing of
whales with it being an old tradition, I don't buy it.'
Paul McCartney

Feast day of Saints Rhipsime, Gaiana and Companions, St Theodota of
Philippolis, and St Michael, St Raphael, and St Gabriel, archangels.

EVENTS

1399 The first monarch to abdicate, Richard II, was replaced by Bolingbroke who
ascended the throne as Henry IV. **1829** The first regular police force in London
was inaugurated; the officers became known as 'bobbies' after Robert Peel, the
Home Secretary who founded the modern police force. **1911** Italy declared war
on Turkey over possession of Tripoli, in Libya. **1916** John D Rockefeller became
the world's first billionaire during the share boom in the USA. **1938** The Munich
Agreement between Germany and France, Italy and Britain was signed. **1944**
Soviet troops entered Yugoslavia. **1950** The first automatic telephone answering
machine was tested by the US Bell Telephone Company. **1991** Haiti's first freely
elected president, Jean-Bertrand Aristide, was ousted in a military coup.

BIRTHS

Miguel de Cervantes, Spanish playwright and novelist, **1547**; Horatio Nelson,
Viscount, English admiral, **1758**; Enrico Fermi, US physicist, **1901**; Jerry Lee
Lewis, US singer and pianist, **1935**; Lech Walesa, Polish leader, **1943**; Sebastian
Coe, English athlete, **1956**.

DEATHS

Winslow Homer, US painter, **1910**; Rudolf Diesel, German engineer, **1913**;
Willem Einthoven, Dutch physiologist, **1927**; Winifred Holtby, English
novelist, **1935**; Bruce Bairnsfather, British cartoonist, **1959**; Carson McCullers,
US author, **1967**.

'Long Island represents the American's idea of what God would
have done with Nature if he'd had the money.'
Ian Fleming

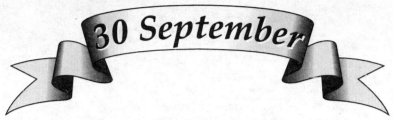

30 September

'I look forward to the day when there is a strike not because
a firm has introduced automation but because it has not.'
Jo Grimond, reported on 30 Sept 1956

National Day of Botswana. Feast day of St Jerome, St Simon of Crépy, St Gregory the Enlightener, and St Honorius of Canterbury.

✎ EVENTS ✎

1791 The first performance of Mozart's *Magic Flute* took place in Vienna. **1888** Jack the Ripper murdered two more women – Liz Stride, found behind 40 Berner Street, and Kate Eddowes in Mitre Square, both in London's East End. **1902** Rayon, or artificial silk, was patented. **1928** Alexander Fleming announced his discovery of penicillin. **1935** George Gershwin's opera *Porgy and Bess* was first performed in Boston. **1939** The USSR and Germany agreed on the partition of Poland. **1952** Cinerama, invented by Fred Waller, was first exhibited in New York. **1987** Keith Best, MP, was sentenced to four months in prison for trying to obtain British Telecom shares by deception.

✎ BIRTHS ✎

Lord Raglan, British field-marshal, **1788**; David Fyodorovich Oistrakh, Russian violinist, **1908**; Deborah Kerr, British actress, **1923**; Truman Capote, US author, **1924**; Angie Dickinson, US actress, **1931**; Johnny Mathis, US singer, **1937**.

✎ DEATHS ✎

James Brindley, British canal engineer, **1772**; Richard Austin Freeman, British crime writer, **1943**; James Dean, US film actor, **1955**; Simone Signoret, French film actress, **1985**; Virgil Thomson, US composer, **1989**.

'I dress for women, and undress for men.'
Angie Dickinson

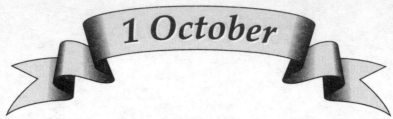

1 October

'We should live our lives as though Christ were coming this afternoon.'
Jimmy Carter

National day of China, Nigeria, and Cyprus. Feast day of St Romanus the Melodist, St Melorus or Mylor, St Bavo or Allowin, St Thérèse of Lisieux.

⚜ EVENTS ⚜

331 BC Alexander the Great defeated Darius III at Arbela. **1795** Belgium became part of the French Republic. **1843** The *News of the World*, Britain's most popular Sunday newspaper, was first published. **1908** The first Model T, produced in Detroit, Michigan, was introduced by Henry Ford. **1918** The Arab forces of Emir Faisal, with British officer T E Lawrence, captured Damascus from the Turks. **1936** General Francisco Franco took office as Head of Spain's Nationalist Government. **1938** German forces entered Sudetenland, Czechoslovakia, annexed by Hitler under the Munich Agreement. **1949** The People's Republic of China was proclaimed, with Mao Zedong as its chairman. **1971** Disneyworld, the world's largest amusement resort, was opened in Florida. **1982** Helmut Kohl became federal chancellor of West Germany, succeeding Helmut Schmidt.

⚜ BIRTHS ⚜

King Henry III, 1207; Paul Dukas, French composer, 1865; Vladimir Horowitz, US pianist, 1904; Walter Matthau, US film actor, 1920; Jimmy Carter, 39th US president, 1924; Richard Harris, British actor, 1933; Julie Andrews, English actress and singer, 1935.

⚜ DEATHS ⚜

Pierre Corneille, French dramatist, 1684; John Blow, British composer, 1708; Edwin Landseer, English painter, 1873; Wilhelm Dilthey, German philosopher, 1911; Louis Seymour Bazett Leakey, English anthropologist, 1972; Roy Harris US composer, 1979.

'I want to say that the Devil is innocent. It's a matter of who has the power and writes the books. You know, the Devil never wrote a book.'
Nawal al-Saadawi

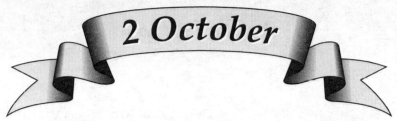

2 October

'There are many reasons why novelists write, but they all
have one thing in common - a need to create an alternative world.'
John Fowles

Feast day of The Guardian Angels, St Leger or Leodegarius, and St Eleutherius
of Nicomedia.

〰 EVENTS 〰

1187 Saladin, the Muslim sultan, captured Jerusalem after its 88-year
occupation by the Franks. **1608** The first telescope was demonstrated by the
Dutch lens maker, Hans Lipperschey. **1836** Charles Darwin returned from his
five-year survey of South American waters aboard the HMS *Beagle*. **1870** Rome
became the capital of the newly unified Italy. **1901** The British Royal Navy's
first submarine, built by Vickers, was launched at Barrow. **1909** The first rugby
football match was played at Twickenham, between Harlequins and Richmond.
1942 The British cruiser *Curacao* sank with the loss of 338 lives, after colliding
with the liner *Queen Mary* off the coast of Donegal. **1983** Neil Kinnock was
elected leader of Britain's Labour Party.

〰 BIRTHS 〰

Mikhail Yurevich Lermontov, Russian poet, **1814**; Paul von Hindenburg,
German field marshal and politician, **1847**; William Ramsay, Scottish chemist,
1852; Mohandas Karamchand Gandhi, Indian leader, **1869**; Graham Greene,
English novelist, **1904**; Sting, English rock singer, **1951**.

〰 DEATHS 〰

Samuel Adams, US statesman, **1803**; Max Bruch, German composer, **1920**;
Marie Stopes, Scottish birth-control campaigner, **1958**; Marcel Duchamp,
French painter, **1968**; Rock Hudson, US film actor, **1985**; Peter Medawar,
British immunologist, **1987**.

'Our worst enemies here are not the ignorant and the simple,
however cruel; our worst enemies are the intelligent and corrupt.'
Graham Greene, *The Human Factor*

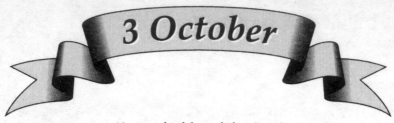

3 October

'A triumph of the embalmer's art.'
Gore Vidal, on Ronald Reagan

Feast day of St Hesychius, St Thomas Cantelupe of Hereford, St Attilanus, St Gerard of Brogne, St Froilan, St Ewald the Fair, and St Ewald the Dark.

❧ EVENTS ❧

1811 The first women's county cricket match began at Newington, between Hampshire and Surrey. **1888** Gilbert and Sullivan's *Yeomen of the Guard* was performed for the first time, at London's Savoy Theatre. **1906** SOS was established as an international distress signal, replacing the call sign CQD. **1929** The Kingdom of Serbs, Croats, and Slovenes was renamed Yugoslavia. **1952** The first British atomic bomb was detonated on the Monte Bello Islands, off W Australia. **1956** The Bolshoi Ballet performed in Britain, at Covent Garden, for the first time. **1990** East and West Germany were officially reunified, with Berlin as the capital.

❧ BIRTHS ❧

Pierre Bonnard, French painter, **1867**; Louis Aragon, French poet, **1897**; Michael Hordern, English actor, **1911**; James Herriot, Scottish author, **1916**; Gore Vidal, US author, **1925**; Chubby Checker, US rock singer, **1941**.

❧ DEATHS ❧

St Francis, Italian founder of the Franciscan order, **1226**; William Morris, English designer, socialist, and poet, **1896**; Woody Guthrie, US singer and composer, **1967**; Malcolm Sargent, British conductor, **1967**; Jean Anouilh, French dramatist, **1987**.

'Tragedy is restful and the reason is that hope, that foul,
deceitful thing, has no part in it.'
Jean Anouilh

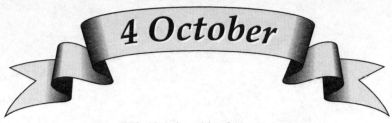

4 October

'In all likelihood world inflation is over.'
Per Jacobsson, managing director of the IMF,
reported on 4 Oct 1959

National Day of Lesotho. Feast day of St Petronius of Bologna, St Francis of Assisi, and St Ammon.

✌ EVENTS ✌

1905 Orville Wright became the first to fly an aircraft for over 33 minutes. **1910** Portugal was proclaimed a republic when King Manuel II was driven from the country by a revolution. **1911** Britain's first public escalator was switched on, at London's Earl's Court underground station. **1957** The USSR's *Sputnik I*, the first space satellite, was launched. **1958** BOAC (now British Airways) began operating the first transatlantic passenger jet service. **1965** Pope Paul VI visited New York to address the UN, becoming the first pope to visit the USA. **1983** A world record speed of 663.5 mph was achieved by Richard Noble in his jet-powered car *Thrust II*, in Nevada.

✌ BIRTHS ✌

Giambattista Piranesi, Italian architect, **1720**; Jean François Millet, French painter, **1814**; Engelbert Dollfuss, Austrian statesman, **1892**; Buster Keaton, US comedian, **1892**; Charlton Heston, US film actor, **1924**; Terence Conran, British designer, **1931**.

✌ DEATHS ✌

Benozzo Gozzoli, Italian painter, **1497**; Rembrandt, Dutch painter, **1669**; John Rennie, Scottish civil engineer, **1821**; Arthur Whitten Brown, pioneer aviator, **1948**; Janis Joplin, US singer, **1970**.

'Goddammit! He beat me to it.'
Janis Joplin, on hearing of Jimi Hendrix's death

5 October

'Most people get into bands for three very simple rock and
roll reasons: to get laid, to get fame, and to get rich.'
Bob Geldof

Feast day of St Flora of Beaulieu, St Maurus, St Magenulf or Meinulf, St
Apollinaris of Valence, and St Galla.

≫ EVENTS ≪

1796 Spain declared war on Britain, during the Revolutionary Wars. **1880** The
earliest 'ball pen', with its own ink supply and retractable tip, was patented by
Alonzo T Cross. **1908** Bulgaria declared its independence from Turkey. **1911**
Italian troops occupied Tripoli, in Libya, during its war with Turkey. **1914** The
first air battle took place between French and German aircraft during World War
I; both sides suffered losses. **1930** The British airship *R101*, the world's largest
dirigible at that time, crashed in France en route to India; the British air minister
was among the 48 killed. **1936** The Jarrow march, of unemployed shipyard
workers, started its southward journey to London. **1967** The first majority
verdict by a jury in Britain was taken, in Brighton. **1970** Anwar Sadat succeeded
Gamal Nasser as president of Egypt.

≫ BIRTHS ≪

Denis Diderot, French philosopher, **1713**; Chester Alan Arthur, 21st US
president, **1830**; Donald Pleasence, English actor, **1919**; Glynis Johns, British
actress, **1923**; Vaclav Havel, Czech dramatist and president, **1936**; Bob Geldof,
Irish musician, **1954**.

≫ DEATHS ≪

Philip III ('the Bold'), King of France, **1285**; Joachim Patinir, Dutch painter,
1524; Jacques Offenbach, French composer, **1880**; Jean Vigo, French film
director, **1934**; Nelson Riddle, US composer and arranger, **1985**.

'There is no doubting my belief in God, but the Church has
driven me close to it.'
David Jenkins, bishop of Durham

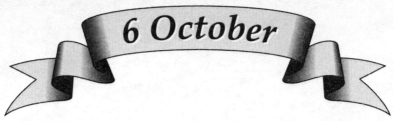
6 October

'We were taught it's us against them. Us were the cops and them were the public.'
Michael Dowd, New York police officer

Feast day of St Mary Frances of Naples, St Faith of Agen, St Nicetas of Constantinople, and St Bruno.

⁊ EVENTS ⁊

1769 English naval explorer Captain James Cook, aboard the *Endeavour*, landed in New Zealand. **1883** The *Orient Express* completed its first run from Paris to Constantinople (now Istanbul) in nearly 78 hours. **1908** Austria annexed Bosnia and Herzegovina. **1927** Warner Brothers' *The Jazz Singer*, the first talking feature film (starring Al Jolson), premiered in New York. **1928** Nationalist General Chiang Kai-shek became president of China. **1968** The first three places in the US Grand Prix were taken by British drivers: Jackie Stewart, Graham Hill, and John Surtees. **1978** London Underground's first woman driver started work. **1981** One day after the 11th anniversary of his election to office, Egyptian President Anwar Sadat was assassinated by Muslim extremists.

⁊ BIRTHS ⁊

Nevil Maskelyne, Astronomer Royal, **1732**; Le Corbusier, Swiss architect, **1887**; Janet Gaynor, US film actress, **1906**; Thor Heyerdahl, Norwegian ethnologist, **1914**; Richie Benaud, Australian cricketer and commentator, **1930**; Melvyn Bragg, English writer and TV presenter, **1939**.

⁊ DEATHS ⁊

William Tyndale, English Bible translator, **1536**; William Henry Smith, English newsagent, bookseller and statesman, **1891**; Alfred Tennyson, English poet, **1892**; George du Maurier, English novelist, **1896**; Denholm Elliott, English actor, **1992**; Cyril Cusack, Irish actor, **1993**.

'Literature is mostly about having sex and not much about having children; life is the other way round.'
David Lodge, *The British Museum is Falling Down*

7 October

'The chances of peaceful change in South Africa are virtually nil.'
Bishop Desmond Tutu, 7 Sept 1985

Feast day of St Justina of Padua, St Mark, pope, St Artaldus or Arthaud, and St Osyth.

EVENTS

1571 The Battle of Lepanto, between Christian allied naval forces and the Ottoman Turks attempting to capture Cyprus from the Venetians, took place. **1806** The first carbon paper was patented by its English inventor, Ralph Wedgwood. **1919** The Dutch airline KLM, the oldest existing airline, was established. **1949** The German Democratic Republic, or East Germany, was formed. **1958** The first photograph of the far side of the Moon was transmitted from the USSR's *Lunik I*. **1985** The Italian liner *Achille Lauro* was seized by Palestinian terrorists; they surrendered two days later, having killed one US passenger. **1988** Grey whales trapped under ice in Alaska became the focus of an international rescue effort.

BIRTHS

William Laud, Archbishop of Canterbury, **1573**; Niels Bohr, Danish physicist, **1885**; Desmond Tutu, Archbishop of Cape Town, **1931**; Clive James, Australian critic and TV presenter, **1939**; Yo Yo Ma, Chinese cellist, **1955**; Jane Torvill, English ice skater, **1957**.

DEATHS

Edgar Allan Poe, US novelist and poet, **1849**; Oliver Wendell Holmes, US writer, **1894**; Marie Lloyd, English music hall comedienne, **1922**; Radclyffe Hall, English author, **1943**; Clarence Birdseye, US deep-freezing inventor, **1967**; Bette Davis, US actress, **1989**; Agnes De Mille, US choreographer, **1993**.

'When you really want love, you will find it waiting for you.'
Oscar Wilde, *De Profundis*

8 October

'Nothing is surely a waste of time when one enjoys the day.'
Arthur Koestler, reported on 8 Oct 1972

Feast day of St Simeon Senex, St Pelagia (or Margaret) the Penitent, St Demetrius, St Keyne, St Thaïs, St Marcellus, and St Reparata of Caesarea.

❧ EVENTS ❧

1085 St Mark's Cathedral in Venice was consecrated. **1871** The Great Fire of Chicago started. It burned until the 11th, killing over 250 people and making 95,000 homeless. **1905** A permanent waving machine was first used on a woman's hair, by Charles Nessler. **1915** The Battle of Loos, in World War I, ended. **1939** Western Poland was incorporated in the Third Reich. **1965** London's Post Office Tower, Britain's tallest building, opened. **1967** A breathalyser was used on a motorist for the first time, in Somerset. **1973** LBC (London Broadcasting), Britain's first legal commercial radio station, began transmitting.

❧ BIRTHS ❧

John Cowper Powys, English novelist, **1872**; Alfred Munnings, British painter, **1878**; Juan Perón, Argentine dictator, **1895**; Betty Boothroyd, British MP, the Speaker,**1929**; Merle Park, British ballerina, **1937**; Jesse Jackson, US politician, **1941**.

❧ DEATHS ❧

Jan Massys, Flemish painter, **1575**; Henry Fielding, English novelist, **1754**; Franklin Pierce, 14th US president, **1869**; Kathleen Ferrier, English contralto, **1953**; Clement Attlee, British statesman, **1967**; Willy Brandt, former German federal chancellor, **1992**.

'Money, it turned out, was exactly like sex, you thought of nothing else
if you didn't have it and thought of other things if you did.'
James Baldwin

9 October

'Lying increases the creative faculties, and expands the ego, lessens the friction of social contacts ... it is only in lies, wholeheartedly and bravely told, that human nature attains through words and speech the forbearance, the nobility, the romance, the idealism, that - being what it is - it falls so short of in fact and in deed.'
Clare Booth Luce

National Day of Uganda. Feast day of St Demetrius of Alexandria, Saints Eleutherius and Rusticus, Saints Andronicus and Athanasia, St Denis or Dionysius of Paris, St Dionysius the Aeropagite, St Savin, St Publia, St Louis Bertrán, and St Ghislain or Gislenus.

❧ EVENTS ❧

1470 Henry VI was restored to the throne after being deposed in 1461. **1779** The first Luddite riots, against the introduction of machinery for spinning cotton, began in Manchester. **1875** The Universal Postal Union was established, with headquarters in Berne, Switzerland. **1888** The massive marble Washington Monument, designed by Robert Mills, was opened. **1934** Alexander, King of Yugoslavia, and French Foreign Minister Louis Barthou were assassinated by Croatian terrorists in Marseilles. **1967** Ernesto 'Che' Guevara, Argentinian-born guerila leader and revolutionary, was murdered in Bolivia.

❧ BIRTHS ❧

Camille Saint-Saëns, French composer, **1835**; Alastair Sim, British actor, **1900**; Jacques Tati, French film director, **1908**; Don McCullin, British war photographer, **1935**; John Lennon, rock singer and songwriter, **1940**; Steve Ovett, English athlete, **1955**.

❧ DEATHS ❧

Gabriel Fallopius, Italian anatomist, **1562**; Pope Pius XII, **1958**; André Maurois, French writer, **1967**; Clare Booth Luce, US writer and politician, **1987**; Jackie Millburn, English footballer, **1988**.

'All You Need Is Love.'
John Lennon & Paul McCartney

10 October

'Mr Heath promised a land of milk and honey - and Mrs
Thatcher stopped the flow of milk.'
John Selway, Labour Party agent 10 Oct 1971

Feast day of St Francis Borgia, St Daniel, St Cerbonius, Saints Eulampius and
Eulampia, St Paulinus of York, St Maharsapor, and St Gereon.

~ EVENTS ~

732 The Franks, under Charles Martel, defeated the Saracens at the Battle of
Tours. **1886** The dinner jacket was first worn in New York by its creator at the
Tuxedo Park Country Club, after which it was named. **1903** Mrs Emmeline
Pankhurst formed the Women's Social and Political Union to fight for women's
emancipation in Britain. **1911** China's Imperial Dynasty was forced to abdicate,
and a republic was proclaimed, under Sun Yat-Sen. **1935** George Gershwin's
Porgy and Bess opened in New York City. **1961** Following a volcanic eruption,
the entire population of the South Atlantic island of Tristan da Cunha was
evacuated to Britain. **1973** US Vice President Spiro Agnew resigned after being
fined US $10,000 for income tax evasion.

~ BIRTHS ~

Jean Antoine Watteau, French painter, **1684**; Henry Cavendish, English
physicist, **1731**; Giuseppe Verdi, Italian composer, **1813**; Thelonious Monk, US
jazz pianist and composer, **1918**; Harold Pinter, British dramatist, **1930**; Charles
Dance, British actor, **1946**.

~ DEATHS ~

Fra Filippo Lippi, Italian painter, **1469**; Edith Piaf, French singer, **1963**; Eddie
Cantor, US actor and entertainer, **1964**; Ralph Richardson, English actor, **1983**;
Orson Welles, US actor and producer, **1985**; Yul Brynner, US film actor, **1985**.

'This is the biggest electric train set any boy ever had!'
Orson Welles, of the RKO studio

11 October

'The twentieth century may not be a very good thing but it's the only century we've got.'
Norman St John Stevas, reported on 11 Oct 1970

Feast day of St Mary Soledad, Saints Andronicus, Tarachus, and Probus, St Agilbert, St Alexander Sauli, St Nectarius of Constantinople, St Bruno the Great of Cologne, St Gummarus or Gomaire, and St Canice or Kenneth.

EVENTS

1521 Pope Leo X conferred the title of 'Defender of the Faith' (Fidei Defensor) on Henry VIII for his book supporting Catholic principles. **1689** Peter the Great, Tsar of Russia, assumed control of the government. **1899** The Anglo-Boer War began. **1923** Rampant inflation in Germany caused the mark to drop to an exchange rate of 10,000,000,000 to the pound. **1968** The US spacecraft *Apollo 7* was launched from Cape Kennedy, with a crew of three. **1980** The Soviet *Salyut 6* returned to earth; its cosmonauts had been in space for a record 185 days. **1982** The *Mary Rose*, which had been the pride of Henry VIII's fleet until it sank in the Solent in 1545, was raised.

BIRTHS

Arthur Phillip, English admiral, **1738**; George Williams, founder of the YMCA, **1821**; François Mauriac, French author, **1885**; Richard Burton, Welsh actor, **1925**; Bobby Charlton, English footballer, **1937**; Dawn French, English actress and comedienne, **1957**.

DEATHS

Huldrych Zwingli, Swiss religious reformer, **1531**; Meriwether Lewis, US explorer, **1809**; James Joule, English physicist, **1889**; Anton Bruckner, Austrian composer, **1896**; 'Chico' Marx, US comedian, **1961**; Jean Cocteau, French poet, dramatist, and film director, **1963**; Jess Thomas, US operatic tenor, **1993**.

'Tact consists in knowing how far we may go too far.'
Jean Cocteau

12 October

'I don't want art for a few, any more than education for a
few, or freedom for a few.'
William Morris

───

Feast day of St Maximilian of Lorch, Saints Felix and Cyprian, St Edwin, St
Wilfrid of York, and St Ethelburga of Barking.

EVENTS

1492 Columbus sighted his first land in discovering the New World, calling it
San Salvador. **1901** US President Theodore Roosevelt renamed the Executive
Mansion 'The White House'. **1928** The first iron lung was used, at Boston
Children's Hospital, Massachusetts. **1948** The first Morris Minor, designed by
Alec Issigonis, was produced at Cowley, Oxfordshire. **1968** The 19th Olympic
Games opened in Mexico City. **1984** During the Tory Party Conference at the
Grand Hotel in Brighton, an IRA bomb exploded in the hotel in an attempt to
murder the British Cabinet. **1986** Queen Elizabeth II became the first British
monarch to visit China.

BIRTHS

King Edward VI, **1537**; Elmer Ambrose Sperry, US inventor, **1860**; James
Ramsay McDonald, British statesman, **1866**; Ralph Vaughan Williams, English
composer, **1872**; Aleister Crowley, British occultist, **1875**; Luciano Pavarotti,
Italian operatic tenor, **1935**.

DEATHS

Piero della Francesca, Italian painter, **1492**; Elizabeth Fry, English prison
reformer, **1845**; Robert Stephenson, English civil engineer, **1859**; Robert E Lee,
US Confederate general, **1870**; Anatole France, French author, **1924**; Tom
Mix, US western film actor, **1940**; Leon Ames, US film actor, **1993**.

───

'There's nothing like tobacco; it is the passion of all decent people;
someone who lives without tobacco does not deserve to live.'
Molière, *Don Juan*

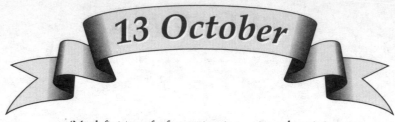

13 October

'My definition of a free society is a society where it is
safe to be unpopular.'
Adlai Stevenson, US politician

Feast day of Saints Januarius and Martial, St Gerald of Aurillac, St Edward the Confessor, St Coloman, St Comgan, St Faustus of Cordova, and St Maurice of Carnoët.

➤ EVENTS ➤

1307 On the orders of Philip IV of France, the arrest of the Templars on charges of heresy took place in Paris. **1792** The cornerstone of the White House, Washington, DC, was laid by President George Washington. **1884** Greenwich was adapted as the universal time meridian of longitude from which standard times throughout the world are calculated. **1894** The first Merseyside 'derby' football match was played at Goodison Park between Liverpool and Everton, with Everton winning 3–0. **1904** Sigmund Freud's *The Interpretation of Dreams* was published. **1923** Ankara replaced Istanbul as the capital of Turkey. **1988** The Cardinal of Turin confirmed reports that the Shroud of Turin, believed to carry the imprint of Christ's face, had been scientifically dated to the Middle Ages.

➤ BIRTHS ➤

Rudolf Virchow, German pathologist, **1821**; Lillie Langtry, British actress, **1853**; Yves Montand, French singer and actor, **1921**; Margaret Thatcher, British politician, **1925**; Paul Simon, US singer and songwriter, **1941**; Marie Osmond, US singer, **1959**.

➤ DEATHS ➤

Claudius I, Roman emperor, **54**; Nicholas de Malebranche, French philosopher, **1715**; Joachim Murat, King of the Two Sicilies, **1815**; Antonio Canova, Italian sculptor, **1822**; Henry Irving, English actor, **1905**; Clifton Webb, US actor, **1966**.

'Happiness and Beauty are by-products.'
George Bernard Shaw, *Maxims for Revolutionists*

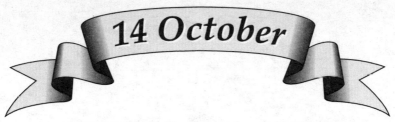
14 October

'I do not dislike the French from the vulgar antipathy
between neighbouring nations, but for their insolent and
unfounded airs of superiority.'
Horace Walpole

National day of Madagascar. Feast day of St Callixtus I, St Angadiama, St Justus of Lyons, St Burchard of Würzburg, St Manaccus, St Manechildis, and St Dominic Lauricatus.

EVENTS

1066 The Battle of Hastings was fought on Senlac Hill, where King Harold was slain as William the Conqueror's troops routed the English army. **1884** Photographic film was patented by US entrepreneur and inventor George Eastman. **1920** Oxford degrees were conferred on women for the first time. **1947** The first supersonic flight (670 mph) was made in California by Charles Yeagar in his *Bell XI* rocket plane. **1971** The US spacecraft *Mariner 9* transmitted the first close-up TV pictures of Mars to Earth. **1982** The largest mass wedding took place in Seoul, South Korea, when 5,837 couples were married simultaneously.

BIRTHS

William Penn, Quaker founder of Pennsylvania, **1644**; Éamon de Valera, Irish statesman, **1882**; Dwight D Eisenhower, 34th US president, **1890**; e e cummings, US poet, **1894**; Lillian Gish, US film actress, **1899**; Cliff Richard, English singer, **1940**.

DEATHS

Erwin Rommel, German field-marshal, **1944**; Errol Flynn, Australian actor, **1959**; Edith Evans, English actress,**1976**; Bing Crosby, US singer and film actor, **1977**; Leonard Bernstein, US conductor and composer, **1990**.

'I mustn't go on singling out names. One must not be a name
dropper, as Her Majesty remarked to me yesterday.'
Norman St John Stevas

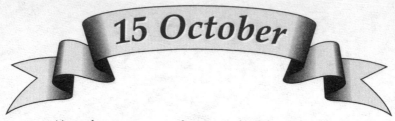

15 October

'A psychiatrist is a man who goes to the Folies Bergère and looks at the audience.'
Mervyn Stockwood, reported on 15 Oct 1961

Feast day of St Teresa of Avila, St Leonard of Vandoeuvre, St Thecla of Kitzingen, and St Euthymius the Younger.

〜 EVENTS 〜

1581 The first major ballet was staged at the request of Catherine de' Medici at the palace in Paris. **1582** The Gregorian calendar was adopted in Italy, Spain, Portugal, and France; 5 Oct became 15 Oct. **1915** In World War I, Bulgaria allied itself with the Central European Powers. **1917** Mata Hari, Dutch spy, was shot in Paris, having been found guilty of espionage for the Germans. **1928** The German airship *Graf Zeppelin*, captained by Hugo Eckener, completed its first transatlantic flight. **1961** The human-rights organization Amnesty International was established in London.

〜 BIRTHS 〜

Virgil, Roman poet, **70 BC**; Evangelista Torricelli, Italian physicist, **1608**; Friedrich Wilhelm Nietzsche, German philosopher, **1844**; P G Wodehouse, English novelist, **1881**; C P Snow, English scientist and novelist, **1905**; Mario Puzo, US novelist, **1920**; HRH the Duchess of York, **1959**.

〜 DEATHS 〜

Antoine de la Mothe Cadillac, French explorer, **1730**; Tadeusz Kościuszko, Polish patriot, **1817**; Raymond Nicolas Landry Poincaré, French statesman, **1934**; Hermann Goering, Nazi leader, **1946**; Cole Porter, US composer and lyricist, **1964**.

'He's a businessman ... I'll make him an offer he can't refuse.'
Mario Puzo, *The Godfather*

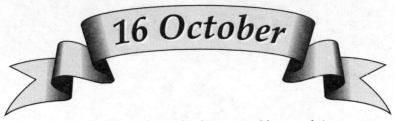
16 October

'I ask you to judge me by the enemies I have made.'
Franklin D Roosevelt, reported on 16 Oct 1932

Feast day of Saints Martinian and Maxima, St Margaret-Mary, St Anastasius of Cluny, St Hedwig, St Bertrand of Comminges, St Becharius, St Mommolinus, St Lull, St Gerard Majella, and St Gall.

EVENTS

1815 Napoleon was exiled to the Atlantic island of St Helena. **1846** The first public surgical operation using ether as an anaesthetic was performed at the Massachusetts General Hospital, Boston. **1902** The first detention centre housing young offenders was opened in Borstal, Kent. **1922** The Simplon II railway tunnel, under the Alps, was completed. **1946** Nazi war criminals, including von Ribbentrop, Rosenberg, and Streicher, were hanged at Nuremberg. **1964** China exploded a nuclear device. **1964** Labour Party leader Harold Wilson became Prime Minister. **1978** Cardinal Karol Wojtyla was elected Pope John Paul II – the first non-Italian pope since 1542. **1987** Southern England was hit by hurricane-force winds, causing 19 deaths and hundreds of millions of pounds' worth of damage.

BIRTHS

Noah Webster, US lexicographer, **1758**; Oscar Wilde, Irish dramatist and author, **1854**; Austen Chamberlain, British statesman, **1863**; David Ben Gurion, Israeli statesman, **1886**; Eugene O'Neill, US dramatist, **1888**; Günter Grass, German novelist, **1927**.

DEATHS

Hugh Latimer, bishop and Protestant martyr, **1555**; Nicholas Ridley, bishop and Protestant martyr, **1555**; Marie Antoinette, Queen of France, **1793**; George Marshall, US general and diplomat, **1959**; Moshe Dayan, Israeli general and politician, **1981**; Cornel Wilde, US film actor, **1989**; Paolo Bortoluzzi, Italian dancer and choreographer, **1993**.

'I have nothing to declare except my genius.'
Oscar Wilde, remark at the New York Customs House

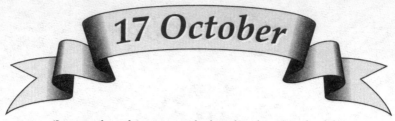

17 October

'It is equality of monotony which makes the strength of the British Isles.'
Eleanor Roosevelt, reported on 17 Oct 1948

Feast day of The Ursuline Martyrs of Valenciennes, Saints Ethelbert and Ethelred, St John the Dwarf, St Anstrudis or Austrude, St Seraphino, St Nothelm, St Ignatius of Antioch, and St Rule.

EVENTS

1651 Charles II, defeated by Cromwell at Worcester, fled to France, destitute and friendless. **1777** British commander General Burgoyne surrendered to General Horatio Gates at Saratoga, a victory for the American colonists. **1914** An earthquake struck Greece and Asia Minor, killing over 3,000 people. **1931** US gangster Al Capone was sentenced to 11 years in prison for income-tax evasion, the only charge that could be sustained against him. **1956** Calder Hall, Britain's first nuclear power station, was opened. **1959** The South African De Beers diamond firm announced that synthetic industrial diamonds had been produced. **1977** A US Supreme Court ruling allowed Concorde to use Kennedy Airport, New York.

BIRTHS

John Wilkes, British political reformer, **1727**; Karen Blixen (Isak Dinesen), Danish author, **1885**; Nathaniel West, US novelist, **1903**; Arthur Miller, US dramatist, **1915**; Rita Hayworth, US film actress, **1918**; Montgomery Clift, US film actor; Ann Jones, English tennis player, **1938**.

DEATHS

Philip Sidney, English poet and soldier, **1586**; Frédéric Chopin, Polish composer, **1849**; Gustav Robert Kirchoff, German physicist, **1887**; Julia Ward Howe, US author, **1910**; S J Perelman, US humorist, **1979**; William Paton, English pharmacologist, **1993**.

'Prison has almost no rehabilitative effect whatever. A great deal of dishonesty in the debate is that contributed by the politicians.'
Bruce Laughland

18 October

'Dictators have only become possible through the invention of
the microphone.'
Sir Thomas Inskip, reported on 18 Oct 1936

Feast day of St Luke, St Gwen of Corwall, and St Justus of Beauvais.

≋ EVENTS ≋

1685 The Edict of Nantes, granting religious freedom to the Huguenots, was revoked by King Louis XIV of France. **1826** Britain's last state lottery was held. **1887** Russia transferred Alaska to the USA for $7.2 million. **1922** The British Broadcasting Company (later Corporation) was officially formed. **1977** Germany's anti-terrorist squad stormed a hijacked Lufthansa aircraft at Mogadishu Airport, Somalia, killing three of the four Palestinian hijackers and freeing all of the hostages. **1989** Following a wave of pro-democracy demonstrations in East Germany, Erich Honecker was replaced as head of state by Egon Krenz. **1989** With the end of Communist rule, Hungary was proclaimed a free republic.

≋ BIRTHS ≋

Canaletto, Italian painter, **1697**; Henri Bergson, French philosopher, **1859**; Pierre Trudeau, Canadian politician, **1919**; Chuck Berry, US singer, **1926**; George C Scott, US film actor, **1927**; Martina Navratilova, Czech tennis player, **1956**.

≋ DEATHS ≋

Lord Palmerston, British politician, **1865**; Charles Babbage, English mathematician, **1871**; Charles François Gounod, French composer, **1893**; Thomas Edison, US inventor, **1931**; Elizabeth Arden, cosmetics company founder, **1966**; Pierre Mendès-France, French statesman, **1982**.

'A woman rang in to say she'd heard there was a hurricane on
the way. Well, don't worry. There isn't.'
Michael Fish, reported on 18 Oct 1987

19 October

'If you stay here much longer you will go back with slitty eyes.'
Duke of Edinburgh, to English students in China,
reported on 19 Oct 1986

Feast day of St Paul of the Cross, St Philip Howard, St Ethbin, St Aquilinus of Evreux, St Cleopatra, St Frideswide, St Peter of Alcántara, St John de Brébeuf, St René Goupil, St Varus, and Saints Ptolemy and Lucius.

✥ EVENTS ✥

1781 Lord Cornwallis surrendered to General Washington at Yorktown, Virginia, marking the end of the American War of Independence. **1813** The Allies defeated Napoleon at the Battle of the Nations at Leipzig. **1860** The first company to manufacture internal combustion engines was formed in Florence. **1864** In the American Civil War, General Sheridan was victorious over the Confederates at the Battle of Cedar Creek. **1872** The Holtermann nugget was mined at Hill End, New South Wales; weighing 630lbs, it was the largest gold-bearing nugget ever found. **1935** The League of Nations imposed sanctions on Italy, following her invasion of Abyssinia (Ethiopia). **1987** Wall Street was struck by 'Black Monday', during which millions were wiped out on stock markets around the world. **1989** After serving 14 years in prison for the IRA Guildford and Woolwich bombings, the 'Guildford Four' had their convictions quashed.

✥ BIRTHS ✥

Thomas Browne, English author and physician, **1605**; Leigh Hunt, English poet and essayist, **1784**; Alfred Dreyfus, French army officer, **1859**; Auguste Marie Lumière, French photographic pioneer, **1862**; John Le Carré, English novelist, **1931**; Peter Tosh, Jamaican reggae musician, **1944**.

✥ DEATHS ✥

King John of England, **1216**; Thomas Browne, English author and physician, **1682**; Jonathan Swift, Irish author, **1745**; George Pullman, US engineer and sleeping-car manufacturer, **1897**; Ernest Rutherford, New Zealand physicist, **1937**; Jacqueline du Pré, British cellist, **1987**.

20 October

'One starts to get young at the age of 60 and then it's too late.'
Pablo Picasso

Feast day of St Artemius, St Andrew the Calybite of Crete, St Caprasius of Agen, St Bertilla Boscardin, and St Acca.

EVENTS

1714 The coronation of King George I took place. **1818** Britain and the USA established the 49th parallel as the boundary between Canada and the USA. **1822** The *Sunday Times* was first published. **1827** The Battle of Navarino, off the coast of Greece, ended with the combined British, French, and Russian fleets completely destroying the Egyptian and Turkish fleets. **1935** Mao Zedong's Long March ended in Yenan, north China. **1944** The Allies captured Aachen, Germany. **1944** US troops landed at Leyte, in the Philippines. **1968** Jacqueline Kennedy, widow of US president Kennedy, married Greek millionaire Aristotle Onassis. **1973** The Sydney Opera House, designed by Danish architect John Utzon, was opened to the public.

BIRTHS

Christopher Wren, English architect, **1632**; Lord Palmerston, British statesman, **1784**; Arthur Rimbaud, French poet, **1854**; James Chadwick, English physicist, **1891**; Anna Neagle, British actress, **1904**; Tom Petty, US guitarist and singer, **1953**.

DEATHS

Thomas Linacre, English physician and humanist, **1524**; Richard Francis Burton, English explorer and scholar, **1890**; Herbert Hoover, 31st US president, **1964**; Bud Flanagan, English comedian, **1968**; Sheila Scott, English aviator, **1988**; Anthony Quayle, English actor, **1989**.

'As for philosophers, they make imaginary laws for imaginary commonwealths, and their discourses are as the stars, which give little light because they are so high.'
Sir Francis Bacon, *The Advancement of Learning*

21 October

'I had nothing to offer except my own confusion.'
Jack Kerouac

Feast day of St Hilarion, St Fintan or Munnu of Taghmon, St Condedus, St Tuda, St John of Bridlington, and St Malchus.

EVENTS

1805 The British defeated the Franco-Spanish fleet at the Battle of Trafalgar. **1858** Offenbach's opera *Orpheus in the Underworld* was first performed, in Paris. **1934** Mao Zedong's Long March, with his 100,000-strong Communist army, began. **1950** Tibet was occupied by Chinese forces. **1960** Britain launched its first nuclear submarine, the HMS *Dreadnought*. **1966** The Welsh village of Aberfan was engulfed by a collapsed slagheap, killing 144, including 116 children. **1967** Egyptian missiles sank the Israeli destroyer *Eilat*, with the loss of over 40 lives. **1984** Niki Lauda became world motor-racing champion for the third time. **1991** Jesse Turner, an American who had been held hostage in Lebanon for just under five years, was freed by his captors.

BIRTHS

Katsushika Hokusai, Japanese artist and printmaker, **1760**; Samuel Taylor Coleridge, English poet, **1772**; Alfred Nobel, Swedish industrialist, **1833**; Georg Solti, British conductor, **1912**; Dizzie Gillespie, US jazz trumpeter, **1917**; Carrie Fisher, US film actress, **1956**.

DEATHS

Pietro Aretino, Italian writer, **1556**; Edmund Waller, English poet, **1687**; Horatio, Viscount Nelson, English admiral, killed at Trafalgar, **1805**; Jack Kerouac, US poet and novelist, **1969**; Bob Todd, English comedy actor, **1992**.

'You cannot shake hands with a clenched fist.'
Indira Gandhi

22 October

'History is littered with wars everybody knew would never happen.'
Enoch Powell, reported on 22 Oct 1967

Feast day of St Philip of Heraclea and his Companions, St Mellon or Mallonus, St Abercius, Saints Nunilo and Alodia, and St Donatus of Ficsole.

EVENTS

1797 The first parachute jump was made by André-Jacques Garnerin from a balloon above the Parc Monceau, Paris. **1878** The first floodlit rugby match took place, Broughton v Swinton, at Broughton, Lancs. **1883** New York's Metropolitan Opera House opened. **1909** French aviator Elise Deroche became the first woman to make a solo flight. **1910** Dr Hawley Crippen was found guilty of poisoning his wife and was sentenced to be hanged on 23 October 1910. **1935** Haiti was struck by a hurricane, causing over 2,000 deaths. **1962** US President Kennedy announced that Soviet missile bases had been installed in Cuba. **1987** The first volume of the Gutenberg Bible was sold at auction in New York for $5.39m/£3.26m – a record price for a printed book.

BIRTHS

Franz Liszt, Hungarian composer, **1811**; Sarah Bernhardt, French actress, **1844**; Doris Lessing, English novelist, **1919**; Robert Rauschenberg, US artist, **1925**; Derek Jacobi, English actor, **1938**; Catherine Deneuve, French film actress, **1943**.

DEATHS

Charles Martel, leader of the Franks, **741**; Thomas Sheraton, English furniture maker, **1806**; Paul Cézanne, French painter, **1906**; Pablo Casals, Spanish cellist, **1973**; Arnold Joseph Toynbee, English historian, **1975**.

'I dedicate this prize to all those who suffer in public and
in private and who never give up dreaming.'
Ben Okri, on receiving the Booker prize on this day 1991

23 October

'If two men on the same job agree all the time then one is useless.
If they disagree all the time, then both are useless.'
Darryl Zanuck, reported on 23 Oct 1949

Feast day of St Severino Boethius, St Severinus or Seurin of Bordeaux, St Elfleda or Ethelfled, St Allucio, St Ignatius of Constantinople, St Theodoret, St Romanus of Rouen, and St John of Capistrano.

≫ EVENTS ≪

1642 The Battle of Edgehill, in the Cotswolds, took place – the first major conflict of the English Civil War. **1922** Andrew Bonar Law took office as British prime minister; he was replaced 22.5.23, making his the shortest term of office in the twentieth century. **1942** The Battle of El Alamein, in Egypt, began. **1946** The first meeting of the United Nations General Assembly took place in New York. **1947** Julie Andrews made her debut in *Starlight Roof*, aged 12. **1956** The Hungarian revolt against Soviet leadership began, in which thousands of demonstrators called for the withdrawal of Soviet forces. **1970** Gary Gabelich achieved the world land speed record of 631.367mph, in his rocket-engine car on Bonneville Salt Flats, Utah. **1987** Former British champion jockey Lester Piggott was sentenced to three years in prison for tax evasion.

≫ BIRTHS ≪

Pierre Larousse, French lexicographer, **1817**; Robert Bridges, British poet, **1844**; Louis Riel, French-Canadian rebel, **1844**; Douglas Jardine, English cricketer, **1900**; Pelé, Brazilian footballer, **1940**; Anita Roddick, British entrepreneur and founder of The Body Shop, **1942**.

≫ DEATHS ≪

Marcus Junius Brutus, Roman soldier, **42 BC**; Théophile Gautier, French poet, **1872**; W G Grace, English cricketer, **1915**; John Boyd Dunlop, Scottish inventor of the pneumatic rubber tyre, **1921**; Zane Grey, US novelist, **1939**; Al Jolson, US singer and actor, **1950**.

'I know that poetry is indispensable but to what I could not say.'
Jean Cocteau, reported on 23 Oct 1955

24 October

'We cannot in any better manner glorify the Lord and Creator of the universe than that in all things ... we contemplate the display of his omnificence and perfections with the utmost admiration.'
Anton van Leeuwenhoek

National Day of Zambia and United Nations Day. Feast day of St Martin or Mark, St Martin of Vertou, St Elesbaan, St Felix of Thibiuca, St Antony Claret, St Evergislus, St Aretas, St Senoch, St Maglorius or Maelor, St Proclus of Constantinople, and The Martyrs of Najran.

≫ EVENTS ≪

1648 The Treaty of Westphalia was signed, ending the Thirty Years' War. **1857** The first football club was formed by a group of Cambridge University Old Boys meeting in Sheffield. **1901** Mrs Ann Edson Taylor braved a descent over Niagara Falls in a padded barrel to help pay the mortgage. **1945** The United Nations charter came into force. **1977** Saudi Arabia purchased the transatlantic liner *France* for use as a floating luxury hotel. **1987** Heavyweight boxing champion Frank Bruno knocked out Joe Bugner in Britain's most hyped boxing match held at White Hart Lane, London. **1989** US television preacher Jim Bakker was sentenced to 45 years in prison and fined $500,000/£272,000 for his multi-million dollar scam.

≫ BIRTHS ≪

Anton van Leeuwenhoek, Dutch microscope pioneer, **1632**; Jacques Lafitte, French banker and politician, **1767**; Sybil Thorndike, English actress, **1882**; Tito Gobbi, Italian baritone, **1915**; Robin Day, English TV presenter, **1923**; Bill Wyman, English bass guitarist, **1941**.

≫ DEATHS ≪

Jane Seymour, 3rd wife of King Henry VIII, **1537**; Tycho Brahe, Danish astronomer, **1601**; Vidkun Quisling, Norwegian politician and Nazi collaborator, **1945**; Franz Lehár, Hungarian composer, **1948**; Christian Dior, French couturier, **1957**; Mary McCarthy, US author, **1989**; Jo Grimond, Scottish politician and writer, **1993**; Jiri Hajek, Czech human-rights campaigner, **1993**.

25 October

'For every woman trying to free women there are probably two
trying to restrict someone else's freedom.'
Brigid Brophy, reported on 25 Oct 1970

Feast day of Saints Crispin and Crispinian, Saints Fronto and George, The Forty
Martyrs of England and Wales, Saints Chrysanthus and Daria, St Richard Gwyn,
and St Gaudentius of Brescia.

EVENTS

1415 The English army, led by King Henry V, defeated the French at the Battle
of Agincourt, during the Hundred Years' War. **1839** *Bradshaw's Railway Guide*,
the world's first railway timetable, was published in Manchester. **1854** Lord
Cardigan led the Charge of the Light Brigade during the Battle of Balaclava in
the Crimean War. **1900** The Transvaal, a region in South Africa which is rich
in minerals, especially gold, was annexed by the British. **1961** The British
satirical magazine *Private Eye* was first published. **1971** Taiwan was expelled
from the UN to allow the admission of the People's Republic of China. **1983**
Over 2,000 US troops invaded Grenada.

BIRTHS

Thomas Babington Macaulay, English historian and essayist, **1800**; Johann
Strauss the Younger, Austrian composer, **1825**; Georges Bizet, French composer,
1838; Pablo Picasso, Spanish artist, **1881**; Richard Evelyn Byrd, US aviator and
explorer, **1888**; Abel Gance, French film director, **1889**.

DEATHS

Geoffrey Chaucer, English poet, **1400**; Giorgione, Italian painter, **1510**;
Evangelista Torricelli, Italian physicist and inventor of the barometer, **1647**;
King George II, **1760**; Frank Norris, US novelist, **1902**; Frederick Rolfe, English
writer, **1913**; Vincent Price, US film actor, **1993**.

'Theirs not to make reply, / Theirs not to reason why,
Theirs but to do and die: / Into the valley of Death
Rode the six hundred.'
Alfred Tennyson, on the Charge of the Light Brigade

26 October

'The Bible and the Church have been the greatest stumbling blocks in the way of women's emancipation.'
Elizabeth Cady Stanton

National Day of Iran and of Austria. Feast day of Saints Lucian and Marcian, St Bean, St Rusticus of Narbonne, St Eata, and St Cedd.

❦ EVENTS ❦

1825 The Erie Canal, linking the Niagara River with the Hudson River, was opened to traffic. **1860** Italian unification leader Giuseppe Garibaldi proclaimed Victor Emmanuel King of Italy. **1881** The legendary 'Gunfight at the OK Corral' took place at Tombstone, Arizona. **1905** Sweden and Norway ended their union and Oscar II, the Norwegian king, abdicated. **1927** Duke Ellington and his orchestra recorded the jazz classic, *Creole Love Song*. **1929** T W Evans of Miami, Florida, became the first woman to give birth aboard an aircraft. **1956** The UN's International Atomic Energy Agency was formed. **1965** Queen Elizabeth presented the Beatles with their MBEs at Buckingham Palace. **1985** A US infant, known as Baby Fae, was given a baboon's heart to replace her malformed one.

❦ BIRTHS ❦

Georges Danton, French revolutionary leader, **1759**; Leon Trotsky, Russian Communist leader, **1879**; François Mitterand, French statesman, **1916**; Mohammed Reza Pahlavi, last Shah of Iran, **1919**; John Arden, English dramatist, **1930**; Bob Hoskins, English actor, **1942**.

❦ DEATHS ❦

Gilles de Rais, French marshal, **1440**; William Hogarth, English artist and engraver, **1764**; Elizabeth Stanton, US feminist, **1902**; Igor Sikorsky, US aeronautical engineer, **1972**; Roger Hollis, British civil servant and alleged double agent, **1973**.

'The love of money is the root of all evil.'
Bible, 1 Timothy 6:10

27 October

'I'm not interested in the bloody system! Why has he no food?
Why is he starving to death?'
Bob Geldof, reported on 27 Oct 1985

Feast day of St Otteran or Odhran of Iona, and St Frumentius of Ethiopia.

∾ EVENTS ∾

1662 Charles II sold Dunkirk to Louis XIV for 2.5 million livres. **1901** In Paris, a 'getaway car' was used for the first time, when thieves robbed a shop and sped away. **1904** The first section of New York City's subway system was opened. **1917** US troops entered the war in France. **1936** Mrs Wallis Simpson was granted a divorce from her second husband, leaving her free to marry King Edward VIII. **1971** The Republic of Congo changed its name to the Republic of Zaire. **1986** The City of London experienced 'Big Bang' day, due to the deregulation of the money market.

∾ BIRTHS ∾

Captain James Cook, English naval explorer, **1728**; Niccolò Paganini, Italian violinist and composer, **1782**; Theodore Roosevelt, 26th US president, **1858**; Dylan Thomas, Welsh poet, **1905**; Roy Lichtenstein, US painter, **1923**; Sylvia Plath, US poet, **1932**; John Cleese, English actor and comedian, **1939**.

∾ DEATHS ∾

Ivan III (the Great), Tsar of Russia, **1505**; George Morland, English painter, **1804**; Lise Meitner, Austrian nuclear physicist, **1968**; Eric Maschwitz, English lyricist, **1969**; James M Cain, US novelist, **1977**.

'We want war with no nation.'
Yosuke Matsuoka, Japanese foreign minister 1940-41,
reported on 27 Oct 1932

28 October

'France is the only place where you can make love in the afternoon without people hammering on your door.'
Barbara Cartland, reported on 28 Oct 1984

Feast day of Saints Anastasia and Cyril, St Faro, St Abraham of Ephesus, St Salvius or Saire, St Simon, St Jude or Thaddeus, and St Fidelis of Como.

✎ EVENTS ✎

1636 Harvard University, the first in the USA, was founded. **1746** An earthquake demolished Lima and Callao, in Peru. **1831** English chemist and physicist Michael Faraday demonstrated the first dynamo. **1886** The Statue of Liberty, designed by Auguste Bartholdi, was presented by France to the USA to mark the 100th anniversary of the Declaration of Independence. **1893** HMS *Havelock*, the Royal Navy's first destroyer, went on trials. **1914** George Eastman, of Eastman Kodak Company, announced the introduction of a colour photographic process. **1971** By a margin of 112 votes, the House of Commons backed Prime Minister Heath's decision to apply for EEC membership. **1982** Felipe González became Spain's first Socialist prime minister, with a sweeping electoral victory.

✎ BIRTHS ✎

Evelyn Waugh, English novelist, **1903**; Francis Bacon, British painter, **1909**; Jonas Salk, US microbiologist, **1914**; Cleo Laine, British singer, **1927**; Carl Davis, US composer, **1936**; Hank Marvin, English guitarist, **1941**.

✎ DEATHS ✎

John Locke, English philosopher, **1704**; John Smeaton, English civil engineer, **1792**; Ottmar Mergenthaler, German inventor of the Linotype, **1899**; Georges Carpentier, French boxer, **1975**; Woody Herman, US bandleader, **1987**; Pietro Annigoni, Italian painter, **1988**.

'It is one thing to show a man that he is in error, and another to put him in possession of the truth.'
John Locke

29 October

'The old boy network works better in Japan than in the United Kingdom.'
Tadao Kato, Japanese ambassador in London, reported on 29 Oct 1978

National Day of Turkey. Feast day of The Martyrs of Douay, St Theuderius or Chef, St Colman of Kilmacduagh, and St Narcissus of Jerusalem.

EVENTS

1618 Sir Walter Raleigh, English navigator, courtier, and once favourite of Elizabeth I, was beheaded at Whitehall for treason. **1787** Mozart's opera *Don Giovanni* was first performed, in Prague. **1863** The International Red Cross was founded by Swiss philanthropist Henri Dunant. **1929** The Wall Street crash known as 'Black Tuesday' took place, leading to the Great Depression. **1964** The union of Tanganyika and Zanzibar was announced, adopting the name of Tanzania. **1967** Expo-67, an international exhibition, opened in Montreal. **1982** In Australia, Lindy Chamberlain was sentenced to life imprisonment for the murder of her nine-week-old baby who, she claimed, had been carried off by a dingo. **1991** Vietnam formally approved a plan to repatriate forcibly tens of thousands of Vietnamese refugees living in camps in Hong Kong.

BIRTHS

James Boswell, Scottish biographer and diarist, **1740**; Wilfred Rhodes, English cricketer, **1877**; Jean Giraudoux, French author, **1882**; Fanny Brice, US singer and entertainer, **1891**; Joseph Goebbels, German Nazi propaganda chief, **1897**; Richard Dreyfuss, US actor, **1947**.

DEATHS

Joseph Pulitzer, US newspaper publisher, **1911**; Frances Hodgson Burnett, English novelist, **1924**; Gustav V, King of Sweden, **1950**; Louis Burt Mayer, US film producer and distributor, **1957**; John Braine, British novelist, **1986**.

'I would warn wives of eminent men to treat their husbands as
if they were not eminent.'
A Clutton Brock, politician, reported on 25 March 1919

30 October

'If anyone thinks £75,000 is a lot of money, he must be in a different world.'
Peter Cadbury, industrialist, reported on 30 Oct 1988

Feast day of St Marcellus the Centurion, St Alphonsus Rodriguez, St Germanus of Capua, St Serapion of Antioch, St Asterius of Amasea, and St Ethelnoth.

EVENTS

1485 The Yeomen of the Guard were established by King Henry VII. **1650** 'Quakers', the more common name for the Society of Friends, came into being during a court case, at which George Fox, the founder, told the magistrate to 'quake and tremble at the word of God'. **1911** P'u-Yi, the boy emperor of China aged five, granted a new constitution, officially ending three centuries of Manchu domination over China. **1918** The Republic of Czechoslovakia was proclaimed. **1925** The Scottish inventor John Baird made the first televised transmission of a moving object (a 15-year-old office boy). **1938** US actor Orson Welles' radio production of *The War of the Worlds* by H G Wells caused panic in the USA. **1965** Brian Jones of the Rolling Stones was jailed for drug offences. **1988** Sun Myung Moon, head of the Unification Church, conducted the marriage of 6,516 couples in a Seoul factory; the couples had first met the day before.

BIRTHS

Richard Brinsley Sheridan, Irish dramatist, **1751**; John Adams, 2nd US president, **1735**; Alfred Sisley, French painter, **1840**; Ezra Pound, US poet, **1885**; Louis Malle, French film director, **1932**; Diego Maradona, Argentinian footballer, **1960**.

DEATHS

Edward Vernon, English admiral, **1757**; Edmund Cartwright, English inventor, **1823**; Andrew Bonar Law, British statesman, **1923**; Pio Baroja, Spanish novelist, **1956**; Jim Mollison, Scottish pioneer aviator, **1959**; Barnes Neville Wallis, British aeronautical engineer, **1979**.

'I have made my contribution to society. I have no plans to work again.'
John Lennon, reported on 30 Oct 1977

31 October

'If poetry comes not as naturally as leaves to a tree it had better not come at all.'
John Keats

All Hallows' Eve (Halloween). Feast day of St Quentin or Quintinus, St Bee or Bega, St Wolfgang, and St Foillan of Fosses.

≈ EVENTS ≈

1517 Martin Luther nailed his theses on indulgences to the church door at Wittenberg, Germany. **1864** Nevada became the 36th state of the Union. **1902** The first telegraph cable across the Pacific Ocean was completed. **1940** The Battle of Britain ended. **1951** Zebra crossings came into effect in Britain. **1952** At Eniwetok Atoll, in the Pacific, the USA detonated the first hydrogen bomb. **1956** British and French troops bombed Egyptian airfields at Suez. **1971** An IRA bomb exploded at the top of the Post Office Tower, London. **1982** The Thames barrier, part of London's flood defences, was raised for the first time.

≈ BIRTHS ≈

Jan Vermeer, Dutch painter, **1632**; John Keats, English poet, **1795**; Joseph Wilson Swan, English inventor of the electric lamp, **1828**; Chiang Kai-shek, Chinese leader, **1887**; Dale Evans, US film actress, **1912**; Michael Collins, US astronaut, **1930**.

≈ DEATHS ≈

Dan Leno, British comedian, **1904**; Harry Houdini, US escapologist, **1926**; Max Reinhardt, Austrian producer and director, **1943**; Augustus John, Welsh painter, **1961**; Indira Gandhi, Indian politician, assassinated, **1984**; River Phoenix, US film actor, **1993**.

'It is not our fault so much of what appears is gloomy.'
David Nicholas, ITN news editor, reported on 2 March 1980

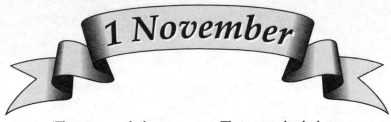

1 November

'There is no such thing as society. There are individual men
and women and there are families.'
Margaret Thatcher, reported on 1 Nov 1987

National Day of Algeria. Feast day of All Saints, St Benignus of Dijon, Saints
Caesarius and Julian, St Austremonius or Stremoine, St Cadfan, St Mary, martyr,
St Vigor, St Marcellus of Paris, and Saint Mathurin or Maturinus.

EVENTS

1755 An earthquake reduced two-thirds of Lisbon to rubble and resulted,
according to accounts, in the death of 60,000 people. **1848** The first W H Smith
railway bookstall opened, at Euston Station, London. **1911** *Woman's Weekly* was
first published. **1914** The British ships *Good Hope* and *Monmouth* were sunk by
the Germans, at the Battle of Coronel. **1940** A prehistoric painting was
discovered in a cave in Lascaux in the Dordogne, France. **1950** Two Puerto
Rican nationalists attempted to assassinate US President Truman. **1959** The
first stretch of the M1 motorway was opened. **1972** Orissa, India, was struck by
a tidal wave which killed 10,000 people and left 5 million homeless.

BIRTHS

Benvenuto Cellini, Italian sculptor and goldsmith, **1500**; Antonio Canova,
Italian sculptor, **1757**; Stephen Crane, US novelist, **1871**; L S Lowry, English
painter, **1887**; Victoria de los Angeles, Spanish soprano, **1923**; Gary Player,
South African golfer, **1935**.

DEATHS

George Gordon, British Protestant agitator, **1793**; Ezra Pound, US poet, **1972**;
King Vidor, US film director, **1982**; Phil Silvers, US comedian and actor, **1985**;
Louis Johnson, New Zealand poet, **1988**.

'Most women know that sex is good for headaches.'
Tom Smith, doctor, reported on 1 Nov 1987

2 November

'What is proposed is a monstrous carbuncle on the face of a much loved and elegant friend.'
Prince Charles, on a proposed extension to the National Gallery, London, reported on 2 Nov 1986

Feast day of All Souls, St Victorinus of Pettau, and Saint Marcian of Cyrrhus.

≈ EVENTS ≈

1785 The first insubmersible lifeboat was patented by Lionel Lakin, a London coach builder. **1871** The 'Rogues Gallery' was started, when photographs of all prisoners in Britain were first taken. **1899** Ladysmith, in Natal, South Africa, was besieged by the Boers. **1917** The Balfour Declaration, stating British support for the Jewish Zionist goal of a homeland in Palestine, was sent to Lord Rothschild. **1930** Ras Tafari, King of Ethiopia, was crowned Emperor Haile Selassie ('Might of the Trinity'). **1957** With eight simultaneous hits in the UK Top 30 chart, Elvis Presley set an all-time record. **1960** A British jury acquitted Penguin Books of obscenity in the matter of publishing D H Lawrence's *Lady Chatterley's Lover*. **1976** James Earl Carter was elected the 39th President of the USA. **1990** Ivana Trump filed for divorce from US millionaire Donald Trump.

≈ BIRTHS ≈

Daniel Boone, US frontiersman, **1734**; Marie Antoinette, Queen of King Louis XVI of France, **1755**; Joseph Radetzky, Austrian field marshal, **1766**; Luchino Visconti, Italian film director, **1906**; Burt Lancaster, US film actor, **1913**; Keith Emerson, English rock musician, **1944**.

≈ DEATHS ≈

Richard Hooker, English theologian, **1600**; Jenny Lind, Swedish soprano, **1887**; William Powell Frith, British painter, **1909**; George Bernard Shaw, Irish dramatist, **1950**; James Thurber, US humorous writer and cartoonist, **1961**.

'The function of the expert is not to be more right than other people, but to be wrong for more sophisticated reasons.'
David Butler, reported on 2 Nov 1969

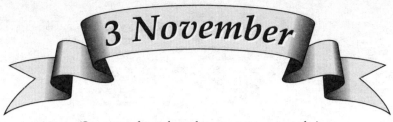
3 November

'Statesmanship is housekeeping on a great scale.'
Sir John Simon, reported on 3 Nov 1922

National Day of Panama. Feast day of St Rumwald, St Malachy of Armagh, St Amicus, St Winifred or Gwenfrewi, St Martin de Porres, and St Pirminus.

☞ EVENTS ☜

1493 Christopher Columbus, on his second voyage of discovery, sighted Dominica, in the West Indies. **1706** A violent earthquake occurred in the Abruzzi, Italy, killing some 15,000 inhabitants. **1927** Turkey adopted the Roman alphabet, abolishing the use of Arabic. **1942** British troops, led by Field Marshal Montgomery, broke through Rommel's front line in Africa. **1957** The Russian dog, Laika, became the first in space aboard *Sputnik 2*. **1975** The North Sea pipeline, the first to be built underwater, was officially opened by Queen Elizabeth II. **1993** A mystery woman paid a record 5 million Swiss francs (£2.2m) for an envelope with two stamps sent from Mauritius to a Bordeaux wine exporter in 1847.

☞ BIRTHS ☜

Vincenzo Bellini, Italian operatic composer, **1801**; Karl Baedeker, German guide-book publisher, **1801**; Charles Bronson, US film actor, **1922**; Roy Emerson, Australian tennis player, **1936**; Larry Holmes, US boxing champion, **1949**; Adam Ant, English rock musician, **1954**.

☞ DEATHS ☜

Constantius II, Roman emperor of the East, **361**; Annie Oakley, US entertainer and markswoman, **1926**; Henri Matisse, French painter, **1954**; Ralph Hodgson, English poet, **1962**; Leon Theremin, Russian inventor, **1993**.

'If you can actually count your money, then you are not
really a rich man.'
John Paul Getty, reported on 3 Nov 1957

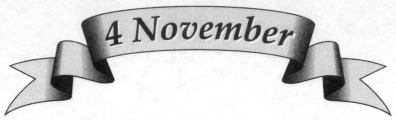
4 November

'I don't make jokes - I just watch the government and report the facts.'
Will Rogers

Feast day of saints Vitalis and Agricola, St Birstan or Brynstan of Winchester, St Pierius, St John Zedazneli, St Charles Borromeo, St Joannicus, and St Clarus.

〜 EVENTS 〜

1605 Guy Fawkes, a Roman Catholic convert and conspirator in the Gunpowder Plot, was arrested in Parliament's cellar. **1862** US inventor Richard Gatling patented the rapid-fire, or machine, gun. **1914** The first fashion show was organized by Edna Woodman Chase of *Vogue* magazine, and held at the Ritz-Carlton Hotel, New York. **1922** British archaeologist Howard Carter discovered the tomb of the Egyptian pharaoh Tutankhamen. **1946** UNESCO was established, with headquarters in Paris. **1979** Iranian students stormed the US Embassy in Teheran and held over 60 staff and US marines hostage. **1980** Ronald Reagan was elected 40th US president. **1991** Imelda Marcos returned to the Philippines after five years of exile in the USA; the government endorsed her return so that she could be tried on corruption and tax evasion charges.

〜 BIRTHS 〜

King William III, **1605**; Augustus Montague Toplady, British clergyman and author, **1740**; Eden Phillpotts, English novelist and dramatist; G E Moore, British philosopher, **1873**; Will Rogers, US humorist and actor, **1879**; Art Carney, US actor, **1918**.

〜 DEATHS 〜

Felix Mendelssohn, German composer, **1847**; Paul Delaroche, French painter, **1856**; Joseph Rowntree, British cocoa manufacturer and philanthropist, **1859**; Wilfred Owen, English poet, **1918**; Gabriel Fauré, French organist and composer, **1924**.

'Of course they have, or I wouldn't be sitting here talking to someone like you.'
Barbara Cartland, when asked in a radio interview whether class barriers had broken down

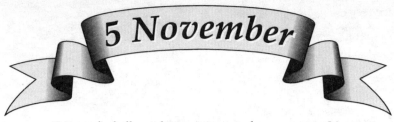
5 November

Guy Fawkes' Night. Feast day of Saints Elisabeth and Zachary, St Galation, St
Bertilla of Chelles, and St Episteme.

∾ EVENTS ∾

1854 The combined British and French armies defeated the Russians at the
Battle of Inkerman during the Crimean War. **1912** The British Board of Film
Censors was appointed. **1914** Cyprus was annexed by Britain on the outbreak of
war with Turkey. **1919** Rudolph Valentino, the archetypal romantic screen
lover, married actress Jean Acker; the marriage lasted less than six hours. **1927**
Britain's first automatic traffic lights began functioning, in Wolverhampton.
1968 Richard Nixon was elected 37th US president. **1990** Rabbi Meir Kahane,
founder of the militant Jewish Defence League and Israel's extremist anti-Arab
Kach party, was assassinated in a New York City hotel.

∾ BIRTHS ∾

James Elroy Flecker, English poet, **1884**; John Haldane, Scottish scientist, **1892**;
Vivien Leigh, British actress, **1913**; Lester Piggott, British jockey, **1935**; Elke
Sommer, German actress, **1940**; Art Garfunkel, US singer and composer, **1941**.

∾ DEATHS ∾

Mack Sennett, US film producer, **1960**; Maurice Utrillo, French painter, **1955**;
Al Capp, US cartoonist, **1979**; Jacques Tati, French film actor and director,
1982; Vladimir Horowitz, US pianist, **1989**; Robert Maxwell, British publishing
and newspaper proprietor, **1991**.

'It is not enough to have a good mind.
The main thing is to use it well.'
René Descartes, *Discourse on Method*

6 November

'Only a fool wants a confrontation and only a fool wants a strike.'
Arthur Scargill, reported on 6 Nov 1977

Feast day of St Demetrian of Khytri, St Melaine, St Barlaam of Khutyn, St Leonard of Noblac, St Winnoc, and St Illtud.

EVENTS

1429 Henry VI was crowned King of England. **1860** Abraham Lincoln was elected 16th US president. **1869** Diamonds were discovered at Kimberley, in Cape Province, South Africa. **1924** British Tory leader Stanley Baldwin was elected prime minister. **1932** In general elections held in Germany, the Nazis emerged as the largest party. **1956** Construction of the Kariba High Dam, on the Zambezi River between Zambia and Zimbabwe, began. **1975** UK punk rock group, the Sex Pistols, gave their first public performance at London's St Martin's College of Art; college authorities cut the concert short – after 10 minutes. **1988** Six thousand US Defense Department computers were crippled by a virus; the culprit was the 23-year-old son of the head of the country's computer security agency.

BIRTHS

Alois Senefelder, Austrian inventor of lithography, **1771**; Adolphe Sax, Belgian inventor of the saxophone, **1814**; John Philip Sousa, US bandmaster and composer, **1854**; John Alcock, British pioneer aviator, **1892**; Mike Nichols, US director, **1931**; Sally Field, US actress, **1946**.

DEATHS

Gustav II, King of Sweden, **1632**; Heinrich Schütz, German composer, **1672**; William Hone, British satirist and editor, **1842**; Peter Ilyich Tchaikovsky, Russian composer, **1893**; Kate Greenaway, British illustrator, **1901**; Gene Eliza Tierney, US film actress, **1991**.

'Words are, of course, the most powerful drug used by mankind.'
Rudyard Kipling

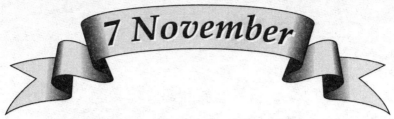
7 November

'I often think how much easier the world would have been to
manage if Herr Hitler and Signor Mussolini had been at Oxford.'
Lord Halifax, reported on 7 Nov 1937

National day of Russia. Feast day of St Herculanus of Perugia, St Engelbert, St
Willibrord, and St Florentius of Strasbourg.

EVENTS

1783 The last public hanging in England took place when John Austin, a forger,
was executed at Tyburn. **1872** The *Marie Celeste*, the ill-fated brigantine, sailed
from New York to be found mysteriously abandoned near the Azores some time
later. **1916** Jeanette Rankin, of the state of Montana, became the first woman
member of US Congress. **1917** The Bolshevik Revolution, led by Lenin,
overthrew Prime Minister Alexander Kerensky's government. **1972** Richard
Nixon was re-elected US president. **1988** In Las Vegas, 'Sugar' Ray Lewis
knocked out Canadian Donny Londe, completing his collection of world titles
at five different weights. **1990** Mary Robinson became the Irish Republic's first
woman president.

BIRTHS

Marie Curie, Polish physicist, **1867**; Leon Trotsky, Russian Communist leader,
1879; Chandrasekhara Venkata Raman, Indian physicist, **1888**; Albert Camus,
French writer, **1913**; Joan Sutherland, operatic soprano, **1926**; Joni Mitchell,
Canadian singer, **1943**.

DEATHS

Godfrey Kneller, German painter, **1723**; Victor McLaglen, English film actor,
1959; Eleanor Roosevelt, US writer and lecturer, **1962**; Gene Tunney, US
heavyweight boxer, **1978**; Steve McQueen, US film actor, **1980**; Alexander
Dubček, Czech statesman; Adelaide Hall, US singer, dancer, and actress, **1993**.

'You know what charm is: getting the answer yes without
having asked any clear question.'
Albert Camus

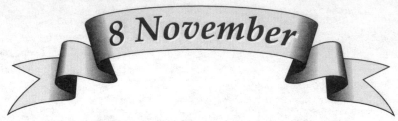
8 November

'Fame is no plant that grows on mortal soil.'
John Milton

Feast day of The Four Crowned Martyrs, St Cuby or Cybi, St Godfrey of Amiens, St Deusdedit, St Willehad, and St Tysilio or Suliau.

EVENTS

1793 The Louvre was opened to the public by the Revolutionary government, although only part of the collection could be viewed. **1895** William Röntgen discovered X-rays during an experiment at the University of Wurzburg. **1923** Hitler led his unsuccessful rising in Munich, known as the Beer Hall Putsch. **1942** Under Eisenhower's command, British and US forces invaded North Africa, in 'Operation Torch'. **1958** *Melody Maker* published the first British album charts. **1987** An IRA bomb went off in Eniskillen, Co Fermanagh, shortly before a Remembrance Day service, killing 11 people. **1991** EC foreign ministers, meeting in Rome, imposed an economic embargo on Yugoslavia in an effort to halt the civil war there.

BIRTHS

Edmond Halley, English astronomer, **1656**; Bram Stoker, Irish writer, **1847**; Herbert Austin, English motor-car manufacturer, **1866**; Margaret Mitchell, US novelist, **1900**, Christiaan Barnard, South African heart transplant pioneer, **1922**; Alain Delon, French film actor, **1935**.

DEATHS

John Milton, English poet, **1674**; Tom Sayers, English bare-knuckle pugilist, **1865**; Fred Archer, English jockey, **1886**; Victorien Sardou, French dramatist, **1908**; Ivan Alexeyevich Bunin, Russian poet, **1953**; Edgard Varèse, French composer, **1965**.

'No one is so completely disenchanted with the world, or knows it so thoroughly, or is so utterly disgusted with it, that when it begins to smile upon him he does not become partially reconciled to it.'
Giacomo Leopardi, *Pensieri*

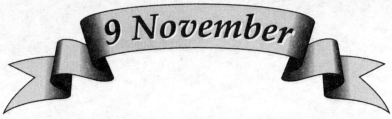

9 November

'The British public seems to abandon all sense of propriety and cleanliness when entering a public cafeteria and instantly assumes dirty habits.'
Egon Ronay, reported on 9 Nov 1975

National Day of Cambodia. Feast day of St Theodore the Recruit, St Vitonus or Vanne, and St Benignus or Benen.

❧ EVENTS ❧

1837 Moses Montefiore became the first Jew to be knighted in England. **1859** Flogging in the British army was abolished. **1908** Britain's first woman mayor, Elizabeth Garrett Anderson, was elected at Aldeburgh. **1918** Following a revolution in Germany, Kaiser William abdicated and fled to Holland. **1925** The SS (Schutzstaffel or 'Protection Squad') was formed in Germany. **1965** Capital punishment was abolished in Britain. **1988** Gary Kasparov became world chess champion after beating Anatoly Karpov, who had held the title for ten years, in Moscow.

❧ BIRTHS ❧

Ivan Turgenev, Russian dramatist, **1818**; King Edward VII, **1841**; Giles Gilbert Scott, English architect, **1880**; Katherine Hepburn, US film actress, **1909**; Hedy Lamarr, US film actress, **1913**; Carl Sagan, US astronomer, **1934**.

❧ DEATHS ❧

Guillaume Apollinaire, French poet, **1918**; James Ramsay MacDonald, British statesman, **1937**; Neville Chamberlain, British statesman, **1940**; Dylan Thomas, Welsh poet, **1953**; Charles de Gaulle, French statesman, **1970**; Yves Montand, French singer and actor, **1991**.

'How can you govern a country which has 246 varieties of cheese?'
Charles de Gaulle

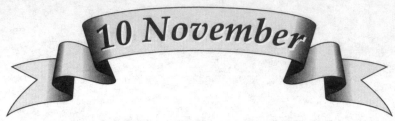
10 November

'This is not the end. It is not even the beginning of the
end. But it is, perhaps, the end of the beginning.'
Winston Churchill, on the Battle for Egypt

Feast day of St Leo the Great, St Justus of Canterbury, St Aedh MacBrice, St
Theoctista, and St Andrew Avellino.

⤜ EVENTS ⤛

1775 The Continental Congress authorised the creation of the 'Continental
Marines', now known as the US Marines. **1862** The first performance of
Giuseppe Verdi's opera *La Forza del Destino* was held in St Petersburg. **1871**
Henry Morton Stanley, who had been sent to track down missing explorer David
Livingstone, met him at Ujiji, on Lake Tanganyika. **1938** Kristallnacht, or
'night of (broken) glass', took place when Nazis burned 267 synagogues and
destroyed thousands of Jewish homes and businesses in Germany. **1928** Hirohito
was crowned Emperor of Japan, at the age of 27. **1989** Bulldozers began
demolishing the 28-year-old Berlin Wall, following the government's
announcement that it would allow free travel between East and West Germany.

⤜ BIRTHS ⤛

Martin Luther, German Protestant reformer, **1483**; François Couperin, French
composer, **1600**; William Hogarth, English painter and engraver, **1697**; Johann
Christoph Friedrich von Schiller, German poet and dramatist, **1759**; Jacob
Epstein, British sculptor, **1880**.

⤜ DEATHS ⤛

Pope Leo I (the Great), **461**; Arthur Rimbaud, French poet, **1891**; Mustapha
Kemal Atatürk, Turkish statesman, **1938**; Dennis Wheatley, English novelist,
1979; Leonid Brezhnev, Soviet political leader, **1982**; Gordon Richards, **1986**.

'There is something the poor know that the rich do not know, something
the sick know that people in good health do not know, something the
stupid know that the intelligent do not know.'
Gerald Brenan, *Thoughts in a Dry Season*

11 November

'If I had the choice between smoked salmon and tinned salmon,
I'd have it tinned. With vinegar.'
Harold Wilson, reported on 11 Nov 1962

Feast day of St Martin of Tours, St Bartholomew of Grottaferata, St Mannas of Egypt, and St Theodore the Studite.

✇ EVENTS ✇

1918 The armistice was signed between the Allies and Germany in Compeigne, France, effectively ending World War I. **1921** The British Legion held its first Poppy Day to raise money for wounded World War I veterans. **1940** The Willys-Overland Company launched a four-wheel drive vehicle for the US Army, named 'Jeep' after GP (general purpose). **1952** The first video recorder was demonstrated in Beverly Hills, California, by its inventors John Mullin and Wayne Johnson. **1965** Ian Smith, Prime Minister of Rhodesia, unilaterally declared his country's independence from Britain. **1975** Angola gained independence from Portugal.

✇ BIRTHS ✇

Louis Antoine de Bougainville, French navigator, **1729**; Fyodor Mikhailovich Dostoevsky, Russian author, **1821**; Edouard Vuillard, French painter, **1868**; Kurt Vonnegut, US novelist, **1922**; Bibi Andersson, Swedish film actress, **1935**; Rodney Marsh, Australian cricketer, **1947**.

✇ DEATHS ✇

Sören Kierkegaard, Danish philosopher, **1855**; Ned Kelly, Australian outlaw, **1880**; Edward German, English composer, **1936**; Jerome Kern, US composer, **1945**; Dimitri Tiomkin, US composer, **1979**; Vyacheslav Mikhailovich Molotov, Russian leader, **1986**.

'My life's work has been accomplished. I did all that I could.'
Mikhail Gorbachev

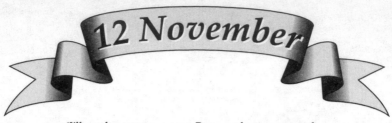

12 November

'I'll not listen to reason ... Reason always means what
someone else has got to say.'
Elizabeth Gaskell

Feast day of St Benedict of Benevento, St Machar or Mochumma, St Astrik or
Anastasius, St Nilus the Elder, St Cadwalader, St Lebuin or Liafwine, St Cunibert,
St Emilian Cucullatus, St Cumian the Tall, St Josephat of Polotsk, and St Livinus.

≋ EVENTS ≋

1660 English author John Bunyan was arrested for preaching without a licence;
refusing to give up preaching, he remained in jail for 12 years. **1847** The first
public demonstration of the use of chloroform as an anaesthetic was given by
James Simpson, at the University of Edinburgh. **1859** Jules Léotard, the daring
young man on the flying trapeze, made his debut at the Cirque Napoléon, in
Paris. **1912** The remains of English explorer Robert Scott and his companions
were found in Antarctica. **1918** The Republic of Austria was declared, thus
ending the Habsburg dynasty. **1944** The RAF bombed and sank the *Tirpitz*, the
last of the major German battleships. **1974** For the first time since the 1840s, a
salmon was caught in the Thames. **1981** The US shuttle *Columbia* became the
first reusable crewed spacecraft, by making its second trip.

≋ BIRTHS ≋

Alexander Borodin, Russian composer, **1833**; Auguste Rodin, French sculptor,
1840; Sun Yat-sen, Chinese nationalist politician, **1866**; Grace Kelly, Princess
Grace of Monaco, **1929**; Neil Young, Canadian rock singer and guitarist, **1946**;
Nadia Comaneci, Romanian gymnast, **1961**.

≋ DEATHS ≋

Canute II (the Great), king of England and Denmark, **1035**; John Sylvan,
French astronomer, **1793**; Elizabeth Gaskell, English novelist, **1865**; Percival
Lowell, US astronomer, **1916**; Baroness Orczy, English novelist, **1947**; Rudolf
Friml, US composer, **1972**; H R Haldeman, US political aide, **1993**.

'I confess I did my best to accommodate as many women as I could.'
'Magic' Johnson, US basketball player

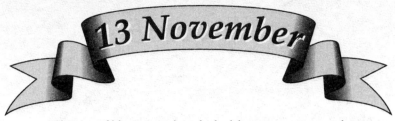
13 November

'The tree of liberty must be refreshed from time to time with
the blood of patriots and tyrants. It is its natural manure.'
Thomas Jefferson

Feast day of At Arcadius, St Didacus or Diego of Seville, St Abbo of Fleury, St
Eugenius of Toledo, St Brice or Britius, St Homobonus, St Nicholas, pope, St
Francis Xavia Cabrini, St Stanislaus Kostka, and St Maxellendis.

✎ EVENTS ✎

1002 The Massacre of the Danes in the southern counties of England took place
by order of Ethelred II. **1851** The telegraph service between London and Paris
began operating. **1907** The first helicopter rose 2 m/6.5 ft above ground in
Normandy. **1914** US heiress Mary Phelps Jacob patented a new female
undergarment, known as the 'backless brassiere'. **1916** In World War I, the Battle
of the Somme ended, having caused the deaths of some 60,000 allied soldiers. **1970**
A cyclone and tidal waves struck East Pakistan, killing over 500,000 people. **1985**
The Colombian volcano Nevado del Ruiz, dormant since 1845, erupted, killing
over 20,000 people. **1987** With a view to encouraging 'safe sex', or AIDS
prevention, the BBC screened its first condom commercial (without a brand name).

✎ BIRTHS ✎

John Moore, British general, **1761**; Charles Frederick Worth, English couturier,
1825; Robert Louis Stevenson, Scottish writer, **1850**; Eugene Ionesco, French
author and dramatist, **1912**; Adrienne Corri, British actress, **1931**; George
Carey, archbishop of Canterbury, **1935**.

✎ DEATHS ✎

Gioacchino Rossini, Italian composer, **1868**; Camille Pissarro, French painter,
1903; Elsa Schiaparelli, Italian couturière, **1973**; Vittorio de Sica, Italian film
director, **1974**; Chesney Allen, British comedian, **1982**.

'The idea that only a male can represent Christ at the altar
is a most serious heresy.'
George Carey, archbishop of Canterbury

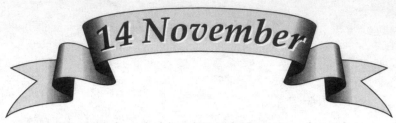

14 November

'Pray, good people, be civil. I am the Protestant whore.'
Nell Gwyn, to a hostile crowd that took her to be Catholic

Feast day of St Laurence O'Toole, St Adeotus Aribert, St Nicholas Tavelic, St Dubricius or Dyfrig, St Stephen of Como, and St Peter of Narbonne.

✎ EVENTS ✎

1770 Scottish explorer James Bruce discovered the source of the Blue Nile in NE Ethiopia, then considered the main stream of the Nile. **1896** The speed limit for motor vehicles in Britain was raised from 4 mph to 14 mph. **1925** An exhibition of Surrealist art opened in Paris, including works by Max Ernst, Man Ray, Joan Miró, and Pablo Picasso. **1940** Enemy bombing destroyed Coventry's medieval cathedral. **1952** Britain's first pop singles chart was published by *New Musical Express*. **1963** The island of Surtsey off Iceland was 'born' by the eruption of an underwater volcano. **1973** Bobby Moore made his 108th (and final) international appearance for England, against Italy at Wembley. **1991** Prince Sihanouk, Cambodia's former head of state, returned to Phnom Penh after nearly 13 years in exile to head the country's interim government.

✎ BIRTHS ✎

Robert Fulton, US engineer, **1765**; Claude Monet, French painter, **1840**; Jawaarlal Nehru, Indian statesman, **1889**; Elisabeth Frink, English sculptor, **1930**; King Hussein of Jordan, **1935**; HRH the Prince of Wales, **1948**.

✎ DEATHS ✎

Nell Gwyn, English actress and mistress of Charles II, **1687**; Gottfried Wilhelm Leibniz, German philosopher, **1716**; Georg Wilhelm Friedrich Hegel, German philosopher, **1831**; Booker T Washington, US educationalist, **1915**; Manuel de Falla, Spanish composer, **1946**; Tony Richardson, British director, **1991**.

'I have caught more ills from people sneezing over me and
giving me virus infections than from kissing dogs.'
Barbara Woodhouse, dog trainer

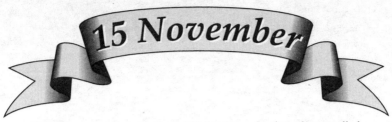

15 November

'Democracy is not convenient. It's not fun to be shoved, controlled, continually questioned ... I caught hell from it, but I kept silent because this was kasha I cooked myself.'
Mikhail Gorbachev

Feast day of St Leopold of Austria, Saints Abibus, Gurias, and Samonas, St Fintan of Rheinau, St Malo or Machutus, St Albert the Great, and St Desiderius or Didier of Cahors.

EVENTS

1837 Pitman's system of shorthand was published, under the title *Stenographic Sound-Hand*. **1889** Dom Pedro was overthrown, and Brazil was proclaimed a republic. **1899** Winston Churchill was captured by the Boers while covering the war as a reporter for the *Morning Post*. **1956** *Love Me Tender*, the first film starring Elvis Presley, premiered in New York. **1968** The Cunard liner *Queen Elizabeth* ended her final transatlantic journey. **1983** An independent Turkish Republic of Northern Cyprus was unilaterally proclaimed, recognized only by Turkey. **1985** UK and Irish premiers, Margaret Thatcher and Garret Fitzerald, signed the Anglo-Irish Agreement in Dublin. **1991** In the wake of increased sectarian violence in Northern Ireland, Britain called up 1,400 reserve troops for full-time active duty.

BIRTHS

William Pitt the Elder, British statesman, **1708**; William Herschel, English astronomer, **1738**; Erwin Rommel, German field marshal, **1891**; Averell Harriman, US diplomat, **1891**; Petula Clark, British singer and actress, **1934**; Daniel Barenboim, Israeli pianist and conductor, **1942**.

DEATHS

George Romney, English painter, **1802**; Henryk Sienkiewicz, Polish novelist, **1916**; Lionel Barrymore, US actor, **1954**; Tyrone Power, US film actor, **1958**; Jean Gabin, French actor, **1976**; Margaret Mead, US anthropologist, **1978**; Luciano Liggio, Italian racketeer, **1993**.

'The parks are the lungs of London.'
William Pitt, *The Elder*

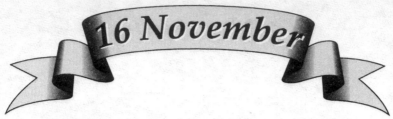
16 November

> 'It is beginning to be hinted that we are a nation of amateurs.'
> **Earl of Rosebery**

Feast day of St Margaret of Scotland, St Agnes of Assisi, St Gertrude of Helfta, St Afan, St Edmund of Abingdon, St Mechtildis of Helfta, St Nikon 'Metanoeite', and St Eucherius of Lyons.

EVENTS

1824 Australian explorer Hamilton Hume discovered the Murray River, the longest river in Australia. **1869** The Suez Canal, which had taken ten years to build, was formally opened. **1913** The first volume of *Remembrance of Things Past*, the classic autobiographical novel by Marcel Proust, was published in Paris. **1918** Hungary achieved independence from the Austro-Hungarian empire and was proclaimed a republic. **1928** In London, obscenity charges were brought against Radclyffe Hall's crusading lesbian novel *The Well of Loneliness*. **1965** The USSR launched *Venus III*, an unmanned spacecraft that successfully landed on Venus. **1993** Amid the tears of its employees and sympathisers, Vladimir Lenin's mausoleum was closed by the Russian authorities; it was the first site in Moscow linked to Lenin to be shut down.

BIRTHS

Tiberius, Roman emperor, **42 BC**; John Bright, British political reformer, **1811**; William Frend de Morgan, English artist and novelist, **1839**; George S Kaufman, US dramatist, **1889**; Willie Carson, English jockey, **1942**; Frank Bruno, British boxer, **1961**.

DEATHS

King Henry III, **1272**; Jack Sheppard, English highwayman, **1724**; Louis Riel, Canadian leader of the Métis rebellion, **1885**; Clark Gable, US film actor, **1960**; William Holden, US film actor, **1981**; Arthur Askey, English comedian, **1983**.

> 'Marriage must be a relation of sympathy or of conquest.'
> **George Eliot**

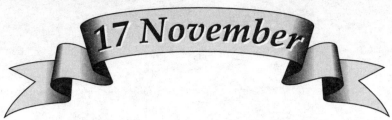

17 November

'I find that the three major administrative problems on a campus are sex for the students, athletics for the alumni and parking for the faculty.'
Clark Kerr, president of the University of California
Time 17 Nov 1958

Feast day of St Hilda, Saints Acisclus and Victoria, St Anianus or Aignan of Orléans, Saints Alphaeus and Zachaeus, St Elizabeth of Hungary, St Gregory of Tours, St Gregory the Wonderworker, St Dionysius of Alexandria, The Martyrs of Paraguay, and St Hugh of Lincoln.

〰 EVENTS 〰

1800 The US Congress met for the first time, in Washington DC. **1880** The first three British women to graduate received their Bachelor of Arts degrees from the University of London. **1922** The last sultan of Turkey was deposed by Kemal Atatürk. **1922** Siberia voted for union with the USSR. **1970** The USSR's *Luna 17* landed on the Sea of Rains on the moon, and released the first moonwalker vehicle. **1970** Stephanie Rahn became the *Sun* newspaper's first Page Three girl. **1988** Benazir Bhutto was elected prime minister of Pakistan, becoming the first female leader of a Muslim state.

〰 BIRTHS 〰

Louis XVIII, King of France, **1755**; Bernard Law Montgomery, British field-marshal, **1887**; Charles Mackerras, Australian conductor, **1925**; Rock Hudson, US film actor, **1925**; Peter Cook, English writer and entertainer, **1937**; Martin Scorsese, US film director, **1942**.

〰 DEATHS 〰

Pico della Mirandola, Italian philosopher, **1497**; Mary I, Queen of England, **1558**; Robert Owen, British socialist, **1856**; Auguste Rodin, French sculptor, **1917**; Heitor Villa-Lobos, Brazilian composer, **1959**; Gladys Cooper, English actress, **1971**.

'The so-called new morality is too often the old immorality condoned.'
Lord Shawcross

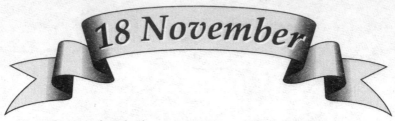

18 November

'It is not the job of any government to lecture the public on moral values. Politicians can best exert their influence in this sphere by example rather than by exhortation.'
Edward Heath, on *Back to Basics* policy

Feast day of St Odo of Cluny, St Romanus of Antioch, and St Mawes or Maudez.

∼ EVENTS ∼

1477 William Caxton's *The Dictes or Sayinges of the Philosophres* was published – the first printed book in England bearing a date. **1626** St Peter's in Rome was consecrated. **1918** Latvia was proclaimed an independent republic. **1928** The first experimental sound cartoon, *Steamboat Willie*, starring Mickey Mouse, was screened in the USA. **1977** President Anwar Sadat became the first Egyptian leader to visit Israel and to address the Knesset (parliament). **1987** A fire broke out at London's King's Cross underground station, killing 30 people. **1991** The Shiite Muslim faction Islamic Jihad freed Church of England envoy Terry Waite (held since Jan 1987) and US university professor Thomas Sutherland (held since June 1985).

∼ BIRTHS ∼

Carl von Weber, German composer, **1786**; Louis Daguerre, French photographic pioneer, **1789**; W S Gilbert, English dramatist and librettist, **1836**; Ignacy Padereweski, Polish pianist, composer and statesman, **1860**; Alan Shepard, US astronaut, **1923**; David Hemmings, English and director, **1941**.

∼ DEATHS ∼

Chester Alan Arthur, 21st US president, **1886**; Marcel Proust, French author, **1922**; Niels Henrik Bohr, Danish physicist, **1962**; Joseph Kennedy, US financier and diplomat, **1969**; Gustáv Husák, Czech politician, **1991**.

'Happiness is salutary for the body but sorrow develops the powers of the spirit.'
Marcel Proust

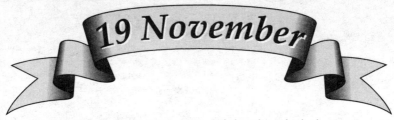
19 November

'Fourscore and seven years ago our fathers brought forth upon
this continent a new nation, conceived in liberty, and
dedicated to the proposition that all men are created equal.'
Abraham Lincoln

Feast day of St Ermenburga, St Barlaam of Antioch, and St Nerses I.

❦ EVENTS ❦

1493 On his second voyage to the New World, Columbus discovered Puerto Rico.
1850 Alfred Tennyson was appointed Poet Laureate. **1863** President Lincoln
delivered his famous Gettysburg address, after the American Civil War. **1942** The
Red Army counter-attacked and surrounded the German army at Stalingrad. **1969**
Brazilian footballer Pelé scored his 1,000th goal in his 909th first class match. **1987**
A record price for a car was reached when a 1931 Bugatti Royale was sold at auction
for £5.5 million.

❦ BIRTHS ❦

Charles I, King of England and Scotland, **1600**; Ferdinand de Lesseps, French
engineer, **1805**; Anton Walbrook, German actor, **1900**; Indira Gandhi, Indian
stateswoman, **1917**; Calvin Klein, US fashion designer, **1942**; Jodie Foster, US
actress, **1963**.

❦ DEATHS ❦

Nicolas Poussin, French painter, **1665**; Thomas Shadwell, English dramatist and
poet, **1692**; Franz Schubert, Austrian composer, **1828**; William Siemens,
German metallurgist, **1883**; Basil Spence, British architect, **1976**; Christina
Onassis, Greek shipowner, **1988**.

'Martyrdom does not end something, it is only a beginning.'
Indira Gandhi

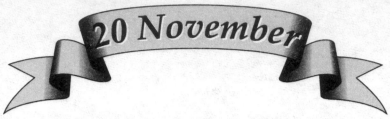
20 November

'All happy families resemble each other, but each unhappy
family is unhappy in its own way.'
Leo Tolstoy

Feast day of St Edmund the Martyr, St Maxentia of Beauvais, St Nerses of Sahgerd,
St Bernward, St Felix of Valois, and St Dasius.

≈ EVENTS ≈

1759 The British fleet under Admiral Hawke defeated the French at the Battle
of Quiberon Bay, thwarting an invasion of England. **1818** Simón Bolívar, known
as 'the Liberator', declared Venezuela to be independent of Spain. **1917** The
Battle of Cambrai began, in which the British deployed large numbers of tanks
for the first time. **1944** The lights of Piccadilly, the Strand, and Fleet Street were
switched back on after five years of blackout. **1945** The Nuremberg trials of 24
chief Nazi war criminals by an international military tribunal began. **1979**
Anthony Blunt, Surveyor of the Queen's Pictures, was stripped of his
knighthood when his past work as a double agent was made public. **1980** The
Solar Challenger was flown for the first time, entirely under solar power.

≈ BIRTHS ≈

Edwin Powell Hubble, US astronomer, **1889**; Alexandra Danilova, Russian
ballerina and choreographer, **1906**; Alistair Cooke, English, journalist and
broadcaster, **1908**; Dulcie Gray, English actress, **1920**, Nadine Gordimer, South
African novelist, **1923**; Robert Kennedy, US politician, **1925**.

≈ DEATHS ≈

Anton Rubinstein, Russian pianist and composer, **1894**; Leo Tolstoy, Russian
novelist, **1910**; Queen Alexandra, consort of Edward VII, **1925**; John
Rushworth Jellicoe, British admiral, **1935**; Francis William Aston, English
physicist, **1945**; Francisco Franco, Spanish dictator, **1975**.

'You can stroke people with words.'
F Scott Fitzgerald

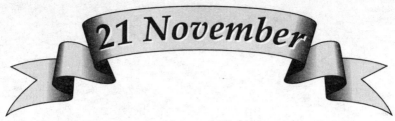
21 November

'Show me a good loser and I'll show you a loser.'
Paul Newman, reported on 21 Nov 1982

Feast day of St Geasius, pope, and St Albert of Louvain.

❧ EVENTS ❧

1783 François de Rozier and the Marquis d'Arlandres made the first human flight when they lifted off from the Bois de Boulogne, Paris, in a hot-air balloon built by the Montgolfier brothers. **1918** The German High Seas Fleet surrendered to the Allies. **1934** Cole Porter's *Anything Goes* was first performed in New York. **1953** The discovery of the Piltdown Man skull by Charles Dawson in Sussex in 1912 was finally revealed as a hoax. **1974** In Birmingham, 20 people were killed and 200 injured by IRA bomb explosions. **1990** Leaders of NATO and Warsaw Pact member states signed the Charter of Paris and a treaty on Conventional Forces in Europe, bringing an end to the Cold War.

❧ BIRTHS ❧

Voltaire, French philosopher and writer, **1694**; Harpo Marx, US comedian, **1888**; René Magritte, Belgian painter, **1898**; Coleman Hawkins, US jazz saxophonist, **1904**; Natalia Makarova, Russian ballerina, **1940**; Goldie Hawn, US film actress, **1945**.

❧ DEATHS ❧

Henry Purcell, English composer, **1695**; James Hogg, Scottish novelist and poet, **1835**; Franz Josef I, Emperor of Austria, **1916**; James Hertzog, South African politician, **1942**; Venkata Raman, Indian physicist, **1970**.

'Fear of the policeman is the beginning of wisdom.'
Charles Pasqua, French politician

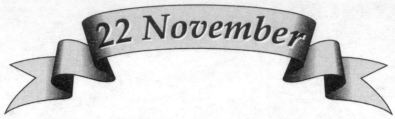

22 November

> 'It's them as take advantage that get advantage i' this world.'
> **George Eliot**

National Day of Lebanon. Feast day of St Cecilia or Cecily, and Saints Philemon and Apphia.

≋ EVENTS ≋

1497 Portuguese navigator Vasco da Gama rounded the Cape of Good Hope in his search for a route to India. **1938** The first coelacanth, a prehistoric fish believed to be extinct, was caught off the South African coast. **1946** Biro ball point pens went on sale in Britain, invented by Hungarian journalist László Biro. **1956** The 16th Olympic Games opened in Melbourne. **1963** John F Kennedy, 35th US president, was assassinated in Dallas, Texas, allegedly by Lee Harvey Oswald. **1975** Two days after the death of General Franco, Juan Carlos I was sworn in as King of Spain. **1986** Mike Tyson, aged 20, defeated Trevor Berbick in Las Vegas, becoming the youngest-ever heavyweight boxing champion. **1990** Prime Minister Margaret Thatcher, who had led Britain since 1979, announced her resignation.

≋ BIRTHS ≋

George Eliot (Mary Ann Evans), English novelist, **1819**; Wassily Kandinsky, Russian painter, **1866**; André Gide, French author, **1869**; Charles de Gaulle, French statesman, **1890**; Benjamin Britten, English composer, **1913**; Billie Jean King, US tennis champion, **1943**; Boris Becker, German tennis champion, **1967**.

≋ DEATHS ≋

Edward Teach (Blackbeard the pirate), English navigator, **1718**; Robert Clive, British general and administrator, **1774**; Arthur Sullivan, English composer, **1900**; Jack London, US novelist, **1916**; Mae West, US film actress, **1980**; Sterling Holloway, US film actor, **1992**.

> 'I wrote the story myself. It's all about a girl who lost her reputation but never missed it.'
> **Mae West**

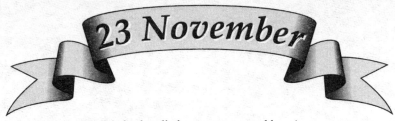
23 November

'My back will always give me problems.'
Denis Thatcher, husband of Margaret Thatcher, on his
golf, reported on 23 Nov 1980

Feast day of St Clement I, pope, St Alexander, prince, St Columbanus, St
Amphilochius, St Trudo or Trond, St Gregory of Girgenti, and St Felicitas.

❧ EVENTS ❧

1670 Molière's *Le Bourgeois Gentilhomme* was performed for the first time in
Paris. **1852** Britain's first pillar boxes were erected, at St Helier, Jersey. **1889**
The first juke box was installed in the Palais Royal Saloon in San Francisco.
1906 Italian operatic tenor Enrico Caruso was fined $10 for sexual harassment.
1921 US President Warren Harding banned doctors from prescribing beer,
eliminating a loophole in the prohibition law. **1963** The first episode of the
BBC TV serial *Dr Who* was broadcast, with William Hartnell as Dr Who and
Anna Ford as his female companion. **1980** A violent earthquake struck
Southern Italy, killing over 4,000 people.

❧ BIRTHS ❧

Billy the Kid, US outlaw, **1859**; Manuel de Falla, Spanish composer, **1876**; Boris
Karloff, English film actor, **1887**; Michael Gough, English actor, **1917**; Lew
Hoad, Australian tennis player, **1934**; Shane Gould, Australian swimmer, **1956**.

❧ DEATHS ❧

Abbé Prévost, French author, **1763**; Dr Hawley Harvey Crippen, US murderer,
executed, **1910**; Arthur Wing Pinero, British dramatist, **1934**; P C Wren,
British novelist, **1941**; André Malraux, French novelist, **1976**; Merle Oberon,
British film actress, **1979**.

'It is not possible for a poet to be a professional. Poetry
is essentially an amateur activity.'
Lord Barrington

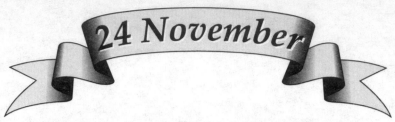

24 November

'Gaiety is the most outstanding feature of the Soviet Union.'
Josef Stalin, reported on 24 Nov 1935

Feast day of Saints Flora and Mary, St Chrysogonus, and St Colman of Cloyne.

∽ EVENTS ∾

1642 Dutch navigator Abel Tasman discovered Van Diemen's Land which he named after his captain, but it was later renamed Tasmania. **1859** Darwin's *The Origin of Species* was published. **1963** Lee Harvey Oswald, charged with the assassination of John F Kennedy, was shot while in police custody by Jack Ruby, a stripclub owner. **1989** Czech politician **Alexander Dubček** made his first public appearance in over 20 years, speaking at a pro-democracy rally in Prague. **1993** The last 14 bottles of Scotch whisky salvaged from the SS *Politician*, wrecked in 1941 and the inspiration of the book and film, *Whisky Galore*, were sold at auction for £11,462 at Christie's.

∽ BIRTHS ∾

Baruch Spinoza, Dutch philosopher, **1632**; Laurence Sterne, Irish novelist, **1713**; Henri de Toulouse-Lautrec, French painter, **1864**; Scott Joplin, US ragtime pianist and composer, **1868**; Billy Connolly, Scottish comedian, **1942**; Ian Botham, English cricketer, **1955**.

∽ DEATHS ∾

John Knox, Scottish religious reformer, **1572**; Erskine Childers, Irish nationalist and novelist, **1922**; Georges Clemenceau, French statesman, **1929**; George Raft, US film actor, **1980**; Freddie Mercury, English rock singer, **1991**; Anthony Burgess, British novelist and critic, **1993**.

'A work of fiction should be, for its author, a journey into the unknown, and the prose should convey the difficulties of the journey.'
Anthony Burgess

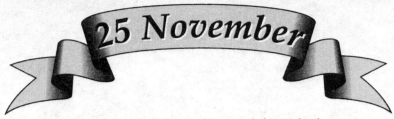
25 November

'I believe in benevolent dictatorship provided I am the dictator.'
Richard Branson, reported on 25 Nov 1984

Feast day of St Moses the Martyr and St Mercurius of Caesarea.

✿ EVENTS ✿

1884 Evaporated milk was patented by John Mayenberg of St Louis, Missouri. **1937** An inter-regional spelling competition became the first British quiz programme to be broadcast. **1941** HMS *Barham* was sunk, with the loss of 868 lives. **1952** The longest-running play, *The Mousetrap* by Agatha Christie, opened in London, at the Ambassador's Theatre. **1969** In protest against Britain's involvement in Biafra and support of US involvement in Vietnam, John Lennon returned his MBE. **1975** Surinam, formerly called Dutch Guiana, became a fully independent republic. **1991** Winston Silcott became the first of the 'Tottenham Three', convicted for the 1985 killing of a policeman in Tottenham, North London, to have his conviction overturned.

✿ BIRTHS ✿

Andrew Carnegie, US industrialist and philanthropist, **1835**; Carl Benz, German engineer and car manufacturer, **1844**; Augusto Pinochet, Chilean dictator, **1915**; Ricardo Montalban, US film actor, **1920**; Imran Khan Niaz, Pakistani cricketer, **1952**.

✿ DEATHS ✿

Isaac Watts, English hymn writer, **1748**; Bojangles (Bill Robinson), US tapdancer and entertainer, **1949**; Myra Hess, British pianist, **1965**; Upton Sinclair, US novelist, **1968**; Yukio Mishima, Japanese novelist, **1970**; Anton Dolin, British dancer and choreographer, **1983**.

'A secret in the Oxford sense:
you may tell it to only one person at a time.'
Oliver Franks

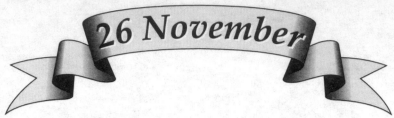
26 November

'Venice is like eating an entire box of chocolate liqueurs at one go.'
Truman Capote

Feast day of St Conrad of Constance, St Peter of Alexandria, St John Berchmans, St Basolus or Basle, St Siricius, St Leonard of Porto Maurizio, and St Silvester Gozzolini.

≈ EVENTS ≈

1703 England was hit by severe gales, known as the Great Storm, in which 8,000 people died. **1789** The American holiday of Thanksgiving was celebrated nationally for the first time. **1906** President Theodore Roosevelt returned to Washington after a trip to Central America, becoming the first US president to travel abroad while in office. **1942** The Soviet forces counter-attacked at Stalingrad, ending the siege and forcing General von Paulus's Sixth Army to retreat. **1949** India became a federal republic within the Commonwealth. **1966** French President Charles de Gaulle opened the world's first tidal power station in Brittany. **1990** Lee Kuan Yew, Singapore's prime minister for 31 years, announced that he was stepping down.

≈ BIRTHS ≈

William Cowper, English poet, **1731**; William George Armstrong, English inventor, **1810**; Emlyn Williams, Welsh actor and dramatist, **1905**; Cyril Cusack, Irish actor, **1910**; Charles Schultz, US cartoonist, **1922**; Tina Turner, US rock singer, **1938**.

≈ DEATHS ≈

Isabella I, Queen of Castile and Aragon, **1504**; John McAdam, Scottish engineer, **1836**; Nicolas Soult, French general, **1851**; Leander Jameson, British colonial administrator, **1917**; Tommy Dorsey, US trombonist and bandleader, **1956**; Arnold Zweig, German novelist, **1968**.

'I never know how much of what I say is true.'
Bette Midler

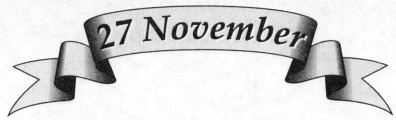
27 November

'But Lord! To see the absurd nature of Englishmen, that
cannot forbear laughing and jeering at everything that looks strange.'
Samuel Pepys, *Diary* 27 Nov 1662

Feast day of St James Intercisus, St Cungar of Somerset, Saints Barlaam and
Josaphat, St Maximus of Riez, St Fergus of Strathern, St Virgil of Salzburg, and
St Secundinus or Sechnall.

EVENTS

1095 Pope Urban began to preach the First Crusade at Clermont, France. **1582**
William Shakespeare, aged 18, married Anne Hathaway. **1914** Britain's first
policewomen went on duty, at Grantham, Lincolnshire. **1940** In Romania, the
pro-fascist group Iron Guard murdered 64 people, including former prime
minister Jorga. **1967** French President Charles de Gaulle rejected British entry
into the Common Market. **1970** The Gay Liberation Front held its first
demonstration in London.

BIRTHS

Anders Celsius, Swedish astronomer and thermometer inventor, **1701**; Fanny
Kemble, English actress, **1809**; Chaim Weizmann, Israeli chemist and Zionist
leader, **1874**; Konosuke Matsushita, Japanese industrialist, **1894**; Alexander
Dubček, Czech statesman, **1920**; Jimi Hendrix, US guitarist and singer, **1942**.

DEATHS

Horace, Roman poet, **8 BC**; Alexandre Dumas *fils*, French novelist and
dramatist, **1895**; Eugene O'Neill, US dramatist, **1953**; Arthur Honegger, Swiss
composer, **1955**; Ross McWhirter, British editor, **1975**.

'Dare to be wise.'
Horace

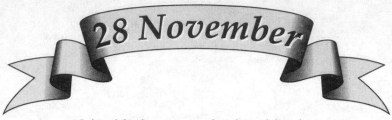
28 November

'O for a life of sensations rather than of thoughts!'
John Keats

Feast day of St Stephen the Younger, St Catherine Labouré, St Simeon Metaphrastes, St James of the March, and St Joseph Pignatelli.

EVENTS

1520 Portuguese navigator Ferdinand Magellan sailed through the Straits at the tip of South America and reached an ocean which he named the Pacific. **1660** The Royal Society was chartered in London. **1905** The Irish political party Sinn Fein was founded by Arthur Griffith in Dublin. **1909** In France, a law was passed allowing women eight weeks' maternity leave. **1948** Edwin Land's first polaroid cameras went on sale in Boston. **1960** Mauritania gained independence. **1978** Amid growing fundamentalist opposition, the Iranian government banned religious rallies. **1993** The Northern Ireland peace process and Prime Minister John Major's credibility were dealt a blow when secret government contacts with the IRA were publicly disclosed.

BIRTHS

Jean Baptiste Lully, Italian/French composer, **1632**; William Blake, English poet and artist, **1757**; Friedrich Engels, German Socialist, **1820**; Alberto Moravia, Italian writer, **1907**; Claude Lévi-Strauss, French anthropologist, **1908**; Randy Newman, US singer and songwriter, **1943**.

DEATHS

Giovanni Lorenzo Bernini, Italian sculptor, **1680**; Washington Irving, US author, **1859**; Enrico Fermi, Italian physicist, **1954**; Enid Blyton, English children's book author, **1968**; Kenneth Connor, English actor, **1993**.

'One often calms one's grief by recounting it.'
Pierre Corneille

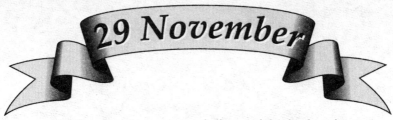

29 November

'Philosopher: A man up in a balloon with his family and
friends holding the ropes which confine him to earth and
trying to haul him down.'
Louisa May Alcott

Feast day of St Radbod, St Brendan of Birr, St Saturninus, martyr, and St
Saturninus or Sernin of Toulouse.

❧ EVENTS ❧

1864 The Sand Creek massacre took place when over 150 Cheyenne and
Arapaho Indians – who had surrendered and were disarmed – were killed by US
cavalry. **1929** US Admiral Richard Byrd became the first man to fly over the
South Pole, with his pilot Bernt Balchen. **1932** Cole Porter's *The Gay Divorcee*,
starring Fred Astaire, was first performed in New York. **1945** Yugoslavia was
proclaimed a Federal People's Republic, under Tito's leadership. **1947** The UN
approved Britain's plan for a partition of Palestine. **1990** The UN Security
Council, at the urging of the USA, authorised the use of force against Iraq if it
did not withdraw totally from Kuwait by 15 January 1991.

❧ BIRTHS ❧

Domenico Donizetti, Italian composer, **1797**; Christian Johann Doppler,
Austrian physicist, **1803**; Louisa May Alcott, US author, **1832**; C S Lewis,
English scholar and writer, **1898**; Jacques Chirac, French statesman, **1932**; John
Mayall, British vocalist and guitarist, **1949**.

❧ DEATHS ❧

Thomas Wolsey, English cardinal and politician, **1530**; Maria Theresa, Empress
of Austria. **1780**; Giacomo Puccini, Italian composer, **1924**; Graham Hill,
English racing driver, **1975**; Natalie Wood, US film actress, **1981**; Ralph
Bellamy, US film actor, **1991**.

'The only time a woman really succeeds in changing a man is
when he's a baby.'
Natalie Wood

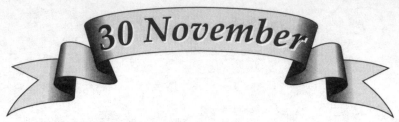

30 November

'Gratitude, like love, is never a dependable international emotion.'
Joseph Alsop, reported on 30 Nov 1952

National Day of Scotland. Feast day of St Andrew the Apostle, St Sapor, and St Cuthbert Mayne.

EVENTS

1840 Napoleon I's remains were returned from St Helena to Paris. **1872** The first international football match was played, Scotland vs England (drawing 0–0). **1914** Charlie Chaplin made his film debut in *Making a Living*, a Mack Sennett one-reeler, without his trademark moustache and cane. **1936** The Crystal Palace at Sydenham, designed by Joseph Paxton and originally constructed in Hyde Park to house the Great Exhibition of 1851, burned down. **1939** The USSR invaded Finland. **1988** PLO leader Yassir Arafat attempted to enter the USA to address the UN General Assembly, but was refused a visa.

BIRTHS

Andrea Palladio, Italian architect, **1508**; Philip Sidney, English poet and soldier, **1554**; Jonathan Swift, Irish author, **1667**; Mark Twain, US author, **1835**; Winston Churchill, British statesman, **1874**; Gary Lineker, English footballer, **1960**.

DEATHS

Oscar Wilde, Irish dramatist, **1900**; Edward John Eyre, Australian explorer, **1901**; Beniamino Gigli, Italian operatic tenor, **1957**; Zeppo Marx, US actor and comedian, **1979**; Cary Grant, US film actor, **1986**; James Baldwin, US writer, **1987**.

'Experience is the name every one gives to their mistakes.'
Oscar Wilde

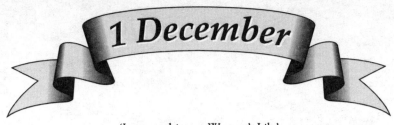

1 December

'I owe nothing to Women's Lib.'
Margaret Thatcher, reported on 1 Dec 1974

World Aids day. Feast day of St Edmund Campion, St Agericus or Airy, St Eligius or Elroy, St Alexander Briant, St Anasanus, St Tudwal, and St Ralph Sherwin.

EVENTS

1640 The Spanish were driven out of Portugal and the country regained its independence. **1919** US-born Lady Nancy Astor became the first woman to take her seat in the House of Commons, as MP for the Sutton division of Plymouth. **1925** The Locarno Pact was signed in London, guaranteeing peace and frontiers in Europe. **1939** *Gone with the Wind* premiered in New York. **1942** The Beveridge Report on Social Security, which formed the basis of the welfare state in Britain, was issued. **1953** The first issue of Hugh Heffner's *Playboy* magazine was published; the centre-spread nude featured Marilyn Monroe. **1989** Pope John Paul II and Mikhail Gorbachev met in Rome, ending 70 years of hostility between the Vatican and the USSR. **1991** France won its first Davis Cup tennis title in 59 years by defeating the USA at the finals in Lyons, France.

BIRTHS

Madame Tussaud, French wax-modeller, **1761**; Alicia Markova, British ballet dancer, **1910**; Woody Allen, US film actor, writer and director, **1935**; Lee Trevino, US golfer, **1939**; Richard Pryor, US comedian and actor, **1940**; Bette Midler, US comedienne and singer, **1945**.

DEATHS

King Henry I, **1135**; Lorenzo Ghiberti, Italian sculptor and goldsmith, **1455**; Vincent d'Indy, French composer, **1931**; J B S Haldane, English scientist and writer, **1964**; David Ben-Gurion, Israeli statesman, **1973**; James Baldwin, US writer, **1987**.

'Too many homes are built on foundations of crushed women.'
Clough Williams-Ellis, reported on 1 Dec 1946

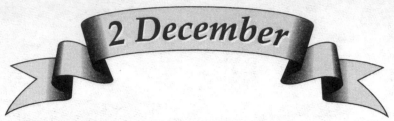
2 December

'This is not like releasing a movie. It is like conducting a military campaign.'
Robert Mitchell, UK marketing director for Walt Disney,
on the release of *Aladdin*

Feast day of St Chromatius of Aquilea, St Silvanus of Constantinople, St Nonnus and St Bibiana or Viviana.

✎ EVENTS ✎

1697 The rebuilt St Paul's Cathedral, work of Sir Christopher Wren, was opened. **1805** Napoleon (crowned Emperor exactly one year earlier) defeated the Austrians and Russians at the Battle of Austerlitz. **1823** US President James Monroe proclaimed the Monroe Doctrine, warning that any further European colonial ambitions in the western hemisphere would be considered threats to US peace and security. **1901** In the USA, King Camp Gillette patented a safety razor with a double-edged disposable blade. **1942** The first nuclear chain reaction took place at the University of Chicago, under physicists Enrico Fermi and Arthur Compton. **1988** In Bangladesh, a cyclone killed thousands of people and left five million homeless. **1990** West German Chancellor Helmut Kohl was elected chancellor of a united Germany.

✎ BIRTHS ✎

Georges Seurat, French painter, **1859**; Ruth Draper, US entertainer, **1884**; John Barbirolli, English conductor, **1899**; Peter Carl Goldmark, US inventor of the LP record, **1906**; Maria Callas, US lyric soprano, **1923**; Alexander Haig, US general and politician.

✎ DEATHS ✎

Hernándo Cortés, Spanish conquistador, **1547**; Gerhardt Mercator, Belgian cartographer, **1594**; Marquis de Sade, French writer and philosopher, **1814**; John Brown, US abolitionist, **1859**; Philip Larkin, English poet, **1985**; Aaron Copland, US composer, **1990**; Pablo Escobar, Colombian racketeer, **1993**.

'There'll always be an England, even if it's in Hollywood.'
Bob Hope, Attr.

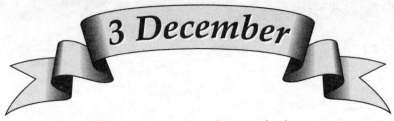

3 December

'A belief in the supernatural source of evil is not
necessary; men alone are quite capable of every wickedness.'
Joseph Conrad

Feast day of Saints Claudius, Hilaria and their Companions, St Birinus, St
Lucius of Britain, St Cassian of Tangier, and St Francis Xavier.

EVENTS

1810 The British captured Mauritius from the French. **1910** Neon lighting was
displayed for the first time at the Paris Motor Show. **1917** The Quebec Bridge,
the world's longest cantilever, over the St Lawrence River, was opened – 87 lives
were lost during its construction. **1961** At the Museum of Modern Art in New
York, Henri Matisse's painting *Le Bateau*, which had been hanging upside-down
for 46 days, was hung the right way up. **1967** At Groote Schurr Hospital, Cape
Town, Dr Christiaan Barnard carried out the world's first heart transplant. **1984**
A chemical leakage at a pesticide factory in Bhopal, India caused the deaths of
over 2,500 people and blinded many thousands.

BIRTHS

Niccolò Amati, Italian violin-maker, **1596**; Joseph Conrad, British novelist,
1857; Anton von Webern, Austrian composer, **1883**; Andy Williams, US
singer, **1930**; Jean-Luc Godard, French film director, **1930**; Franz Klammer,
Austrian skier, **1953**.

DEATHS

Frederick VI, King of Denmark, **1839**; Robert Louis Stevenson, Scottish
novelist, **1894**; Mary Baker Eddy, US founder of Christian Science, **1910**; Pierre
Auguste Renoir, French painter, **1919**; Oswald Mosley, English fascist leader,
1980; Lewis Thomas, US physician and biologist, **1993**; Frank Zappa, US
composer and guitarist, **1993**.

'For my part, I travel not to go anywhere, but to go. I
travel for travel's sake. The great affair is to move.'
Robert Louis Stevenson

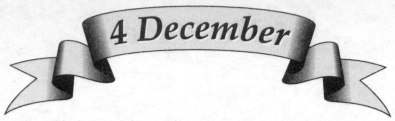

4 December

'The history of the world is but the biography of great men.'
Thomas Carlyle

Feast day of St Maruthas, St Bernard of Parma, St Sola, St Osmund, St Anno, St Barbara, virgin-martyr, and St John of Damascus.

EVENTS

1154 The only Englishman to become a pope, Nicholas Breakspear, became Adrian IV. **1791** Britain's oldest Sunday paper, the *Observer*, was first published. **1798** William Pitt the Younger first introduced income tax in Britain, to finance the wars with revolutionary France. **1808** Napoleon abolished the Inquisition in Spain. **1829** Under British rule, suttee (whereby a widow commits suicide by joining her husband's funeral pyre) was made illegal in India. **1947** The first performance of Tennessee Williams' *A Streetcar Named Desire* starring Marlon Brando and Jessica Tandy, in New York. **1961** Birth control pills became available on the NHS. **1991** News correspondent Terry Anderson, the longest-held Western hostage in Lebanon (2,454 days in captivity), was freed by Islamic Jihad.

BIRTHS

Thomas Carlyle, Scottish author, **1795**; Edith Cavell, English nurse, **1865**; Rainer Maria Rilke, German poet, **1875**; Francisco Franco, Spanish dictator, **1892**; Ronnie Corbett, British comedian, **1930**; Jeff Bridges, US film actor, **1949**.

DEATHS

Cardinal Richelieu, French politician, **1642**; John Gay, English poet and dramatist, **1732**; Luigi Galvani, Italian physiologist, **1798**; Jack Payne, British bandleader, **1969**; Benjamin Britten, English composer, **1976**.

'Many, if not most, of our Indian wars have had their origin
in broken promises and injustice on our part.'
Rutherford B Hayes, speech

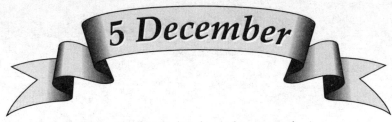

5 December

'Pornography is only a form of sentimentality.'
Grahame Greene, reported on 5 Dec 1937

The national day of Thailand. Feast day of St Christian, St Sabas, St Justinian or Iestin, St Crispina, St Nicetius of Trier, St Sigiramnus or Cyran, and St John Almond.

EVENTS

1766 James Christie, founder of the famous auctioneers, held his first sale in London. **1904** The Russian fleet was destroyed by the Japanese at Port Arthur, during the Russo-Japanese War. **1908** The first American football game in which players were numbered was played, at Pittsburgh. **1933** Prohibition was repealed in the USA after more than 13 years. **1958** Britain's first motorway, the Preston by-pass, was opened by Prime Minister Macmillan. **1993** The single by Mr Blobby, a pink-and-yellow spotted BBC television star, reached number one in the charts.

BIRTHS

Christina Georgina Rossetti, English poet, **1830**; Fritz Lang, Austrian film director, **1890**; Walt Disney, US filmmaker and animator, **1901**; Otto Preminger, Austrian film director, **1906**; Little Richard, US rock 'n' roll pioneer, **1935**; José Carreras, Spanish operatic tenor, **1946**.

DEATHS

Wolfgang Amadeus Mozart, Austrian composer, **1791**; Alexandre Dumas *père*, French novelist, **1870**; Henry Tate, English businessman and philanthropist, **1899**; Claude Monet, French painter, **1926**; Jan Kubelik, Czech violinist, **1940**; Robert Aldrich, US film director, **1983**.

'We have stopped losing the war in Vietnam.'
Robert McNamara, US defense secretary,
reported on 5 Dec 1965

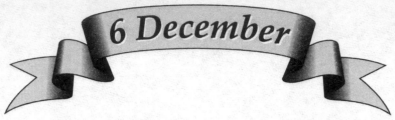

6 December

'Every time thought is driven underground even if it is bad thought, it is a danger to society.'
Ramsay Macdonald, reported on 6 Dec 1925

National Day of Finland. Feast day of St Gertrude the Elder, St Abraham of Kratia, St Nicholas of Bari, St Asella, and Saints Dionysia, Majoricus and their Companions.

≈ EVENTS ≈

1492 Columbus discovered Hispaniola, now Haiti and the Dominican Republic. **1774** Austria became the first nation to introduce a state education system. **1877** With a recording of himself reciting *Mary Had a Little Lamb* Thomas Edison demonstrated the first gramophone, in New Jersey, USA. **1907** In Monongah, West Virginia 361 people were killed in America's worst mine disaster. **1917** Finland proclaimed independence from Russia. **1921** The Irish Free State was formally created, as a result of the Anglo-Irish Treaty. **1926** Mussolini introduced a tax on bachelors. **1990** Saddam Hussein announced that he would free all of the 2,000 foreign hostages held in Iraq and occupied Kuwait.

≈ BIRTHS ≈

King Henry VI, **1421**; George Monck, English admiral, **1608**; Warren Hastings, British administrator, **1732**; Osbert Sitwell, English writer, **1892**; Ira Gershwin, US lyricist, **1896**; Dave Brubeck, US jazz musician, **1920**.

≈ DEATHS ≈

Jean-Baptiste-Siméon Chardin, French painter, **1779**; Madame du Barry, mistress of King Louis XV of France, **1793**; Anthony Trollope, English novelist, **1882**; Ernst Werner von Siemens, German inventor, **1892**; Roy Orbison, US singer and songwriter.

'You don't lead people by following them, but by saying what they want to follow.'
Enoch Powell, reported on 6 Dec 1970

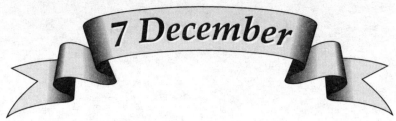

7 December

'The good of the people is the chief law.'
Cicero

Feast day of St Martin of Saujon, St Ambrose of Milan, St Eutychianus, St Servus, and St Buithe or Boethius.

EVENTS

1431 In Paris, Henry VI of England was crowned King of France. **1732** The original Covent Garden Theatre Royal (now the Royal Opera House) was opened. **1787** Delaware became the first of the United States. **1907** At London's National Sporting Club, Eugene Corri became the first referee to officiate from inside a boxing ring. **1941** The Japanese attacked the US fleet in Pearl Harbor. **1982** The first execution by lethal injection took place at Fort Worth Prison, Texas. **1988** An earthquake in Armenia killed thousands and caused widespread destruction. **1990** A week-long succession of violent clashes between Hindus and Muslims in several Indian cities began, resulting in about 300 deaths and 3,000 arrests.

BIRTHS

Giovanni Lorenzo Bernini, Italian sculptor, **1598**; Pietro Mascagni, Italian composer, **1863**; Eli Wallach, US film actor, **1915**; Mario Soares, Portuguese politician, **1924**; Ellen Burstyn, US actress, **1932**; Geoff Lawson, Australian cricketer, **1958**.

DEATHS

Cicero, Roman orator, **43 BC**; William Bligh, captain of the Bounty, **1817**; Ferdinand de Lesseps, French engineer, **1894**; Kirsten Flagstad, Norwegian operatic soprano, **1962**; Thornton Wilder, US novelist, **1975**; Robert Graves, English poet and author, **1985**; Wolfgang Paul, German nuclear physicist, **1993**.

'Marriage is a bribe to make a housekeeper think she's a householder.'
Thornton Wilder

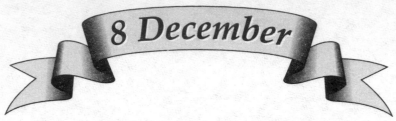

8 December

'Then, with that faint fleeting smile playing about his lips, he faced
the firing squad; erect and motionless, proud and disdainful,
Walter Mitty, the undefeated, inscrutable to the last.'
James Thurber, *My World and Welcome to It* 'The Secret Life of Walter Mitty'

Feast day of the Immaculate Conception, St Romaric, St Eucharius, St
Sophronius of Cyprus, and St Patapius.

EVENTS

1854 Pope Pius IX declared the dogma of the Immaculate Conception of the
Blessed Virgin Mary to be an article of faith. **1863** Tom King of England
defeated American John Heenan, becoming the first world heavyweight
champion. **1941** The USA, Britain, and Australia declared war on Japan, one
day after the attack on Pearl Harbor. **1987** US President Reagan and Soviet
President Gorbachev signed the Intermediate Nuclear Forces treaty in
Washington DC, the first nuclear arms reduction agreement. **1991** The leaders
of Russia, Byelorussia, and the Ukraine signed an agreement forming a
'Commonwealth of Independent States' to replace the USSR; the decision was
denounced by President Gorbachev as unconstitutional.

BIRTHS

Horace, Roman poet, **65 BC**; Mary Stuart, Queen of Scots, **1542**; Bjørnstjerne
Bjørnson, Norwegian poet and dramatist, **1832**; James Thurber, US wit and
cartoonist, **1894**; Sammy Davis Jr, US singer, actor, and dancer, **1925**; Jim
Morrison, US singer, **1943**.

DEATHS

Thomas de Quincey, English author, **1859**; Herbert Spencer, British philosopher
and writer, **1903**; Simon Marks, English retailer, **1964**; Golda Meir, Israeli
politician, **1978**; John Lennon, British rock singer and songwriter, **1980**.

'Not in vain is Ireland pouring itself all over the earth ...
The Irish, with their glowing hearts and reverent credulity,
are needed in this cold age of intellect and scepticism.'
Lydia M Child, US anti-slavery campaigner

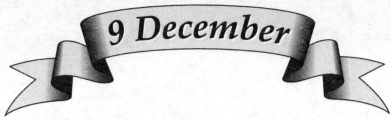
9 December

'Good taste is the worst vice ever invented.'
Dame Edith Sitwell

The national day of Tanzania. Feast day of The Seven Martyrs of Samosata, St Peter Fourier, St Budoc or Beuzec, St Gorgonia, and St Leocadia.

✿ EVENTS ✿

1783 The first executions at Newgate Prison took place. **1868** Gladstone was elected prime minister of Britain, beginning the first of his four terms. **1917** The British captured Jerusalem from the Turks, during World War I. **1955** Sugar Ray Robinson knocked out Carl Olson, regaining his world middleweight boxing title. **1960** The first episode of *Coronation Street* was screened on ITV. **1987** The first martyrs of the 'intifada' in the Gaza Strip were created when an Israeli patrol attacked the Jabaliya refugee camp. **1990** Lech Walesa, leader of the once-outlawed Solidarity labour movement, was elected president of Poland.

✿ BIRTHS ✿

John Milton, English poet, **1608**; Clarence Birdseye, US inventor of deep-freezing process, **1886**; Douglas Fairbanks Jr, US film actor, **1909**; Kirk Douglas, US film actor, **1918**; Robert Hawke, Australian politician, **1929**; Joan Armatrading, English singer and songwriter, **1950**.

✿ DEATHS ✿

Anthony Van Dyck, Flemish painter, **1641**; Joseph Bramah, English inventor of the hydraulic press, **1814**; Juan de la Cierva, Spanish enginer, **1963**; Edith Sitwell, English poet and author, **1964**; Karl Barth, Swiss theologian, **1968**; Bernice Abbott, US photographer, **1991**; Danny Blanchflower, Irish footballer, **1993**.

'The men who really wield, retain and covet power are the kind who answer bedside telephones while making love.'
Nicholas Pileggi

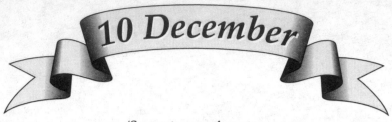

10 December

'Success is counted sweetest
By those who ne'er succeed.'
Emily Dickinson

Feast day of St Gregory, pope, St Edmund Gerhings, St Eustace White, St John Roberts, St Eulalia of Merida, St Swithin Wells, Saints Mannas, Hermogenes and Eugrphus, St Polydore Plaaden, and St Melchiades or Miltiades.

⤳ EVENTS ⤳

1768 The Royal Academy of Arts was founded in London by George III, with Joshua Reynolds as its first president. **1845** Pneumatic tyres were patented by Scottish civil engineer Robert Thompson. **1898** Cuba became independent of Spain following the Spanish-American War. **1901** Nobel prizes were first awarded. **1941** The Royal Naval battleships *Prince of Wales* and *Repulse* were sunk by Japanese aircraft in the Battle of Malaya. The leaders of the 12 EC nations ended their two-day summit and agreed on the treaty of Maastricht, pledging closer political and economic union.

⤳ BIRTHS ⤳

César Franck, Belgian composer, **1822**; Emily Dickinson, US poet, **1830**; William Plomer, South African author, **1903**; Olivier Messiaen, French composer and organist, **1908**; Dorothy Lamour, US film actress, **1914**; Kenneth Branagh, British actor and director, **1960**.

⤳ DEATHS ⤳

Paolo Uccello, Italian painter, **1475**; Leopold I, King of the Belgians, **1865**; Alfred Nobel, Swedish industrialist and philatropist, **1896**; Damon Runyon, US writer, **1946**; Otis Redding, US soul singer and songwriter, **1967**; Jascha Heifetz, US violinist, **1987**.

'We must use time as a tool, not as a couch.'
John F Kennedy

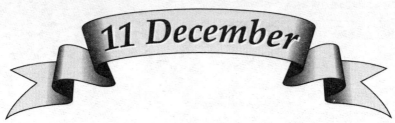
11 December

'God grant me the serenity to accept the things I cannot change, courage to change the things I can, and wisdom always to tell the difference.'
Kurt Vonnegut, *Slaughterhouse Five*

Feast day of St Daniel the Stylite, St Damasus, pope, Saints Fuscianus, Victoricus and Gentianus, and St Barsabas.

❧ EVENTS ❧

1769 Edward Beran of London patented venetian blinds. **1844** Nitrous oxide, or laughing gas, was first used for a tooth extraction. **1894** The first motor show opened in Paris, with nine exhibitors. **1941** Germany and Italy declared war on the USA. **1987** Charlie Chaplin's trademark cane and bowler hat were sold at Christie's for £82,500. **1991** Salman Rushdie, under an Islamic death sentence for blasphemy, made his first public appearance since 1989 in New York, at a dinner marking the 200th anniversary of the First Amendment (which guarantees freedom of speech).

❧ BIRTHS ❧

Pope Leo X, **1475**; Hector Berlioz, French composer, **1803**; Carlo Ponti, Italian film director and producer, **1913**; Alexander Solzhenitsyn, Russian author, **1918**; Kenneth MacMillan, Scottish choreographer, **1929**; Brenda Lee, US pop singer, **1944**.

❧ DEATHS ❧

Llewlyn ap Gruffydd, last native Prince of Wales, **1282**; Bernardino Pinturicchio, Italian painter, **1513**; Olive Schreiner, South African novelist, **1920**; Ed Murrow, US journalist and broadcaster, **1965**.

'Football isn't a matter of life and death - it's much more important than that.'
Bill Shankly

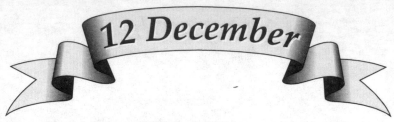

12 December

'Women must come off the pedestal. Men put us up there to get
us out of the way.'
Lady Rhondda, reported on 12 Dec 1920

National Day of Kenya. Feast day of St Jane Frances de Chantel, St Corentin or
Cury, Saints Epimachus and Alexander, St Edburga of Minster, St Vicelin, and
St Finnian of Clonard.

✑ EVENTS ✑

1896 Guglielmo Marconi gave the first public demonstration of radio at
Toynbee Hall, London. **1915** The first all-metal aircraft, the German *Junkers J1*,
made its first flight. **1925** The world's first motel, in San Luis Obispo, California,
opened. **1955** Bill Haley and the Comets recorded 'See You Later Alligator' at
Decca Recording Studios, New York. **1955** British engineer Christopher
Cockerell patented the first hovercraft. **1989** US billionairess Leona Helmsley,
dubbed the 'Queen of Greed', was fined $7 million and sentenced to four years
in prison for tax evasion.

✑ BIRTHS ✑

Gustave Flaubert, French novelist, **1821**; Edvard Munch, Norwegian painter,
1863; Edward G Robinson, US film actor, **1893**; Frank Sinatra, US singer and
actor, **1915**; Dionne Warwick, US singer, **1941**; Emerson Fittipaldi, Brazilian
racing driver, **1960**.

✑ DEATHS ✑

Robert Browning, English poet, **1889**; Douglas Fairbanks, Sr, US film actor,
1939; Peter Fraser, New Zealand politician, **1950**; Tallulah Bankhead, US
actress, **1968**; Anne Baxter, US film actress, **1985**.

'A little uncertainty is good for everyone.'
Henry Kissinger, reported on 12 Dec 1976

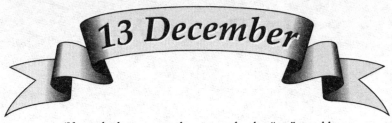
13 December

'If man had time to study one word only, "wit" would
perhaps be the best word he could choose.'
C S Lewis

Feast day of St Lucy, St Aubert of Cambrai, St Othilia or Odilia, St Eustratius of
Sebastea, and St Judocus or Josse.

☙ EVENTS ☙

1577 Francis Drake began his journey from Plymouth in the *Golden Hind* that was
to take him around the world. **1642** Dutch navigator Abel Tasman discovered
New Zealand. **1903** Moulds for ice cream cones were patented by Italo Marcione
of New York. **1904** The Metropolitan Underground railway in London went
electric. **1967** A military coup replaced the monarchy in Greece, sending King
Constantine II into exile. **1973** Due to the Arab oil embargo and the coalminers'
slowdown, the British government ordered a three-day work week.

☙ BIRTHS ☙

Heinrich Heine, German poet and journalist, **1797**; John Piper, English painter
and writer, **1903**; Laurens van der Post, South African writer and explorer,
1906; Balthazar Johannes Vorster, South African politician, **1915**; Christopher
Plummer, US film actor, **1929**; Howard Brenton, English dramatist, **1942**.

☙ DEATHS ☙

Maimonides, Jewish philosopher, **1204**; Donatello, Italian sculptor, **1466**; Dr
Samuel Johnson, English lexicographer, **1784**; Wassily Kandinsky, Russian
painter, **1944**; Grandma Moses, US primitive painter (aged 101), **1961**; Mary
Renault, English novelist, **1983**.

'Jealousy is no more than feeling alone against smiling enemies.'
Elizabeth Bowen

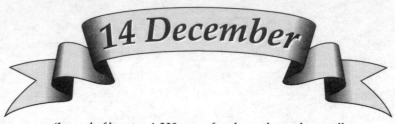
14 December

'Instead of burning 1,000 tons of coal, our descendants will
take the energy out of an ounce or two of matter.'
Sir Oliver Lodge, reported on 14 Dec 1919

Feast day of St John of the Cross, Saints Fingar or Gwinnear and Phiala, St
Spiridion, St Venantius Fortunatus, and St Nicasius of Reims.

EVENTS

1900 Professor Max Planck of Berlin University revealed his revolutionary
Quantum Theory. **1911** A Norwegian expedition led by Roald Amundsen
became the first to reach the South Pole – 35 days ahead of Captain Scott. **1918**
For the first time in Britain women (over 30) voted in a General Election. **1959**
Archbishop Makarios was elected Cyprus' first president. **1962** US *Mariner II*
sent the first close-up pictures of the planet Venus back to Earth. **1990** After 30
years in exile, ANC president Oliver Tambo returned to South Africa.

BIRTHS

Nostradamus, French physician and astrologer, **1503**; Tycho Brahe, Danish
astronomer and mathematician, **1546**; Roger Fry, English painter and critic,
1866; King George VI, **1895**; Lee Remick, US actress, **1935**; Stan Smith, US
tennis player, **1946**.

DEATHS

George Washington, 1st US president, **1799**; Prince Albert, consort of Queen
Victoria, **1861**; Stanley Baldwin, British politician, **1947**; Stanley Spencer,
English painter, **1959**; Andrei Sakharov, Russian physicist and human-rights
campaigner, **1989**.

'In Hollywood they don't feel guilt.'
Agnieszka Holland, Polish director

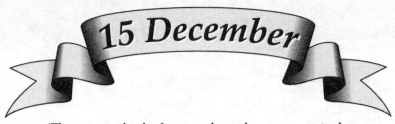
15 December

'There are two kinds of women: those who want power in the
world, and those who want power in bed.'
Jacqueline Kennedy Onassis

Feast day of St Nino, St Valerian, St Mary di Rosa, and St Paul of Latros.

✑ EVENTS ✑

1654 A meteorological office established in Tuscany began recording daily
temperature readings. **1791** The Bill of Rights' ten amendments became part of
the US Constitution. **1916** In World War I, the first Battle of Verdun ended;
over 700,000 German and Allied soldiers died in the action. **1939** Nylon was
first produced commercially in Delaware, USA. **1961** Nazi official Adolph
Eichmann was found guilty of crimes against the Jewish people and sentenced to
death, after a trial in Jerusalem. **1982** Gibraltar's frontier with Spain was opened
to pedestrian use after 13 years. **1992** Bettino Craxi, the leader of Italy's Socialist
Party, was informed that he was under investigation in a burgeoning corruption
scandal that had racked the northern city of Milan.

✑ BIRTHS ✑

Nero, Roman emperor, **37**; George Romney, English painter, **1734**; Gustave
Eiffel, French engineer, **1832**; John Paul Getty, US oil billionaire, **1892**; Edna
O'Brien, Irish novelist, **1936**; Dave Clark, English pop drummer, **1942**.

✑ DEATHS ✑

Jan Vermeer, Dutch painter, **1675**; Izaak Walton, English author of *The
Compleat Angler*, **1683**; Sitting Bull, chief of the Sioux Indians, **1890**; Fats
Waller, US jazz pianist, **1943**; Charles Laughton, English actor, **1962**; Walt
Disney, US filmmaker and animator, **1966**.

'They came to see me bat not to see you bowl.'
W G Grace, on refusing to leave the crease after
being bowled out first ball

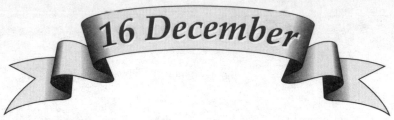
16 December

'For what do we live, but to make sport for our neighbours,
and laugh at them in our turn.'
Jane Austen

Feast day of St Irenion, Saints Ananiah, Azariah, and Michael, and St Adelaide.

✺ EVENTS ✺

1653 Oliver Cromwell became Lord Protector of England. **1773** The Boston Tea Party, a protest against British taxation, took place off Griffin's Wharf in Boston harbour. **1809** Napoleon divorced his wife Josephine, because she had not produced children. **1838** The Zulu chief Dingaan was defeated by a small force of Boers at Blood River – celebrated in South Africa as 'Dingaan's Day'. **1850** The first immigrant ship, the *Charlotte Jane*, arrived at Lyttleton, New Zealand. **1944** The Battle of the Bulge, in the Ardennes, began with a strong counter-attack by the Germans under General von Rundstedt. **1990** Jean-Bertrand Aristide, a leftist priest, was elected president in Haiti's first democratic elections. **1991** The UN General Assembly voted to repeal its 1975 resolution equating Zionism with racism.

✺ BIRTHS ✺

Catherine of Aragon, 1st wife of King Henry VIII, **1485**; Jane Austen, English novelist, **1775**; Jack Hobbs, English cricketer, **1882**; Noël Coward, English dramatist, actor and composer, **1889**; Margaret Mead, US anthropologist, **1901**; Liv Ullmann, Norwegian actress, **1938**.

✺ DEATHS ✺

Wilhelm Grimm, German philologist and folklorist, **1859**; Camille Saint-Saëns, French composer, **1921**; Glenn Miller, US trombonist and bandleader, **1944**; William Somerset Maugham, British novelist, **1965**; Kakuei Tanaka, Japanese politician, **1993**.

'Mad dogs and Englishmen
Go out in the midday sun.'
Noël Coward

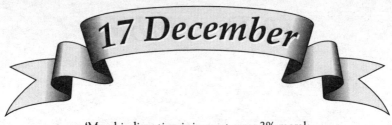

17 December

'Moral indignation is in most cases 2% moral,
48% indignation and 50% envy.'
Vittorio de Sica, reported on 17 Dec 1961

Feast day of St Lazarus, St Sturmi, St Begga, St Wivina, and St Olympias.

❧ EVENTS ❧

1843 *A Christmas Carol* by Charles Dickens was published. **1892** Tchaikovsky's *The Nutcracker* was first performed, in St Petersburg by the Russian Imperial Ballet. **1903** Orville Wright made the first successful controlled flight in a powered aircraft, at Kill Devil Hill, near Kitty Hawk, North Carolina, USA. **1939** The German battleship *Graf Spee* was scuttled by British warships off Montvideo, Uruguay, after the Battle of the River Plate. **1973** Thirty-one people were killed at Rome airport after Arab guerillas hijacked a German airliner. **1986** At Papworth Hospital, Cambridge, Davina Thompson became the world's first recipient of a heart, lungs, and liver transplant. **1992** Israel deported over 400 Palestinians to Lebanese territory in an unprecedented mass expulsion of suspected militants.

❧ BIRTHS ❧

Domenico Cimarosa, Italian composer, **1749**; Humphry Davy, English chemist and inventor, **1778**; William Lyon MacKenzie King, Canadian statesman, **1874**; Erskine Caldwell, US novelist, **1903**; Tommy Steele, British singer and actor, **1936**; Peter Snell, New Zealand athlete, **1938**.

❧ DEATHS ❧

Simón Bolívar, South American revolutionary leader, **1830**; Alphonse Daudet, French novelist, **1897**; Elizabeth Garrett Anderson, first English woman physician, **1917**; Harold Holt, Australian politician, **1967**; Sy Oliver, US composer, **1988**.

'Scrooge! a squeezing, wrenching, grasping, scraping,
clutching, covetous old sinner!'
Charles Dickens, *A Christmas Carol*

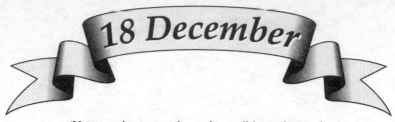

18 December

'Happy is the man with a wife to tell him what to do
and a secretary to do it.'
Lord Mancroft, reported on 18 Dec 1966

Feast day of Saints Rufus and Zosimus, St Flannan, St Winebald, St Gatian, and St Samthan

∼ EVENTS ∼

1865 The USA officially abolished slavery with the ratification of the 13th Amendment. **1903** The Panama Canal Zone was acquired 'in perpetuity' by the USA, for an annual rent. **1912** The immigration of illiterate persons to the USA was prohibited by Congress. **1912** The discovery of the Piltdown Man in East Sussex was announced; it was proved to be a hoax in 1953. **1969** The death penalty for murder was abolished in Britain. **1970** Divorce became legal in Italy. **1979** The sound barrier on land was broken for the first time by Stanley Barrett, driving at 739.6 mph, in California.

∼ BIRTHS ∼

Joseph Grimaldi, English clown, **1779**; Paul Klee, Swiss painter, **1879**; Willy Brandt, German statesman, **1913**; Betty Grable, US film actress, **1916**; Keith Richards, British guitarist, **1943**; Steven Spielberg, US film director, **1947**.

∼ DEATHS ∼

Antonio Stradivari, Italian violin maker, **1737**; John Alcock, English aviator, **1919**; Dorothy L Sayers, English author, **1957**; Bobby Jones, US golfer, **1971**; Ben Travers, British dramatist, **1980**; Paul Tortelier, French cellist, **1990**.

'It is a gentleman's first duty to remember in the morning
who it was he took to bed with him.'
Dorothy L Sayers

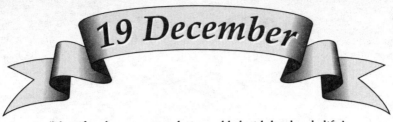
19 December

'My wife, who, poor wretch, is troubled with her lonely life.'
Samuel Pepys, 19 Dec 1662

Feast day of St Timothy, St Gregory of Auxerre, St Anastasius I of Antioch, and St Nemesius of Alexandria.

✑ EVENTS ✑

1154 Henry II became King of England. **1562** The Battle of Dreux was fought between the Huguenots and the Catholics, beginning the French Wars of Religion. **1842** Hawaii's independence was recognised by the USA. **1955** 'Blue Suede Shoes' was recorded by Carl Perkins in Memphis, Tennessee. **1957** An air service between London and Moscow was inaugurated. **1984** Ted Hughes was appointed Poet Laureate. **1984** Britain and China signed an agreement in Beijing, in which Britain agreed to transfer full sovereignty of Hong Kong to China in 1997. **1991** Bob Hawke was deposed as Australia's prime minister by his parliamentary colleagues and replaced by Paul Keating.

✑ BIRTHS ✑

William Edward Parry, English Arctic explorer, **1790**; Albert Abraham Michelson, US physicist, **1852**; Ralph Richardson, English actor, **1902**; Leonid Brezhnev, Soviet leader, **1906**; Jean Genet, French dramatist and essayist, **1910**; Edith Piaf, French singer, **1915**.

✑ DEATHS ✑

Vitus Bering, Danish navigator, **1741**; Emily Brontë, English novelist, **1848**; Joseph Turner, English painter, **1851**; Robert Andrews Millikan, US physicist, **1953**; Alexei Nikolaievich Kosygin, Soviet politician, **1980**; Stella Gibbons, English author, **1989**.

'Television has brought back murder into the home - where it belongs.'
Alfred Hitchcock, reported on 19 Dec 1925

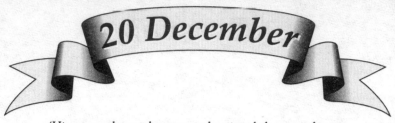

20 December

'History teaches us that men and nations behave wisely once
they have exhausted all other alternatives.'
Abba Eban, reported on 20 Dec 1970

Feast day of St Dominic of Silos, St Ammon and his Companions, St Ursicinus,
and St Philogonius.

☙ EVENTS ☙

1860 South Carolina seceded from the American Union, and joined the
Confederacy. **1915** The ANZACS, Australian and New Zealand forces with
British troops were evacuated from Gallipoli, after their expedition against the
Turks went seriously wrong. **1933** *Flying Down to Rio*, the first film to feature
Fred Astaire and Ginger Rogers, was first shown in New York. **1957** Elvis
Presley, at the height of his stardom, received his draft papers. **1989** General
Noriega, Panama's former dictator, was overthrown by a US invasion force
invited by the new civilian government. **1990** Soviet Foregn Minister
Shevardnadze resigned, complaining of conservative attacks on his policies.

☙ BIRTHS ☙

Robert Menzies, Australian politician, **1894**; James Leasor, English author,
1923; Geoffrey Howe, British politician, **1926**; Uri Geller, Israeli
psychic/illusionist, **1946**; Jenny Agutter, English actress, **1952**; Billy Bragg,
English rock singer, **1958**.

☙ DEATHS ☙

Erich Ludendorff, German general, **1937**; James Hilton, English novelist, **1954**;
John Steinbeck, US novelist, **1968**; Artur Rubinstein, US pianist, **1982**; Bill
Brandt, British photographer, **1983**.

'I know this - a man got to do what he got to do.'
John Steinbeck

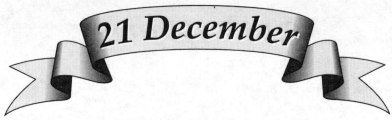

21 December

'I think that a judge should be looked on rather as a sphinx than as a person - you shouldn't be able to imagine a judge having a bath.'
H C Leon, judge, reported on 21 Dec 1975

Feast day of St Thomas the Apostle, Saints Themistocles and Dioscorus, St John Vincent, St Anastasius II of Antioch, St Peter Canisius, and St Glycerius.

∽ EVENTS ∽

1620 The Pilgrim Fathers, aboard the *Mayflower*, landed at Plymouth Rock, Massachusetts. **1879** Ibsen's *A Doll's House* was first performed in Copenhagen, with a revised happy ending. **1925** Eisenstein's film *Battleship Potemkin* was first shown in Moscow. **1937** Walt Disney's *Snow White and the Seven Dwarfs* was shown in Los Angeles, the first full-length animated talking picture. **1958** Charles de Gaulle became President of France. **1988** A Pan Am jet blew up in mid-flight and crashed in Lockerbie, Scotland, killing all 259 passengers aboard and 11 people on the ground; the terrorist bomb had been concealed within a radio. **1990** In a German television interview, Saddam Hussein declared that he would not withdraw from Kuwait by the UN deadline.

∽ BIRTHS ∽

Benjamin Disraeli, British politician, **1804**; Joseph Stalin, Soviet leader, **1879**; Heinrich Böll, German author, **1917**; Jane Fonda, US film actress, **1937**; Frank Zappa, US rock singer and composer, **1940**; Chris Evert, US tennis player, **1954**.

∽ DEATHS ∽

Giovanni Boccaccio, Italian author, **1375**; James Parkinson, British neurologist, **1824**; F Scott Fitzgerald, US novelist, **1940**; George Patton, US military leader, **1945**; Jack Hobbs, English cricketer, **1963**.

'Churchill was fundamentally what the English call unstable - by which they mean anybody who has that touch of genius which is inconvenient in normal times.'
Harold Macmillan, reported on 21 Dec 1975

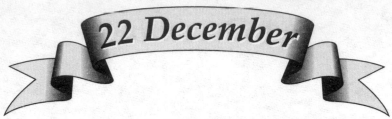

22 December

'I have often found that a man who trusts nobody is apt to be
the kind of man that nobody trusts.'
Harold Macmillan, reported on 22 Dec 1963

Feast day of St Flavian of Tuscany, St Zeno, St Chaeremon and Others, and St
Ischyrion.

🌿 EVENTS 🌿

1715 James Stuart, the 'Old Pretender', landed at Petershead after his exile in
France. **1894** Alfred Dreyfus, the French officer who was falsely convicted for
selling military secrets, was sent to Devil's Island. **1895** German physicist
Wilhelm Röntgen made the first X-ray, of his wife's hand. **1961** James Davis
became the first US soldier to die in Vietnam, while US involvement was still
limited to the provision of military advisers. **1989** Romanian dictator Nicolae
Ceausçescu was overthrown in a bloody revolutionary coup. **1991** Eleven of the
12 Soviet republics (excluding Georgia) agreed, in Alma Ata, Kazakhstan, on the
creation of a Commonwealth of Independent States.

🌿 BIRTHS 🌿

John Crome, English painter, **1768**; John Nevil Maskelyne, English stage
magician, **1839**; Giacomo Puccini, Italian composer, **1858**; Peggy Ashcroft,
English actress, **1907**; Noel Edmonds, English TV presenter, **1910**; Maurice and
Robin Gibb, Australian pop musicians, **1949**.

🌿 DEATHS 🌿

George Eliot, English novelist, **1880**; Beatrix Potter, English author and artist,
1943; Harry Langdon, US silent-film comedian, **1944**; Richard Dimbleby,
British broadcaster, **1965**; Samuel Beckett, Irish author and dramatist, **1989**.

'You mustn't think that I advocate perpetual sex. Far from it. Nothing
nauseates me more than promiscuous sex in and out of season.'
D H Lawrence

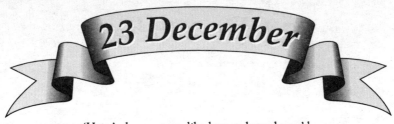
23 December

'Heav'n has no rage, like love to hatred turn'd,
Nor hell a fury, like a woman scorn'd.'
William Congreve

Feast day of The Ten Martyrs of Crete, St Dagobert II of Austria, St John of Kanti, Saints Victoria and Anatolia, St Frithebert, St Servulus, and St Thorlac.

✒ EVENTS ✒

1834 English architect Joseph Hansom patented his 'safety cab', better known as the Hansom cab. **1888** Following a quarrel with Paul Gauguin, Dutch painter Vincent Van Gogh cut off part of his own earlobe. **1922** The BBC began daily news broadcasts. **1948** General Tojo and six other Japanese military leaders were executed, having been found guilty of crimes against humanity. **1953** Soviet secret police chief Lavrenti Beria and six of his associates were shot for treason following a secret trial. **1986** Dick Rutan and Jeana Yeager made the first non-stop flight around the world without refueling, piloting the US plane *Voyager*. **1965** A 70-mph speed limit was introduced in Britain. **1990** Elections in Yugoslavia ended, leaving four of its six republics with non-Communist governments.

✒ BIRTHS ✒

Richard Arkwright, English inventor, **1732**; Alexander I, tsar of Russia, **1777**; Samuel Smiles, Scottish author, **1812**; J Arthur Rank, British film magnate, **1888**; Maurice Denham, English actor, **1909**; Helmut Schmidt, German statesman, **1918**.

✒ DEATHS ✒

Michael Drayton, English poet, **1631**; Thomas Robert Malthus, English economist, **1834**; George Catlin, US painter and explorer, **1872**; Charles Dana Gibson, US artist and illustrator, **1944**; Henry Cotton, British golfer, **1987**; Ernst Krenek, US composer, **1991**.

'We are inclined to believe those whom we do not know because they have never deceived us.'
Samuel Johnson

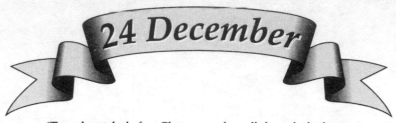

24 December

'Twas the night before Christmas, when all through the house
Not a creature was stirring, not even a mouse;
The stockings were hung by the chimney with care,
In hopes that St Nicholas soon would be there.'
Clement Clarke Moore, 'A Visit from St Nicholas'

Feast day of St Gregory of Spoleto, Saints, Tharsilla and Emiliana, St Adela, St Irmina, St Delphinus, and St Sharbel Makhlouf.

❧ EVENTS ❧

1814 The War of 1812 between the USA and Britain was brought to an end with the signing of the Treaty of Ghent. **1828** William Burke who, with his partner William Hare, dug up the dead and murdered to sell the corpses for dissection, went on trial in Edinburgh. **1871** Verdi's *Aida* was first performed in Cairo. **1914** The first air raid on Britain was made when a German airplane dropped a bomb on the grounds of a rectory in Dover. **1951** Libya achieved independence as the United Kingdom of Libya, under King Idris. **1965** A meteorite landed on Leicestershire; it weighed about 100lbs. **1979** Afghanistan was invaded by Soviet troops as the Kabul government fell.

❧ BIRTHS ❧

King John, **1167**; Ignatius of Loyola, Spanish founder of the Jesuits, **1491**; Matthew Arnold, English poet and critic, **1822**; Howard Hughes, US tycoon, **1905**; Ava Gardner, US film actress, **1922**; Colin Cowdrey, English cricketer, **1932**.

❧ DEATHS ❧

Vasco da Gama, Portuguese explorer and navigator, **1524**; W M Thackeray, English novelist, **1863**; Leon Bakst, Russian painter and stage designer, **1924**; Alban Berg, Austrian composer, **1935**; Frank Richards, English writer, **1961**; Karl Doenitz, German naval commander, **1980**.

'What is the use of a new-born child?'
Benjamin Franklin, when asked the same question of a new invention

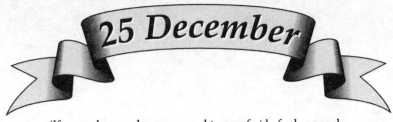

25 December

'If a man has good manners and is not afraid of other people,
he will get by even if he is stupid.'
Sir David Eccles, reported on 25 Dec 1955

Christmas Day. Feast day of The Martyrs of Nicomedia, St Eugenia, St Alburga,
and St Anastasia of Sirmium.

❧ EVENTS ❧

800 Charlemagne was crowned first Holy Roman Emperor in Rome by Pope Leo
III. **1066** William the Conqueror was crowned king of England at Westminster
Abbey. **1914** During World War I, British and German troops observed an
unofficial truce, even playing football together on the Western Front's 'no man's
land'. **1926** Hirohito succeeded his father Yoshihito as emperor of Japan. **1941**
Hong Kong surrendered to the Japanese. **1972** The Nicaraguan capital Managua
was devastated by an earthquake which killed over 10,000 people. **1989**
Dissident playwright Vaclav Havel was elected president of Czechoslovakia.
1991 Unable to maintain control over a disintegrating Soviet Union, Mikhail
Gorbachev announced his resignation as president.

❧ BIRTHS ❧

Isaac Newton, English scientist, **1642**; Maurice Utrillo, French painter, **1883**;
Humphrey Bogart, US film actor, **1899**; Anwar Sadat, Egyptian statesman, **1918**;
Sissy Spacek, US film actress, **1949**; Annie Lennox, British pop singer, **1954**.

❧ DEATHS ❧

Karel Čapek, Czech dramatist, **1938**; W C Fields, US actor and screenwriter,
1946; Charlie Chaplin, English actor and director, **1977**; Joan Miró, Spanish
artist, **1983**; Nicolae Ceauşcescu, Romanian politician, executed, **1989**.

'A lovely thing about Christmas is that it's compulsory, like
a thunderstorm, and we all go through it together.'
Garrison Keillor, *Leaving Home* 'Exiles'

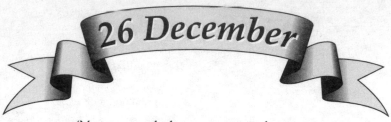
26 December

'Men are so made they can resist sound argument
and yet yield to a glance.'
Honoré de Balzac, Attr.

Boxing Day (Handsel Day in Scotland). Feast day of St Stephen, St Dionysius, pope, St Archelaus of Kashkar, St Vicentia Lopez, St Zosimus, pope, and St Tathai or Athaeus.

❧ EVENTS ❧

1898 Marie and Pierre Curie discovered radium. **1908** Texan boxer 'Galveston Jack' Johnson knocked out Tommy Burns in Sydney, Australia, to become the first black boxer to win the world heavyweight title. **1943** The German battlecruiser *Scharnhorst* was sunk in the North Sea, during the Battle of North Cape. **1956** Fidel Castro attempted a secret landing in Cuba to overthrow the Batista regime; all but 11 of his supporters were killed. **1959** The first charity walk took place, along Icknield Way, in aid of the World Refugee Fund. **1991** The Soviet Union's parliament formally voted the country out of existence.

❧ BIRTHS ❧

Thomas Gray, English poet, **1716**; Charles Babbage, English mathematician, **1792**; Henry Miller, US novelist, **1891**; Mao Zedong, Chinese Communist leader, **1893**; Richard Widmark, US film actor, **1914**; June Lapotaire, English actress, **1944**.

❧ DEATHS ❧

John Wilkes, British politician and journalist, **1797**; Heinrich Schliemann, German archaeologist, **1890**; Charles Pathé, French film pioneer, **1957**; Harry S Truman, 33rd US president, **1972**; Jack Benny, US comedian, **1974**.

'A hurtful act is the transference to others of the
degradation which we bear in ourselves.'
Simone Weil

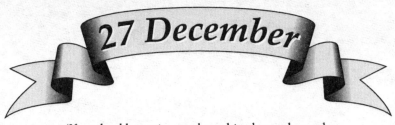

27 December

'If we should promise people nothing better than only
revolution, they would scratch their heads and say: "Is it
not better to have good goulash?" '
Nikita Khrushchev, reported on 27 Dec 1964

Feast day of St John the Evangelist, St Fabiola, Saints Theodore and
Theophanes Graptoi, and St Nicarete.

✑ EVENTS ✑

1703 The Methuen Treaty was signed between Portugal and England, giving
preference to the import of Portuguese wines into England. **1831** Charles
Darwin set sail in the *Beagle* on his voyage of scientific discovery. **1904** James
Barrie's *Peter Pan* premiered in London. **1927** Defeated in his struggle for power
against Stalin, Leon Trotsky was expelled from the Communist Party. **1965** The
BP oil rig Sea Gem capsized in the North Sea, with the loss of 13 lives. **1978**
With the adoption of a new constitution, Spain became a democracy after 40
years of dictatorship.

✑ BIRTHS ✑

Johannes Kepler, German astronomer, **1571**; George Cayley, British aviation
pioneer, **1773**; Louis Pasteur, French chemist and microbiologist, **1822**; Sydney
Greenstreet, English film actor, **1878**; Marlene Dietrich, German singer and
actress, **1901**; Gerard Depardieu, French film actor, **1948**.

✑ DEATHS ✑

Charles Lamb, English essayist and critic, **1834**; Max Beckmann, German
painter, **1950**; Lester Pearson, Canadian statesman, **1972**; Houari Boumédienne,
Algerian politician, **1978**; Hoagy Carmichael, US composer, singer, and pianist,
1981; Hervé Guibert, French novelist and photographer, **1992**.

'At 20 you have many desires that hide the truth,
but beyond 40 there are only real and fragile
truths - your abilities and your failings.'
Gerard Depardieu

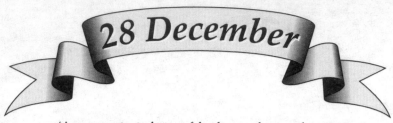
28 December

'A compromise is the art of dividing a cake in such a way
that everyone believes that he has got the biggest piece.'
Ludwig Erhard, reported on 28 Dec 1958

Feast day of the Holy Innocents, St Antony of Lérins, and St Theodore the
Sanctified.

✎ EVENTS ✎

1065 Westminster Abbey was consecrated under Edward the Confessor. **1836**
Mexico's independence was recognised by Spain. **1879** The central portion of
the Tay Bridge collapsed as a train was passing over it, killing 75 people. **1908**
An earthquake killed over 75,000 at Messina in Sicily. **1926** The highest
recorded cricket innings score of 1,107 runs was hit by Victoria, against New
South Wales, in Melbourne. **1937** The Irish Free State became the Republic of
Ireland when a new constitution established the country as a sovereign state
under the name of Eire. **1950** The Peak District became Britain's first designated
National Park. **1989** Alexander Dubček, who had been expelled from the
Communist Party in 1970, was elected speaker of the Czech parliament.

✎ BIRTHS ✎

Woodrow Wilson, 28th US president, **1856**; Arthur Stanley Eddington, English
astronomer, **1882**; Earl Hines, US jazz pianist, **1905**; Lew Ayres, US film actor,
1908, Maggie Smith, English actress, **1934**; Nigel Kennedy, English violinist, **1956**.

✎ DEATHS ✎

Queen Mary II, **1694**; Rob Roy, Scottish clan chief, **1734**; Gustave Eiffel,
French engineer, **1923**; Maurice Ravel, French composer, **1937**; Max Steiner,
US film music composer, **1971**; Sam Peckinpah, US film director, **1984**.

'If drama shows people dealing nobly with their misery, it
disenfranchises those who cannot cope like that.'
Juliet Stevenson, actress

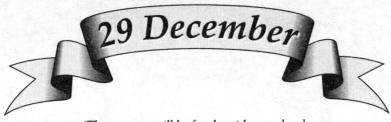

29 December

'The next war will be fought with atom bombs
and the one after that with spears.'
Harold Wrey, reported on 29 Dec 1946

Feast day of St Thomas of Canterbury, St Ebrulf or Evroult, St Trophimus of
Arles, and St Maroellus Akimetes.

∽ EVENTS ∾

1170 St Thomas à Becket, the 40th Archbishop of Canterbury, was murdered in
his own cathedral by four knights acting on Henry II's orders. **1860** HMS *Warrior*,
Britain's first seagoing iron-clad warship, was launched. **1890** The massacre at
Wounded Knee, the last major battle between Native American Indians and US
troops, took place. **1895** The Jameson Raid from Mafikeng into Transvaal, which
attempted to overthrow Kruger's Boer government, started. **1911** Sun Yat-sen
became the first president of a republican China, following the Revolution. **1989**
Following Hong Kong's decision to forcibly repatriate some Vietnamese refugees,
thousands of Vietnamese 'boat people' battled with riot police.

∽ BIRTHS ∾

Marquise de Pompadour, mistress of King Louis XV, **1721**; Charles Goodyear,
US inventor, **1800**; William Gladstone, English statesman, **1809**; Pablo Casals,
Spanish cellist, **1876**; Jon Voight, US film actor, **1938**; Marianne Faithfull,
English singer and actress, **1946**.

∽ DEATHS ∾

Thomas Sydenham, English physician, **1689**; Jacques Louis David, French
painter, **1825**; Christina Georgina Rossetti, English poet, **1894**; Rainer Maria
Rilke, German poet, **1926**; James Fletcher Henderson, US jazz pianist and
composer, **1952**; Harold Macmillan, British politician, **1986**.

'It's better to be unfaithful than faithful without wanting to be.'
Brigitte Bardot, reported on 29 Dec 1968

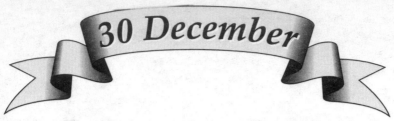
30 December

'The industrial nations will have to realise that this era
of terrific progress and even more terrific wealth based on
cheap oil is finished.'
Shah of Iran, reported on 30 Dec 1973

Feast day of St Sabinus of Spoleto, St Anysia, St Anysius, and St Egwin.

✎ EVENTS ✎

1460 At the Battle of Wakefield, in the Wars of the Roses, the Duke of York was defeated and killed by the Lancastrians. **1879** Gilbert and Sullivan's *The Pirates of Penzance* was first performed, at Paignton, Devon. **1880** The Transvaal was declared a republic by Paul Kruger, who became its first president. **1887** A petition to Queen Victoria with over one million names of women appealing for public houses to be closed on Sundays was handed to the home secretary. **1919** Lincoln's Inn, in London, admitted the first female bar student. **1922** The Union of Soviet Socialist Republics was formed. **1947** King Michael of Romania abdicated in favour of a Communist Republic. **1988** Colonel Oliver North subpoenaed President Reagan and Vice President Bush to testify at the Irangate hearings.

✎ BIRTHS ✎

André Messager, French composer, **1853**; Rudyard Kipling, English author and poet, **1865**; Carol Reed, English film director, **1906**; Bo Diddley, US rhythm and blues singer, **1928**; Tracey Ullman, English comedienne, **1959**; Ben Johnson, Canadian athlete, **1961**.

✎ DEATHS ✎

Robert Boyle, Irish physicist and chemist, **1691**; Amelia Bloomer, US social reformer, **1894**; Grigoriy Efimovich Rasputin, Siberian mystic, **1916**; Trygve Lie, Norwegian politician and diplomat, **1968**; Richard Rodgers, US composer, **1979**.

'There can be no whitewash at the White House.'
Richard Nixon, reported on 30 Dec 1973

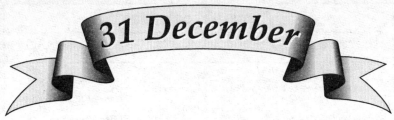

31 December

'I'd not know what I may appear to the world; but to myself I seem to have been only a boy playing on the sea-shore and diverting myself in now and then finding a smoother pebble or a prettier shell than ordinary, whilst the great ocean of truth lay all undiscovered before me.'
Sir Isaac Newton

New Year's Eve. Feast day of St Silvester I, pope, St Melania the Younger, and St Columba of Sens.

✤ EVENTS ✤

1687 The first Huguenots set sail from France for the Cape of Good Hope, where they would later create the South African wine industry with the vines they took with them on the voyage. **1695** The window tax was imposed in Britain, which resulted in many being bricked up. **1891** New York's new Immigration Depot was opened at Ellis Island, to provide improved facilities for the massive numbers of arrivals. **1923** The chimes of Big Ben were first broadcast by the BBC. **1960** The farthing coin, which had been in use in Great Britain since the 13th century, ceased to be legal tender. **1990** Titleholder Gary Kasparov of the USSR won the world chess championship match against his countryman Anatoly Karpov.

✤ BIRTHS ✤

Charles Edward Stuart, the Young Pretender, **1720**; Henri Matisse, French painter, **1869**; George Marshall, US general, **1880**; Anthony Hopkins, Welsh actor, **1937**; Ben Kingsley, British actor, **1943**; Donna Summer, US singer, **1948**.

✤ DEATHS ✤

John Flamsteed, first Astronomer Royal, **1719**; Gustave Courbet, French painter, **1877**; Miguel de Unamuno, Spanish writer, **1936**; Malcolm Campbell, British racing driver, **1948**; Maxim Litvinov, Soviet leader, **1951**; Rick Nelson, US rock and country singer, **1985**.

'Snowy, Flowy, Blowy, / Showery, Flowery, Bowery,
Hoppy, Croppy, Droppy, / Breezy, Sneezy, Freezy.'
George Ellis (Sir George Gander), the twelve months of the year

Perpetual calendar

The number shown for each year indicates which Gregorian calendar to use

1821 — 2	1847 — 6	1873 — 4	1899 — 1	1925 — 5	1951 — 2	1977 — 7	2003 — 4	2029 — 2	2055 — 6
1822 — 3	1848 —14	1874 — 5	1900 — 2	1926 — 6	1952 —10	1978 — 1	2004 —12	2030 — 3	2056 —14
1823 — 4	1849 — 2	1875 — 6	1901 — 3	1927 — 7	1953 — 5	1979 — 2	2005 — 7	2031 — 4	2057 — 2
1824 —12	1850 — 3	1876 —14	1902 — 4	1928 — 8	1954 — 6	1980 —10	2006 — 1	2032 —12	2058 — 3
1825 — 7	1851 — 4	1877 — 2	1903 — 5	1929 — 3	1955 — 7	1981 — 5	2007 — 2	2033 — 7	2059 — 4
1826 — 1	1852 —12	1878 — 3	1904 —13	1930 — 4	1956 — 8	1982 — 6	2008 —10	2034 — 1	2060 —12
1827 — 2	1853 — 7	1879 — 4	1905 — 1	1931 — 5	1957 — 3	1983 — 7	2009 — 5	2035 — 2	2061 — 7
1828 —10	1854 — 1	1880 —12	1906 — 2	1932 —13	1958 — 4	1984 — 8	2010 — 6	2036 —10	2062 — 1
1829 — 5	1855 — 2	1881 — 7	1907 — 3	1933 — 1	1959 — 5	1985 — 3	2011 — 7	2037 — 5	2063 — 2
1830 — 6	1856 —10	1882 — 1	1908 —11	1934 — 2	1960 —13	1986 — 4	2012 — 8	2038 — 6	2064 —10
1831 — 7	1857 — 5	1883 — 2	1909 — 6	1935 — 3	1961 — 1	1987 — 5	2013 — 3	2039 — 7	2065 — 5
1832 — 8	1858 — 6	1884 —10	1910 — 7	1936 —11	1962 — 2	1988 —13	2014 — 4	2040 — 8	2066 — 6
1833 — 3	1859 — 7	1885 — 5	1911 — 1	1937 — 6	1963 — 3	1989 — 1	2015 — 5	2041 — 3	2067 — 7
1834 — 4	1860 — 8	1886 — 6	1912 — 9	1938 — 7	1964 —11	1990 — 2	2016 —13	2042 — 4	2068 — 8
1835 — 5	1861 — 3	1887 — 7	1913 — 4	1939 — 1	1965 — 6	1991 — 3	2017 — 1	2043 — 5	2069 — 3
1836 —13	1862 — 4	1888 — 8	1914 — 5	1940 — 9	1966 — 7	1992 —11	2018 — 2	2044 —13	2070 — 4
1837 — 1	1863 — 5	1889 — 3	1915 — 6	1941 — 4	1967 — 1	1993 — 6	2019 — 3	2045 — 1	2071 — 5
1838 — 2	1864 —13	1890 — 4	1916 —14	1942 — 5	1968 — 9	1994 — 7	2020 —11	2046 — 2	2072 —13
1839 — 3	1865 — 1	1891 — 5	1917 — 2	1943 — 6	1969 — 4	1995 — 1	2021 — 6	2047 — 3	2073 — 1
1840 —11	1866 — 2	1892 —13	1918 — 3	1944 —14	1970 — 5	1996 — 9	2022 — 7	2048 —11	2074 — 2
1841 — 6	1867 — 3	1893 — 1	1919 — 4	1945 — 2	1971 — 6	1997 — 4	2023 — 1	2049 — 6	2075 — 3
1842 — 7	1868 —11	1894 — 2	1920 —12	1946 — 3	1972 —14	1998 — 5	2024 — 9	2050 — 7	2076 —11
1843 — 1	1869 — 6	1895 — 3	1921 — 7	1947 — 4	1973 — 2	1999 — 6	2025 — 4	2051 — 1	2077 — 6
1844 — 9	1870 — 7	1896 —11	1922 — 1	1948 —12	1974 — 3	2000 —14	2026 — 5	2052 — 9	2078 — 7
1845 — 4	1871 — 1	1897 — 6	1923 — 2	1949 — 7	1975 — 4	2001 — 2	2027 — 6	2053 — 4	2079 — 1
1846 — 5	1872 — 9	1898 — 7	1924 —10	1950 — 1	1976 —12	2002 — 3	2028 —14	2054 — 5	2080 — 9

1

```
JANUARY                 FEBRUARY                MARCH
S  M  T  W  T  F  S      S  M  T  W  T  F  S     S  M  T  W  T  F  S
         1  2  3  4  5               1  2  3  4            1  2  3  4
6  7  8  9 10 11 12      5  6  7  8  9 10 11     5  6  7  8  9 10 11
13 14 15 16 17 18 19    12 13 14 15 16 17 18    12 13 14 15 16 17 18
20 21 22 23 24 25 26    19 20 21 22 23 24 25    19 20 21 22 23 24 25
27 28 29 30 31          26 27 28                26 27 28 29 30 31

APRIL                   MAY                     JUNE
S  M  T  W  T  F  S      S  M  T  W  T  F  S     S  M  T  W  T  F  S
                  1         1  2  3  4  5  6               1  2  3
2  3  4  5  6  7  8      7  8  9 10 11 12 13     4  5  6  7  8  9 10
9 10 11 12 13 14 15    14 15 16 17 18 19 20    11 12 13 14 15 16 17
16 17 18 19 20 21 22    21 22 23 24 25 26 27    18 19 20 21 22 23 24
23 24 25 26 27 28 29    28 29 30 31             25 26 27 28 29 30
30

JULY                    AUGUST                  SEPTEMBER
S  M  T  W  T  F  S      S  M  T  W  T  F  S     S  M  T  W  T  F  S
                  1            1  2  3  4  5                  1  2
2  3  4  5  6  7  8      6  7  8  9 10 11 12     3  4  5  6  7  8  9
9 10 11 12 13 14 15    13 14 15 16 17 18 19    10 11 12 13 14 15 16
16 17 18 19 20 21 22    20 21 22 23 24 25 26    17 18 19 20 21 22 23
23 24 25 26 27 28 29    27 28 29 30 31          24 25 26 27 28 29 30
30 31

OCTOBER                 NOVEMBER                DECEMBER
S  M  T  W  T  F  S      S  M  T  W  T  F  S     S  M  T  W  T  F  S
1  2  3  4  5  6  7               1  2  3  4                  1  2
8  9 10 11 12 13 14     5  6  7  8  9 10 11     3  4  5  6  7  8  9
15 16 17 18 19 20 21    12 13 14 15 16 17 18    10 11 12 13 14 15 16
22 23 24 25 26 27 28    19 20 21 22 23 24 25    17 18 19 20 21 22 23
29 30 31                26 27 28 29 30          24 25 26 27 28 29 30
                                                31
```

2

```
JANUARY                 FEBRUARY                MARCH
S  M  T  W  T  F  S      S  M  T  W  T  F  S     S  M  T  W  T  F  S
1  2  3  4  5  6                  1  2  3                  1  2  3
7  8  9 10 11 12 13     4  5  6  7  8  9 10     4  5  6  7  8  9 10
14 15 16 17 18 19 20    11 12 13 14 15 16 17    11 12 13 14 15 16 17
21 22 23 24 25 26 27    18 19 20 21 22 23 24    18 19 20 21 22 23 24
28 29 30 31             25 26 27 28             25 26 27 28 29 30 31

APRIL                   MAY                     JUNE
S  M  T  W  T  F  S      S  M  T  W  T  F  S     S  M  T  W  T  F  S
1  2  3  4  5  6  7            1  2  3  4  5                  1  2
8  9 10 11 12 13 14     6  7  8  9 10 11 12     3  4  5  6  7  8  9
15 16 17 18 19 20 21    13 14 15 16 17 18 19    10 11 12 13 14 15 16
22 23 24 25 26 27 28    20 21 22 23 24 25 26    17 18 19 20 21 22 23
29 30                   27 28 29 30 31          24 25 26 27 28 29 30

JULY                    AUGUST                  SEPTEMBER
S  M  T  W  T  F  S      S  M  T  W  T  F  S     S  M  T  W  T  F  S
1  2  3  4  5  6  7            1  2  3  4                     1
8  9 10 11 12 13 14     5  6  7  8  9 10 11     2  3  4  5  6  7  8
15 16 17 18 19 20 21    12 13 14 15 16 17 18     9 10 11 12 13 14 15
22 23 24 25 26 27 28    19 20 21 22 23 24 25    16 17 18 19 20 21 22
29 30 31                26 27 28 29 30 31       23 24 25 26 27 28 29
                                                30

OCTOBER                 NOVEMBER                DECEMBER
S  M  T  W  T  F  S      S  M  T  W  T  F  S     S  M  T  W  T  F  S
   1  2  3  4  5  6               1  2  3                        1
7  8  9 10 11 12 13     4  5  6  7  8  9 10     2  3  4  5  6  7  8
14 15 16 17 18 19 20    11 12 13 14 15 16 17     9 10 11 12 13 14 15
21 22 23 24 25 26 27    18 19 20 21 22 23 24    16 17 18 19 20 21 22
28 29 30 31            25 26 27 28 29 30        23 24 25 26 27 28 29
                                                30 31
```

3

JANUARY

S	M	T	W	T	F	S
		1	2	3	4	5
6	7	8	9	10	11	12
13	14	15	16	17	18	19
20	21	22	23	24	25	26
27	28	29	30	31		

FEBRUARY

S	M	T	W	T	F	S
					1	2
3	4	5	6	7	8	9
10	11	12	13	14	15	16
17	18	19	20	21	22	23
24	25	26	27	28		

MARCH

S	M	T	W	T	F	S
					1	2
3	4	5	6	7	8	9
10	11	12	13	14	15	16
17	18	19	20	21	22	23
24	25	26	27	28	29	30
31						

APRIL

S	M	T	W	T	F	S
	1	2	3	4	5	6
7	8	9	10	11	12	13
14	15	16	17	18	19	20
21	22	23	24	25	26	27
28	29	30				

MAY

S	M	T	W	T	F	S
			1	2	3	4
5	6	7	8	9	10	11
12	13	14	15	16	17	18
19	20	21	22	23	24	25
26	27	28	29	30	31	

JUNE

S	M	T	W	T	F	S
						1
2	3	4	5	6	7	8
9	10	11	12	13	14	15
16	17	18	19	20	21	22
23	24	25	26	27	28	29
30						

JULY

S	M	T	W	T	F	S
	1	2	3	4	5	6
7	8	9	10	11	12	13
14	15	16	17	18	19	20
21	22	23	24	25	26	27
28	29	30	31			

AUGUST

S	M	T	W	T	F	S
				1	2	3
4	5	6	7	8	9	10
11	12	13	14	15	16	17
18	19	20	21	22	23	24
25	26	27	28	29	30	31

SEPTEMBER

S	M	T	W	T	F	S
1	2	3	4	5	6	7
8	9	10	11	12	13	14
15	16	17	18	19	20	21
22	23	24	25	26	27	28
29	30					

OCTOBER

S	M	T	W	T	F	S
		1	2	3	4	5
6	7	8	9	10	11	12
13	14	15	16	17	18	19
20	21	22	23	24	25	26
27	28	29	30	31		

NOVEMBER

S	M	T	W	T	F	S
					1	2
3	4	5	6	7	8	9
10	11	12	13	14	15	16
17	18	19	20	21	22	23
24	25	26	27	28	29	30

DECEMBER

S	M	T	W	T	F	S
1	2	3	4	5	6	7
8	9	10	11	12	13	14
15	16	17	18	19	20	21
22	23	24	25	26	27	28
29	30	31				

4

JANUARY

S	M	T	W	T	F	S
			1	2	3	4
5	6	7	8	9	10	11
12	13	14	15	16	17	18
19	20	21	22	23	24	25
26	27	28	29	30	31	

FEBRUARY

S	M	T	W	T	F	S
						1
2	3	4	5	6	7	8
9	10	11	12	13	14	15
16	17	18	19	20	21	22
23	24	25	26	27	28	

MARCH

S	M	T	W	T	F	S
						1
2	3	4	5	6	7	8
9	10	11	12	13	14	15
16	17	18	19	20	21	22
23	24	25	26	27	28	29
30	31					

APRIL

S	M	T	W	T	F	S
		1	2	3	4	5
6	7	8	9	10	11	12
13	14	15	16	17	18	19
20	21	22	23	24	25	26
27	28	29	30			

MAY

S	M	T	W	T	F	S
				1	2	3
4	5	6	7	8	9	10
11	12	13	14	15	16	17
18	19	20	21	22	23	24
25	26	27	28	29	30	31

JUNE

S	M	T	W	T	F	S
1	2	3	4	5	6	7
8	9	10	11	12	13	14
15	16	17	18	19	20	21
22	23	24	25	26	27	28
29	30					

JULY

S	M	T	W	T	F	S
		1	2	3	4	5
6	7	8	9	10	11	12
13	14	15	16	17	18	19
20	21	22	23	24	25	26
27	28	29	30	31		

AUGUST

S	M	T	W	T	F	S
					1	2
3	4	5	6	7	8	9
10	11	12	13	14	15	16
17	18	19	20	21	22	23
24	25	26	27	28	29	30
31						

SEPTEMBER

S	M	T	W	T	F	S
	1	2	3	4	5	6
7	8	9	10	11	12	13
14	15	16	17	18	19	20
21	22	23	24	25	26	27
28	29	30				

OCTOBER

S	M	T	W	T	F	S
			1	2	3	4
5	6	7	8	9	10	11
12	13	14	15	16	17	18
19	20	21	22	23	24	25
26	27	28	29	30	31	

NOVEMBER

S	M	T	W	T	F	S
						1
2	3	4	5	6	7	8
9	10	11	12	13	14	15
16	17	18	19	20	21	22
23	24	25	26	27	28	29
30						

DECEMBER

S	M	T	W	T	F	S
	1	2	3	4	5	6
7	8	9	10	11	12	13
14	15	16	17	18	19	20
21	22	23	24	25	26	27
28	29	30	31			

5

JANUARY

S	M	T	W	T	F	S
				1	2	3
4	5	6	7	8	9	10
11	12	13	14	15	16	17
18	19	20	21	22	23	24
25	26	27	28	29	30	31

FEBRUARY

S	M	T	W	T	F	S
1	2	3	4	5	6	7
8	9	10	11	12	13	14
15	16	17	18	19	20	21
22	23	24	25	26	27	28

MARCH

S	M	T	W	T	F	S
1	2	3	4	5	6	7
8	9	10	11	12	13	14
15	16	17	18	19	20	21
22	23	24	25	26	27	28
29	30	31				

APRIL

S	M	T	W	T	F	S
			1	2	3	4
5	6	7	8	9	10	11
12	13	14	15	16	17	18
19	20	21	22	23	24	25
26	27	28	29	30		

MAY

S	M	T	W	T	F	S
					1	2
3	4	5	6	7	8	9
10	11	12	13	14	15	16
17	18	19	20	21	22	23
24	25	26	27	28	29	30
31						

JUNE

S	M	T	W	T	F	S
	1	2	3	4	5	6
7	8	9	10	11	12	13
14	15	16	17	18	19	20
21	22	23	24	25	26	27
28	29	30				

JULY

S	M	T	W	T	F	S
			1	2	3	4
5	6	7	8	9	10	11
12	13	14	15	16	17	18
19	20	21	22	23	24	25
26	27	28	29	30	31	

AUGUST

S	M	T	W	T	F	S
						1
2	3	4	5	6	7	8
9	10	11	12	13	14	15
16	17	18	19	20	21	22
23	24	25	26	27	28	29
30	31					

SEPTEMBER

S	M	T	W	T	F	S
		1	2	3	4	5
6	7	8	9	10	11	12
13	14	15	16	17	18	19
20	21	22	23	24	25	26
27	28	29	30			

OCTOBER

S	M	T	W	T	F	S
				1	2	3
4	5	6	7	8	9	10
11	12	13	14	15	16	17
18	19	20	21	22	23	24
25	26	27	28	29	30	31

NOVEMBER

S	M	T	W	T	F	S
1	2	3	4	5	6	7
8	9	10	11	12	13	14
15	16	17	18	19	20	21
22	23	24	25	26	27	28
29	30					

DECEMBER

S	M	T	W	T	F	S
		1	2	3	4	5
6	7	8	9	10	11	12
13	14	15	16	17	18	19
20	21	22	23	24	25	26
27	28	29	30	31		

6

JANUARY

S	M	T	W	T	F	S
					1	2
3	4	5	6	7	8	9
10	11	12	13	14	15	16
17	18	19	20	21	22	23
24	25	26	27	28	29	30
31						

FEBRUARY

S	M	T	W	T	F	S
	1	2	3	4	5	6
7	8	9	10	11	12	13
14	15	16	17	18	19	20
21	22	23	24	25	26	27
28						

MARCH

S	M	T	W	T	F	S
	1	2	3	4	5	6
7	8	9	10	11	12	13
14	15	16	17	18	19	20
21	22	23	24	25	26	27
28	29	30	31			

APRIL

S	M	T	W	T	F	S
				1	2	3
4	5	6	7	8	9	10
11	12	13	14	15	16	17
18	19	20	21	22	23	24
25	26	27	28	29	30	

MAY

S	M	T	W	T	F	S
						1
2	3	4	5	6	7	8
9	10	11	12	13	14	15
16	17	18	19	20	21	22
23	24	25	26	27	28	29
30	31					

JUNE

S	M	T	W	T	F	S
		1	2	3	4	5
6	7	8	9	10	11	12
13	14	15	16	17	18	19
20	21	22	23	24	25	26
27	28	29	30			

JULY

S	M	T	W	T	F	S
				1	2	3
4	5	6	7	8	9	10
11	12	13	14	15	16	17
18	19	20	21	22	23	24
25	26	27	28	29	30	31

AUGUST

S	M	T	W	T	F	S
1	2	3	4	5	6	7
8	9	10	11	12	13	14
15	16	17	18	19	20	21
22	23	24	25	26	27	28
29	30	31				

SEPTEMBER

S	M	T	W	T	F	S
			1	2	3	4
5	6	7	8	9	10	11
12	13	14	15	16	17	18
19	20	21	22	23	24	25
26	27	28	29	30		

OCTOBER

S	M	T	W	T	F	S
					1	2
3	4	5	6	7	8	9
10	11	12	13	14	15	16
17	18	19	20	21	22	23
24	25	26	27	28	29	30
31						

NOVEMBER

S	M	T	W	T	F	S
	1	2	3	4	5	6
7	8	9	10	11	12	13
14	15	16	17	18	19	20
21	22	23	24	25	26	27
28	29	30				

DECEMBER

S	M	T	W	T	F	S
			1	2	3	4
5	6	7	8	9	10	11
12	13	14	15	16	17	18
19	20	21	22	23	24	25
26	27	28	29	30	31	

7

JANUARY
S	M	T	W	T	F	S
						1
2	3	4	5	6	7	8
9	10	11	12	13	14	15
16	17	18	19	20	21	22
23	24	25	26	27	28	29
30	31					

FEBRUARY
S	M	T	W	T	F	S
		1	2	3	4	5
6	7	8	9	10	11	12
13	14	15	16	17	18	19
20	21	22	23	24	25	26
27	28					

MARCH
S	M	T	W	T	F	S
		1	2	3	4	5
6	7	8	9	10	11	12
13	14	15	16	17	18	19
20	21	22	23	24	25	26
27	28	29	30	31		

APRIL
S	M	T	W	T	F	S
					1	2
3	4	5	6	7	8	9
10	11	12	13	14	15	16
17	18	19	20	21	22	23
24	25	26	27	28	29	30

MAY
S	M	T	W	T	F	S
1	2	3	4	5	6	7
8	9	10	11	12	13	14
15	16	17	18	19	20	21
22	23	24	25	26	27	28
29	30	31				

JUNE
S	M	T	W	T	F	S
			1	2	3	4
5	6	7	8	9	10	11
12	13	14	15	16	17	18
19	20	21	22	23	24	25
26	27	28	29	30		

JULY
S	M	T	W	T	F	S
					1	2
3	4	5	6	7	8	9
10	11	12	13	14	15	16
17	18	19	20	21	22	23
24	25	26	27	28	29	30
31						

AUGUST
S	M	T	W	T	F	S
	1	2	3	4	5	6
7	8	9	10	11	12	13
14	15	16	17	18	19	20
21	22	23	24	25	26	27
28	29	30	31			

SEPTEMBER
S	M	T	W	T	F	S
					1	2
3						
4	5	6	7	8	9	10
11	12	13	14	15	16	17
18	19	20	21	22	23	24
25	26	27	28	29	30	

OCTOBER
S	M	T	W	T	F	S
						1
2	3	4	5	6	7	8
9	10	11	12	13	14	15
16	17	18	19	20	21	22
23	24	25	26	27	28	29
30	31					

NOVEMBER
S	M	T	W	T	F	S
		1	2	3	4	5
6	7	8	9	10	11	12
13	14	15	16	17	18	19
20	21	22	23	24	25	26
27	28	29	30			

DECEMBER
S	M	T	W	T	F	S
				1	2	3
4	5	6	7	8	9	10
11	12	13	14	15	16	17
18	19	20	21	22	23	24
25	26	27	28	29	30	31

8

JANUARY
S	M	T	W	T	F	S
1	2	3	4	5	6	7
8	9	10	11	12	13	14
15	16	17	18	19	20	21
22	23	24	25	26	27	28
29	30	31				

FEBRUARY
S	M	T	W	T	F	S
			1	2	3	4
5	6	7	8	9	10	11
12	13	14	15	16	17	18
19	20	21	22	23	24	25
26	27	28	29			

MARCH
S	M	T	W	T	F	S
					1	2
3						
4	5	6	7	8	9	10
11	12	13	14	15	16	17
18	19	20	21	22	23	24
25	26	27	28	29	30	31

APRIL
S	M	T	W	T	F	S
1	2	3	4	5	6	7
8	9	10	11	12	13	14
15	16	17	18	19	20	21
22	23	24	25	26	27	28
29	30					

MAY
S	M	T	W	T	F	S
		1	2	3	4	5
6	7	8	9	10	11	12
13	14	15	16	17	18	19
20	21	22	23	24	25	26
27	28	29	30	31		

JUNE
S	M	T	W	T	F	S
					1	2
3	4	5	6	7	8	9
10	11	12	13	14	15	16
17	18	19	20	21	22	23
24	25	26	27	28	29	30

JULY
S	M	T	W	T	F	S
1	2	3	4	5	6	7
8	9	10	11	12	13	14
15	16	17	18	19	20	21
22	23	24	25	26	27	28
29	30	31				

AUGUST
S	M	T	W	T	F	S
			1	2	3	4
5	6	7	8	9	10	11
12	13	14	15	16	17	18
19	20	21	22	23	24	25
26	27	28	29	30	31	

SEPTEMBER
S	M	T	W	T	F	S
						1
2	3	4	5	6	7	8
9	10	11	12	13	14	15
16	17	18	19	20	21	22
23	24	25	26	27	28	29
30						

OCTOBER
S	M	T	W	T	F	S
	1	2	3	4	5	6
7	8	9	10	11	12	13
14	15	16	17	18	19	20
21	22	23	24	25	26	27
28	29	30	31			

NOVEMBER
S	M	T	W	T	F	S
				1	2	3
4	5	6	7	8	9	10
11	12	13	14	15	16	17
18	19	20	21	22	23	24
25	26	27	28	29	30	

DECEMBER
S	M	T	W	T	F	S
						1
2	3	4	5	6	7	8
9	10	11	12	13	14	15
16	17	18	19	20	21	22
23	24	25	26	27	28	29
30	31					

9

JANUARY
S	M	T	W	T	F	S
	1	2	3	4	5	6
7	8	9	10	11	12	13
14	15	16	17	18	19	20
21	22	23	24	25	26	27
28	29	30	31			

FEBRUARY
S	M	T	W	T	F	S
				1	2	3
4	5	6	7	8	9	10
11	12	13	14	15	16	17
18	19	20	21	22	23	24
25	26	27	28	29		

MARCH
S	M	T	W	T	F	S
					1	2
3	4	5	6	7	8	9
10	11	12	13	14	15	16
17	18	19	20	21	22	23
24	25	26	27	28	29	30
31						

APRIL
S	M	T	W	T	F	S
	1	2	3	4	5	6
7	8	9	10	11	12	13
14	15	16	17	18	19	20
21	22	23	24	25	26	27
28	29	30				

MAY
S	M	T	W	T	F	S
			1	2	3	4
5	6	7	8	9	10	11
12	13	14	15	16	17	18
19	20	21	22	23	24	25
26	27	28	29	30	31	

JUNE
S	M	T	W	T	F	S
						1
2	3	4	5	6	7	8
9	10	11	12	13	14	15
16	17	18	19	20	21	22
23	24	25	26	27	28	29
30						

JULY
S	M	T	W	T	F	S
	1	2	3	4	5	6
7	8	9	10	11	12	13
14	15	16	17	18	19	20
21	22	23	24	25	26	27
28	29	30	31			

AUGUST
S	M	T	W	T	F	S
				1	2	3
4	5	6	7	8	9	10
11	12	13	14	15	16	17
18	19	20	21	22	23	24
25	26	27	28	29	30	31

SEPTEMBER
S	M	T	W	T	F	S
1	2	3	4	5	6	7
8	9	10	11	12	13	14
15	16	17	18	19	20	21
22	23	24	25	26	27	28
29	30					

OCTOBER
S	M	T	W	T	F	S
		1	2	3	4	5
6	7	8	9	10	11	12
13	14	15	16	17	18	19
20	21	22	23	24	25	26
27	28	29	30	31		

NOVEMBER
S	M	T	W	T	F	S
					1	2
3	4	5	6	7	8	9
10	11	12	13	14	15	16
17	18	19	20	21	22	23
24	25	26	27	28	29	30

DECEMBER
S	M	T	W	T	F	S
1	2	3	4	5	6	7
8	9	10	11	12	13	14
15	16	17	18	19	20	21
22	23	24	25	26	27	28
29	30	31				

10

JANUARY
S	M	T	W	T	F	S
		1	2	3	4	5
6	7	8	9	10	11	12
13	14	15	16	17	18	19
20	21	22	23	24	25	26
27	28	29	30	31		

FEBRUARY
S	M	T	W	T	F	S
					1	2
3	4	5	6	7	8	9
10	11	12	13	14	15	16
17	18	19	20	21	22	23
24	25	26	27	28	29	

MARCH
S	M	T	W	T	F	S
						1
2	3	4	5	6	7	8
9	10	11	12	13	14	15
16	17	18	19	20	21	22
23	24	25	26	27	28	29
30	31					

APRIL
S	M	T	W	T	F	S
		1	2	3	4	5
6	7	8	9	10	11	12
13	14	15	16	17	18	19
20	21	22	23	24	25	26
27	28	29	30			

MAY
S	M	T	W	T	F	S
				1	2	3
4	5	6	7	8	9	10
11	12	13	14	15	16	17
18	19	20	21	22	23	24
25	26	27	28	29	30	31

JUNE
S	M	T	W	T	F	S
1	2	3	4	5	6	7
8	9	10	11	12	13	14
15	16	17	18	19	20	21
22	23	24	25	26	27	28
29	30					

JULY
S	M	T	W	T	F	S
		1	2	3	4	5
6	7	8	9	10	11	12
13	14	15	16	17	18	19
20	21	22	23	24	25	26
27	28	29	30	31		

AUGUST
S	M	T	W	T	F	S
					1	2
3	4	5	6	7	8	9
10	11	12	13	14	15	16
17	18	19	20	21	22	23
24	25	26	27	28	29	30
31						

SEPTEMBER
S	M	T	W	T	F	S
	1	2	3	4	5	6
7	8	9	10	11	12	13
14	15	16	17	18	19	20
21	22	23	24	25	26	27
28	29	30				

OCTOBER
S	M	T	W	T	F	S
			1	2	3	4
5	6	7	8	9	10	11
12	13	14	15	16	17	18
19	20	21	22	23	24	25
26	27	28	29	30	31	

NOVEMBER
S	M	T	W	T	F	S
						1
2	3	4	5	6	7	8
9	10	11	12	13	14	15
16	17	18	19	20	21	22
23	24	25	26	27	28	29
30						

DECEMBER
S	M	T	W	T	F	S
	1	2	3	4	5	6
7	8	9	10	11	12	13
14	15	16	17	18	19	20
21	22	23	24	25	26	27
28	29	30	31			

11

JANUARY
```
S  M  T  W  T  F  S
         1  2  3  4
 5  6  7  8  9 10 11
12 13 14 15 16 17 18
19 20 21 22 23 24 25
26 27 28 29 30 31
```

FEBRUARY
```
S  M  T  W  T  F  S
                  1
 2  3  4  5  6  7  8
 9 10 11 12 13 14 15
16 17 18 19 20 21 22
23 24 25 26 27 28 29
```

MARCH
```
S  M  T  W  T  F  S
 1  2  3  4  5  6  7
 8  9 10 11 12 13 14
15 16 17 18 19 20 21
22 23 24 25 26 27 28
29 30 31
```

APRIL
```
S  M  T  W  T  F  S
         1  2  3  4
 5  6  7  8  9 10 11
12 13 14 15 16 17 18
19 20 21 22 23 24 25
26 27 28 29 30
```

MAY
```
S  M  T  W  T  F  S
               1  2
 3  4  5  6  7  8  9
10 11 12 13 14 15 16
17 18 19 20 21 22 23
24 25 26 27 28 29 30
31
```

JUNE
```
S  M  T  W  T  F  S
    1  2  3  4  5  6
 7  8  9 10 11 12 13
14 15 16 17 18 19 20
21 22 23 24 25 26 27
28 29 30
```

JULY
```
S  M  T  W  T  F  S
         1  2  3  4
 5  6  7  8  9 10 11
12 13 14 15 16 17 18
19 20 21 22 23 24 25
26 27 28 29 30 31
```

AUGUST
```
S  M  T  W  T  F  S
                  1
 2  3  4  5  6  7  8
 9 10 11 12 13 14 15
16 17 18 19 20 21 22
23 24 25 26 27 28 29
30 31
```

SEPTEMBER
```
S  M  T  W  T  F  S
    1  2  3  4  5
 6  7  8  9 10 11 12
13 14 15 16 17 18 19
20 21 22 23 24 25 26
27 28 29 30
```

OCTOBER
```
S  M  T  W  T  F  S
               1  2  3
 4  5  6  7  8  9 10
11 12 13 14 15 16 17
18 19 20 21 22 23 24
25 26 27 28 29 30 31
```

NOVEMBER
```
S  M  T  W  T  F  S
 1  2  3  4  5  6  7
 8  9 10 11 12 13 14
15 16 17 18 19 20 21
22 23 24 25 26 27 28
29 30
```

DECEMBER
```
S  M  T  W  T  F  S
    1  2  3  4  5
 6  7  8  9 10 11 12
13 14 15 16 17 18 19
20 21 22 23 24 25 26
27 28 29 30 31
```

12

JANUARY
```
S  M  T  W  T  F  S
            1  2  3
 4  5  6  7  8  9 10
11 12 13 14 15 16 17
18 19 20 21 22 23 24
25 26 27 28 29 30 31
```

FEBRUARY
```
S  M  T  W  T  F  S
 1  2  3  4  5  6  7
 8  9 10 11 12 13 14
15 16 17 18 19 20 21
22 23 24 25 26 27 28
29
```

MARCH
```
S  M  T  W  T  F  S
    1  2  3  4  5  6
 7  8  9 10 11 12 13
14 15 16 17 18 19 20
21 22 23 24 25 26 27
28 29 30 31
```

APRIL
```
S  M  T  W  T  F  S
            1  2  3
 4  5  6  7  8  9 10
11 12 13 14 15 16 17
18 19 20 21 22 23 24
25 26 27 28 29 30
```

MAY
```
S  M  T  W  T  F  S
                  1
 2  3  4  5  6  7  8
 9 10 11 12 13 14 15
16 17 18 19 20 21 22
23 24 25 26 27 28 29
30 31
```

JUNE
```
S  M  T  W  T  F  S
    1  2  3  4  5
 6  7  8  9 10 11 12
13 14 15 16 17 18 19
20 21 22 23 24 25 26
27 28 29 30
```

JULY
```
S  M  T  W  T  F  S
            1  2  3
 4  5  6  7  8  9 10
11 12 13 14 15 16 17
18 19 20 21 22 23 24
25 26 27 28 29 30 31
```

AUGUST
```
S  M  T  W  T  F  S
 1  2  3  4  5  6  7
 8  9 10 11 12 13 14
15 16 17 18 19 20 21
22 23 24 25 26 27 28
29 30 31
```

SEPTEMBER
```
S  M  T  W  T  F  S
         1  2  3  4
 5  6  7  8  9 10 11
12 13 14 15 16 17 18
19 20 21 22 23 24 25
26 27 28 29 30
```

OCTOBER
```
S  M  T  W  T  F  S
               1  2
 3  4  5  6  7  8  9
10 11 12 13 14 15 16
17 18 19 20 21 22 23
24 25 26 27 28 29 30
31
```

NOVEMBER
```
S  M  T  W  T  F  S
    1  2  3  4  5  6
 7  8  9 10 11 12 13
14 15 16 17 18 19 20
21 22 23 24 25 26 27
28 29 30
```

DECEMBER
```
S  M  T  W  T  F  S
         1  2  3  4
 5  6  7  8  9 10 11
12 13 14 15 16 17 18
19 20 21 22 23 24 25
26 27 28 29 30 31
```

13

JANUARY
```
S  M  T  W  T  F  S
               1  2
 3  4  5  6  7  8  9
10 11 12 13 14 15 16
17 18 19 20 21 22 23
24 25 26 27 28 29 30
31
```

FEBRUARY
```
S  M  T  W  T  F  S
    1  2  3  4  5  6
 7  8  9 10 11 12 13
14 15 16 17 18 19 20
21 22 23 24 25 26 27
28 29
```

MARCH
```
S  M  T  W  T  F  S
    1  2  3  4  5
 6  7  8  9 10 11 12
13 14 15 16 17 18 19
20 21 22 23 24 25 26
27 28 29 30 31
```

APRIL
```
S  M  T  W  T  F  S
                  1  2
 3  4  5  6  7  8  9
10 11 12 13 14 15 16
17 18 19 20 21 22 23
24 25 26 27 28 29 30
```

MAY
```
S  M  T  W  T  F  S
 1  2  3  4  5  6  7
 8  9 10 11 12 13 14
15 16 17 18 19 20 21
22 23 24 25 26 27 28
29 30 31
```

JUNE
```
S  M  T  W  T  F  S
         1  2  3  4
 5  6  7  8  9 10 11
12 13 14 15 16 17 18
19 20 21 22 23 24 25
26 27 28 29 30
```

JULY
```
S  M  T  W  T  F  S
               1  2
 3  4  5  6  7  8  9
10 11 12 13 14 15 16
17 18 19 20 21 22 23
24 25 26 27 28 29 30
31
```

AUGUST
```
S  M  T  W  T  F  S
    1  2  3  4  5  6
 7  8  9 10 11 12 13
14 15 16 17 18 19 20
21 22 23 24 25 26 27
28 29 30 31
```

SEPTEMBER
```
S  M  T  W  T  F  S
                  1  2  3
 4  5  6  7  8  9 10
11 12 13 14 15 16 17
18 19 20 21 22 23 24
25 26 27 28 29 30
```

OCTOBER
```
S  M  T  W  T  F  S
                     1
 2  3  4  5  6  7  8
 9 10 11 12 13 14 15
16 17 18 19 20 21 22
23 24 25 26 27 28 29
30 31
```

NOVEMBER
```
S  M  T  W  T  F  S
         1  2  3  4  5
 6  7  8  9 10 11 12
13 14 15 16 17 18 19
20 21 22 23 24 25 26
27 28 29 30
```

DECEMBER
```
S  M  T  W  T  F  S
            1  2  3
 4  5  6  7  8  9 10
11 12 13 14 15 16 17
18 19 20 21 22 23 24
25 26 27 28 29 30 31
```

14

JANUARY
```
S  M  T  W  T  F  S
                  1
 2  3  4  5  6  7  8
 9 10 11 12 13 14 15
16 17 18 19 20 21 22
23 24 25 26 27 28 29
30 31
```

FEBRUARY
```
S  M  T  W  T  F  S
    1  2  3  4  5
 6  7  8  9 10 11 12
13 14 15 16 17 18 19
20 21 22 23 24 25 26
27 28
```

MARCH
```
S  M  T  W  T  F  S
         1  2  3  4
 5  6  7  8  9 10 11
12 13 14 15 16 17 18
19 20 21 22 23 24 25
26 27 28 29 30 31
```

APRIL
```
S  M  T  W  T  F  S
                  1
 2  3  4  5  6  7  8
 9 10 11 12 13 14 15
16 17 18 19 20 21 22
23 24 25 26 27 28 29
30
```

MAY
```
S  M  T  W  T  F  S
    1  2  3  4  5  6
 7  8  9 10 11 12 13
14 15 16 17 18 19 20
21 22 23 24 25 26 27
28 29 30 31
```

JUNE
```
S  M  T  W  T  F  S
            1  2  3
 4  5  6  7  8  9 10
11 12 13 14 15 16 17
18 19 20 21 22 23 24
25 26 27 28 29 30
```

JULY
```
S  M  T  W  T  F  S
                  1
 2  3  4  5  6  7  8
 9 10 11 12 13 14 15
16 17 18 19 20 21 22
23 24 25 26 27 28 29
30 31
```

AUGUST
```
S  M  T  W  T  F  S
         1  2  3  4  5
 6  7  8  9 10 11 12
13 14 15 16 17 18 19
20 21 22 23 24 25 26
27 28 29 30 31
```

SEPTEMBER
```
S  M  T  W  T  F  S
                  1  2
 3  4  5  6  7  8  9
10 11 12 13 14 15 16
17 18 19 20 21 22 23
24 25 26 27 28 29 30
```

OCTOBER
```
S  M  T  W  T  F  S
 1  2  3  4  5  6  7
 8  9 10 11 12 13 14
15 16 17 18 19 20 21
22 23 24 25 26 27 28
29 30 31
```

NOVEMBER
```
S  M  T  W  T  F  S
         1  2  3  4
 5  6  7  8  9 10 11
12 13 14 15 16 17 18
19 20 21 22 23 24 25
26 27 28 29 30
```

DECEMBER
```
S  M  T  W  T  F  S
                  1  2
 3  4  5  6  7  8  9
10 11 12 13 14 15 16
17 18 19 20 21 22 23
24 25 26 27 28 29 30
31
```

Months

The month names in most European languages were probably derived as follows:

January	Janus, Roman god	July	Julius Caesar, Roman general
February	Februar, Roman festival of purification	August	Augustus, Roman emperor
March	Mars, Roman god	September	Latin *septem*, 'seven'
April	Latin *aperire*, 'to open'	October	Latin *octo*, 'eight'
May	Maia, Roman goddess	November	Latin *novem*, 'nine'
June	Juno, Roman goddess	December	Latin *decem*, 'ten'

September, October, November, December were originally the seventh, eighth, ninth, and tenth months of the Roman year.

Days of the week

The names of the days are derived as follows:

English	Latin	Saxon	English	Latin	Saxon
Sunday	Dies Solis	Sun's Day	Thursday	Dies Jovis	Thor's Day
Monday	Dies Lunae	Moon's Day	Friday	Dies Veneris	Frigg's Day
Tuesday	Dies Martis	Tiu's Day	Saturday	Dies Saturni	Saeternes' Day
Wednesday	Dies Mercurii	Woden's Day			

Tiu: Anglo-Saxon counterpart of Nordic Tyr, son of Odin, God of War, closest to Mars (Greek Ares), son of Roman God Jupiter (Greek Zeus); *Woden*: Anglo-Saxon counterpart of Odin, Nordic dispenser of victory, closest to Mercury (Greek Hermes), Roman messenger of victory; *Thor*: Nordic God of Thunder, eldest son of Odin, closest to Roman Jupiter (Greek Zeus); *Frigg* (or *Freyja*): wife of Odin, the Nordic Goddess of Love, equivalent to Venus (Greek Aphrodite)

Wedding anniversaries

In many Western countries, different wedding anniversaries have become associated with gifts of different materials. There is variation between countries.

Anniversary	Material	Anniversary	Material	Anniversary	Material
1st	cotton	9th	pottery, willow	25th	silver
2nd	paper	10th	tin	30th	pearl
3rd	leather	11th	steel	35th	coral
4th	fruit, flowers	12th	silk, linen	40th	ruby
5th	wood	13th	lace	45th	sapphire
6th	sugar	14th	ivory	50th	gold
7th	copper, wool	15th	crystal	55th	emerald
8th	bronze, pottery	20th	china	60th	diamond
				70th	platinum

Signs of the zodiac

Spring

Aries
The Ram
21 March-20 April

Taurus
The Bull
21 April-21 May

Gemini
The Twins
22 May-21June

Summer

Cancer
The Crab
22 June-23 July

Leo
The Lion
24 July-23 Aug

Virgo
The Virgin
24 Aug-23 Sept

Autumn

Libra
The Balance
24 Sept-23 Oct

Scorpio
The Scorpion
24 Oct-22 Nov

Sagittarius
The Archer
23 Nov-21 Dec

Winter

Capricorn
The Goat
22 Dec-20 Jan

Aquarius
The Water Bearer
21 Jan-19 Feb

Pisces
The Fishes
20 Feb-20 March

Movable Christian feasts 1995 – 2025

	Ash Wednesday	Easter Day	Ascension Day	Pentecost (Whit Sunday)	Advent Sunday
1995	1 Mar	16 Apr	25 May	4 Jun	3 Dec
1996	21 Feb	7 Apr	16 May	26 May	1 Dec
1997	12 Feb	30 Mar	8 May	18 May	30 Nov
1998	25 Feb	12 Apr	21 May	31 May	29 Nov
1999	17 Feb	4 Apr	13 May	23 May	28 Nov
2000	8 Mar	23 Apr	1 Jun	11 Jun	3 Dec
2001	28 Feb	15 Apr	24 May	3 Jun	2 Dec
2002	13 Feb	31 Mar	9 May	19 May	1 Dec
2003	5 Mar	20 Apr	29 May	8 Jun	30 Nov
2004	25 Feb	11 Apr	20 May	30 May	28 Nov
2005	9 Feb	27 Mar	5 May	15 May	27 Nov
2006	1 Mar	16 Apr	25 May	4 Jun	3 Dec
2007	21 Feb	8 Apr	17 May	27 May	2 Dec
2008	6 Feb	23 Mar	1 May	11 May	30 Nov
2009	25 Feb	12 Apr	21 May	31 May	29 Nov
2010	17 Feb	4 Apr	13 May	23 May	28 Nov
2011	9 Mar	24 Apr	2 Jun	12 Jun	27 Nov
2012	22 Feb	8 Apr	17 May	27 May	2 Dec
2013	13 Feb	31 Mar	9 May	19 May	1 Dec
2014	5 Mar	20 Apr	29 May	8 Jun	30 Nov
2015	18 Feb	5 Apr	14 May	24 May	29 Nov
2016	10 Mar	27 Mar	5 May	15 May	27 Nov
2017	1 Mar	16 Apr	25 May	4 Jun	3 Dec
2018	14 Feb	1 Apr	10 May	20 May	2 Dec
2019	6 Mar	21 Apr	30 May	9 Jun	1 Dec
2020	26 Feb	12 Apr	21 May	31 May	29 Nov
2021	17 Feb	4 Apr	13 May	23 May	28 Nov
2022	2 Mar	17 Apr	26 May	5 Jun	27 Nov
2023	22 Feb	9 Apr	18 May	28 May	3 Dec
2024	14 Feb	31 Mar	9 May	19 May	1 Dec
2025	5 Mar	20 Apr	29 May	8 Jun	30 Nov

Advent Sunday is the fourth Sunday before Christmas Day.
Ash Wednesday is the first day of Lent, and falls in the seventh week before Easter.
Holy Week is the week before Easter Day, and includes Palm Sunday, Maundy Thursday, Good Friday, and Easter Eve.
Ascension Day is 40 days after Easter Day.
Pentecost (Whit Sunday) is seven weeks after Easter Day.
Trinity Sunday is eight weeks after Easter Day.

Patron saints

Saint	Occupation	Saint	Occupation
Adam	gardeners	Ivo	lawyers
Albert the Great	scientists	James	labourers
Alphonsus Liguori	theologians	Jean-Baptiste Vianney	priests
Amand	brewers, hotelkeepers	Jerome	librarians
		Joan of Arc	soldiers
Andrew	fishermen	John Baptist	teachers
Angelico	artists	de la Salle	
Anne	miners	John Bosco	labourers
Apollonia	dentists	John of God	book trade, nurses, printers
Augustine	theologians		
Barbara	builders, miners	Joseph	carpenters
Bernadino (Feltre)	bankers	Joseph (Arimathea)	gravediggers, undertakers
Bernadino of Siena	advertisers		
Camillus de Lellis	nurses	Joseph (Cupertino)	astronauts
Catherine of Alexandria	librarians, philosophers	Julian the Hospitaler	hotelkeepers
		Lawrence	cooks
Cecilia	musicians, poets, singers	Leonard	prisoners
		Louis	sculptors
Christopher	motorists, sailors	Lucy	glassworkers, writers
Cosmas and Damian	barbers, chemists, doctors, surgeons		
		Luke	artists, butchers, doctors, glassworkers, sculptors, surgeons
Crispin	shoemakers		
Crispinian	shoemakers		
David	poets		
Dismas	undertakers	Martha	cooks, housewives, servants, waiters
Dominic	astronomers		
Dorothy	florists		
Eligius	blacksmiths, jewellers, metalworkers	Martin of Tours	soldiers
		Matthew	accountants, bookkeepers, tax collectors
Erasmus	sailors		
Fiacre	gardeners, taxi drivers		
		Michael	grocers, policemen
Florian	firemen		
Francis de Sales	authors, editors, journalists	Our Lady of Loreto	aviators
		Peter	fishermen
Francis of Assisi	merchants	Raymond Nonnatus	midwives
Francis of Paola	sailors	Sebastian	athletes, soldiers
Gabriel	messengers, postal workers, radio workers, television workers	Thérèse of Lisieux	florists
		Thomas (Apostle)	architects, builders
		Thomas Aquinas	philosophers, scholars, students, theologians
Genesius	actors, secretaries		
George	soldiers	Thomas More	lawyers
Gregory	singers	Vitus	actors, comedians, dancers
Gregory the Great	musicians, teachers		
Homobonus	tailors	Wenceslaus	brewers
Honoratus	bakers	Zita	servants
Isidore	farmers		

Christian festivals and holy days

1 January	The naming of Jesus
	The Circumcision of Christ
	The Solemnity of Mary Mother of God
6 January	Epiphany
25 January	The Conversion of St Paul
2 February	The Presentation of Christ in the Temple
19 March	St Joseph of Nazareth, husband of the Blessed Virgin Mary
25 March	The Annunciation of Our Lord to the Blessed Virgin Mary
25 April	St Mark the Evangelist
1 May	St Philip and St James, Apostles
14 May	St Matthias the Apostle
31 May	The Visitation of the Blessed Virgin Mary
11 June	St Barnabas the Apostle
24 June	The Birth of St John the Baptist
29 June	St Peter and St Paul, Apostles
3 July	St Thomas the Apostle
22 July	St Mary Magdalen
25 July	St James the Apostle
6 August	The Transfiguration of our Lord
24 August	St Bartholomew the Apostle
1 September	New Year (Eastern Orthodox Church)
8 September	The Nativity of the Blessed Virgin Mary
14 September	The Exaltation of the Holy Cross
21 September	St Matthew the Apostle
29 September	St Michael and All Angels (Michaelmas)
18 October	St Luke the Evangelist
28 October	St Simon and St Jude, Apostles
1 November	All Saints
21 November	Presentation of the Blessed Virgin Mary in the Temple
30 November	St Andrew the Apostle
8 December	The Immaculate Conception of the Blessed Virgin Mary
25 December	Christmas
26 December	St Stephen the first Martyr
27 December	St John the Evangelist
28 December	The Holy Innocents

Birthstones

Month	Stone	Quality
January	garnet	constancy
February	amethyst	sincerity
March	bloodstone	courage
April	diamond	innocence and lasting love
May	emerald	success and hope
June	pearl	health and purity
July	ruby	love and contentment
August	agate	married happiness
September	sapphire	wisdom
October	opal	hope
November	topaz	fidelity
December	turquoise	harmony

Index of Events and People

antibiotic, 22 Feb, 30 Sept
Antietam, 17 Sept
Antioch, 3 June
Antonescu, Ion, 1 June
Antonio of Padua, St, 13 June
Antwerp, 4 Sept
ANZAC, 20 Dec
apartheid, 29 June
Apollinaire, Guillaume, 9 Nov
Apollo, 27 Jan
Apollo, 17 July
Apollo 7, 11 Oct
Apollo 9, 3 Mar
Apollo 11, 21 July
Apollo 16, 16 April
appendix, 4 Jan
Appleton, Edward, 6 Sept
Appomatox, 9 April
Aquinas, St Thomas, 7 Mar
Aquino, Benigno, 21 Aug
Arab League, 22 Mar
Arafat, Yassir, 3 Feb, 17 Feb, 30 Nov
Aragon, Louis, 3 Oct
Arbela, 1 Oct
Arbuckle, 'Fatty', 24 Mar
Archer, Fred, 11 Jan, 8 Nov
Archer, Jeffrey, 15 April
Arden, Elizabeth, 18 Oct
Arden, John, 26 Oct
Ardennes, 16 Dec; Offensive, 6 Jan
Ardiles, Osvaldo, 3 Aug
Aretino, Pietro, 21 Oct
Argentina, 24 Feb, 2 April, 9 July,
    23 Sept
Argyropoulos, Joannes, 15 June
Arif, Abdul Salam, 13 April
Ariosto, Ludovico, 8 Sept
Aristide, Jean-Bertrand, 29 Sept,
    16 Dec
Arizona, 18 April, 26 Oct
Arkansas, 15 June
Arkwright, Richard, 3 Aug, 23 Dec
Armada, Spanish, 29 July
Armatrading, Joan, 9 Dec
Armenia, 7 Dec
arms reduction, 31 July, 8 Dec
Armstrong, Louis, 4 July, 6 July
Armstrong, Neil, 5 Aug
Armstrong, William, 26 Nov
Arne, Thomas, 12 Mar
Arnhem, 17 Sept
Arnold, Matthew, 15 April, 24 Dec
Arnold, Thomas, 12 June, 13 June
Arras, Battle of, 9 April
Artaud, Antonin, 4 Sept
Arthur, Chester Alan, 5 Oct, 18 Nov
Ascot, 7 Aug
Ashdown, Battle of, 6 Jan
Ashe, Arthur, 6 Feb, 10 July
Asher, Jane, 20 July
Ashkenazy, Vladimir, 6 July
Ashley, Laura, 17 Sept
Ashmole, Elias, 18 May, 23 May
Ashton, Frederick, 19 Aug, 17 Sept
Asimov, Isaac, 2 Jan, 6 April
Askey, Arthur, 16 Nov

aspirin, 6 Mar
Asquith, Herbert Henry, 15 Feb, 8
    April, 12 Sept
assassination, 2 Mar, 29 July, 6 Sept,
    9 Oct, 5 Nov, 22 Nov;
    attempted, 2 Mar, 30 Mar, 20
    May, 20 July, 12 Oct
Ashcroft, Peggy, 22 Dec
Astaire, Fred, 10 May, 22 June,
    29 Nov, 20 Dec
Astley, Rick, 6 Feb
Aston, Francis, 1 Sept, 20 Nov
Astor, Nancy, 24 Feb, 2 May, 1 Dec
Aswan High Dam, 15 Jan
Atatürk, Kemal, 12 Mar, 13 Aug,
    10 Nov
Atbara, Battle of, 8 April
Athenagoras I, Patriarch, 5 Jan
Athens, 6 April, 26 Sept
Atkinson, Rowan, 6 Jan
Atlantic Charter, 11 Aug
Atlantic Ocean, 22 April, 25 April,
    18 June, 12 July
atomic energy, 26 Oct
Attenborough, David, 8 May
Attenborough, Richard, 29 Aug
Attila, 20 Sept
Attlee, Clement, 3 Jan, 8 Oct
Auber, Daniel, 14 May
Aubrey, John, 12 Mar, 23 June
Auchinleck, Claude, 23 Mar, 21 June
Auckland, 10 July
auction, 3 April, 19 Nov, 24 Nov, 5
    Dec, 11 Dec
Auden, W H, 21 Feb, 11 Sept,
    28 Sept
Audubon, John, 27 Jan, 26 April
Augsburg, Diet of, 20 June
Augustine, St, 26 May
Augustus, 19 Aug, 23 Sept
Augustus II of Poland, 12 May
Aurangzeb, 20 Feb, 26 May, 15 June
Aurelius, Marcus, 17 Mar, 26 April
aurora borealis, 25 Jan
Austen, Jane, 18 July, 16 Dec
Austerlitz, Battle of, 2 Dec
Austin, Alfred, 2 June
Austin, Herbert, 8 Nov
Australia, 1 Jan, 18 Jan, 9 Feb,
    12 Feb, 2 Mar, 19 Mar, 20
    April, 28 April, 21 May, 20 July,
    17 Sept, 19 Oct, 29 Oct,
    16 Nov, 19 Dec
Austria, 7 Feb, 9 Feb, 13 Feb, 20 Feb,
    12 Mar, 6 Oct, 12 Nov, 6 Dec
Austria-Hungary, 13 July
Authorized Version, 2 May
Avalon, Frankie, 8 Sept, 18 Sept
Avignon, 17 Jan
Avilés, Pedro de, 15 Feb
Ayatollah Khomeini, 1 Feb, 14 Feb
Ayckbourn, Alan, 12 April
Aylmer, John, 3 June
Ayres, Lew, 28 Dec
Aznavour, Charles, 22 May
Azores, 11 Aug

Aztec empire, 13 Aug

Babbage, Charles, 18 Oct, 26 Dec
Babur, 20 April
Bacall, Lauren, 16 Sept
Bach, Johann Sebastian, 21 Mar,
    28 July
Bacon, Francis, 22 Jan, 9 April
Bacon, Francis, 28 April, 28 Oct
Badel, Alan, 19 Mar
Baden-Powell, Robert, 22 Feb
Bader, Douglas, 5 Sept
Badminton Horse Trials, 20 April
Baedecker, Karl, 3 Nov
Baez, Joan, 9 Jan
Bagnold, Enid, 31 Mar
Bailey, David, 2 Jan
Bailey, Nathaniel, 27 June
Bailey, Pearl, 29 Mar
Baillie, Isobel, 24 Sept
Baird, John Logie, 27 Jan, 14 June,
    13 Aug, 30 Oct
Bairnsfather, Bruce, 9 July, 29 Sept
Baker, Henry, 8 May
Baker, Janet, 21 Aug
Baker, Josephine, 4 Feb, 12 April
Baker, Richard, 15 June
Bakker, Jim, 24 Oct
Bakst, Leon, 24 Dec
Balanchine, George, 9 Jan, 30 April
Balboa, Vasco, 25 Sept
Balchen, Bernt, 29 Nov
Balcon, Michael, 19 May
Baldwin, James, 2 Aug, 30 Nov
Baldwin, Stanley, 16 May, 22 May,
    3 Aug, 14 Dec
Balfour, Arthur, 19 Mar, 25 July
Balfour Declaration, 2 Nov
Balkan states, 30 May
Ballantyne, R B, 8 Feb
Ballesteros, Severiano, 9 April,
    13 April
ballet, 2 Mar, 4 Mar, 15 Oct
Ballo in Maschera, Un, 17 Feb
balloon, 27 Aug, 15 Sept, 19 Sept,
    24 Sept, 21 Nov
Balmain, Pierre, 18 May
Baltic states, 17 June
Balzac, Honoré de, 20 May, 17 Aug
banana, 10 April
Bancroft, Anne, 17 Sept
Bancroft, Squire, 14 May
Banda, Hastings, 14 May
Bandaranaike, Sirimavo, 17 April,
    21 July
Banér, John, 23 June
Bangladesh, 19 April, 2 Dec
bank, 1 Aug;
    error, 13 Sept;
    notes, 16 July;
    raid, 13 Feb
Bank of England, 14 Feb, 26 Feb,
    27 July
Bankhead, Tallulah, 12 Dec
bankruptcy, 20 Feb
Banks, Joseph, 28 April, 9 June,

Blackpool, 18 Sept
'Black Tuesday', 29 Oct
Blackwell, Elizabeth, 23 Jan
Blake, Robert, 7 Aug
Blake, William, 12 Aug, 28 Nov
Blanchflower, Danny, 9 Dec
Blanc, Mont, 8 Aug
Blasco Ibáñez, Vicente, 28 Jan
Blavatsky, Helena, 9 May
Blenheim, Battle of, 13 Aug
Blériot, Louis, 1 July, 25 July, 2 Aug
Bligh, William, 28 April, 7 Dec
Bliss, Arthur, 2 Aug
Blitz, 23 Aug
Blixen, Karen, 17 Oct
Blondin, Charles, 19 Feb
blood transfusion, 27 Mar, 25 Sept
Blood, Thomas, 24 Aug
'Bloody Sunday', 30 Jan
Bloom, Claire, 15 Feb
Bloomer, Amelia, 27 May, 19 July
Blow, John, 1 Oct
Blücher, Gebhard von, 12 Sept
Bluebird, 24 Feb, 3 Sept
Blue Danube, The, 13 Feb
Blue Nile, 14 Nov
Blum, Léon, 30 Mar
Blunt, Anthony, 27 Mar, 20 Nov
Blyton, Enid, 11 Aug, 28 Nov
board game, 14 Sept
boat race, 24 Mar, 28 Mar, 10 June
Boccaccio, Giovanni, 21 Dec
Boccherini, Luigi, 19 Feb
Boccioni, Umberto, 16 Aug
Bodley, Thomas, 28 Jan, 2 Mar
Bodoni, Giambattista, 16 Feb
Boeing 747, 12 Jan, 8 Feb
Boer War, 31 May, 11 Oct
Bogarde, Dirk, 28 Mar
Bogart, Humphrey, 14 Jan, 25 Dec
Bohème, La, 1 Feb
Bohr, Niels, 7 Oct, 18 Nov
Bojangles (Bill Robinson), 25 Nov
Boldrewood, Rolf, 11 Mar
Boleyn, Anne, 25 Jan, 2 May,
    12 May, 17 May
Bolívar, Simón, 22 June, 24 July,
    10 Sept, 17 Dec
Bolivia, 5 Feb
Böll, Heinrich, 21 Dec
Bologna, 2 Aug
Bolshevik, 8 Feb, 16 July
Bolshoi Ballet, 3 Oct
Bolt, Robert, 15 Aug
Bolton, John, 6 July
bomb, 8 Sept, 22 Sept, 31 Oct,
    8 Nov, 21 Nov, 21 Dec, 24 Dec;
    atomic, 13 Feb, 16 July, 6 Aug,
    9 Aug, 3 Oct;
    flying, 13 June;
    hydrogen, 17 Jan, 1 Mar, 29 Aug,
    31 Oct;
    thermonuclear, 15 May;
    V2, 28 Mar
Bombay, 12 Jan
bombing, 9 May, 23 June, 2 Aug,

23 Aug, 30 Aug, 10 Sept, 12 Oct,
    19 Oct, 14 Nov
Bonaparte, Joseph, 7 Jan
Bond, Michael, 13 Jan
Bondfield, Margaret, 16 June
Bonhoeffer, Dietrich, 9 April
Bonington, Chris, 6 Aug
Bonnard, Pierre, 23 Jan, 3 Oct
Bonneville Salt Flats, 3 Sept, 23 Oct
book, 18 Nov
Boomplatz, 29 Aug
Boone, Daniel, 26 Sept, 2 Nov
Boot, Jesse, 13 June
Booth, William, 10 April, 2 July,
    20 Aug
Boothroyd, Betty, 8 Oct
Borden, Lizzie, 19 July
Border, Alan, 27 July
Bordet, Jules, 6 April
Borg, Björn, 6 June, 5 July
Borge, Victor, 3 Jan
Borges, Jorge Luis, 14 June
Borgia, Cesare, 12 Mar
Borgia, Lucrezia, 18 April, 24 June
Borgnine, Ernest, 24 Jan
Boris Godunov, 19 Mar
Borodin, Alexander, 27 Feb, 12 Nov
Borodino, Battle of, 7 Sept
Borrow, George, 5 May, 26 July
borstal, 16 Oct
Bortoluzzi, Paolo, 16 Oct
Bosanquet, Bernard, 14 June
Bosch, Karl, 26 April
Bosnia, 8 Jan
Bosnia-Herzegovina, 6 Oct, 13 July
Boston, 12 Feb, 28 Nov, 16 Dec;
    Massacre, 5 Mar;
    Tea Party, 16 Dec
Boswell, James, 19 May, 29 Oct
Botany Bay, 9 April
Botha, P W, 12 Jan, 3 Feb
Botha, Louis, 27 Aug, 27 Sept
Botham, Ian, 24 Nov
Bothwell Bridge, 22 June
Bothwell, Earl of, 15 May
Botticelli, Sandro, 17 May, 20 May
Boucher, François, 30 May
Bougainville, Louis de, 11 Nov
Bouguereau, Adolphe, 20 Aug
Boulez, Pierre, 26 Mar
Boult, Adrian, 23 Feb, 8 April
Boumédienne, Houari, 19 June,
    27 Dec
Bounty, 28 April
Bourgeois, Léon, 29 May
Bow, Clara, 27 Sept
Bowdler, Thomas, 24 Feb
Bowen, Elizabeth, 22 Feb
Bowie, David, 8 Jan
Boxer Rebellion, 13 June, 14 Aug,
    7 Sept
boxing, 1 Mar, 17 Mar, 16 Aug,
    24 Oct, 7 Nov, 22 Nov, 7 Dec,
    8 Dec, 9 Dec, 26 Dec
Boyce, William, 7 Feb
Boyer, Charles, 26 Aug

Boyle, Robert, 25 Jan
Boyne, Battle of, 1 July
Boy Scouts, 4 Sept
Brabham, Jack, 2 April
Bracken, Brendan, 20 May
Bradbury, Ray, 22 Aug
Bradford, William, 9 May
Bradley, James, 13 July
Bradman, Donald, 12 July, 27 Aug
Bradshaw, George, 8 Sept
Brady, Matthew, 15 Jan
Brady, Nicholas, 20 May
Brady, Scott, 17 April
Braganza, Catherine de, 21 May
Bragg, Billy, 20 Dec
Bragg, Melvyn, 6 Oct
Bragg, William Henry, 2 July
Brahe, Tycho, 24 Oct, 14 Dec
Brahms, Johannes, 3 April, 7 May
Braille, Louis, 4 Jan
Braine, John, 13 April, 29 Oct
Bramah, Joseph, 9 Dec
Bramante, Donato, 11 April
Branagh, Kenneth, 10 Dec
Brando, Marlon, 3 April, 4 Dec
Brandt, Bill, 20 Dec
Brandt, Willy, 8 Oct, 18 Dec
Brandywine Creek, Battle of, 11 Sept
Brangwyn, Frank, 11 June
Branson, Richard, 18 July
Braque, Georges, 31 Aug
Brasília, 21 April
Braun, Eva, 30 April
Braun, Wernher von, 23 Mar
Brazil, 26 Jan, 21 April, 22 April,
    13 May, 15 Nov
Brazil, Angela, 13 Mar
Bream, Julian, 15 July
Brearley, Mike, 28 April
breathalyser, 8 Oct
Brecht, Bertolt, 10 Feb, 14 Aug
Brendel, Alfred, 5 Jan
Brennan, Walter, 25 July, 21 Sept
Brentano, Franz, 16 Jan
Brenton, Howard, 13 Dec
Brents, Willem, 30 June
Brezhnev, Leonid, 7 May, 22 May,
    16 June, 10 Nov, 19 Dec
Brice, Fanny, 29 Oct
Bridge, Frank, 26 Feb
Bridges, Jeff, 4 Dec
Bridges, Lloyd, 15 Jan
Bridges, Robert, 23 Oct
Bright, John, 16 Nov
Brightman, Sarah, 14 Aug
Brighton, 9 Aug, 11 Sept, 5 Oct,
    12 Oct
Brindley, James, 30 Sept
Britain, 6 Feb, 10 Feb, 12 Feb,
    13 Feb, 19 Feb, 28 Mar, 21
    May, 4 June, 16 June, 28 June,
    5 July, 14 July, 19 Aug, 5 Oct,
    19 Dec, 24 Dec
British Airways, 4 Oct
British Board of Film Censors, 5 Nov
British Citizenship Act, 30 May

18 July, 28 Sept
carbon paper, 7 Oct
Cardano, Geronimo, 24 Sept
Cardiff, Jack, 18 Sept
Cardin, Pierre, 7 July
Carey, George, 13 Nov
Carl XVI Gustav of Sweden,
  30 April
Carlisle, 28 June
Carlos I, 1 Feb
Carlson, Chester, 19 Sept
Carlyle, Thomas, 5 Feb, 4 Dec
Carmen, 3 Mar
Carmichael, Hoagy, 27 Dec
Carmichael, Ian, 18 June
Carnegie, Andrew, 11 Aug, 25 Nov
Carney, Art, 4 Nov
Carnot, Lazare, 13 May
Carnot, Nicolas, 1 June, 24 Aug
Caroline, Princess of Monaco, 23 Jan
Caroline, Princess of Wales, 6 June
Carothers, Wallace, 29 April
Carpenter, Karen, 4 Feb
Carpentier, Georges, 28 Oct
carpet sweeper, 19 Sept
Carradine, John, 5 Feb
Carreras, José, 5 Dec
Carroll, Lewis, 14 Jan
Carrott, Jasper, 14 Mar
Carson, Willie, 16 Nov
Cartagena, Pact of, 16 May
Carter, Howard, 2 Mar, 9 May,
  4 Nov
Carter, Jimmy, 1 Oct, 2 Nov
Carter, Lynda, 24 July
Cartier, Jacques, 24 July, 1 Sept
Cartier-Bresson, Henri, 22 Aug
Cartland, Barbara, 9 July
Cartwright, Edmund, 30 Oct
Caruso, Enrico, 13 Jan, 25 Feb,
  2 Aug, 23 Nov
Cary, Joyce, 29 Mar
Casablanca, 14 Jan
Casals, Pablo, 22 Oct
Casals, Rosemary, 19 Sept
Casanova, Giovanni, 4 June
Casement, Roger, 3 Aug, 1 Sept
Cash, Johnny, 26 Feb
Cassavetes, John, 3 Feb
Cassini, Giovanni, 8 June, 11 Sept
Casson, Hugh, 23 May
Castillon, Battle of, 17 July
Castro, Fidel, 1 Jan, 3 Jan, 16 Feb,
  21 Feb, 13 Aug, 26 Dec
cat show, 13 July
Cather, Willa, 24 April
Catherine of Aragon, 7 Jan, 17 May,
  11 June, 16 Dec
Catherine I of Russia, 8 Feb
Catherine II 'the Great', 2 May
Catholic Emancipation Act, 13 April
Catlin, George, 23 Dec
Cato Street conspiracy, 23 Feb
'cat's-eyes', 4 April
Causley, Charles, 24 Aug
Cavafy, Constantinos, 29 April

Cavalier, Jean, 31 May
Cavalli, Francesco, 14 Feb
Cavell, Edith, 4 Dec
Cavendish, Henry, 24 Feb, 10 Oct
Cavour, Count (Camillo Benso),
  10 Aug
Cawley, Yvonne, 31 July
Cawnpore, Massacre of, 15 July
Caxton, William, 18 Nov
Cayley, Arthur, 16 Aug
Cayley, George, 27 Dec
CD-video, 2 Sept
Cézanne, Paul, 19 Jan, 22 Oct
Ceauşçescu, Nicolae, 22 Dec, 25 Dec
Cecil, Robert, 24 May
Cedar Creek, 19 Oct
Ceefax, 23 Sept
Cellini, Benvenuto, 13 Feb, 1 Nov
celluloid, 15 June
Celsius, Anders, 25 April, 27 Nov
census, 10 Mar
Ceres, 1 Jan
Cervantes Saavedra, Miguel de,
  23 April, 29 Sept
Cetewayo, 14 Aug
Châlons-sur-Marne, 20 Sept
Chabrier, Alexis-Emmanuel, 13 Sept
Chabrol, Claude, 24 June
Chad, 11 Aug
Chadwick, James, 24 July, 20 Oct
Chagall, Marc, 28 Mar, 7 July
Chain, Ernst, 19 June
Chaliapin, Fyodor, 13 Feb, 12 April
Challenger, 28 Jan
Chamberlain, Austen, 16 Mar,
  16 Oct
Chamberlain, Joseph, 8 July
Chamberlain, Neville, 20 Feb,
  18 Mar, 22 May, 9 Nov
Chambers, Ephraim, 15 May
Champlain, Samuel, 3 July
Champollion, Jean-François, 4 Mar
Chancellorsville, Battle of, 5 May
Chandler, Raymond, 26 Mar, 23 July
Chandrasekhar, Bhagwat, 17 May
Chanel, Coco, 10 Jan, 19 Aug
Chaney, Lon, 1 April
Chang, 11 May
Channel Tunnel, 6 Feb
Chaplin, Charlie, 16 April, 30 Nov,
  25 Dec, 11 Dec
Chaplin, Geraldine, 31 July
Chapman, George, 12 May
Chappell, Greg, 7 Aug
Chappell, Ian, 26 Sept
Chardin, Jean, 22 June, 6 Dec
charity walk, 26 Dec
Charlemagne, 28 Jan, 2 April,
  25 Dec
Charles, Prince of Wales, 29 July,
  14 Nov
Charles the Bold, 5 Jan
Charles I of Great Britain, 30 Jan,
  18 June, 19 Nov
Charles II of Great Britain, 4 Mar,
  22 April, 21 May, 29 May,

10 Aug, 17 Oct, 27 Oct
Charles IV, Holy Roman Emperor,
  16 May
Charles V, Holy Roman Emperor,
  24 Feb, 25 May, 26 May, 20 June,
  24 June, 28 June
Charles VI, Holy Roman Emperor,
  27 May
Charles VIII of France, 30 June
Charles XII of Sweden, 17 June
Charles, Bonnie Prince, 21 Sept
Charles, Cardinal of Lorraine,
  18 May
Charles, Duke of Bourbon, 5 May
Charles Martel, 10 Oct, 22 Oct
Charles of Orleans, 26 May
Charles, Ray, 23 Sept
Charleston, 17 Feb
Charlton, Bobby, 19 April, 11 Oct
chart, music, 4 Jan, 20 July, 2 Nov,
  8 Nov, 14 Nov, 5 Dec
Chartist Movement, 16 June
Chateaubriand, François, 4 Sept
Chatham, 12 June
Chatterton, Thomas, 24 Aug
Chaucer, Geoffrey, 25 Oct
Chavez, Carlos, 2 Aug
Chayefsky, Paddy, 29 Jan
Checker, Chubby, 3 Oct
Cheke, John, 16 June
Chekhov, Anton, 30 Jan, 15 July
Chelsea Hospital, Royal, 11 Mar
cheque, 16 Feb; traveller's, 5 Aug
Chequers Court, 8 Jan
Cherbourg, 27 June
Chernenko, Constantin, 10 Mar
Chernobyl, 26 April
Cheshire, Leonard, 31 July
chess, 1 Sept, 9 Nov
Chester, 11 May
Chesterton, G K, 29 May, 14 June
Chevalier, Maurice, 1 Jan, 12 Sept
chewing gum, 23 Sept
Chiang Kai-shek, 5 April, 16 May,
  11 Aug, 13 Sept, 6 Oct, 31 Oct
Chicago, 14 Feb, 22 July, 8 Oct;
  University, 2 Dec
Child, Josiah, 22 June
Childers, Erskine, 24 Nov
Chile, 11 Feb, 12 Sept, 18 Sept
chimney sweeps, 7 Aug
China, 12 Jan, 23 Jan, 12 Feb,
  21 Feb, 2 May, 16 May, 18 May,
  30 May, 13 June, 24 June, 11 July,
  28 July, 11 Aug, 2 Sept, 18 Sept,
  1 Oct, 6 Oct, 10 Oct, 12 Oct,
  16 Oct, 20 Oct, 21 Oct, 25 Oct,
  30 Oct, 19 Dec
Chippendale, Thomas, 28 May
Chirac, Jacques, 29 Nov
Chirico, Giorgio de, 10 July
chloroform, 7 April
Chopin, Frédéric, 1 Mar, 17 Oct
Chorus Line, A, 22 July
Chotusitz, 17 May
Chrisholm, Judith, 8 July

Christian X of Denmark, 20 April
Christian, Fletcher, 28 April
Christians, 24 Feb
Christie, Agatha, 12 Jan, 15 Sept
Christie, James, 5 Dec
Christie's, 11 Jan, 24 Nov, 11 Dec
Christmas Carol, A, 17 Dec
Christmas Island, 15 May
Christoff, Boris, 28 June
Churchill, John, 16 June, 24 June
Churchill, Randolph, 24 Jan
Churchill, Winston, 14 Jan, 24 Jan,
   4 Feb, 5 Mar, 5 April, 9 May,
   29 June, 11 Aug, 15 Nov, 30 Nov
Cicero, Marcus Tullius, 3 Jan, 7 Dec
Cid, El, 10 July
Cierva, Juan de la, 9 Dec
cigarette, 31 July
Cimarosa, Domenico, 17 Dec
cinema, 22 Mar, 24 Sept
Cinerama, 30 Sept
Citizens' Charter, 22 July
'Citizen King', 7 Aug, 26 Aug
Civil Defence, 21 Aug
Civil Rights Act, US, 13 June, 2 July
Civil War, American, 9 April,
   12 April, 5 May, 26 May, 1 July,
   21 July, 30 Aug, 17 Sept, 19 Oct,
   19 Nov;
      English, 14 June, 25, June, 28
         June, 2 July, 22 Aug, 23 Oct;
      Spanish, 26 Jan, 28 Mar,
         26 April, 18 May, 18 July;
      Yugoslavian, 7 Sept
Clapton, Eric, 30 Mar
Clare, John, 20 May
Clark, Dave, 15 Dec
Clark, Jim, 7 April
Clark, Petula, 15 Nov
Clarke, Samuel, 17 May
Clarke, Kenneth, 2 July
Claude, Duc de Villars, 17 June
Claudel, Paul, 6 Aug
Claudius, 1 Aug, 13 Oct
Clay, Henry, 12 April
Cleese, John, 27 Oct
Clémenceau, Georges, 28 Sept,
   24 Nov
Clement XIII, Pope, 2 Feb
Cleopatra, 30 Aug
Cleopatra's Needle, 12 Sept
Cleveland, Stephen Grover, 24 June
Clift, Montgomery, 17 Oct
Clinton, Bill, 19 Aug
Clive, Robert, 23 June, 22 Nov
Clore, Charles, 26 July
Clough, Brian, 21 Mar
Clydebank, 20 Sept, 26 Sept
CND, 17 Feb, 4 April
Cobb, Lee J, 11 Feb
Cobbett, William, 9 Mar
Cobden, Richard, 2 April, 3 June
Coburn, James, 31 Aug
Coca Cola, 29 Mar, 31 Aug
Cochise, 9 June
Cochran, C B, 31 Jan

Cockcroft, John, 18 Sept
Cockerell, Christopher, 4 June,
   12 Dec
Cockroft, John, 27 May
Cocteau, Jean, 5 July, 11 Oct
cod war, 19 Feb
Cody, William, 26 Feb
Coe, Sebastian, 29 Sept
coelacanth, 22 Nov
Coke, Thomas William, 6 May
Colbert, Claudette, 13 Sept
Colbert, Jean-Baptiste, 6 Sept
Cold War, 21 Nov
Cole, Nat 'King', 15 Feb, 17 Mar
Cole, George, 22 April
Coleridge, Samuel Taylor, 25 July,
   21 Oct
Colette, 3 Aug
Collins, Joan, 23 May
Collins, Phil, 30 Jan
Collins, Michael, 22 Aug, 31 Oct
Collins, Wilkie, 8 Jan, 23 Sept
Collins, William, 12 June
Colman, Ronald, 9 Feb
Cologne, 14 Aug
Colombia, 18 May, 4 July, 28 July,
   13 Nov
Colombo, 15 July
Colt, Samuel, 10 Jan, 19 July
Coltrane, John, 23 Sept
Colum, Padraic, 11 Jan
Columbia, 12 April, 12 Nov
Columbus, Christopher, 20 May,
   3 Aug, 31 July, 1 Aug, 3 Nov,
   12 Oct, 19 Nov, 6 Dec
Comaneci, Nadia, 12 Nov
Cominform, 28 June
Common Market, 22 Jan, 17 Feb,
   27 Nov
Commons, House of, 19 Jan, 10 May,
   11 May, 25 May, 1 Dec
Commonwealth, English, 30 Jan
Commonwealth of Independent
   States, 8 Dec, 22 Dec
Communist Party, 27 Feb, 29 Aug,
   27 Dec;
      Manifesto, 4 July
Comnenus, Alexius, 13 May
Compton, Arthur, 2 Dec
Comte, Auguste, 5 Sept
concentration camp, 11 April
concert, charity, 13 July
Concorde, 9 Jan, 21 Jan, 2 Mar, 9
   April, 17 Oct
Confederate States of America, 4 Feb
Confucius, 27 Aug
Congo, 8 May, 12 May, 10 June,
   27 Oct
Congreve, William, 19 Jan
Connecticut, 23 April
Connery, Sean, 25 Aug
Connolly, Billy, 24 Nov
Connolly, Maureen, 17 Sept
Connor, Kenneth, 19 Oct
Connors, Jimmy, 2 Sept
Conrad, Joseph, 3 Aug, 3 Dec

Conran, Terence, 4 Oct
conscription, 24 Jan, 27 April, 2 Sept
Constable, John, 31 Mar, 11 June
Constantine, 27 Feb
Constantine I of Greece, 27 Sept
Constantine II of Greece, 21 April,
   13 Dec
Constantinople, 12 April, 16 May,
   18 June, 29 May
Constantinus, Flavius Valerius,
   25 July
Constantius II, 3 Nov
constitution,
   German, 5 May;
   Irish, 28 Dec;
   Siamese, 27 June;
   Spanish, 27 Dec;
   US, 21 June, 28 July, 17 Sept,
   15 Dec
Continental Congress, 5 Sept
contraceptive, 20 Feb, 18 Aug, 4 Dec
Cooder, Ry, 15 Mar
Coogan, Jackie, 1 Mar
Cook, James, 18 Jan, 17 Jan, 14 Feb,
   28 April, 9 April, 20
   April, 11 July, 6 Oct, 27 Oct
Cook, Peter, 17 Nov
Cook, Thomas, 18 July
Cooke, Alistair, 20 Nov
Cookson, Catherine, 20 June
Coolidge, Calvin, 5 Jan, 26 May
Cooper, Alice, 4 Feb
Cooper, Gary, 7 May, 13 May
Cooper, Gladys, 17 Nov
Cooper, Henry, 3 May
Cooper, James Fenimore, 14 Sept
Cooper, Jilly, 21 Feb
Cooper, Tommy, 15 Mar
Copenhagen, 15 Aug;
   Battle of, 2 April
Copernicus, Nicolaus, 19 Feb,
   24 May
Copland, Aaron, 2 Dec
Coppola, Francis Ford, 7 April
Corbett, Harry H, 21 Mar
Corbett, Ronnie, 4 Dec
Corday, Charlotte, 13 July, 17 July
Corelli, Arcangelo, 17 Feb, 13 June
Corn Laws, 26 May
Corneille, Pierre, 6 June, 1 Oct
Corneille, Thomas, 20 Aug
Cornelius, Henry, 3 May
Cornell, Ezra, 11 Jan
cornflakes, 19 Feb
Cornwall, 3 May
Coronation Street, 9 Dec
Coronel, Battle of, 1 Nov
Corot, Jaen-Baptiste, 22 Feb
Corporation Act, 9 May
Correggio, Antonio, 5 Mar
Corri, Adrienne, 13 Nov
Corsica, 12 July
Cortés, Hernándo, 13 Aug, 2 Dec
Corunna, Battle of, 16 Jan
Corvinus, Matthias, 31 May
Cosby, Bill, 12 July

Costa Rica, 8 June
Costello, John, 20 June
Costello, Lou, 3 Mar
Cotman, John Sell, 16 May
Cotton, Henry, 23 Dec
Cotton, Robert, 6 May
Coubertin, Pierre de, 2 Sept
Coulomb, Charles de, 14 June,
  23 Aug
coup, 21 Aug, 13 Dec
Couperin, François, 12 Sept, 10 Nov
Coupole, La, 6 Jan
Courbet, Gustave, 10 June
Court, Margaret, 16 July
Courtneidge, Cicely, 26 April
Cousins, Robin, 17 Aug
Cousteau, Jacques, 11 June
Covenanters, 22 June
Covent Garden, 5 July, 3 Oct, 7 Dec
Coventry, 14 Nov
Coward, Noël, 26 Mar, 24 Sept,
  16 Dec
Cowdrey, Colin, 24 Dec
Cowley, 12 Oct
Cowper, William, 25 April, 26 Nov
Cox, David, 7 June
Cozzens, James Gould, 8 Aug
Cranach, Lucas (the Younger),
  25 Jan
Crane, Harold Hart, 27 April
Crane, Stephen, 5 June, 1 Nov
Cranmer, Thomas, 21 Mar, 2 July
Crashaw, Richard, 21 Aug
Crawford, Broderick, 26 April
Crawford, Joan, 23 Mar, 10 May
Craxi, Bettino, 15 Dec
Crébillon, Prosper de, 17 June
Crécy, Battle of, 26 Aug
cremation, 26 Mar
Crete, 20 May
cricket, 12 July, 26 July, 12 Aug, 29
  Aug, 6 Sept, 28 Dec;
  women's, 3 Oct
Crimea, 27 June
Crimean War, 30 Mar, 11 Sept,
  20 Sept, 5 Nov
Crippen, Hawley, 31 July, 22 Oct,
  23 Nov
Cripps, Richard Stafford, 21 April
Croatia, 15 Jan
Crockett, Davy, 17 Aug
Crome, John, 22 April, 22 Dec
Crompton, Richmal, 11 Jan
Cromwell, Oliver, 25 April, 13 May,
  25 May, 14 June, 2 July, 3 Sept,
  16 Dec
Cromwell, Richard, 25 May, 13 July
Cromwell, Thomas, 28 July
Cronin, A J, 6 Jan, 19 July
Crookes, William, 17 June
Crosby, Bing, 2 May, 14 Oct
Crosby, Bob, 9 Mar
crossword puzzle, 1 Feb
Crowley, Aleister, 12 Oct
Cruft, Charles, 10 Sept
Cruft's Dog Show, 10 Mar

Cruikshank, Andrew, 29 April
Cruikshank, George, 27 Sept
Cruyff, Johann, 25 April
Cruze, James, 4 Aug
Crystal Palace, 13 July, 4 Sept,
  30 Nov
Cuba, 1 Jan, 15 Feb, 16 Feb, 21 Feb,
  17 April, 4 June, 5 June, 12 June,
  12 Aug, 22 Oct, 10 Dec, 26 Dec
Cudworth, Ralph, 26 June
Cukor, George, 24 Jan, 7 July
Culver, Roland, 29 Feb
cummings, e e, 3 Sept, 14 Oct
Curaçao, 2 Oct
Curie, Marie, 4 July, 7 Nov, 26 Dec
Curie, Pierre, 19 April, 15 May,
  26 Dec
Curry, John, 9 Sept
Curwen's Act, 19 June
Cusack, Cyril, 6 Oct, 26 Nov
Cushing, Peter, 26 May
Custer, George, 25 June
Cuvier, Georges, 13 May
cycling, 19 July, 23 July, 26 July
cyclone, 2 Dec, 13 Nov
Cyprus, 19 Feb, 9 Mar, 1 May,
  20 May, 4 June, 9 June, 11 June,
  12 July, 16 Aug, 5 Nov, 15 Nov,
  14 Dec
Czech Republic, 1 Jan
Czechoslovakia, 1 Jan, 19 Jan,
  21 Feb, 27 Feb, 29 June, 20 Aug,
  1 Oct, 30 Oct, 25 Dec

D'Amboise, Georges, 25 May
D'Annunzio, Gabriele, 12 Sept
Daguerre, Louis, 10 July, 18 Nov
Dahl, Johan Siegwald, 16 Aug
Dahomey, 22 June
Daily Courant, 11 Mar
Daily Mail, 4 May
Daily News, 21 Jan
Daily Worker, 21 Jan
Daimler, Gottlieb, 6 Mar
Daladier, Edouard, 18 June
Dalai Lama, 22 Feb, 31 Mar, 6 July,
  7 Sept
Dalberg, John, 19 June
Dalgleish, Kenny, 4 Mar
Dali, Salvador, 23 Jan
Dallapiccola, Luigi, 19 Feb
Dallas, 22 Nov
Dalton, John, 27 July, 6 Sept
Daltrey, Roger, 1 Mar
Damascus, 24 Mar, 1 Oct
Damien, Father, 15 April
Damietta, 22 May, 29 May
Dampier, William, 3 June
Dana, Richard, 1 Aug
Dance, Charles, 10 Oct
Daniels, Paul, 6 April
Danilova, Alexandra, 20 Nov
Dankworth, John, 20 Sept
Danton, Georges, 5 April, 26 Oct
Darby, Abraham, 8 Mar
Darling, Grace, 7 Sept

Darrow, Clarence, 18 April
Dartmoor Prison, 20 Mar
Darwin, Charles, 12 Feb, 23 Mar,
  19 April, 1 July, 2 Oct, 24 Nov,
  27 Dec
Darwin, Erasmus, 18 April
Daubenton, Louis, 29 May
Daudet, Alphonse, 13 May, 17 Dec
Daumier, Honoré, 11 Feb, 20 Feb
Daventry, 26 Feb
David, Jacques, 30 Aug
Davidson, Emily, 4 June
Davis, Bette, 5 April, 7 Oct
Davis, Carl, 28 Oct
Davis, Colin, 25 Sept
Davis, Dwight, 5 July
Davis, Fred, 14 Aug
Davis, Joe, 15 April
Davis, Miles, 25 May
Davis, Sammy Jr, 8 Dec
Davy, Humphry, 29 May, 17 Dec
Day, Doris, 3 April
Day, Robin, 24 Oct
Day-Lewis, Cecil, 27 April, 22 May
Dayan, Moshe, 20 May, 16 Oct
Daytona Beach, 24 Feb
Dead Sea Scrolls, 7 Feb
Dean, Christopher, 27 July
Dean, James, 8 Feb, 8 Mar, 30 Sept
De Forest, Lee, 26 Aug
de la Mare, Walter, 25 April, 22 June
de la Roche, Mazo, 12 July
de la Tour, Georges, 19 Mar
De Launay, Marguerite, 15 June
De Laurentis, Dino, 8 Aug
De Mille, Agnes, 7 Oct
De Mille, Cecil B, 21 Jan, 12 Aug
De Niro, Robert, 17 Aug
De Quincey, Thomas, 15 Aug
De Rita, Joe, 3 July
de Savary, Peter, 11 July
de Valera, éamon, 16 Feb, 29 Aug,
  14 Oct
death duties, 2 Aug
death penalty, 28 June
Debussy, Claude, 25 Mar, 30 April,
  22 Aug
debutante, 26 July
decimal currency, 15 Feb, 23 April
Declaration of Independence,
  American, 4 July
Dee, John, 13 July
Defoe, Daniel, 24 April
Degas, Edgar, 19 July, 27 Sept
Deighton, Len, 18 Feb
Delacroix, Eugène, 13 Aug, 26 April
Delaroche, Paul, 4 Nov
Delaware, 7 Dec, 15 Dec
Delhi, 1 Jan, 20 April
Delibes, Léo, 16 Jan
Delille, Jacques, 22 June
Delisle, Joseph, 12 May
Delius, Frederick, 10 June
Dell, Ethel, 2 Aug
della Porta, Giambattista, 4 Feb
della Robbia, Luca, 10 Feb

Delon, Alain, 8 Nov
Delors, Jacques, 20 July
Deneuve, Catherine, 22 Oct
Denham, Maurice, 23 Dec
Denmark, 22 Jan, 17 May
Denning, Alfred, 23 Jan
Dennis, Sandy, 27 April
Depardieu, Gerard, 27 Dec
Depression, 29 Oct
Derain, André, 8 Sept
Derby, 4 May
Desai, Shri Morarji, 29 Feb
Descartes, René, 1 Feb, 31 Mar
'Desert Island Discs', 29 Jan
Desmond, Florence, 16 Jan
DeSylva, Buddy, 11 July
Detroit, 21 Aug, 1 Oct
Dev, Kapil, 6 Jan
Devereux, Robert, 25 Feb
Dewar, James, 27 Mar
Dexter, Ted, 15 May
Diaghilev, Sergei, 19 Mar, 19 Aug
diamond, 26 Jan, 17 Oct, 6 Nov
Diamond, Neil, 24 Jan
Diaz, Bartholomeu, 3 Feb
Diaz de Novaes, Bartholomew,
   29 May
Diaz, Porfirio, 25 May
Dickens, Charles, 21 Jan, 7 Feb,
   9 June, 17 Dec
Dickinson, Angie, 30 Sept
Dickinson, Emily, 15 May, 10 Dec
dictionary, 14 April, 15 April
Diderot, Denis, 1 July, 30 July, 5 Oct
Dien Bien Phu, 7 May
Dieppe, 19 Aug
Diesel, Rudolf, 18 Mar, 29 Sept
Dietrich, Marlene, 6 May, 27 Dec
Dietz, Howard, 30 July
Digby, Kenelm, 11 June
Diller, Phyllis, 17 July
Dillinger, John, 22 July
Dilthey, Wilhelm, 1 Oct
DiMaggio, Joe, 14 Jan
Dimbleby, Richard, 22 Dec
'Dingaan's Day', 16 Dec
Dior, Christian, 21 Jan, 24 Oct
dirigible, 5 Oct
disco, 11 Jan
Disney, Walt, 5 Dec, 15 Dec, 21 Dec
Disneyland, 18 July
Disneyworld, 1 Oct
Disraeli, Benjamin, 19 April, 21 Dec
diving, 16 Aug; suit, 10 Feb
divorce, 18 July, 18 Dec
Doddridge, Philip, 26 June
Doenitz, Karl, 24 Dec
Dolin, Anton, 27 July, 25 Nov
Dollfuss, Engelbert, 25 July, 4 Oct
Dollond, John, 10 June
Doll's House, A, 21 Dec
Dolmetsch, Arnold, 24 Feb
Domingo, Placido, 21 Jan
Dominica, 3 Nov
Dominican Republic, 3 Sept, 6 Dec
Domino, 'Fats', 26 Feb

Donald Duck, 9 June
Donat, Robert, 18 Mar
Donatello, 13 Dec
Doncaster, 24 Sept
Don Giovanni, 29 Oct
Donizetti, Domenico, 8 April,
   29 Nov
Donleavy, James, 23 April
Donne, John, 31 Mar
Donoghue, Steve, 23 Mar
Doppler, Christian, 17 Mar, 29 Nov
Doré, Gustave, 6 Jan
Dors, Diana, 4 May
Dorsey, Jimmy, 29 Feb
Dorsey, Tommy, 26 Nov
Dostoevsky, Fyodor, 9 Feb, 11 Nov
Dotrice, Michele, 27 Sept
Doubleday, Frank, 30 Jan
Douglas, James, 2 June
Douglas, Kirk, 9 Dec
Douglas, Michael, 25 Sept
Douglas-Home, William, 28 Sept
Doumer, Paul, 7 May
Dover, 24 Dec
Downing Street, 22 Sept
Doyle, Arthur Conan, 22 May, 7 July
Drabble, Margaret, 5 June
Drake, Francis, 28 Jan, 4 April,
   19 April, 17 June, 13 Dec
Draper, Ruth, 2 Dec
Drayton, Michael, 23 Dec
Dresden, Battle of, 27 Aug
Dreux, Battle of, 19 Dec
Dreyfus, Alfred, 13 Jan, 23 Feb,
   11 July, 19 Oct, 22 Dec
Dreyfuss, Richard, 29 Oct
Drinkwater, John, 1 June
driving test, 26 Mar
Drumclog, 1 June
drunken driving, 10 Sept
Drury Lane Theatre, 28 Sept
Dr Who, 23 Nov
Dryden, John, 13 April, 1 May,
   19 Aug
Dubček, Alexander, 7 Nov, 24 Nov,
   27 Nov, 28 Dec
Dublin, 2 Feb, 24 April, 22 May,
   15 Nov, 28 Nov
Duchamp, Marcel, 28 July, 2 Oct
Dudley, Robert, 24 June
duel, 3 May
Dufy, Raoul, 23 Mar
Duhamel, Georges, 30 June
Dukas, Paul, 18 May, 1 Oct
Dulles, John, 24 May
Dumas, Alexandre, fils, 27 July,
   27 Nov
Dumas, Alexandre, père, 24 July,
   5 Dec
du Maurier, Daphne, 13 May
du Maurier, George, 6 Oct
Dunaway, Faye, 14 Jan
Dunbar, Battle of, 27 April, 3 Sept
Duncan, Isadora, 14 Sept
Dunkirk, 29 May, 27 Oct
Dunkirk, Dunes of, 1 June

Dunlop, John, 23 Oct
du Pré, Jacqueline, 19 Oct
Durante, Jimmy, 29 Jan
Duras, Marguerite, 4 April
Dürer, Albrecht, 6 April
Durrell, Gerald, 7 Jan
Durrell, Lawrence, 27 Feb
Dusseldorf, 10 Sept
Dutch East India Company, 20 Mar,
   2 June
Duvalier, François 'Papa Doc',
   14 April, 25 Sept
Duvall, Robert, 5 Jan
Dvořák, Antonin, 1 May, 8 Sept
Dylan, Bob, 24 May, 26 Sept
dynamite, 14 July
dynamo, 28 Oct

Earhart, Amelia, 18 June, 2 July,
   24 July
Earp, Wyatt, 19 Mar
Earth, orbit of, 20 Feb, 12 April
earthquake, 14 Jan, 23 Jan, 26 Feb,
   29 Feb, 6 April, 10 April, 18 April,
   16 July, 28 July, 9 Aug, 11 Aug,
   13 Aug, 17 Aug, 1 Sept, 6 Sept,
   9 Sept, 22 Sept, 17 Oct, 28 Oct,
   1 Nov, 3 Nov, 23 Nov, 7 Dec,
   25 Dec, 28 Dec
EastEnders, 19 Feb
Easter, 25 Aug
Easter Rising, 24 April
East India Company, 2 June, 2 Aug
Eastman, George, 14 Mar, 12 July,
   14 Oct, 8 Oct
Eastwood, Clint, 31 May
Eccles, John, 27 Jan
Echegaray, José, 15 Sept
Eck, Johann, 26 June
Eckstine, Billy, 8 July
eclipse, solar, 19 Mar
Ecuador, 13 Aug
Edberg, Stefan, 19 Jan
Eddington, Arthur Stanley, 28 Dec
Eddy, Mary Baker, 3 Dec
Eddy, Nelson, 29 June
Eden, Anthony, 20 Feb, 12 June,
   23 June
Ederle, Gertrude, 6 Aug
Edgar, King of England, 11 May
Edgehill, Battle of, 23 Oct
Edinburgh, 24 May, 18 June, 27 Aug
Edison, Thomas, 27 Jan, 11 Feb,
   19 Feb, 15 April, 18 Oct, 6 Dec
Edmonds, Noel, 22 Dec
Edrich, Bill, 24 April
education, 6 Dec
Edward, Prince of the UK, 10 Mar
Edward I of England, 27 April,
   17 June, 24 June, 7 July, 19 Aug
Edward II of England, 7 Feb, 24 June,
   21 Sept
Edward III of England, 23 April,
   21 June, 26 Aug
Edward IV of England, 9 April,
   28 April

Fisher, Geoffrey, 15 Sept
Fisher, St John, 7 June, 22 June
fish fingers, 26 Sept
Fishguard, 22 Feb
fishing limits, 1 June
Fittipaldi, Emerson, 12 Dec
Fitzgerald, Edward, 14 June
Fitzgerald, Ella, 25 April
Fitzgerald, F Scott, 24 Sept, 21 Dec
Fitzherbert, Maria, 29 Mar
Fitzroy, Robert, 30 April
Fitzsimmons, Bob, 17 Mar
Fiume, 12 Sept
Flagstaad, Kirsten, 7 Dec
Flamborough Head, Battle of,
  23 Sept
Flamsteed, John, 19 Aug
Flanagan, Bud, 20 Oct
Flaubert, Gustave, 8 May, 12 Dec
Flecker, James Elroy, 5 Nov
Fledermaus, Die, 5 April
Fleming, Alexander, 11 Mar, 6 Aug,
  30 Sept
Fleming, Ian, 28 May, 12 Aug
Fleming, Victor, 23 Feb
Fletcher, Phineas, 8 May
Fleury, André-Hercule de, 22 June
flight, 5 Sept; non-stop, 7 Mar;
  supersonic, 14 Oct
flirting, 9 Jan
Flodden Field, Battle of, 9 Sept
flogging, 9 Nov
flood, 2 Mar, 21 Sept
Florence, 19 Oct
Florey, Howard, 21 Feb, 24 Sept
Florida, 22 Feb, 8 April, 30 June,
  1 Oct
Flynn, Errol, 20 June, 14 Oct
Foch, Ferdinand, 20 Mar
Fokine, Michel, 26 April, 22 Aug
Fonda, Peter, 23 Feb
Fonda, Henry, 16 May, 12 Aug
Fonda, Jane, 21 Dec
Fontanne, Lynn, 30 July
Fonteyn, Margot, 21 Feb
football, 13 Feb, 10 Mar, 22 Mar,
  23 Mar, 25 Mar, 13 April,
  19 April, 28 April, 13 July, 20 July,
  30 July, 8 Sept, 14 Sept, 21 Sept,
  13 Oct, 24 Oct, 19 Nov, 30 Nov,
  5 Dec
Forbes, Bryan, 22 July
Ford, Ford Madox, 26 June
Ford, Gerald, 14 July, 9 Aug
Ford, Glenn, 1 May
Ford, Harrison, 13 July
Ford, Henry, 7 April, 30 July
Ford, John, 1 Feb, 31 Aug
Ford, John, 17 April
Ford, Model T, 1 Oct
Foreman, George, 22 Jan
Forester, C S, 2 April
Forfarshire, 7 Sept
Formby, George, 6 Mar
Formosa, 16 May

Forster, E M, 1 Jan, 7 June
Fort St George, 27 May
Fort Sumter, 12 April
Forth railway bridge, 4 Mar
Fort Worth, Texas, 18 April
Forza del Destino, La, 10 Nov
Fosse, Bob, 23 Sept
Foster, Jodie, 19 Nov
Foster, Stephen, 13 Jan
Foucault, Jean, 18 Sept
Fowles, John, 31 Mar
Fox, Charles James, 13 Sept
Fox, George, 13 Jan, 30 Oct
Fox, William, 1 Jan, 1 May
Fra Angelico, 18 Feb, 18 Mar
Fracastoro, Girolamo, 8 Aug
Fragonard, Jean Honoré, 22 Aug
France, 24 Oct
France, 5 Feb, 6 Feb, 7 Feb, 9 Feb,
  13 Feb, 19 Feb, 23 Feb, 12 Mar,
  20 Mar, 6 May, 28 May, 21 June,
  28 June, 2 July, 15 July, 1 Aug,
  3 Aug, 14 Aug, 19 Aug, 4 Sept,
  18 Sept, 22 Sept, 27 Oct, 28 Oct,
  28 Nov
France, Anatole, 12 Oct
Francesca, Piero della, 12 Oct
Francesco de Paolo, St, 15 June
Francis, St, 3 Oct
Francis I of France, 31 Mar, 4 June
Francis, Trevor, 19 April
Franck, César, 10 Dec
Franco, Francisco, 1 Oct, 20 Nov,
  4 Dec
Franco-Prussian War, 28 Jan
Frank, Anne, 12 Mar, 12 June
Frankenstein, 4 Jan
Franklin, Aretha, 25 Mar
Franklin, Benjamin, 17 Jan, 17 April
Franklin, John, 16 April, 11 June
Franz Ferdinand, Archduke, 28 June
Franz Josef I, 18 Aug, 21 Nov
Fraser, Dawn, 4 Sept
Fraser, Peter, 12 Dec
fraud, 13 Aug, 24 Oct
Frazer, James, 7 May
Frazier, Joe, 22 Jan, 22 Jan, 8 Mar
Frémont, John, 13 July
Frears, Stephen, 20 June
Frederick VI of Denmark, 3 Dec
Frederick I of Prussia, 11 July
Frederick II 'the Great' of Prussia,
  24 Jan, 17 Aug
Frederick William I of Prussia,
  31 May
Freischutz, Der, 7 Mar
Freeman, Edward Augustus, 16 May
Freeman, Morgan, 1 June
Freeman, Richard, 30 Sept
Fremont, John, 21 Jan
French, Dawn, 11 Oct
French Foreign Legion, 9 Mar
French, John, 22 May
French language, 5 Jan
French Resistance, 22 Mar
French Sudan, 17 Jan

French Togoland, 27 April
Frescobaldi, Girolamo, 1 Mar
Freud, Sigmund, 6 May, 23 Sept,
  13 Oct
Freund, Karl, 3 May
Friedman, Milton, 31 July
Friendship 7, 20 Feb
Friml, Rudolf, 12 Nov
Frink, Elisabeth, 18 April, 14 Nov
Frith, William Powell, 2 Nov
Frobisher, Martin, 11 Aug
Froebel, Friedrich, 21 April, 21 June
Frost, David, 7 April
Frost, Robert, 26 Mar
Froude, William, 4 May
frozen food, 6 Mar
Fry, Elizabeth, 21 May, 12 Oct
Fry, Roger, 14 Dec
Fry, Stephen, 24 Aug
Fuad I of Egypt, 28 April
Fuchs, Klaus, 28 Jan
Fuchs, Leonhard, 10 May
Fuchs, Vivian, 11 Feb
Fugard, Athol, 11 June
Fuller, Thomas, 19 June
Fulton, Robert, 14 Nov
Funk, Walther, 31 May
Furtwängler, Wilhelm, 25 Jan

Gabin, Jean, 15 Nov
Gable, Clark, 1 Feb, 16 Nov
Gabor, Zsa Zsa, 6 Feb
Gabriel, Peter, 13 Feb
Gabrieli, Giovanni, 12 Aug
Gagarin, Yuri, 9 Mar, 12 April
Gaillard, Slim, 26 Feb
Gainsborough, Thomas, 2 Aug
Gaitskell, Hugh, 18 Jan, 9 April
Galilei, Galileo, 7 Jan, 8 Jan, 15 Feb
Galle, Johann, 23 Sept
Gallico, Paul, 15 July
Gallipoli, 8 Jan, 25 April, 20 Dec
Galsworthy, John, 31 Jan, 14 Aug
Galton, Francis, 17 Jan, 16 Feb
Galvani, Luigi, 9 Sept, 4 Dec
Galveston, 8 Sept
Gama, Vasco da, 8 July, 22 Nov,
  24 Dec
Gambia, 18 Feb, 24 April
Gance, Abel, 25 Oct
Gandhi, Indira, 19 Jan, 31 Oct,
  19 Nov
Gandhi, Mohandas 'Mahatma',
  30 Jan, 8 Mar, 12 Mar, 18 Mar,
  2 Oct
Gandhi, Rajiv, 22 May
Ganges, 12 May
Garbo, Greta, 18 Sept
Gardini, Raul, 23 July
Gardner, Ava, 25 Jan, 24 Dec
Gardner, Erle Stanley, 11 Mar,
  17 July
Garfield, James, 19 Sept
Garfunkel, Art, 5 Nov
Garibaldi, Giuseppe, 2 June, 4 July,
  26 Oct

Garland, Judy, 10 June
Garnerin, André, 18 Aug
Garrick, David, 19 Feb
Garter, Knights of the, 13 May;
 Order of the, 23 April
gas chamber, 8 Feb
gas light, 28 Jan
gas masks, 9 July
Gascoigne, George, 18 May
Gascon rebellion, 2 May
Gaskell, Elizabeth, 12 Nov
Gatling, Richard, 26 Feb, 12 Sept,
 4 Nov
Gatting, Mike, 6 June
Gaudier-Brzeska, Henri, 5 June
Gauguin, Paul, 7 June
Gaulle, Charles de, 8 Jan, 28 April,
 14 June, 9 Nov, 22 Nov, 27 Nov,
 21 Dec
Gauss, Karl, 23 Feb, 30 April
Gautier, Théophile, 23 Oct
Gay, John, 29 Jan, 4 Dec
Gay Liberation Front, 27 Nov
Gay-Lussac, Louis-Joseph, 9 May
Gaye, Marvin, 1 April
Gay News, 11 July
Gaynor, Janet, 6 Oct
Gaza, 5 July, 9 Dec
Gazzara, Ben, 28 Aug
Geldof, Bob, 5 Oct
Geller, Uri, 20 Dec
Gemmill, Archie, 24 Mar
General Motors, 16 Sept
Genet, Jean, 19 Dec
Geneva, 3 April; Convention,
 22 Aug
Genoa, 6 June, 27 May
Gentili, Alberico, 19 June
Gentry, Bobbie, 27 July
George I of Great Britain, 28 Mar,
 28 May, 11 June, 1 Aug, 20 Oct
George II of Great Britain, 25 Oct
George III of Great Britain, 29 Jan,
 4 June
George IV of Great Britain, 12 Aug
George V of Great Britain, 20 Jan,
 6 May
George VI of Great Britain, 26 April,
 3 May, 8 June, 14 Dec
George Cross, 15 April, 23 Sept
George, Duke of Clarence, 18 Feb
George Medal, 23 Sept
Georgia, 9 Sept
Gere, Richard, 29 Aug
Géricault, Théodore, 26 Sept
German, Edward, 11 Nov
Germany, 30 Jan, 2 Feb, 26 Feb,
 27 Feb, 5 Mar, 12 Mar, 15 Mar,
 21 Mar, 28 Mar, 6 April, 25 April,
 9 May, 12 May, 13 May, 5 June,
 21 June, 25 June, 30 June, 1 July,
 31 July, 3 Aug, 8 Aug, 13 Aug,
 19 Aug, 23 Aug, 30 Aug, 6 Sept,
 8 Sept, 15 Sept, 1 Oct, 3 Oct,
 7 Oct, 11 Oct, 18 Oct, 6 Nov,
 9 Nov, 10 Nov, 2 Dec,

Geronimo, 17 Feb, 4 Sept
Gershwin, George, 11 July, 26 Sept,
 30 Sept, 10 Oct
Gershwin, Ira, 17 Aug, 6 Dec
Gerulaitis, Vitas, 26 July
Getty, John Paul, 15 Dec
Gettysburg Address, 19 Nov
Gettysburg, Battle of, 1 July, 3 July
Getz, Stan, 2 Feb
Ghana, 6 Mar, 21 Mar
Ghent, 3 May; Treaty of, 24 Dec
Ghiberti, Lorenzo, 1 Dec
Giacometti, Alberto, 11 Jan
Gibb, Maurice, 22 Dec
Gibb, Robin, 22 Dec
Gibberd, Frederick, 9 Jan
Gibbon, Edward, 27 April
Gibbons, Grinling, 4 April
Gibbons, Orlando, 5 June
Gibbons, Stella, 5 Jan, 19 Dec
Gibraltar, 6 Mar, 11 April, 24 July,
 15 Dec
Gibson, Charles Dana, 23 Dec
Gide, André, 19 Feb, 22 Nov
Gielgud, John, 14 April
Giffaud, Henri, 24 Sept
Gigli, Beniamino, 20 Mar, 30 Nov
Gilbert, Cass, 17 May
Gilbert, Humphrey, 5 Aug
Gilbert, William, 24 May
Gilbert, W S, 14 Mar, 29 May,
 3 Oct, 18 Nov
Gilette, King Camp, 9 July, 2 Dec
Gill, Eric, 22 Feb
Gillespie, Dizzy, 6 Jan, 21 Oct
Gillray, James, 1 June
Gilmore, Gary, 17 Jan
Gingold, Hermione, 24 May
Giorgione, 25 Oct
Giraudoux, Jean, 31 Jan, 29 Oct
Girl Guides, 12 Mar
Gish, Lillian, 27 Feb, 14 Oct
Gladstone, William, 19 May, 9 Dec
Glazunov, Alexander, 21 Mar
Glencoe massacre, 13 Feb, 9 May
Glendower, 14 June
Glenn, John, 20 Feb, 18 July
Glinka, Mikhail, 15 Feb, 1 June
Glitter, Gary, 14 July
Globe Theatre, 29 June
Glück, Christoph, 2 July
Glubb, John, 17 Mar
goal net, 23 Mar
Gobbi, Tito, 5 Mar, 24 Oct
Godard, Lean-Luc, 3 Dec
Godfrey of Bouillon, 5 May
Godunov, Boris, 13 April
Godwin-Austin, Mount, (K2),
 31 July
Goebbels, Joseph, 1 May, 29 Oct
Goering, Hermann, 12 Jan, 15 Oct
Goethe, Johann, 22 Mar, 28 Aug
Gogh, Vincent van, 30 Mar, 29 July,
 23 Nov
Gogol, Nikolai, 21 Feb, 4 Mar,
 31 Mar

Golan Heights, 15 Feb
gold, 24 Jan, 12 Feb, 21 May,
 17 Aug, 8 Sept, 19 Oct, 25 Oct
Goldberg, Szymon, 19 July
Gold Coast, 21 Mar, 15 June
gold disc, 10 Feb
Golden Hind, 13 Dec
Golding, William, 19 Sept
Goldmark, Peter, 2 Dec
Goldoni, Carlo, 6 Feb, 25 Feb
Goldsmith, Oliver, 4 April
Goldwyn, Samuel, 31 Jan, 27 Aug
golf, 13 April, 15 Sept
Goncharov, Ivan, 27 Sept
Goncourt, Edmond de, 26 May
Gone with the Wind, 1 Mar, 1 Dec
González, Felipe, 28 Oct
Gooch, Graham, 23 July
Goodhew, Duncan, 27 Mar
Good Hope, 1 Nov
Goodman, Benny, 30 May, 13 June
Goodman, Steve, 25 July
Goodwin Sands, 17 Mar
Goodyear, Charles, 1 July
Googe, Barnabe, 11 June
Gorbachev, Mikhail, 2 Mar, 11 Mar,
 21 Aug, 1 Dec, 8 Dec, 25 Dec
Gordimer, Nadine, 20 Nov
Gordon, Charles, 26 Jan
Gordon, George, 1 Nov
Gordon Riots, 2 June
Gorky, Maxim, 14 Mar, 18 June
Gosse, Edmund, 21 Sept
Gossens, Salvador Allende, 11 Sept
Götterdämmerung, 17 Aug
Gough, Michael, 23 Nov
Gould, Shane, 23 Nov
Gounod, Charles, 17 June, 18 Oct
Gow, Ian, 30 July
Gower, David, 1 April
Goya, Francisco de, 30 Mar, 16 April
Gozzoli, Benozzo, 4 Oct
Grable, Betty, 2 July, 18 Dec
Grace, Princess of Monaco (Grace
 Kelly), 19 April, 14 Sept, 12 Nov
Grace, W G, 23 Oct
Graf Spee, 17 Dec
Graf, Steffi, 14 June
Graham, David, 11 Sept
Graham, Martha, 3 April
Grahame, Kenneth, 8 Mar, 6 July
Grainger, Percy, 20 Feb, 8 July
gramophone, 26 Sept, 6 Dec
Granada, 2 Jan
Grand National, 26 Feb, 24 Mar,
 31 Mar
Grand Prix, 7 Aug, 6 Oct
Granger, Stewart, 16 Aug
Grant, Cary, 18 Jan, 30 Nov
Grant, J A, 23 Feb
Grant, Ulysses S, 9 April, 27 April,
 23 July
Grantham, 13 May 27 Nov
Grappelli, Stephane, 26 Jan
Grass, Günther, 16 Oct
Graves, Robert, 7 Dec

Gray, Dulcie, 20 Nov
Gray, Elisha, 21 Jan
Gray, Thomas, 26 Dec
Great Britain, 13 Feb
Great Eastern, 31 Jan, 27 July
Great Exhibition, 1 May
Great Frost, 8 Feb
Great Lakes, 25 April
Great Ormond Street, 14 Feb
Great Storm, 26 Nov
Great Western, 8 April, 19 July
Greece, 2 Feb, 19 Feb, 17 April,
    21 April, 7 May, 11 June, 24 Aug,
    27 Sept, 17 Oct, 13 Dec
Greenaway, Kate, 17 Mar, 6 Nov
Greene, Graham, 3 April, 2 Oct
Greenland, 24 May
Greenpeace, 10 July
Greenstreet, Sydney, 18 Jan, 27 Dec
Greenwich, 10 Aug, 13 Oct; Mean
Time, 29 Jan; Observatory, 5 Feb
Greenwood, Joan, 2 Mar
Greenwood, Walter, 16 Sept
Greer, Germaine, 29 Jan
Gregory, St, 12 Mar
Gregory VII, Pope, 9 Mar
Gregory XIII, Pope, 24 Feb
Gregory, Augusta, 5 Mar
Grenada, 7 Feb, 13 Mar, 25 Oct
Grenoble, 17 Feb
Gresham, Thomas, 23 Jan
Grey, Joel, 11 April
Grey, Lady Jane, 12 Feb, 10 July
Grey, Thomas, 30 July
Grey, Zane, 31 Jan, 23 Oct
Grieg, Edvard, 15 June
Griffith, D W, 22 Jan, 23 July
Grimaldi, Joseph, 31 May, 18 Dec
Grimm, Jakob, 20 Sept
Grimm, Wilhelm, 24 Feb, 16 Dec
Grimond, Jo, 24 Oct
Gris, Juan, 23 Mar
Grock, 14 July
Grolier, Jean, 14 May
Gropius, Walter, 18 May, 5 July
Grossbeeren, Battle of, 23 Aug
Grossmith, George, 1 Mar
Grote, George, 18 June
Grotius, Hugo, 28 Aug
Grufydd, Llewelyn ap, 11 Dec
Guadalcanal, 7 Aug
Guam, 21 July
Guardian, The, 24 Aug
Guernica, 10 Sept
Guernica, 26 April
Guernsey, 1 July
Guevara, Che, 14 June, 9 Oct
Guibert, Hervé, 27 Dec
Guicciardini, Francesco, 6 May
'Guildford Four', 19 Oct
Guillotin, Joseph, 28 May
guillotine, 25 April, 28 July, 18 Sept
Guinness, Alec, 2 April
Guitry, Sacha, 24 Feb
Gulf War, 9 Jan, 24 Jan, 29 Jan,
    2 Feb, 27 Feb

Gunpowder Plot, 31 Jan, 4 Nov
Gustav I of Sweden, 7 June
Gustav II of Sweden, 6 Nov
Gustav V of Sweden, 16 June, 29 Oct
Gustav VI of Sweden, 15 Sept
Guthrie, Arlo, 10 July
Guthrie, Woody, 14 July, 3 Oct
Guthrum, 23 May
Gutteridge, Jeff, 27 July
Guy's Hospital, 24 July
Guyana, 23 Feb
Gwyn Nell, 2 Feb, 14 Nov

Haakon VII of Norway, 3 Aug,
    21 Sept
Habgood, John, 23 June
Habsburgs, 12 Nov
Hackman, Gene, 30 Jan
Hadlee, Richard, 3 July
Hadrian, 24 Jan, 10 July, 8 Aug
Haeckel, Ernst, 16 Feb
Haggard, Henry Rider, 14 May,
    22 June
Hagman, Larry, 21 Sept
Hahn, Otto, 8 Mar, 28 July
Haig, Alexander, 2 Dec
Haig, Douglas, 29 Jan, 19 June
Haile Selassie, 3 April, 2 May,
    23 July, 27 Aug, 12 Sept, 2 Nov
Hailwood, Mike, 23 Mar
Hair, 27 Sept
Haiti, 25 Sept, 29 Sept, 22 Oct,
    6 Dec, 16 Dec
Haitink, Bernard, 4 Mar
Hajek, Jiri, 24 Oct
Haldane, John, 3 May, 5 Nov, 1 Dec
Haldeman, H R, 12 Nov
Hale, George Ellery, 21 Feb, 29 June
Hale, Nathan, 22 Sept
Haley, Bill, 9 Feb, 6 July, 12 Dec
Hall, Adelaide, 7 Nov
Hall, Asaph, 11 Aug
Hall, Radclyffe, 7 Oct, 16 Nov
Hall, Wesley, 12 Sept
Hallé, Charles, 11 April
Halley, Edmond, 14 Jan, 8 Nov
Hals, Frans, 26 Aug
Hamburg, 1 Aug
Hamilton, Emma, 15 Jan
Hamilton, George, 12 Aug
Hamilton, Patrick, 29 Feb
Hamlin, Vincent, 14 June
Hammarskjöld, Dag, 29 July, 18 Sept
Hammerstein II, Oscar, 23 Aug
Hammett, Dashiel, 10 Jan
Hampden, John, 18 June
Hampton Court Palace, 31 Mar,
    12 July
Hampton, Lionel, 12 April
Hamsun, Knut, 4 Aug
Hancock, Tony, 25 June
Handel, George, 23 Feb, 14 April,
    27 April
Handley, Tommy, 9 Jan
Handy, W C, 28 Mar
hanging, 13 Aug

Hani, Chris, 10 April
Hanover, 20 June
Hansom, Joseph, 23 Dec
Hardenburg, Karl August von,
    31 May
Hardie, James Keir, 26 Sept
Hardrada, Harald, 25 Sept
Hardy, Oliver, 18 Jan, 7 Aug
Hardy, Thomas, 11 Jan, 2 June
Hare, David, 5 June
Hare, William, 24 Dec
Hargreaves, James, 22 April
Harlow, Jean, 3 Mar, 7 June
Harmsworth, Alfred, 14 Aug
Harold II of England, 27 May,
    25 Sept
Harriman, Averell, 26 July, 15 Nov
Harris, Joel Chandler, 3 July
Harris, Richard, 1 Oct
Harris, Roy, 1 Oct
Harrison, Benjamin, 20 Aug
Harrison, George, 25 Feb
Harrison, Rex, 5 Mar, 2 June
Harte, Francis Bret, 5 May
Harthacnut, 8 June
Harvard University, 28 Oct
Harvey, William, 1 April, 3 June
Hasek, Jaroslav, 3 Jan, 30 April
Hastings, Battle of, 14 Oct
Hastings, Michael, 2 Sept
Hastings, Warren, 6 Dec
Hathaway, Anne, 6 Aug
Hathaway, Henry, 12 Feb, 13 Mar
Hatley, Robert, 21 May
Haughey, Charles, 16 Sept
Hauptmann, Gerhart, 8 June
Havel, Vaclav, 21 Feb, 5 Oct, 25 Dec
Havilland, Geoffrey de, 21 May
Havilland, Olivia de, 1 July
Hawaii, 18 Jan, 14 Feb, 14 July,
    21 Aug, 19 Dec
Hawke, Robert, 9 Dec, 19 Dec
Hawking, Stephen, 8 Jan
Hawkins, Jack, 18 July, 14 Sept
Hawkins, Coleman, 21 Nov
Hawks, Howard, 30 May
Hawksmoor, Nicholas, 25 Mar
Hawn, Goldie, 21 Nov
Hawthorn, Mike, 22 Jan
Hawthorne, Nathaniel, 19 May,
    4 July
Hay, Will, 18 April
Haydn, Franz Joseph, 31 Mar,
    31 May
Hayle, Barbara, 18 April
Hayward, Tom, 19 July
Hayworth, Rita, 15 May, 17 Oct
Hazlitt, William, 10 April, 18 Sept
Healey, Denis, 30 Aug
Healy, Timothy, 17 May
Heaney, Seamus, 13 April
Hearne, Thomas, 10 June
Hearst, Patricia, 5 Feb
Hearst, William Randolph, 14 Aug
Heath, Edward, 9 July, 28 Oct
Heathrow airport, 9 Sept

Hume, Basil, 2 Mar
Hume, David, 7 May, 25 Aug
Humperdinck, Engelbert, 1 Sept, 27 Sept
Humphrey, Hubert, 13 Jan, 27 May
Humphreys, Christmas, 13 April
Humphries, Barry, 17 Feb
Hundred Years' War, 28 May, 17 July, 19 Sept, 25 Oct
Hungary, 27 June, 12 Aug, 10 Sept, 18 Oct, 23 Oct, 16 Nov
Hunt, John, 22 June
Hunt, Leigh, 28 Aug, 19 Oct
Hunt, William, 7 Sept
Hunter, John, 13 Feb
Hunter, William, 30 Mar, 23 May
Hurd, Douglas, 8 Mar
hurricane, 3 Sept, 21 Sept, 16 Oct, 22 Oct
Hurt, John, 22 Jan
Husák, Gustáv, 18 Nov
Huskisson, William, 15 Sept
Hussein, King of Jordan, 11 Aug, 14 Nov
Hussein, Saddam, 29 April, 17 July, 6 Dec, 21 Dec
Huston, John, 5 Aug, 28 Aug
Hutton, James, 3 June
Huxley, Aldous, 26 July
Huxley, Julian, 14 Feb, 2 June
Huxley, T H, 4 May, 29 June
Huygens, Christiaan, 14 April, 8 June
Huysmans, Joris, 12 May
Hyde Park, London, 5 July
Hyder Ali, 19 June

IBM, 8 Jan, 19 Jan
Ibrox Park, 2 Jan
Ibsen, Henrik, 20 Mar, 23 May, 21 Dec
Ibuse, Masuji, 10 July
ice cream, 13 Dec
Iceland, 28 Jan, 19 Feb, 1 June, 14 Nov
Iglesias, Julio, 23 Sept
Ignatius of Loyola, 31 July
IJselmeer, 28 May
Il Trovatore, 19 Jan
Ilyushin, Sergei, 9 Feb
Importance of Being Earnest, The, 14 Feb
India, 1 Jan, 19 Jan, 26 Jan, 10 Feb, 16 Feb, 20 Feb, 28 Feb, 8 Mar, 12 Mar, 10 May, 28 May, 29 May, 30 June, 2 Aug, 15 Aug, 6 Sept, 23 Sept, 1 Nov, 26 Nov, 3 Dec, 4 Dec, 7 Dec
Indian War, 28 Aug
Indy, Vincent d', 27 May, 1 Dec
inflation, 11 Oct
Ingres, Jean, 14 Jan, 29 Aug
Inkerman, Battle of, 5 Nov
Innes, Hammond, 15 July
Innocent II, Pope, 24 Sept
Innocent III, Pope, 27 May, 16 July

Inquisition, 5 May, 4 Dec
insulin, 11 Jan, 15 April, 24 July
internal combustion engine, 19 Oct
International Justice, Court of, 15 Feb
intifada, 9 Dec
Ionesco, Eugene, 13 Nov
IRA, 10 Jan, 17 Jan, 7 Feb, 20 Feb, 6 Mar, 24 July, 30 July, 22 Sept, 12 Oct, 19 Oct, 31 Oct, 8 Nov, 21 Nov, 28 Nov
Iran, 1 Feb, 10 April, 16 Sept, 28 Nov
Iran-Contra affair, 5 July, 16 Sept
Iran-Iraq War, 3 July, 24 Sept
Iraq, 12 Jan, 16 Jan, 27 Feb, 8 July, 14 July, 2 Aug, 23 Aug, 29 Nov, 6 Dec
Ireland, 26 Mar, 23 May, 4 June
Ireland, John, 12 June
Ireland, Republic of, 22 Jan, 16 Feb, 20 Feb, 18 April, 28 Dec
Irish Free State, 2 Sept, 6 Dec
Irish Home Rule bill, 25 May, 18 Sept
Irish Rebellion, 21 June
iron curtain, 5 Mar
Iron Guard, 27 Nov
iron lung, 12 Oct
Irons, Jeremy, 19 Sept
Irvine, Andy, 16 Sept
Irving, Washington, 3 April, 28 Nov
Irving, Henry, 13 Oct
Isabella I, Queen of Castile, 14 Mar, 26 Nov
Isandhlwana, 22 Jan
Isherwood, Christopher, 4 Jan, 26 Aug
Isle of Wight, 4 Feb
Israel, 4 Jan, 17 Mar, 26 Mar, 11 May, 12 May, 14 May, 5 June, 3 July, 5 July, 17 Dec
Istanbul, 28 Mar, 9 Aug
Italy, 18 Feb, 23 Feb, 29 Feb, 7 April, 2 May, 9 May, 14 May, 26 May, 3 June, 10 July, 25 July, 29 July, 4 Aug, 3 Sept, 9 Sept, 20 Sept, 29 Sept, 2 Oct, 19 Oct, 26 Oct, 3 Nov, 23 Nov, 15 Dec, 18 Dec
ITV, 22 Sept
Ivan III 'the Great', 22 Jan, 27 Oct
Ivan IV 'the Terrible', 16 Jan, 18 Mar, 25 Aug
Ives, Charles, 19 May
Ivory Coast, 7 Aug
Ivory, James, 7 June
Iwerks, Ub, 24 Mar

Jack the Ripper, 31 Aug, 30 Sept
Jacklin, Tony, 7 July, 15 Sept
Jackson, Andrew, 15 Mar, 18 June, 31 July
Jackson, Geoffrey, 9 Sept
Jackson, Glenda, 9 May
Jackson, Jesse, 8 Oct
Jackson, Mahalia, 27 Jan

Jackson, Michael, 29 Aug
Jackson, 'Stonewall', 21 Jan, 5 May
Jacobi, Derek, 22 Oct
Jacquerie, 28 May
Jagger, Mick, 26 July
Jahangir, 31 Aug
Jamaica, 14 Jan, 6 Aug
James I of Great Britain (James VI of Scotland), 24 Mar, 27 Mar, 17 June, 19 June
James I of Scotland, 20 Feb
James II of Scotland, 3 Aug
James IV of Scotland, 9 Sept
James V of Scotland, 10 April, 11 May
James, Clive, 7 Oct
James, Duke of Berwick, 12 June
James, Henry, 28 Feb, 15 April
James, Jesse, 3 April
James, Marquess of Montrose, 21 May
Jameson, Leander, 26 Nov
Janáček, Leoš, 3 July
Janning, Emil, 2 Jan
Jansen, Cornelius, 6 May
Japan, 19 Jan, 4 Feb, 18 May, 27 May, 7 July, 6 Aug, 9 Aug, 13 Aug, 22 Aug, 28 Aug, 8 Sept, 18 Sept, 8 Dec, 23 Dec, 25 Dec
Jardine, Douglas, 23 Oct
Jarrow March, 5 Oct
Jaunpur, 12 May
Jaurès, Jean, 3 Sept
Jay, Peter, 7 Feb
Jazz Singer, The, 6 Oct
Jeans, James Hopwood, 11 Sept
Jeddah, treaty of, 20 May
jeep, 11 Nov
Jefferson, Thomas, 13 April, 4 July
Jeffreys, George, 18 April
Jellicoe, John, 20 Nov
Jenkins, Clive, 2 May
Jenner, Edward, 26 Jan, 17 May
Jerome, Jerome K, 2 May, 14 June
Jersey, 23 Nov
Jerusalem, 11 April, 15 July, 1 Sept, 2 Oct, 9 Dec
Jervis, John, 14 Feb, 14 Mar
Jespersen, Otto, 30 April
Jesuit order, 4 April, 15 Aug
Jewison, Norman, 21 July
Jews, 14 Mar, 6 Sept, 15 Sept, 10 Nov
Jiang Qing, 25 Jan
Joachim, Joseph, 15 Aug
Joan of Arc, 6 Jan, 29 April, 23 May, 30 May, 18 June
Johannesburg, 8 Sept, 30 Aug
John XXIII, Pope, 3 Jan
John, King of England, 17 May, 4 June, 19 Oct, 24 Dec
John, Augustus, 4 Jan, 31 Oct
John, Elton, 25 Mar
John of Gaunt, 3 Feb
John of the Cross, St, 24 June
John Paul I, Pope, 26 Aug, 28 Sept

John Paul II, Pope, 16 Oct, 1 Dec
Johns, Glynis, 5 Oct
Johnson, Amy, 5 Jan
Johnson, Ben, 26 Sept
Johnson, Celia, 25 April
Johnson, Louis, 1 Nov
Johnson, Lyndon B, 22 Jan, 2 July, 27 Aug
Johnson, Samuel, 15 April, 18 Sept, 13 Dec
Jolson, Al, 26 May, 6 Oct, 23 Oct
Jones, Ann, 17 Oct
Jones, Bobby, 18 Dec
Jones, Brian, 3 July, 30 Oct
Jones, Henry, 20 Sept
Jones, Inigo, 21 June, 15 July
Jones, John Paul, 23 Sept
Jonson, Ben, 11 June, 6 Aug
Joplin, Janis, 19 Jan, 4 Oct
Joplin, Scott, 1 April, 24 Nov
Jordan, 22 Mar, 2 June, 11 Aug
Jordan, River, 7 Feb
Joseph I, Holy Roman Emperor, 17 April
Joule, James, 11 Oct
Joyce, James, 13 Jan, 2 Feb
Joyce, William, 24 April, 18 Sept, 19 Sept
Juan Carlos I of Spain, 5 Jan, 22 Nov
Juarez, Benito, 11 Jan
juke box, 23 Nov
Jules et Jim, 24 Jan
Juliana, Queen of the Netherlands, 30 April
Jung, Carl Gustav, 6 June, 26 July
Junkers J1, 12 Dec
Jupiter, 7 Jan, 20 Aug
Jutland, Battle of, 31 May
Juxon, William, 4 June

K2, 31 July
Kästner, Erich, 23 Feb
Kafka, Franz, 3 June, 3 July
Kahane, Meir, 5 Nov
Kalinin, Mikhail, 3 June
Kandinsky, Wassily, 22 Nov, 13 Dec
Kant, Immanuel, 12 Feb, 22 April
Karajan, Herbert von, 5 April, 16 July
Karamanlis, Constantine, 11 June
Karas, Anton, 10 Jan
Kariba High Dam, 17 May, 6 Nov
Karl Franz Josef of Austria, 1 April
Karloff, Boris, 3 Feb, 23 Nov
Karpov, Anatoly, 9 Nov
Karsavina, Tamara, 10 Mar
Kasparov, Gary, 13 April, 9 Nov
Kaufman, George S, 16 Nov
Kaunda, Kenneth, 28 April
Kaye, Danny, 18 Jan, 3 Mar
Kazan, Elia, 7 Sept
Kean, Edmund, 17 Mar
Keating, Paul, 19 Dec
Keating, Tom, 12 Feb
Keaton, Buster, 1 Feb, 4 Oct
Keaton, Diane, 5 Jan

Keats, John, 23 Feb, 31 Oct
Keegan, Kevin, 14 Feb
Keeler, Christine, 5 Sept
Keith, Penelope, 2 April
Keller, Helen, 27 June
Kellogg, William, 19 Feb
Kellogg-Briand Pact, 27 Aug
Kelly, Grace, (Princess Grace of Monaco) 19 April, 14 Sept, 12 Nov
Kelly, Gene, 23 Aug
Kelly, Ned, 11 Nov
Kemble, Fanny, 27 Nov
Kemble, John, 26 Feb
Kennedy Airport, 17 Oct
Kennedy, Jacqueline, 20 Oct
Kennedy, John F, 20 Jan, 25 May, 29 May, 22 Nov
Kennedy, Joseph, 18 Nov
Kennedy, Nigel, 28 Dec
Kennedy, Robert, 6 June, 20 Nov
Kent, William, 12 April
Kentner, Louis, 22 Sept
Kentucky, 1 June
Kenya, 8 April, 4 Aug
Kenyatta, Jomo, 8 April
Kepler, Johannes, 27 Dec
Keppel, Henry, 14 June
Kerensky, Alexander, 11 June, 15 Sept
Kern, Jerome, 27 Jan, 11 Nov
Kerouac, Jack, 21 Oct
Kerr, Deborah, 30 Sept
Keynes, John Maynard, 21 April, 5 June
Khaddhafi, Moamer al, 16 Jan, 1 Sept
Khama, Seretse, 13 July
Khan, Genghis, 18 Aug
Khan Niaz, Imran, 25 Nov
Khartoum, 2 Sept
Khmer Rouge, 17 April
Khrushchev, Nikita, 14 Feb, 27 Mar, 17 April, 11 Sept
Kidd, William, 23 May
Kielce, Poland, 14 May
Kierkegaard, Sören, 5 May, 11 Nov
Killigrew, Thomas, 19 Mar
Killy, Jean-Claude, 17 Feb, 30 Aug
Kimberley, 6 Nov
kinetoscope, 15 April
King, B B, 16 Sept
King, Billie Jean, 22 Nov
King, Carole, 9 Feb
King, Mackenzie, 22 July
King, Martin Luther, 15 Jan, 10 Mar, 4 April, 28 Aug
King, Stephen, 21 Sept
King, William Lyon MacKenzie, 17 Dec
King's Cross Station, 18 Nov
Kingsley, Charles, 12 June
Kingston, 14 Jan
Kinnear, Roy, 19 Sept
Kinnock, Neil, 28 Mar, 2 Oct
Kinski, Nastassja, 24 Jan

Kipling, Rudyard, 18 Jan
Kirchoff, Gustav, 17 Oct
Kirov Ballet, 6 Aug
Kissinger, Henry, 27 May
Kitchener, Horatio, 8 April, 5 June, 24 June, 2 Sept
Kitt, Eartha, 26 Jan
Klammer, Franz, 3 Dec
Klee, Paul, 29 June, 18 Dec
Klein, Calvin, 19 Nov
Klein, Melanie, 30 Mar
Klemperer, Otto, 14 May, 6 July
Klimt, Gustav, 6 Feb
KLM, 7 Oct
Kneller, Godfrey, 8 Aug, 7 Nov
Knopfler, Mark, 12 Aug
Knox, Alexander, 16 Jan
Knox, John, 24 Nov
Knox, Ronald, 24 Aug
Knox-Johnston, Robin, 17 Mar, 22 April
Königsberg, 6 June
Koch, Robert, 27 May
Koestler, Arthur, 3 Mar, 5 Sept
Kohl, Helmut, 3 April, 1 Oct, 2 Dec
Kokoschka, Oskar, 22 Feb
Koldewey, Robert, 4 Feb
Korda, Alexander, 16 Sept
Korea, 11 April, 8 May, 23 June, 27 July, 22 Aug; North, 28 June, 17 Sept; South, 29 June, 15 Aug, 17 Sept
Kościuszko, Tadeusz, 15 Oct
Kossuth, Lajos, 20 Mar, 19 Sept
Kosygin, Alexei, 19 Dec
Krakatoa, 26 Aug
Kramer, Jack, 1 Aug
Kreisler, Fritz, 29 Jan
Krenek, Ernst, 23 Dec
Krenz, Egon, 18 Oct
Kristallnacht, 10 Nov
Kropotkin, Peter, 8 Feb
Kruger, Paul, 16 April, 14 July
Krupp, Alfred, 14 July
Kubelik, Jan, 5 Dec
Kubrick, Stanley, 26 July
Kuchatov, Igor, 7 Feb
Kurosawa, Akira, 23 Mar
Kuwait, 12 Jan, 16 Jan, 27 Feb, 17 July, 2 Aug, 6 Dec, 29 Nov, 21 Dec

Labour Party, 13 Jan, 30 May, 26 July, 2 Oct
Labrador, 20 April
la Bruyère, Jean de, 10 May
Ladd, Alan, 29 Jan, 3 Sept
Lady Chatterley's Lover, 2 Nov
Ladysmith, 28 Feb, 2 Nov
Laemmle, Carl, 7 Jan
Laënnec, René, 13 Aug
Lafayette, Marquis de, 6 Sept
Lafitte, Jacques, 24 Oct
la Fontaine, Jean de, 13 April, 8 July
Lagos Bay, Battle of, 18 Aug
Lagrange, Joseph-Louis, 10 April

Laika, 9 Mar, 3 Nov
Laine, Cleo, 28 Oct
Laker Airways, 5 Feb
Lal, Madan, 20 Mar
Lamarck, Jean Baptiste de, 1 Aug
Lamarr, Hedy, 9 Nov
Lamartine, Alphonse de, 28 Feb
Lamb, Charles, 27 Dec
Lamb, William, 15 Mar
Lambert, Leonard Constant, 21 Aug
Lammennais, Félicité Robert de,
   19 June
Lamour, Dorothy, 10 Dec
Lancaster, Burt, 2 Nov
Lancaster, James, 9 May
Lancaster, Osbert, 27 July, 4 Aug
Land, Edwin, 28 Nov
Landseer, Edwin, 1 Oct
Landseer, John, 29 Feb
Lane, Edward, 10 Aug
Lanfranc, 28 May
Lang, Andrew, 20 July
Lang, Fritz, 10 Jan, 2 Aug, 5 Dec
Langdon, Harry, 22 Dec
Langtry, Lillie, 12 Feb, 13 Oct
Lansbury, George, 7 May
Laos, 19 July
Lapotaire, Jane, 26 Dec
Larkin, Philip, 9 Aug, 2 Dec
La Rochelle, 2 June
Larousse, Pierre, 3 Jan, 23 Oct
La Scala, 3 Aug
Lascaux, 1 Nov, 12 Sept
Las Vegas, 15 Feb, 7 Nov
Laski, Harold, 30 June
Laski, Marghanita, 6 Feb
Lateran Treaty, 7 July
Latimer, Hugh, 16 Oct
Latvia, 3 Mar, 17 May, 3 Aug,
   17 Sept, 21 Sept, 18 Nov
Laud, William, 7 Oct
Lauda, Niki, 21 Oct
Lauder, Harry, 26 Feb
Laughton, Charles, 1 July, 15 Dec
launderette, 18 April
Laurel, Stan, 23 Feb, 16 June
Laver, Rod, 9 Aug
Lavoisier, Antoine, 8 May
Law, Andrew Bonar, 23 Oct, 30 Oct
law, English, 21 June
Lawford, Peter, 7 Sept
Lawrence, D H, 2 Mar, 11 Sept,
   2 Nov
Lawrence, Ernest Orlando, 8 Aug,
   28 Aug
Lawrence, Gertrude, 4 July, 6 Sept
Lawrence, T E, 19 May, 15 Aug,
   1 Oct
Lawson, Geoff, 7 Dec
Lawson, Nigel, 11 Mar
Layard, Austen Henry, 5 July
Leachman, Cloris, 30 April
League of Nations, 10 Jan, 3 Feb,
   8 April, 28 April, 8 Sept, 18 Sept
Leakey, Louis, 7 Aug, 1 Oct
Lean, David, 25 Mar, 16 April

Leasor, James, 20 Dec
Lebanon, 23 May, 1 Sept, 21 Oct,
   4 Dec, 17 Dec
Le Carré, John, 19 Oct
Le Corbusier, 27 Aug, 6 Oct
Le Fanu, Sheridan, 7 Feb
Léger, Fernand, 4 Feb, 17 Aug
Lehár, Franz, 30 April, 24 Oct
Léotard, Jules, 12 Nov
Lévi-Strauss, Claude, 28 Nov
Lee, Ann, 29 Feb
Lee, Brenda, 11 Dec
Lee, Bruce, 20 July
Lee, Laurie, 26 June
Lee, Robert E, 9 April, 12 Oct
Leeuwenhoek, Anton van, 26 Aug,
   24 Oct
Legrand, Michel, 24 Feb
Leibnitz, Gottfried, 14 Nov
Leicestershire, 24 Dec
Leigh, Janet, 6 July
Leigh, Vivien, 1 Mar, 8 July, 5 Nov
Leipzig, 26 June, 19 Oct
Lely, Peter, 14 Sept
Lemmon, Jack, 8 Feb
Lendl, Ivan, 7 Mar
Lend-Lease Bill, 11 Mar
Lenglen, Suzanne, 4 July
Lenin, Vladimir, 21 Jan, 9 Mar,
   7 Nov, 16 Nov
Leningrad, Siege of, 18 Jan, 30 Aug
Lennon, John, 4 Aug, 9 Oct, 25 Nov,
   8 Dec
Lennox, Annie, 25 Dec
Leno, Dan, 31 Oct
Leo I, Pope, 10 Nov
Leo III, Pope, 25 Dec
Leo X, Pope, 3 Jan, 15 June, 11 Oct,
   11 Dec
Leo XIII, Pope, 20 July
Leon, Juan Ponce de, 8 April
Leonard, Sugar Ray, 17 May
Leonardo da Vinci, 2 May
Leoncavallo, Ruggiero, 8 May, 9 Aug
Leopardi, Giacomo, 29 June
Leopold I, King of the Belgians,
   10 Dec
Leopold III, Holy Roman Emperor,
   5 May
Lepanto, Battle of, 7 Oct
Lepsius, Karl, 10 July
Lermontov, Mikhail, 2 Oct
Lesage, Alain, 8 May
Lesseps, Ferdinand de, 25 April,
   19 Nov, 7 Dec
Lessing, Doris, 22 Oct
Lessing, Gotthold Ephraim, 15 Feb
Levellers, 15 May
Leverrier, Urbain, 11 Mar
Levinson, Barry, 2 June
Lewes, Battle of, 14 May
Lewis, Carl, 1 July
Lewis, C S, 29 Nov
Lewis, Jerry, 16 Mar
Lewis, Jerry Lee, 29 Sept
Lewis, Meriwether, 11 Oct

Lewis, Percy Wyndham, 7 Mar
Lewis, Sinclair, 10 Jan, 7 Feb
Lexington, Massachusetts, 19 April
Leyden, 30 June
Leyte, Philippines, 20 Oct
Lhasa, Tibet, 22 Feb, 3 Aug
libel, 28 Jan
Liberace, 4 Feb
Liberia, 26 July
Liberté, 25 Sept
library, 24 May, 6 Sept
Library of Congress, US, 24 April
Libya, 16 Jan, 1 Sept, 24 Dec
Lice, Turkey, 6 Sept
licence, pilot's, 8 Mar
Lichtenstein, Roy, 27 Oct
Liddell, Eric, 20 Aug
Liddell, Alice, 4 May
Lidice, 10 June
Liebermann, Max, 8 Feb
Liebig, Justus von, 12 May
Liechtenstein, 2 Feb
lifeboat, 30 Jan, 2 Nov
Liggio, Luciano, 15 Nov
Light Brigade, Charge of the, 25 Oct
lightning, 9 July
Ligurian Republic, 6 June
Lilienthal, Otto, 23 May, 10 Aug
Lilly, William, 9 June
Lima, 28 Oct
Linacre, Thomas, 20 Oct
Lincoln, Abraham, 12 Feb, 4 Mar,
   15 April, 22 Sept, 6 Nov, 19 Nov
Lind, Jenny, 7 Mar, 2 Nov
Lindbergh, Charles, 4 Feb, 26 Aug
Lineker, Gary, 30 Nov
Linnaeus, Carolus, (Carl von Linné),
   10 Jan, 23 May
Lipchitz, Jacques, 22 Aug
Lipperschey, Hans, 2 Oct
Lippi, Fra Filippo, 10 Oct
Lisbon, 26 Feb, 1 Nov
Liszt, Franz, 31 July, 22 Oct
Lithuania, 9 Feb, 17 Sept
Little Big Horn, Battle of, 25 June
Little Richard, 13 Sept, 5 Dec
Litvinov, Maxim, 17 July
Lively Lady, 4 July
Lively, Penelope, 17 Mar
Liverpool, 30 July
Livingstone, David, 9 Feb, 19 Mar,
   1 May, 23 July, 16 Sept, 10 Nov
Livonia, 21 June
Livy, 2 Jan
Llewelyn, Gruffyd ap, 4 June
Lloyd, Harold, 8 Mar, 20 April
Lloyd, Marie, 7 Oct, 12 Feb
Lloyd George, David, 17 Jan, 25 Feb
Lloyd Webber, Andrew, 22 Mar
loaf, national, 24 Mar
Locarno Pact, 1 Dec
Lochore, Brian, 3 Sept
Locke, John, 29 Aug, 28 Oct
Lockerbie, 21 Dec
Lockwood, Margaret, 15 July
Lodge, Henry Cabot, 27 Feb

Manson, Charles, 25 Jan
Mantegna, Andrea, 13 Sept
Mao Zedong, 9 Sept, 1 Oct, 20 Oct, 21 Oct, 26 Dec
Maradona, Diego, 30 Oct
Marat, Jean-Paul, 24 May, 13 July
Marathon, Battle of, 28 Sept
Marceau, Marcel, 22 Mar
Marcellus II, Pope, 6 May
March, Fredric, 31 Aug
Marciano, Rocky, 31 Aug, 1 Sept
Marconi, Guglielmo, 25 April, 20 July, 12 Dec
Marcos, Ferdinand, 11 Jan
Marcos, Imelda, 4 Nov
Marengo, Battle of, 14 June
Margaret, Countess of Richmond, 29 June
Margaret, Princess of the UK, 21 Aug
margarine, 15 July
Maria Theresa, 17 May, 29 Nov
Marie Antoinette, 16 May, 16 Oct, 2 Nov
Marie Celeste, 7 Nov
Marienburg, 6 June
Mariner, 15 July
Mariner 9, 14 Oct
Mariner 10, 29 Mar
Mariner II, 14 Dec
Markov, Georgi, 11 Sept
Markova, Alicia, 1 Dec
Marks, Simon, 8 Dec
Marks and Spencer, 28 Sept
Markstein, George, 18 Jan
Marley, Bob, 5 Feb
Marlowe, Christopher, 6 Feb, 30 May
Marne, Battle of the, 4 Aug, 5 Sept, 12 Sept
Marquand, John P, 16 July
Marriage of Figaro, The, 1 May
Marriner, Neville, 15 April
Mars, 15 July, 20 July, 11 Aug, 3 Sept, 14 Oct
Marsden, Gerry, 24 Sept
Marseillaise, 15 July
Marseille, 28 Mar, 9 Oct
Marsh, Ngaio, 23 April
Marsh, Rodney, 11 Nov
Marshall Aid, 5 June
Marshall, George, 28 Aug, 16 Oct
Marshall Islands, 1 Mar, 17 Sept
Marshall, Malcolm, 18 April
Marston, John, 25 June
Marston Moor, Battle of, 2 July
Martineau, Harriet, 12 June
Martinique, 8 May
Martyr, Peter, 8 May
Marvell, Andrew, 31 Mar
Marvin, Hank, 28 Oct
Marvin, Lee, 19 Feb, 29 Aug
Marx, 'Chico', 11 Oct
Marx, 'Groucho', 19 Aug
Marx, 'Harpo', 21 Nov
Marx, Karl, 14 Mar, 5 May, 4 July, 28 Sept

Marx, 'Zeppo', 30 Nov
Mary I of England, 18 Feb, 4 June, 6 July, 17 Nov
Mary II of Great Britain, 13 Feb, 11 April, 28 Dec
Mary of Modena, 7 May
Mary of Teck, Princess, 26 May
Mary, Queen of Scots, 8 Feb, 24 April, 15 May, 16 June, 8 Dec
Mary Rose, 19 July, 11 Oct
Masaryk, Jan, 10 Mar, 14 Sept
Masaryk, Tomas, 7 Mar
Mascagni, Pietro, 7 Dec
Maschwitz, Eric, 27 Oct
Masefield, John, 12 May
Maskell, Dan, 11 April
Maskelyne, Nevil, 9 Feb, 6 Oct, 22 Dec
Mason, James, 15 May, 27 July
Massachusetts, 21 Dec
Massena, André, 6 May
Massenet, Jules, 12 May
Massey, Anna, 11 Aug
Massey, Raymond, 29 July, 30 Aug
Massine, Léonide, 9 Aug
Massys, Jan, 8 Oct
Masters, Edgar Lee, 23 Aug
Mastroianni, Marcello, 28 Sept
Mata Hari, 13 Feb, 25 July, 7 Aug, 15 Oct
matches, 7 April
maternity leave, 28 Nov
Mather, Cotton, 13 Feb
Mather, Increase, 21 June
Mathis, Johnny, 30 Sept
Matilda, 17 June
Matisse, Henri, 3 Nov, 3 Dec
Matsushita, Konusuke, 27 Nov
Matthau, Walter, 1 Oct
Matthews, Stanley, 1 Feb
Mature, Victor, 29 Jan
Maugham, William Somerset, 25 Jan, 16 Dec
Maupassant, Guy de, 6 July, 5 Aug
Mauriac, François, 1 Sept, 11 Oct
Mauritania, 28 Nov
Mauritius, 3 Dec
Maurois, André, 9 Oct
Maximilian I, Holy Roman Emperor, 12 Jan, 6 Feb, 22 Mar
Maximilian, Archduke of Austria, 10 April
Maximilian, Emperor of Mexico, 19 June
Maxwell, James Clerk, 13 June
Maxwell, Robert, 5 Nov
Mayall, John, 29 Nov
Mayall, Rik, 7 Mar
Mayer, Louis, 29 Oct
Mayer, Robert, 9 Jan
Mayerling, 30 Jan
Mayflower, 21 Dec
Mayhew, Henry, 25 July
Mayo, Charles, 26 May, 19 July
Mazarin, Jules, 9 Mar
Mazowiecki, Tadeuz, 19 Aug

Mazzini, Giuseppe, 10 Mar, 22 June
Mboya, Thomas Joseph, 5 July
McAdam, John, 21 Sept, 26 Nov
McCarthy, John, 8 Aug
McCarthy, Joseph, 2 May, 20 May
McCarthy, Mary, 24 Oct
McCullers, Carson, 29 Sept
McCullin, Don, 9 Oct
McDonald, James Ramsay, 12 Oct
McEnroe, John, 16 Feb
McGraw, Ali, 1 April
McGuigan, Barry, 28 Feb
McIlroy, Sammy, 2 Aug
McIndoe, Archibald, 11 April
McKellen, Ian, 25 May
McKern, Leo, 16 Mar
McKinley, William, 6 Sept
McLaglen, Victor, 7 Nov
McLaren, Malcom, 20 Jan
McLaughlin, John, 4 Jan
McQueen, Steve, 24 Mar, 7 Nov
McWhirter, Ross, 27 Nov
Mead, Margaret, 15 Nov, 16 Dec
measles, 14 July
Mecca, 2 July, 16 July
Medawar, Peter, 28 Feb, 2 Oct
Medici, Catherine de', 5 Jan, 15 Oct
Medici, Lorenzo de', 1 Jan, 9 April
Medici, Marie de', 3 July
Medina, 16 July
Medway, River, 12 June
Megiddo, Battle of, 18 Sept
Mehta, Zubin, 29 April
Mein Kampf, 18 July
Meir, Golda, 17 Mar, 3 May, 8 Dec
Meitner, Lise, 27 Oct
Melba, Nellie, 23 Feb, 19 May
Melbourne, 29 Aug, 22 Nov
Melly, George, 17 Aug
Melville, Herman, 1 Aug, 28 Sept
Memling, Hans, 11 Aug
Memphis, Tennessee, 19 Dec
Mendès-France, Pierre, 18 Oct
Mendel, Gregor, 6 Jan, 22 July
Mendeleyev, Dmitri, 2 Feb
Mendelssohn, Felix, 3 Feb, 26 Aug, 4 Nov
Mendoza, Pedro de, 23 June
Menelek, Emperor, 14 May
Menuhin, Yehudi, 22 April
Menzies, Robert, 20 Dec
Mercator, Gerardus, 5 Mar, 5 May, 2 Dec
Mercury, 29 Mar
Mercury, Freddie, 5 Sept, 15 Sept, 24 Nov
Meredith, George, 12 Feb, 18 May
Mergenthaler, Ottmar, 28 Oct
Mérimée, Prosper, 28 May, 23 Sept, 28 Sept
Merman, Ethel, 16 Jan, 15 Feb
Mersey Railway Tunnel, 20 Jan
Mesmer, Friedrich, 5 Mar, 23 May
Messiaen, Olivier, 28 April, 10 Dec
Messina, 28 Dec
meteorite, 24 Dec

meteorological office, 11 Feb, 15 Dec
Methuen Treaty, 27 Dec
metric system, 1 Aug
Metro, 10 July
Metropolis, 10 Jan
Metropolitan Opera House, 22 Oct
Metternich, Clemens, 15 May,
    11 June
Metz, Siege of, 1 Sept
Mexico, 11 Jan, 23 Feb, 13 May,
    25 May, 19 June, 9 Sept, 22 Sept,
    27 Sept, 28 Dec
Mexico City, 12 Oct
Meyerbeer, Giacomo, 5 Sept
Michelin, André, 16 Jan, 4 April
Michelson, Albert, 19 Dec
Michener, James, 3 Feb
Mickey Mouse, 18 Nov
Midler, Bette, 1 Dec
Midway, Battle of, 3 June
Mies van der Rohe, Ludwig, 27 Mar,
    17 Aug
Mignet, François, 8 May
Mihajlovic, Dragolub, 17 July
Mikado, 14 Mar
Milan, 3 May, 26 May, 3 Aug,
    15 Dec
Military Academy, US, 16 Mar;
Sandhurst, 2 April
Mill, John Stuart, 8 May, 20 May
Millais, John Everett, 8 June, 13 Aug
Milland, Ray, 3 Jan, 10 Mar
Millburn, Jackie, 9 Oct
Miller, Arthur, 17 Oct
Miller, Glenn, 5 Feb, 10 Feb, 1 Mar,
    16 Dec
Miller, Henry, 7 June, 26 Dec
Miller, Joe, 16 Aug
Miller, Jonathan, 21 July
Miller, Roger, 2 Jan
Millet, Jean, 4 Oct
Milligan, Spike, 16 April
Millikan, Robert, 19 Dec
Mills, Hayley, 18 April
Mills, John, 22 Feb
Millwall, 31 Jan
Milne, A A, 18 Jan, 31 Jan
Milner, Alfred, Lord, 12 May
Milton, John, 8 Nov, 9 Dec
mine, 6 Dec; coal, 20 May
Minnelli, Lisa, 12 Mar
Minnelli, Vincente, 28 Feb
Minorca, 5 Feb
mint, US, 2 April
Minter, Alan, 17 Aug
Minuit, Peter, 6 May
Mirabeau, Honoré, 2 April
Mirandola, Pico della, 17 Nov
Miró, Joan, 20 April, 25 Dec
Mishima, Yukio, 25 Nov
Missouri, 13 Feb, 28 Feb
'Miss World' contest, 19 April
Mistral, Frédéric, 25 Mar
Mitchell, Joni, 7 Nov
Mitchell, Margaret, 16 Aug, 8 Nov
Mitchum, Robert, 9 Feb, 6 Aug

Mitford, Nancy, 30 June
Mitterrand, François, 26 Oct
Mix, Tom, 12 Oct
Modigliani, Amedeo, 24 Jan, 12 July
Mogadishu, 18 Oct
Mohács, Battle of, 12 Aug, 29 Aug
Mohammed, 16 July
Molière, 15 Jan, 17 Feb, 23 Nov
Mollison, Jim, 30 Oct
Molotov, Vyacheslav, 9 Mar, 11 Nov
Monaco, 19 April;
    Grand Prix, 14 April
Mona Lisa, 21 Aug
Monash, John, 27 June
Monck, George, 6 Dec
Mondrian, Piet, 1 Feb, 7 Mar
Monet, Claude, 14 Nov, 5 Dec
Mongols, 25 May
Monk, Thelonious, 17 Feb, 10 Oct
Monmouth, 1 Nov
Monongah, 6 Dec
Monroe Doctrine, 2 Dec
Monroe, James, 28 April, 4 July,
    2 Dec
Monroe, Marilyn, 14 Jan, 1 June,
    5 Aug, 1 Dec
Mons, Battle of, 14 Aug
Mont Blanc road tunnel, 16 July
Montagu, Edward, 21 May, 1
Montagu, Lady Mary Wortley,
    26 May
Montaigne, Michel Eyquem de,
    13 Sept
Montalban, Ricardo, 25 Nov
Montand, Yves, 13 Oct, 9 Nov
Montaperti, Battle of, 4 Sept
Monte Bello Islands, 3 Oct
Monte Carlo 21 Jan, 14 April
Monte Cassino, 4 Jan, 18 May
Montefiore, Moses, 9 Nov
Montenegro, 13 July
Montespan, Marquise de, 27 May
Montessori, Maria, 31 Aug
Monteverdi, Claudio, 12 May
Montevideo, 17 Dec
Montezuma II, 30 June
Montfort, Simon de, 2 May
Montgolfier, Jacques, 2 Aug, 19 Sept
Montgolfier, Joseph-Michel, 26 June,
    19 Sept
Montgomery, 4 Feb
Montgomery, Bernard, 24 Mar,
    3 Nov, 17 Nov
Montherlant, Henri de, 21 April
Montreal, 29 Oct
Moon, 2 Jan, 31 July, 7 Oct, 17 Nov;
    landing, 3 Feb, 14 Sept;
    walk on, 21 July
Moon, Keith, 23 Aug, 7 Sept
Moon, Sun Myung, 30 Oct
Moore, Bobby, 24 Feb, 12 April,
    14 Nov
Moore, Dudley, 19 April
Moore, G E, 4 Nov
Moore, Henry, 30 July, 31 Aug
Moore, John, 13 Nov

Moore, Marianne, 5 Feb
Moore, Patrick, 4 Mar, 26 April
Moore, Thomas, 28 May
Moorgate, London, 28 Feb
Moravia, Alberto, 26 Sept, 28 Nov
More, Kenneth, 12 July
More, Thomas, 7 Feb, 6 July
Moreau, Gustave, 6 April
Moreau, Jean, 11 Aug
Moreau, Jeanne, 23 Jan
Morgan, William de, 16 Nov
Morland, George, 27 Oct
Mormon Church, 6 April, 30 June
Morocco, 29 Feb
Morris, Desmond, 24 Jan
Morris, William
Morris Minor, 12 Oct
Morris, William, 24 Mar, 3 Oct
Morris, William Richard, 22 Aug
Morrison, Jim, 3 July, 8 Dec
Morrison, Robert, 1 Aug
Morse, Samuel, 2 April, 27 April
Mortimer, John, 21 April
Morton, Jelly Roll, 10 July, 20 Sept
Moscow, 19 May, 7 Sept, 14 Sept,
    15 Sept, 9 Nov, 16 Nov, 19 Dec
Moses, Edwin, 31 Aug
Moses, Grandma, 13 Dec
Mosley, Oswald, 8 June, 3 Dec
Moss, Stirling, 17 Sept
Mossal Bay, 3 Feb
motel, 12 Dec
Motley, John Lothrop, 29 May
motor racing, 7 Aug, 7 Sept, 21 Oct
motorway, 1 Nov, 5 Dec
Moulin, Jean, 8 July
Mount, Peggy, 2 May
Mount St Helens, 18 May
Mountbatten, Louis, 20 Feb, 25 June,
    27 Aug
Mousetrap, The, 13 Sept, 25 Nov
Mozambique, 25 June, 26 June
Mozart, Wolfgang Amadeus, 27 Jan,
    1 May, 16 July, 10 Aug, 30 Sept,
    29 Oct, 5 Dec
Mr Blobby, 5 Dec
Mugabe, Robert, 21 Feb
Muggeridge, Malcolm, 24 Mar
Munch, Edvard, 23 Jan, 12 Dec
Munich, 4 Feb, 5 Sept, 6 Feb,
    22 Sept;
    Agreement, 29 Sept
Municipal Corporations Act, British,
    9 Sept
Munnings, Alfred, 8 Oct
Murat, Joachim, 13 Oct
Murdoch, Iris, 15 July
Murdoch, Rupert, 11 Mar
Murdock, William, 21 Aug
Murillo, Bartolomé, 3 April
Murphy, Eddy, 3 April
Murray, George, 2 Jan
Murray River, 9 Feb, 16 Nov
Murrow, Ed, 11 Dec
Murry, John Middleton, 13 Mar
Mussolini, Benito, 20 Feb, 23 Feb,

23 Mar, 28 April, 23 June, 25 July, 29 July, 12 Sept, 6 Dec
Mussorgsky, Modest, 19 Mar
Muti, Riccardo, 28 July
mutiny, 15 April, 23 June, 24 June, 30 June; Indian, 10 May, 15 July
My Lai massacre, 29 Mar

Nabokov, Vladimir, 2 July
Nagasaki, 9 Aug
Nagy, Imre, 17 June
Naipaul, V S, 17 Aug
Nanak, Guru, 15 April
Nancy, Battle of, 5 Jan
Nanking, Treaty of, 29 Aug
Nansen, Fridtjof, 13 May
Nantes, Edict of, 13 April, 18 Oct
Naoraji, Dadabhai, 6 July
Napier, Charles, 10 Aug
Napier, John, 4 April
Napoleon, 19 Feb, 26 Feb, 9 Mar, 20 Mar, 11 April, 5 May, 16 May, 26 May, 6 June, 14 June, 24 June, 9 July, 21 July, 15 Aug, 18 Aug, 27 Aug, 14 Sept, 16 Oct, 19 Oct, 30 Nov, 2 Dec, 4 Dec, 16 Dec
Napoleon III, 9 Jan, 14 Jan, 4 Sept
Napoleonic Wars, 9 Jan
NASA, 13 Jan
Naseby, Battle of, 14 June
Nash, John, 13 May
Nash, Ogden, 19 May, 19 Aug
Nash, Paul, 11 May, 11 July
Nash, Richard 'Beau', 3 Feb
Nasmyth, James, 19 Aug
Nasser, Gamal, 15 Jan, 24 June, 26 July
Nastase, Ilie, 19 July
Natal, 28 Feb, 10 May, 20 June
national anthem, British, 28 Sept
National Gallery, 22 Mar
National Health Service, 21 Mar, 5 July
National Maritime Museum, Greenwich, 27 April
National Park, 28 Dec
NSPCC, 8 July
nationalisation, 20 May
Nations, Battle of the, 19 Oct
NATO, 4 April, 21 Nov
Natural History Museum, London, 18 April
Navarino, Battle of, 20 Oct
Navigation Acts, 26 June
Navratilova, Martina, 7 July, 9 Sept, 18 Oct
Nazi Party, 4 Feb, 5 Mar, 21 Mar, 30 June, 16 Oct, 6 Nov, 10 Nov
Neagle, Anna, 20 Oct
Neal, Patricia, 20 Jan
Neer, Eglon van der, 3 May
Negri, Pola, 4 Aug
Neguib, Mohammed, 23 July
Negulesco, Jean, 18 July
Nehru, Jawaharlal, 27 May, 14 Nov
Nelson, Horatio, 14 Feb, 2 April,

12 July, 1 Aug, 29 Sept, 21 Oct
neon light, 3 Dec
Neptune, 25 Aug, 23 Sept
Neri, Philip, 26 May
Nero, Tiberius Claudius, 16 Mar, 15 Dec
Neruda, Pablo, 23 Sept
Nerva, Marcus Cocceius, 25 Jan
Netherlands, 13 Feb, 28 May, 6 June, 15 June, 9 July, 25 July, 25 Aug; Revolt of the, 23 May
Nevada, 26 April, 4 Oct, 31 Oct
Nevile, Richard, 14 April
Neville, Richard, 29 May
New Amsterdam, 8 Sept
Newbolt, Henry, 6 June
Newcomen, Thomas, 5 Aug
New Delhi, 10 Feb
New England, 19 May, 28 Aug
New England Company, 19 Mar
Newfoundland, 11 April, 5 Aug
New Guinea, 17 May, 29 June
New Hampshire, 21 June
New Jersey, 1 Feb, 6 May
Newman, John Henry, 21 Feb, 11 Aug
Newman, Paul, 26 Jan
Newman, Randy, 28 Nov
New Mexico, 16 July, 22 Aug
New Orleans, Battle of, 8 Jan
News of the World, 1 Oct
New Statesman, 21 Feb
New World, 3 May
New York, 19 Mar, 1 May, 6 July, 8 Sept, 12 Sept, 13 Sept, 26 Sept, 30 Sept, 4 Oct, 22 Oct, 23 Oct, 27 Oct, 4 Nov, 7 Nov, 3 Dec, 11 Dec, 12 Dec, 13 Dec
New York State, 9 Jan
New York Times, 18 Sept
New York Tribune, 10 April
New Zealand, 7 Feb, 3 May, 21 May, 10 July, 19 Sept, 26 Sept, 6 Oct, 13 Dec, 16 Dec
Newton, Isaac, 20 Mar, 25 Dec
Newton, Olivia, 26 Sept
Ney, Michel, 10 Jan
Niagara Falls, 24 Oct
Niagara frontier, 27 May
Niagara River, 26 Oct
Nicaea, Council of, 25 Aug
Nicaragua, 2 May, 8 June, 28 June, 9 July, 25 Dec
Nichol, Peter, 31 July
Nicholas I, Tsar, 15 Mar, 25 June, 6 July
Nicholas II, Tsar, 16 July
Nichols, Mike, 6 Nov
Nicholson, Jack, 22 April
Nicklaus, Jack, 21 Jan
Nicolson, Harold, 1 May
Nietzsche, Friedrich, 25 Aug, 15 Oct
Nightingale, Florence, 12 May, 13 Aug
Nijinsky, Vaslav, 12 Mar

Nile, Battle of the, 1 Aug
Nile, River, 15 Jan, 23 Feb, 3 Aug
Nimoy, Leonard, 26 Mar
Nin, Anaïs, 14 Jan
Niven, David, 1 Mar, 29 July
Nixon, Richard, 9 Jan, 15 Jan, 21 Feb, 22 May, 8 Aug, 8 Sept, 5 Nov, 7 Nov
Nkrumah, Kwame, 21 Mar, 27 April, 15 June
Nobel, Alfred, 14 July, 21 Oct, 10 Dec
Nobel prize, 10 Dec
Noble, Richard, 4 Oct
Norbert of Xanten, St, 6 June
Nore mutiny, 30 June
Noriega, Manuel, 20 Dec
Norman, Greg, 10 Feb
Norman, Jessye, 15 Sept
Normandy, 13 Nov
Norris, Frank, 25 Oct
Norris, John, 30 May
North, Frederick, 5 Aug
Northampton, Battle of, 10 July
North Atlantic Treaty Organization, 4 April
North Carolina, 17 Dec
North Cape, Battle of, 26 Dec
Northern Ireland, 14 Aug, 15 Nov, 28 Nov
North German Confederation, 18 Aug
North, Oliver, 5 July, 16 Sept
North Pole, 6 April, 3 Aug
North Sea, 27 Dec; pipeline, 3 Nov
Northwest Passage, 25 Mar, 11 Aug, 2 Sept
Norway, 16 Feb, 17 May, 10 Sept, 25 Sept, 26 Oct
Nostradamus, 2 July, 14 Dec
Nottingham, 22 Aug; sheriff of, 10 Feb
Novello, Ivor, 6 Mar
Novgorod, 29 May
Noyes, Alfred, 28 June
nuclear accident, 28 Mar, 26 April
nuclear power, 20 Aug, 17 Oct
nuclear reaction, 2 Dec
nuclear submarine, 21 Jan, 16 Feb, 3 Aug, 21 Oct
nuclear testing, 26 April
nuclear warship, 14 July
nuclear weapons, 26 Jan, 8 July, 5 Aug, 16 Oct
Nunn, Trevor, 14 Jan
Nuremberg, 16 Oct; trials, 20 Nov
Nureyev, Rudolf, 6 Jan, 17 Mar
Nutcracker, The, 17 Dec
Nyasa, Lake, 16 Sept
Nyasaland, 11 June
nylon, 16 Feb, 24 Feb, 15 Dec
Nystad, Peace of, 10 Sept

Oakley, Annie, 3 Nov
Oates, Lawrence, 17 Mar
Oates, Titus, 12 July, 15 Sept

Rickenbacker, Eddie, 23 July
Riddle, Nelson, 5 Oct
Ridley, Nicholas, 16 Oct
Riel, Louis, 23 Oct, 16 Nov
Rigg, Diana, 20 July
Rights of Man, Declaration of,
    26 Aug
Riley, Bridget, 24 April
Rilke, Rainer Maria, 4 Dec
Rimbaud, Arthur, 20 Oct, 10 Nov
Rimsky-Korsakov, Nikolai, 18 Mar,
    20 June
riot, 15 Aug
Ritter, Tex, 2 Jan
River Plate, Battle of the, 17 Dec
Rivonia trial, 12 June
Rizzio, David, 9 Mar
Röntgen, Wilhelm, 8 Nov, 22 Dec
Rob Roy, 28 Dec
Robbins, Harold, 21 May
Robert I 'the Bruce', 25 Mar, 7 June,
    24 June, 11 July
Robert III of Scotland, 1 April
Roberts, John, 14 April
Robeson, Paul, 23 Jan, 9 April
Robespierre, Maximilien, 6 May,
    28 July
Robinson, Edward G, 26 Jan, 12 Dec
Robinson, Mary, 7 Nov
Robinson, Sugar Ray, 3 May
Robinson, William Heath, 31 May
Robson, Flora, 28 Mar, 7 July
Rockefeller, John, 8 July, 29 Sept
Rockefeller, Nelson, 26 Jan
rocket, 16 Mar
Roddick, Anita, 23 Oct
Rodin, Auguste, 12 Nov, 17 Nov
Roethke, Theodore, 1 Aug
Roger I of Sicily, 22 June
Roger II of Sicily, 26 Feb
Rogers, Ginger, 16 July, 20 Dec
Rogers, Richard, 23 July
Rogers, Will, 15 Aug, 4 Nov
Roget, Peter, 18 Jan, 12 Sept
'Rogues' Gallery', 2 Nov
Rokeby Venus, 10 Mar
Rolfe, Frederick, 25 Oct
roller skating, 2 Aug
Rolling Stones, 5 Feb, 5 July
Rollins, Sonny, 7 Sept
Rolls, Charles, 12 July
Romains, Jules, 26 Aug
Romania, 9 May, 27 June, 13 July,
    27 Nov, 22 Dec
Romberg, Sigmund, 29 July
Rome, 17 Jan, 21 April, 6 May,
    4 June, 18 July, 8 Aug, 24 Aug,
    20 Sept, 2 Oct, 8 Nov, 17 Dec,
    25 Dec;
    Treaty of, 25 Mar
Rommel, Erwin, 21 June, 14 Oct,
    3 Nov, 15 Nov
Romney, George, 15 Nov, 15 Dec
Ronsard, Pierre de, 11 Sept
Ronstadt, Linda, 15 July
Röntgen, Wilhelm von, 10 Feb

Rooke, George, 24 July
Rooney, Mickey, 23 Sept
Roosevelt, Eleanor, 7 Nov
Roosevelt, Franklin, 14 Jan, 30 Jan,
    4 Feb, 12 April, 11 Aug
Roosevelt, Theodore, 6 Jan, 14 Sept,
    27 Oct, 26 Nov
Rose, Alec, 4 July
Rose, Billy, 10 Feb
Rose Lee, Gypsy, 9 Jan, 26 April
Roses, Wars of the, 4 May, 22 May,
    10 July
Ross, Annie, 25 July
Ross, Diana, 26 Mar
Ross, James Clark, 3 April
Ross, John, 30 Aug
Ross, Katharine, 29 Jan
Ross, Ronald, 13 May
Rosselini, Isabella, 18 June
Rossetti, Christina, 5 Dec
Rossetti, Dante Gabriel, 9 April, 12 May
Rossini, Gioacchino, 29 Feb, 13 Nov
Rostand, Edmond, 1 April
Rostropovich, Mstislav, 27 Mar
Rothko, Mark, 25 Feb, 25 Sept
Rothschild, Meyer, 19 Sept
Rothschild, Nathan, 28 July
Rotrou, Jean de, 28 June
Rouault, Georges, 13 Feb
Rouen, 30 May, 20 June
Rouget de Lisle, Claude, 16 May
Rousseau, Henri, 2 Sept
Rousseau, Jean-Jacques, 28 June,
    2 July
rowing, 22 April
Rowlandson, Thomas, 22 April
Rowntree, Joseph, 24 May, 4 Nov
Royal Academy of Arts, 10 Dec
Royal Aeronautical Society, 12 Jan
Royal Air Force, 1 April
Royal Charles, 12 June
Royal Exchange, 23 Jan
Royal Navy, 27 May
Royal Observatory, Greenwich,
    10 Aug
Royal Society, 22 April, 28 Nov
Royal William, 17 Aug
Royce, Henry, 27 Mar
rubber galoshes, 12 Feb
Rubbra, Edmund, 23 May
Rubens, Peter Paul, 30 May, 29 June
Rubinstein, Anton, 20 Nov,
Rubinstein, Artur, 20 Dec
Ruby, Jack, 24 Nov
Rudolph, Crown Prince, 30 Jan
rugby, 15 Jan, 27 Mar, 2 Oct, 22 Oct
Rugby Football Union, 26 Jan
Rugby League, 29 Aug
Runyon, Damon, 10 Dec
Rupert, Prince of England, 2 July
Rushdie, Salman, 14 Feb, 19 June,
    12 July, 11 Dec
Ruskin, John, 20 Jan, 8 Feb
Russell, Bertrand, 2 Feb, 18 May
Russell, Jane, 21 June
Russell, Ken, 3 July

Russell, Lord John, 28 May
Russell, Lord William, 21 June
Russell, Willy, 23 Aug
Russia, 16 Jan, 26 Jan, 8 Feb, 27 Feb,
    9 Mar, 15 Mar, 29 May, 17 June,
    21 June, 24 June, 27 June, 3 July,
    16 July, 10 Sept, 15 Sept, 8 Dec
Russo-Japanese War, 4 Feb, 10 Aug,
    5 Dec
Ruthenia, 29 June
Rutherford, Ernest, 30 Aug, 19 Oct
Rutherford, Margaret, 11 May
Ruyter, Michiel de, 7 June, 12 June
Ryder Cup, 15 Sept
Rye House Plot, 12 June

saccharin, 27 Feb
Sacco, Nicola, 23 Aug
Sacheverell, Henry, 5 June
Sachs, Hans, 19 Jan
Sackville West, Vita, 9 Mar, 2 June
Sadat, Anwar, 2 April, 5 Oct, 6 Oct,
    18 Nov, 25 Dec
Sade, Marquis de, 2 Dec
'safety cab', 23 Dec
safety pin, 10 April
Sagan, Carl, 9 Nov
Sagan, Françoise, 21 June
Sahara, 13 Feb
St Albans, 22 May; Battle of, 17 Feb
St Bartholomew, Massacre of,
    24 Aug
Saint-Exupéry, Antoine de, 29 June
Saint-Germain, Treaty of, 10 Sept
St Gotthard tunnel, 29 Feb, 5 Sept
St Helena, 22 April, 16 Oct
St James' Palace, 10 Feb
Saint Laurent, Yves, 30 Jan
St Lawrence River, 16 June, 3 Dec
St Lawrence Seaway, 25 April
St Leger, 24 Sept
St Louis, 25 Nov
St Lucia, 27 June
St Paul's Cathedral, 2 Dec
St Peter's, Rome, 18 Nov
St Petersburg, 22 Jan, 17 Feb,
    17 Dec;
    Alliance of, 28 Sept;
    Treaty of, 5 May
Saint-Saëns, Camille, 9 Oct, 16 Dec
Saints, Battle of the, 12 April
St Valentine's Day Massacre, 14 Feb
St Vincent, Battle of, 14 Feb
Sakharov, Andrei, 14 Dec
Sakkaria River, Battle of the, 24 Aug
Saladin, 4 Mar, 2 Oct
Salamanca, Battle of, 22 July, 6 Aug,
Salamis, Battle of, 23 Sept
Salerno, 3 Sept, 9 Sept
Salieri, Antonio, 18 Aug
Salinger, J D, 1 Jan
Salk, Jonas, 28 Oct
Salt March, 12 Mar
Salvation Army, 2 July
Salyut 6, 11 Oct
Salyut 7, 6 Feb

Sand, George, 8 June, 1 July
Sandburg, Carl, 6 Jan, 22 July
Sand Creek massacre, 29 Nov
Sandhurst, 2 April
Sandinista, 9 July
San Domingo, 5 May
Sandwich Islands, 18 Jan, 14 Feb
San Francisco, 18 April, 29 Aug,
   8 Sept, 23 Nov
San Salvador, 12 Oct
Santa Anna, Antonio de, 21 Feb
Santa Cruz Bay, 20 April
Santander, 26 June
Santo Domingo, 3 Sept
Santos-Dumont, Alberto, 20 July
Saragossa, Battle of, 20 Aug
Sarajevo, 28 June
Saratoga, 17 Oct
Sardinia, 13 Feb
Sardou, Victorien, 5 Sept, 8 Nov
Sargent, John, 12 Jan
Sargent, Malcolm, 3 Oct
Sarto, Andrea del, 16 July, 28 Sept
Sartre, Jean-Paul, 15 April, 21 June
SAS, 6 Mar
Sassoon, Siegfried, 1 Sept, 8 Sept
satellite, communications, 6 April,
   10 July, 12 Aug, 4 Oct;
   lunar, 10 Aug;
   weather, 1 April
Satie, Erik, 17 May, 1 July
Saturn, 20 Aug
Saudi Arabia, 20 May, 23 June,
   24 Oct
Saunders, Jennifer, 12 July
Savonarola, Girolamo, 22 May,
   23 May, 21 Sept
Savoy Hotel, London, 6 Aug
Sax, Adolphe, 7 Feb, 6 Nov
Sayers, Dorothy L, 18 Dec
Sayers, Tom, 8 Nov
Sayle, Alexei, 7 Aug
Scales, Prunella, 22 June
Scapa Flow, 21 June
Scarlatti, Domenico, 23 July
Scharnhorst, 26 Dec
Scheele, Karl, 21 May
Schelling, Friedrich von, 20 Aug
Schiaparelli, Elsa, 13 Nov
Schiller, Johann von, 10 Nov
Schlesinger, John, 16 Feb
Schliemann, Heinrich, 26 Dec
Schmidt, Helmut, 23 Dec
Schnitzler, Arthur, 15 May
Schoenberg, Arnold, 13 July, 13 Sept
school-leaving age, 1 April
Schopenhauer, Arthur, 22 Feb,
   21 Sept
Schreiner, Olive, 11 Dec
Schubert, Franz, 19 Nov
Schultz, Charles, 26 Nov
Schuman, Robert, 4 Sept
Schumann, Clara, 20 May
Schumann, Robert, 8 June, 29 July
Schütz, Heinrich, 6 Nov
Schweitzer, Albert, 14 Jan, 4 Sept

Scorsese, Martin, 17 Nov
Scotland, 29 Jan, 24 Mar, 1 May
Scott, George C, 18 Oct
Scott, George Gilbert, 27 Mar,
   13 July
Scott, Giles Gilbert, 9 Nov
Scott, John, 4 June
Scott, Peter, 14 Sept
Scott, Randolph, 2 Mar
Scott, Robert Falcon, 17 Jan, 29 Mar,
   6 June, 12 Nov
Scott, Sheila, 20 Oct
Scott, Walter, 15 Aug, 21 Sept
screw bottle top, 10 Aug
Scudamore, Peter, 13 June
Seagrave, Henry, 13 June
seaplane, 28 Mar
Searle, Ronald, 3 Mar
Sears Tower, Chicago, 4 May
seat belt, 31 Jan
Sebastopol, 24 June, 11 Sept
Seberg, Jean, 8 Sept
Sedaka, Neil, 13 Mar
Sedgemoor, Battle of, 6 July
Seferis, George, 20 Sept
Segal, George, 13 Feb
Segovia, Andrés, 18 Feb, 2 June
Seine, River, 20 June
Selfridge, Gordon, 11 Jan, 15 Mar,
   8 May
Sellers, Peter, 24 July, 8 Sept
Selznick, David O, 10 May
Sendak, Maurice, 10 June
Seneca Falls, New York, 19 July
Senefelder, Alois, 6 Nov
Senegal, 17 Jan, 20 Aug
Senior, Nassau, 4 June
Senna, Ayrton, 21 Mar
Sennet, Mack, 23 Sept, 5 Nov,
   30 Nov
Seoul, 28 June, 14 Oct
Serbia, 13 July
Sessions, John, 11 Jan
Seurat, Georges, 29 Mar, 2 Dec
Severn Railway Tunnel, 8 Jan
Severn Road Bridge, 8 Sept
Severn Tunnel, 1 Sept
Severus, Lucius Septimius, 4 Feb
Seveso, 10 July
Sévigné, Mme de, 17 April
Seville, 20 Sept
Seward, Anna, 25 Mar
Sex Pistols, 2 Jan, 6 Nov
Seymour, Jane, 15 Feb, 30 May,
   8 June, 24 Oct
Seymour, Lynn, 8 Mar
Seymour, Thomas, 20 Mar
Sforza, Caterina, 20 May
Shackleton, Ernest, 10 May
Shackleton, Henry, 5 Jan
Shadwell, Thomas, 19 Nov
Shakespeare, William, 23 April,
   16 Sept, 27 Nov;
   Memorial Theatre, 23 April
Shankar, Ravi, 7 April
Shannon, Del, 8 Feb

Shanxi Province, 23 Jan
Sharaff, Irene, 16 Aug
Sharif, Omar, 10 April
Sharp, Cecil, 23 June
Sharpeville Massacre, 21 Mar
Shaw, George Bernard, 26 July,
   2 Nov
Sheen, Martin, 3 Aug
Sheene, Barry, 11 Sept
Sheerness, 12 June
Sheffield, 24 Oct
Shelley, Mary Wollstoncraft, 1 Feb,
   30 Aug
Shelley, Percy Bysshe, 8 July, 4 Aug
Shepard, Alan, 18 Nov
Sheppard, Jack, 16 Nov
Sheraton, Thomas, 22 Oct
Sheridan, Richard Brinsley, 7 July,
   30 Oct
Sherlock, William, 19 June
Sherman, William, 8 Feb, 14 Feb
Shevardnadze, Edvard, 25 Jan,
   20 Dec
Shilton, Peter, 18 Sept
Shinwell, Emmanuel, 8 May
Sholes, Christopher, 14 Feb
Sholokhov, Mikhail, 20 Feb, 11 May
Shore, Jane, 22 June
shorthand, 15 Nov
Shostakovich, Dmitri, 9 Aug,
   25 Sept
Shreveport, 26 May
Shute, Nevil, 12 Jan, 17 Jan
Siam, 11 May, 27 June
Sibelius, Jean, 20 Sept
Siberia, 14 July, 17 Nov
Sica, Vittorio de, 7 July, 13 Nov
Sicilian Vespers, 31 Mar
Sicily, 28 Dec
Siddons, Sarah, 8 June, 5 July
Sidney, Philip, 17 Oct, 30 Nov
Siemens, Ernst von, 6 Dec
Siemens, William, 4 April, 19 Nov
Sienkiewicz, Henryk, 15 Nov
Sierra Leone, 27 April, 22 Aug
Sieyès, Emmanuel, 20 June
Sigismund of Luxembourg, 28 June
Signac, Paul, 15 Aug
Signoret, Simone, 30 Sept
Sihanouk, Prince, 14 Nov
Sikorsky, Igor, 26 Oct
Silcott, Winston, 25 Nov
Silesia, Upper, 15 May
Silvers, Phil, 1 Nov
Sim, Alastair, 9 Oct
Simenon, Georges, 13 Feb, 4 Sept
Simmons, Jean, 31 Jan
Simon, Neil, 4 July
Simon, Paul, 13 Oct
Simone, Nina, 21 Feb
Simplon Tunnel, 24 Feb, 16 Oct
Simpson, James, 7 June, 12 Nov
Simpson, Tony, 23 July
Simpson, Wallis, (Duchess of
   Windsor), 26 June, 27 Oct
Simpson's Desert, 20 July

28 Feb, 7 Mar, 10 Mar, 5 April, 30 April, 22 June, 4 Oct, 6 Oct, 13 Dec; Paris, 10 July
Underhill, Evelyn, 15 June
underwear, 13 Nov
UNESCO, 4 Nov
Unification Church, 30 Oct
Uniformity, Act of, 8 May, 19 May
Union Jack, 12 April
United Arab Emirates, 17 July
United Arab Republic, 1 Feb
United Kingdom, 22 Jan
United Nations, 10 Jan, 16 Jan, 23 Oct, 24 Oct, 25 Oct, 16 Dec
Universal Postal Union, 9 Oct
University Test Act, 16 June
Upper Volta, 5 Aug
Uranus, 13 Mar
Urban, Pope, 27 Nov
Urbino, Donato de, 20 May
Uruguay, 9 Sept, 17 Dec
USA, 3 Jan, 16 Jan, 27 Jan, 8 Feb, 11 Feb, 22 Feb, 24 Feb, 3 Mar, 12 Mar, 6 April, 30 April, 13 May, 19 May, 8 June, 12 June, 28 June, 4 July, 5 July, 9 Aug, 12 Aug, 26 Aug, 30 Aug, 3 Sept, 18 Sept, 20 Oct, 28 Oct, 5 Dec, 18 Dec, 24 Dec
US Air Force, 27 Jan, 23 June
US Congress, 7 Nov, 17 Nov
US Marines, 10 Nov
US navy, 27 Mar
USS Enterprise, 24 Sept
USS George Washington, 9 June
USS Housatonic, 17 Feb
USS Long Beach, 14 July
USS Maine, 15 Feb
USS Nautilus, 21 Jan, 3 Aug
USS Vincennes, 3 July
Ussher, James, 21 Mar
USSR, 16 Jan, 31 Jan, 2 Feb, 13 Feb, 3 Mar, 11 Mar, 12 Mar, 27 Mar, 31 May, 23 June, 27 June, 29 June, 3 Aug, 8 Aug, 21 Aug, 23 Aug, 26 Aug, 29 Aug, 30 Aug, 17 Sept, 18 Sept, 30 Nov, 23 Dec, 25 Dec, 26 Dec
Ustinov, Peter, 16 April
Utah, 23 Oct
Utica, 22 Feb
Utrecht, Treaty of, 11 April
Utrillo, Maurice, 5 Nov, 25 Dec

vacuum cleaner, 30 Aug
Vadim, Roger, 26 Jan
Valentino, Rudolph, 23 Aug, 5 Nov
Vallee, Rudy, 3 July, 28 July
Valois, Marguerite de, 14 May
Valois, Ninette de, 6 June
Vanbrugh, John, 26 Mar
van Buren, Martin, 24 July
Vance, Cyrus, 27 Mar
van de Graff, Robert, 16 Jan
van den Vondel, Joost, 5 Feb
van Dyck, Anthony, 22 Mar, 9 Dec

Vane, Henry (the Younger), 26 May, 14 June
Van Heusen, Jimmy, 26 Jan, 7 Feb
Van Morrison, 31 Aug
Van Tromp, Cornelius, 29 May
Vanzetti, Bartolomeo, 23 Aug
Varèse, Edgard, 8 Nov
Vasari, Giorgio, 27 June, 30 July
VAT, 1 April
Vatican City State, 7 July
Vatican Council, 18 July
Vaughan, Frankie, 3 Feb
Vaughan, Sarah, 27 Mar
Vaughan Williams, Ralph, 4 Jan, 12 Oct
vehicle registration plates, 14 Aug
Velázquez, Diego, 6 June, 6 Aug
venereal disease, 31 Jan
venetian blind, 11 Dec
Venezuela, 20 Nov
Venice, 2 May, 27 May, 28 Aug, 8 Oct
Venus, 1 Mar, 16 Nov, 14 Dec
Venus III, 16 Nov
Verdi, Giuseppe, 19 Jan, 27 Jan, 17 Feb, 10 Oct, 10 Nov, 24 Dec
Verdun, Battle of, 21 Feb, 15 Dec
Vereeniging, Peace of, 31 May
Verga, Giovanni, 27 Jan, 2 Sept
Verity, Hedley, 31 July
Verlaine, Paul, 8 Jan, 30 Mar
Vermeer, Jan, 25 Aug, 31 Oct, 15 Dec
Verne, Jules, 8 Feb, 24 Mar
Vernon, Edward, 30 Oct
Veronese, Paolo, 19 April
Versailles Peace Conference, 18 Jan
Versailles, Treaty of, 10 Jan
Verwoerd, Hendrik, 6 Sept
Vespasian, 23 June
Vespucci, Amerigo, 22 Feb
Vesuvius, 7 April, 24 Aug
Vicious, Sid, 2 Feb
Vico, Giovanni Battista, 23 June
Victor Emmanuel II of Italy, 18 Feb, 26 Oct
Victor Emmanuel III of Italy, 9 May
Victoria, Queen, 1 Jan, 22 Jan, 10 Feb, 2 Mar, 7 April, 1 May, 24 May, 20 June, 21 June, 13 July
Victoria Cross, 29 Jan, 20 Sept
Victoria, Lake, 23 Feb, 3 Aug
Vidal, Gore, 3 Oct
video recorder, 11 Nov
Vidor, King, 1 Nov
Vienna, 13 Feb, 5 April, 1 June, 16 July, 21 Sept
Vietnam, 15 Jan, 27 Jan, 12 Feb, 8 Mar, 29 Mar, 30 April, 8 June, 13 Aug, 29 Oct, 22 Dec
Vignola, Giacomo da, 7 July
Vigo, Jean, 5 Oct
Viking I, 20 July
Viking 2, 3 Sept
Vikings, 1 June, 18 June, 20 June
Villa, Pancho, 5 June, 20 June

Villa-Lobos, Heitor, 5 Mar, 17 Nov
Villars, Claude de, 8 May
Vilnius, 13 Jan
Vimiero, Battle of, 21 Aug
Vimy Ridge, 9 April
Virchow, Rudolf, 13 Oct
Virgil, 21 Sept, 15 Oct
Virgin Islands, 25 Jan
Virginia, 25 June
virus, computer, 6 Nov
Visigoths, 24 Aug
Vittoria, 21 June
Vivaldi, Antonio, 4 Mar, 28 July
Vives, Jean Louis, 6 May
volcano, 7 April, 8 May, 18 May, 24 Aug, 26 Aug, 10 Oct, 13 Nov, 14 Nov
Volga-Don Canal, 31 May
Volkswagen, 26 Feb
Volta, Alessandro, 18 Feb, 5 Mar
Voltaire, 20 Feb, 24 May, 30 May, 21 Nov
von Bülow, Hans, 12 Feb
Vonnegut, Kurt, 11 Nov
Vorster, Balthazar Johannes, 10 Sept, 13 Dec
vote, 2 Feb, 6 Feb, 7 Mar, 17 April, 7 May, 19 May, 7 June, 26 Aug, 19 Sept, 14 Dec
Voyager, 20 Aug, 25 Aug, 23 Dec
Vuillard, Jean-Edouard, 21 June, 11 Nov

Wagner, Richard, 13 Feb, 18 Feb, 22 May, 17 Aug, 22 Sept
Wagner, Robert, 10 Feb
Waitangi, Treaty of, 6 Feb
Waite, Terry, 20 Jan, 31 May, 18 Nov
Wajda, Andrzej, 6 Mar
Wakefield, Edward Gibbon, 16 May
Waksman, Selman, 22 Feb, 22 July
Walbrook, Anton, 19 Nov
Walcher, Bishop, 14 May
Wales, 5 Mar, 14 June, 24 June, 21 Oct
Wales, Prince of, 29 July, 14 Nov
Wales, Princess of, 1 July
Walesa, Lech, 22 Sept, 29 Sept, 9 Dec
Wall, Max, 12 Mar
Wall Street, 19 Oct, 29 Oct
Wallace, Edgar, 10 Feb
Wallace, William, 23 Aug
Wallach, Eli, 7 Dec
Waller, Edmund, 21 Oct
Waller, Fats, 21 May, 15 Dec
Wallis, Barnes, 30 Oct
Walpole, Horace, 2 Mar, 24 Sept
Walpole, Hugh, 13 Mar, 1 June
Walpole, Robert, 18 Mar, 3 April, 26 Aug, 22 Sept
Walsingham, Francis, 6 April
Walton, Izaak, 9 Aug, 15 Dec
Walton, William, 29 Mar
Ward, Leslie, 15 May